Driven Apart

Annis May Timpson

Driven Apart:
Women's Employment Equality
and Child Care in Canadian
Public Policy

UBC Press · Vancouver · Toronto

Printed in Canada on acid-free paper ∞

ISBN 0-7748-0820-9 (hardcover)
ISBN 0-7748-0821-7 (paperback)

Canadian Cataloguing in Publication Data

Timpson, Annis May
  Driven apart

  Includes bibliographical references and index.
  ISBN 0-7748-0820-9 (bound); ISBN 0-7748-0821-7 (pbk)

  1. Affirmative action programs – Government policy – Canada.
2. Child care – Government policy – Canada. 3. Women – Canada –
Economic conditions. I. Title.
HQ1236.5.C2T55 2001   305.4'0971   C00-910732-0

This book has been published with the help of a grant from the International
Council for Canadian Studies, through its Canadian Studies Publishing Fund.

UBC Press acknowledges the financial support of the Government of Canada
through the Book Publishing Industry Development Program (BPIDP) for our
publishing activities.
Canadä

We also gratefully acknowledge the support of the Canada Council for the Arts
for our publishing program, as well as the support of the British Columbia Arts
Council.

Printed and bound in Canada by Friesens
Set in Stone by Brenda and Neil West, BN Typographics West
Copy editor: Valerie Adams
Proofreader: Gail Copeland
Indexer: Patricia Buchanan

UBC Press
The University of British Columbia
2029 West Mall
Vancouver, BC V6T 1Z2
(604) 822-5959
Fax: (604) 822-6083
E-mail: info@ubcpress.ubc.ca
www.ubcpress.ubc.ca

For Patricia and Michael Timpson
– two wonderful parents –
with special love

Contents

Tables

Preface

On the last day that I conducted interviews for this project, I went from the Canadian Human Rights Commission in Ottawa across the river to Human Resources Development Canada in Hull. After negotiating its electronic security system, making my way to the tenth floor and speaking once more with the director of Labour Standards and Workplace Equity, I went back down to the eighth floor to meet with a senior bureaucrat in the Children's Task Team of HRDC. As I looked out from her office down the Ottawa River I could see, rising at the edge of Tunney's Pasture, the tower block that housed the public servants who were preparing Health Canada's contribution to the new National Children's Agenda. In the course of those two fascinating interviews, I learned that while the bureaucrats in the Workplace Equity Program had strong links with the Canadian Human Rights Commission, those working on the "kids' file" in HRDC were in frequent contact with their counterparts on the Child Health Program in Health Canada. As our conversations proceeded, I realized that the bureaucrats in the Workplace Equity Program and the Children's Task Team – working just two floors apart in HRDC – hardly knew each other. To me this verified how, by the late 1990s, questions about women's employment equality and child care in federal public policy had been driven apart. What I seek to do in this book is explain why.

Acknowledgments

I would like to acknowledge the extensive help I received from Martha Friendly and Michelle Turiano at the Childcare Research and Resource Unit in the University of Toronto, and Bruce Pearce and Vicki Skelton at the U of T's Newman Industrial Relations Library. It is perhaps indicative of the way that questions about child care and women's employment equality have been driven apart in Canadian public policy that I spent so much time in these two different libraries. Thanks to each one of you for all your help. It was great fun working with you over the years.

In the course of my research, I benefited enormously from interviews with activists and policy makers. These conversations spurred my analysis and helped me make connections that I might otherwise have ignored. My thanks to all those people who gave up time in their busy schedules to talk with me about their work. Every effort has been made to obtain permission from all interviewees cited in this volume.

This book would not have been published without a subvention from the International Council for Canadian Studies and research funds from the Canadian Commonwealth Scholarship Fund, the Foundation for Canadian Studies in the UK, the British Association for Canadian Studies, and the Canadian Studies Program Development grants administered by the Department of Foreign Affairs and International Trade Canada. My thanks to all these organizations and the officers who manage them, in particular Guy Leclair, Deirdre Roser, Jodie Robson, Michael Hellyer, and Vivien Hughes.

I am grateful for permission granted to use material I published previously in "Royal Commissions as Sites of Resistance: Women's Challenges on Child Care in the Royal Commission on the Status of Women," *International Journal of Canadian Studies* 20 (Fall 1999): 123-48; "The Politics of Employment Inequality in Canada: Gender and the Public Sector," in *Women and Career: Themes and Issues in Advanced Industrial Societies*, ed.

Julia Evetts (Longman: London, 1994), 44-58; and "Between the Royal Commissions: Women's Employment Equality in Canada 1966-1986," *London Journal of Canadian Studies* 4 (1987): 68-81.

Driven Apart would never have seen the light of day without the hard work of staff at UBC Press and the anonymous readers who kindly reviewed my manuscript. In particular, I would like to thank Emily Andrew, who worked with me from the outset and proved to be a fabulous acquisitions editor, and Camilla Jenkins, who brought her impressive professional skills to the production of this volume. In addition, I would like to thank Valerie Adams, Patricia Buchanan, Neil and Brenda West, Gail Copeland, Leon Phillips, Berit Kraus, and Janice Williams for the different skills they brought to the production of this book.

My research into Canadian public policy evolved with the support of academics on both sides of the Atlantic. In particular, I would like to take this opportunity to thank Professor Miriam David who, as my personal undergraduate tutor at the University of Bristol, helped lay the foundations for my subsequent studies of social policy. I would also like to express my deep appreciation for the academic guidance I received from Professors Ronald Manzer, Sylvia Bashevkin, and David Rayside, when I worked with them as their doctoral student at the University of Toronto. Their knowledge and their rigour helped me develop the thesis that preceded this book.

For broader academic collegiality and help in developing my ideas, I would also like to thank Caroline Andrew, Jane Arscott, Kathy Brock, Janine Brodie, Sandra Burt, Alan Cairns, David Cameron, Stephen Clarkson, Diana Coole, Alexandra Dobrowolski, Joe Fletcher, Christina Gabriel, Lise Gotell, Rod Haddow, Vivien Hart, Linda Kealey, Tom Klassen, Evert Lindquist, Rianne Mahon, Ingrid Makus, Kenneth McRoberts, Robert O'Brien, Peter Russell, Susan Solomon, Katherine Swinton, Christine Sypnowich, Ted Tapper, Sylvia Van Kirk, Rob Vipond, Albert Weale, Graham White, and my students of Canadian politics at the University of Sussex.

For assistance in tracking down and checking all manner of material, I would like to thank Catherine Hatt, Natalie Rose, Jane Lynch, Harriet Sonne, and Eveline Houtman at the University of Toronto, James Whalen, Edwige Munn, Michael Eamon, and Martin Ruddy at the National Archives and National Library of Canada, Nancy Miller Chenier in the Library of Parliament, Iva Caccia at the Human Rights Research and Education Centre at the University of Ottawa, Freida Forman and Peggy Bristow at the former Women's Resource Centre at the Ontario Institute for Studies in Education, Ann Molgat at the National Action Committee on the Status of Women, Fiona Bladen and Marie-Louise Paradis at the Archives of the Committees and Parliamentary Associations Directorate in Ottawa,

Neil Gavigan and Penny Hammell at Human Resources Development Canada, Rhys Phillips at the Canadian Human Rights Commission, and Elizabeth Bertoldi at the Treasury Board Secretariat. My thanks also to Emmanuel Kattan and Denis Turcotte at the Quebec Government Offices in London for taking a fine-toothed comb through my translations from French. However, any errors of interpretation in this book remain mine alone.

Many other people helped and supported me in all sorts of different ways. For their invaluable support in Robarts Library I would like to thank Elaine Genius, Hormos Khakpour, Svetka Vucina, and Adrienne Thierry-Broad. For their kindnesses at different times in Toronto I would like to thank Peter and Sue Russell, Mary and Mark Endress, Tim Warner and Tita Ang-Angco, Molly Godfrey, David Silcox, Steven Ovadya, Duane Rudy, Marc Saurette, Stuart Mutch, and Vaia and Kitsa at the original Swiss Chalet. For their neighbourly support, here in England, I would like to thank Mrs. Heaven, Kathy Simmonds and Roger Tufft. And for their support at the University of Sussex, my thanks to Andrew Crozier, Peter Nicholls, Tania Golds, Sue Catt, Keith Fowler, and all the Porters in Arts B.

Throughout the time I have worked on this book, I have been sustained by many close and important friends. For their special kindness I particularly want to thank Lise Gotell, Barbara Oram and Robert Snell, Helen Shea, Christine Sypnowich and David Backhurst, Mary St Aubyn, Catherine Reynolds, Jilly Jennings, and David Butlin. For wonderful connections over the years I also want to honour, in Canada – Lois Pineau, Anna and Tony Luengo, Suzanne Ellenbogen, John Donner, Janine Brodie, Christina Gabriel, Hamish and Ann Kimmins, Nancy Kendrew, and Nada Conic; and in England – Michael Pushkin, Vincent Quinn, Rosemary Chapman, Lindsay Davies, John Stobbs, Julian Cooper, Maureen McNeil, Desmond and Barbara Vowles, Ann and John Vidler, Judith Forshaw, Liz Robinson, Helen de Freitas, June MacBride, and Bill and Kevin Read.

Underpinning all my endeavours have been the strength and confidence of my family. My partner, Ian Read, has loved and supported me in so many different ways and shown me the fullness of care. My lively and loving sisters, Rosie and Val, have helped me through every twist and turn that a project like this involves. But above all, it is the love, enthusiasm, kindness, and generosity of my parents, Michael and Patricia Timpson, that has enabled and encouraged me throughout my life.

Abbreviations

ATF	Action travail des femmes
CACSW	Canadian Advisory Council on the Status of Women
CAP	Canada Assistance Plan
CAP-C	Community Action Program for Children
CCAAC	Child Care Advocacy Association of Canada
CCED	Child Care Expense Deduction
CCSD	Canadian Council for Social Development
CCTC	Child Care Tax Credit
CDCAA	Canadian Day Care Advocacy Association
CEIC	Canadian Employment and Immigration Commission
CEW	Committee for the Equality of Women in Canada
CFBPWC	Canadian Federation of Business and Professional Women's Clubs
CFUW	Canadian Federation of University Women
CHRA	Canadian Human Rights Act
CHRC	Canadian Human Rights Commission
CHST	Canada Health and Social Transfer
CLC	Canadian Labour Congress
CNR	Canadian National Railway
EEA	Employment Equity Act
EIC	Employment and Immigration Commission
EOW	Equal Opportunities for Women
FFQ	Fédération des femmes du Québec
FCP	Federal Contractors Program
FPS	Federal public service
HRDC	Human Resources Development Canada
IDC	Interdepartmental Committee on the Status of Women
ILO	International Labour Organization
LIP	Local Initiatives Project

NAC	National Action Committee on the Status of Women
NAHAC	National Ad Hoc Action Committee on the Status of Women
NAWAL	National Association of Women and the Law
NCA	National Children's Agenda
NCB	National Child Benefit
NDP	New Democratic Party
OECD	Organization for Economic Co-operation and Development
OFL	Ontario Federation of Labour
PSC	Public Service Commission of Canada
RCEE	Royal Commission on Equality in Employment
RCSW	Royal Commission on the Status of Women in Canada
SPCCC	Special Parliamentary Committee on Child Care
SSR	Social Security Review
UN	United Nations
WISE	Women in Science and Engineering

Driven Apart

1
The Double-Edged Nature of Women's Employment Inequality

Debates about women's rights at work and the gendered dimensions of employment inequality were notable and contested features of Canadian political discourse throughout the second half of the twentieth century. Concern about these issues took root during the 1940s, when women experienced dramatic shifts in their employment opportunities as a result of being drawn into and later jettisoned from the reserve army of wartime labour.[1] Pressure to improve women's employment conditions, particularly in the burgeoning public sector, recurred in the mid-1950s.[2] However, it was in the 1960s, once the second wave of feminism took root in Canada, that women began to develop a sustained critique of the employment inequalities they experienced and pressure their governments to address the problem through policy innovation and change.[3]

From the outset of second-wave feminism, women advanced analyses of employment inequality that took account of their labour in both the public and domestic spheres. As Roberta Hamilton noted, activists "drew attention, as had never been done before, to the fundamental incompatibility between reproductive labour and child care, on the one hand, and paid work on the other, as well as to the profound consequences of this incompatibility."[4] While liberal, radical, and socialist feminists approached this issue from different ideological vantage points, they shared a common belief that the causes of gender inequality in employment were not rooted solely in the workplace. Only, they claimed, if questions about women's employment in the public sphere were addressed in tandem with questions about their labour in the domestic sphere would the gendered dimensions of employment inequality be fully understood.[5] In particular, feminists thought that women's maternal work had to be recognized in discussions about promoting gender equality in the workplace.[6] As Pat Schulz, a well-known socialist feminist, once argued, "As long as women have the primary responsibility for maintenance of the home and for child care, we will be less than able to pursue job opportunities and our domestic commitments will be used to justify discriminatory employment practices."[7]

Growing awareness of the need to link questions about production and reproduction in analyses of women's economic position was by no means unique to Canadian feminism. It was, for example, well established in the early writing of second-wave feminists in Britain and the United States.[8] What did, however, distinguish Canadian feminists from their counterparts in these other liberal democracies was an ability to work together, despite ideological differences, in order to advance this double-edged critique of gender inequality in employment.[9] Right from the start of the contemporary women's movement, Canadian feminists engaged with the state, demanding policies that recognized the link between women's employment opportunities and the provision of child care.[10]

Canadian feminists lobbied both federal and provincial governments about the need to improve women's employment opportunities and expand the provision of child care. It was in the federal arena, however, that women (outside Quebec) focused their demands for the development of policies that acknowledged the link between these two issues.[11] In some respects, this federal focus was surprising. After all, only one-tenth of the Canadian labour force is regulated by the federal government, and even at the start of second-wave feminism both federal and provincial governments had been involved in employment opportunity and child care initiatives.[12] Moreover, even though the federal government has the constitutional capacity to use its spending power to underwrite the provision of state-subsidized child care, it is the provinces that retain constitutional control over the delivery of this service.

The federal focus of women's campaigns was encouraged by the fact that the renaissance of Canadian feminism occurred within the context of a broader social project to achieve universal welfare guarantees, assured by the Canadian state.[13] It was reinforced by the government of Canada's decision to establish the 1967 Royal Commission on the Status of Women (RCSW) to inquire how best the federal government could ensure that women enjoyed "equal opportunities with men in all aspects of Canadian society."[14] It has since been sustained by the work of activists in national organizations, in particular the National Action Committee on the Status of Women (NAC), founded in 1972, and the Canadian Day Care Advocacy Association (CDCAA), established in 1982 and renamed the Child Care Advocacy Association of Canada (CCAAC) in 1992.

However, despite a long history of feminist engagement with the federal state, women's repeated campaigns for the development of policies to address the double-edged nature of gender inequality in employment, and the clear recognition of these demands in reports of royal commissions and task forces, the federal policy response has been uneven. Policies to eradicate sex discrimination at work and promote women's employment opportunities have been developed and implemented in the federal policy sphere. By contrast, the federal government has not developed policies to promote a publicly funded system of child care in order to enhance women's employment opportunities, save as emergency measures during the Second World War or as an element of broader initiatives to get "welfare mothers" out to work. Instead it has treated child care as a fiscal issue for which parents can receive subsidies through federal taxation.

This book examines why a double-edged interpretation of women's employment inequality, which recognizes the public and domestic dimensions of women's work, has not been fully absorbed into federal policies to promote gender equality in the sphere of employment. The analysis follows the development of debates about women's rights at work from the period of reconstruction after the Second World War, when questions about eradicating employment discrimination against worker-citizens first emerged in Canadian political debate, through to the close of the twentieth century. It examines federal policy developments under Liberal and Conservative governments, showing that even though the reports of federal royal commissions and task forces encoded feminist demands for a double-edged attack on employment inequality, questions about promoting women's employment equality and child care were continually driven apart in the federal policy process.

Organization of the Book
While the book focuses on policy developments since the establishment of the 1967 Royal Commission on the Status of Women, it sets the demands voiced by women during that inquiry in a broader historical context. Chapter 2 examines how the fluctuations in women's employment during the Second World War and in the period of reconstruction that followed generated demands that women, like men, should be able to assume the rights and duties of worker-citizenship in the postwar welfare state. It shows how policy developments in that period of reconstruction created a political context that made it relatively easy for women to call for anti-discrimination measures to ensure their equal treatment with men in the public sphere, yet relatively difficult for them to get their concerns about child care recognized as integral to the promotion of gender equality in employment.

Chapter 3 explores how the RCSW opened up a critical political space for women to articulate publicly how workplace discrimination and the limited provision of child care worked in tandem to constrain their employment opportunities. It shows how even though the commissioners were instructed to focus on questions of women's employment, rather than those of child care, women used the inquiry to articulate their concerns about both these issues, as well as the connection between them. Nevertheless, this process was not straightforward. Indeed, the chapter shows how women used the RCSW not simply as a forum in which to articulate the link between gender equality in employment and the provision of child care but also as a site in which to debate and challenge each other's ideas about the legitimacy of young mothers (as they were then called) working outside the home.

Chapters 4 and 5 focus on policy developments during the Liberal government of Pierre Trudeau. Chapter 4 examines the Trudeau government's response to the report of the RCSW, focusing on how it addressed questions about women's employment, sex discrimination, and child care in the 1970s. Chapter 5 examines the way issues about employment equality and child care were reactivated and redefined in the early 1980s. It looks first at the development of a more systemic approach to employment discrimination in the 1980s, arguing that this was reinforced not only by the entrenchment of equality clauses in the 1982 Charter of Rights and Freedoms but also by competition between the Canadian Human Rights Commission (CHRC) and the Canadian Employment and Immigration Commission (CEIC) to develop affirmative action policies in the federal domain. The chapter then examines how demands for a federal policy on child care were reactivated in the early 1980s by the birth of a national child care movement, a development that in itself reinforced the distinction between questions about women's employment and those of child care.

Chapter 6 returns to the question of how women mobilized around royal commissions by analyzing how they addressed questions about employment opportunity and child care in submissions to the 1983 Royal Commission on Equality in Employment (RCEE). The chapter highlights how women used a royal commission, once again, to argue that child care was essential for them to enjoy equal employment opportunities with men. It also shows how this claim was much less contested than it had been when women raised the issue in the inquiries of the RCSW.

Chapters 7 and 8 focus on policy developments during the Conservative government of Brian Mulroney. Chapter 7 examines the first Mulroney government's response to the report of the RCEE. It shows how the Conservative legislative agenda disconnected questions of employment equity and child care, even though these had been linked again in the report of the RCEE. Chapter 8 analyzes the more limited policy agenda that characterized Mulroney's second term, showing first how the government cautiously extended employment equity into the federal public service and second how it shifted attention away from questions of child care to those of child poverty.

Chapter 9 examines how questions about women's employment and child care were addressed in the 1990s, during the Liberal government of

Jean Chrétien. It argues that while the link between women's employment and child care was re-established by the Liberals, this was not done out of concern to promote gender equality in the workforce but first and foremost to address child poverty and get welfare mothers out to work. Chapter 10 then offers some final reflections on why questions of women's employment equality and child care have been driven apart, rather than linked, in Canadian public policy.

Previous Scholarship on Women's Paid and Caring Work

While this is by no means the first time that scholars have considered the relationship between Canadian women's work inside and outside the home, it is noticeable how the link between these two aspects of women's labour was explored by historians and sociologists before being addressed by analysts of public policy. In the late 1970s, members of the Women's History Collective at the Ontario Institute for Studies in Education and the Clio Collective in Montreal pioneered research in Canada on how women's labour had shifted from the unpaid domestic sphere into the world of paid employment. In the process, they unearthed textual and oral histories that demonstrated how, despite this transition, women still faced the double-bind of a double-day in which they went out to work for pay and home to work for love.[15] Their findings were reinforced in late 1970s and 1980s by sociological analyses of women's work arguing that because women so often entered employment while maintaining primary responsibility for the care of their children, they frequently found themselves concentrated in low-paid, low-status employment.[16]

Despite the fact that historians, sociologists, and feminist activists drew attention to the "double ghetto" of women's working lives, discussions about policies to promote women's employment opportunities and improve the provision of child care evolved as distinct scholarly debates. The literature on policies to promote Canadian women's employment opportunities emerged within the context of broader discussions and debates about the development of policies to root out discrimination in the workplace.[17] By contrast, the literature on Canadian child care policy evolved around questions about the development, cost, and politics of implementing public policies to promote the welfare, education, care, and development of young children.[18] In recent years, however, policy analysts have paid much greater attention to the link between women's paid and caring work.[19] Nonetheless, no one has yet considered why Canadian government policies to promote women's employment opportunities and improve the provision of child care have been developed at such different rates and, despite repeated calls to the contrary, not linked in the design of public policies to promote gender equality in federally regulated employment. This pattern of inquiry is understandable, given the discrete historical development of policies concerned with child care and those concerned with women's employment. However, it unduly limits our understanding of the gendered dimensions of employment inequality in Canada and fails to capture the empirical reality of many women's working lives.

Empirical Perspectives on the Double-Edged Nature of Women's Employment Inequality

Why did women's double-edged demand for equal employment opportunities and child care emerge in Canada in the 1960s and 1970s? After all, from the mid-1950s Canada experienced one of the fastest rates of labour force feminization in the Western industrialized world.[20] The decline of manufacturing industries and the concomitant growth of the tertiary sector in the 1950s and 1960s meant that while industries that had traditionally attracted men closed down, those demanding support skills that had long characterized women's traditional domestic roles expanded.[21] Moreover, in countries like Canada, where welfare states were being established, the growth in women's employment intensified most quickly.[22]

The much trumpeted rise in female labour force participation rates did not, however, mean that women engaged in paid employment on the same terms as men. The occupational segregation of Canadian men and women persisted in both horizontal and vertical forms.[23] In fact, this process intensified with the increased participation of women in the paid labour force.[24] As a result, the vast majority of women found themselves working in poorly paid occupations, situated in the lower echelons of private companies and public sector organizations.[25] Moreover, as Elisabeth Hagen and Jane Jenson have noted, although the creation of welfare states meant that "women as a group had more employment opportunities open up for them than men" in the mid-twentieth century, the growth in women's employment was in the part-time sector of the labour force, which was increasingly dominated by women in all OECD (Organization for Economic Co-operation and Development) countries.[26] This simply intensified the inequalities of employment opportunity that women experienced because part-time work is concentrated in the least-skilled, lowest-paid, and most poorly organized sections of the labour force, where benefits are usually more limited than in the full-time sector.[27]

The rapid growth in women's participation in part-time rather than full-time employment reflects two other factors about the feminization of the Canadian labour force. On the one hand, it relates to the type of work that the service sector has generated and to the increasing flexibility demanded of its employees. On the other hand, it reflects the fact that the greatest increase in female labour force participation rates since the 1960s has been among women with young children.[28] In the early 1960s, most female employees in Canada would leave the workforce when their first child was born and return only when their youngest child had entered school.[29] By the mid-1980s most women with young children went out to work (Table 1.1). Indeed, as Paul Phillips and Erin Phillips have noted, "By 1991 all traces of the reproduction function had disappeared with [female labour force] participation rates peaking in the major family-rearing age categories, 25-34."[30]

The double burden that women experience from juggling their employment while continuing to care for their children has been reinforced by the limited provision of subsidized child care spaces in Canada. In the late 1960s, when women began to pressure the federal government to address the minimal provision of child care for working women, federal subsidies for child care were limited to support for welfare mothers under the 1966 Canada Assistance Plan. This pattern changed very little in the course of the twentieth century, although federal subsidies to support child care for low-income families became increasingly tied to efforts to get mothers receiving welfare out to work.[31] Although recent federal publications on the status of day care in Canada boast "a twenty-five-fold increase" in child care spaces since the government first gathered these data in 1971, in fact the proportion of children of working mothers who have access to regulated child care remains very low (Table 1.2).[32] As a result, most working parents remain highly dependent on informal, unregulated child care. Indeed, as Kristin Colwell noted, in the mid-1990s "children in informal

Table 1.1

Labour force participation rates of women by age of youngest child, 1975-98

Year	Youngest child under 3 (%)	Youngest child 3-5 (%)	Youngest child 6-15 (%)
1975	31.2	40.0	48.2
1978	37.6	46.1	54.3
1981	44.5	52.4	61.1
1985	53.5	59.5	66.2
1991	61.5	68.2	76.2
1997	64.1	68.8	77.7
1998	64.0	70.0	78.0

Note: Figures for 1998 presented to the nearest whole number.
Sources: For 1975 to 1985: Morley Gunderson, *Implications of Daycare Policies on Female Labour Market Behaviour,* Report prepared for the Special Parliamentary Committee on Child Care, 1986, 14. For 1991: Statistics Canada, *Women in the Labour Force, 1994 Edition,* Catalogue no. 75-507E (Ottawa: Statistics Canada, 1994), Table 6.3, p. 52. For 1997: Gordon Cleveland and Michael Krashinsky, *The Benefits and Costs of Good Child Care: The Economic Rationale for Public Investment in Young Children* (Toronto: Childcare Resource and Research Unit, 1998), 42. For 1998: Data prepared by Richard Shillington for the Child Care Resource Unit using Statistics Canada's annual data collection on mothers in the labour force (Facsimile from Richard Shillington to Martha Friendly, 13 October 1999, 6).

Table 1.2

Children in full-time regulated care with mothers in the labour force, 1984-96

Age	Number	Percentage
1984		
0 to 17 months	204,869	5.7
18 to 36 months	215,557	10.7
Between 3 and 6 years	419,727	24.9
Between 6 and 12 years	1,612,567	2.0
1990		
0 to 17 months	307,063	5.4
18 to 36 months	316,277	9.7
Between 3 and 6 years	641,893	27.7
Between 6 and 12 years	1,720,310	5.6
1996		
0 to 17 months	327,005	11.0
18 to 36 months	338,321	14.0
Between 3 and 6 years	715,199	32.0
Between 6 and 13 years	1,595,450	8.0

Sources: Health and Welfare Canada, *Status of Day Care in Canada 1984* (Ottawa: Supply and Services, 1985), Tables 7-10; Health and Welfare Canada, *Status of Day Care in Canada 1990* (Ottawa: Supply and Services, 1991), Tables 7-10; Human Resources Development Canada, *Status of Day Care in Canada 1995 and 1996* (Ottawa: Supply and Services, 1997), Tables 7-10.

child care arrangements account[ed] for eighty per cent of all child care used by parents in Canada."[33]

Theoretical Perspectives on the Double-Edged Nature of Women's Employment Inequality

This book brings to light different ways in which Canadian women have campaigned for public policies that span the public and domestic spheres of their working lives. While its primary purpose is to fill a lacuna in the policy literature on women's employment opportunities and child care, it also throws light on two broad theoretical debates about Canadian public philosophy.

First, the book explores a fundamental tension in Canadian liberalism between the pursuit of equal opportunity and self-development, on the one hand, and the desire for economic efficiency and progress, on the other.[34] As the chapters unfold we will see how the decisions made by politicians and policy makers in the federal government have been shaped by these two competing strands in Canadian public philosophy. While questions about promoting equal employment opportunities for women and men have been a continuous feature of policy development since the

1970s, they have rarely been addressed without consideration of the way that such policies might affect the economy. In other words, the double edge of Canadian liberalism has shaped, and in many respects constrained, the development of policies to promote equal employment opportunities for women and men.

At the same time, this book shows how women have repeatedly challenged and contested the narrowness of Canadian liberalism, not least for its reluctance to move beyond a focus on the public sphere and to develop a complex, substantive notion of equality that takes differences between men and women into account. One of the key questions with which this book is concerned is why equal employment opportunity, anti-discrimination, and employment equity policies have been developed and implemented so much more easily than those of child care. Phrased another way, it asks why the federal state in Canada has addressed questions about promoting equal employment opportunities for men and women in the public sphere with relative ease but has failed to recognize that this project cannot be achieved without addressing the questions of child care that affect so many women's working lives.

While the reasons for this are complex, some insights from feminist theory may help us to begin this exploration. In recent years, a number of feminist theorists have discussed how the concept of worker-citizenship that took root as welfare states were developed in countries such as Canada did not take account of the different contexts in which women and men often assumed employment.[35] As Anna Shola Orloff has noted, "Just as the independent male householder [served] as the ideal-type citizen in classical liberal and democratic theory, the male worker [has served] as the ideal citizen in the literature on social rights."[36] As a result, when questions about promoting equal employment opportunities for men and women began to emerge in the 1950s and '60s, they were framed in terms of women achieving the *same* opportunities as men. Yet as Elizabeth Meehan and Selma Sevenhuijsen have asked, "How can equality policies which assume the possibility of gender-neutrality in politics and at work improve the lives of women who, by and large, are not in the same situation as men with respect to family obligations [and] the labour market?"[37]

This question is important, not least because we live in an era when the meaning of citizenship is strongly tied to an individual's participation in the labour force.[38] This, as Joan Tronto has noted, has posed particular problems because "the moral boundaries that surround a world constituted by the work ethic cannot recognize the importance of care."[39] As a result, "the image of what constitutes responsible human action misses entirely the care work that is necessary to keep human society functioning, except in so far as it is also paid work."[40] Thus, in order to create a concept of worker-citizenship that takes women's interests into account, we need to think about how care responsibilities can more effectively be reconciled with paid work.

Throughout this book, we shall see how Canadian women have repeatedly lobbied the federal government to develop a national system of child care that not only provides quality care for young children but also ensures that the context in which many women engage in paid labour is acknowledged in federal policies to promote gender equality in employment. Indeed, they have tried to develop a more nuanced concept of worker-citizenship that not only respects the objective of equality of opportunity but also takes workers' particular circumstances into account and, in the case of women, enables them to integrate their paid and caring work better. In the process, women have argued that a state that upholds the principle of gender equality must develop policies that take account of the interconnectedness of the public and domestic spheres and recognize the different contexts in which men and women often assume employment.

Nonetheless, although Canadian feminists have a long history of active engagement with the state, developed through a "visible and articulate women's movement" that has successfully placed issues on the political agenda, the result, more often than not, has been that their demands have been contained within a limited set of reforms.[41] As a result, those aspects of gender discrimination in the workplace that concern practices within the public sphere have been acknowledged through the introduction of anti-discrimination and employment equity policies. By contrast, women have had more difficulty getting their proposals for policies that transcend the public/private divide, by linking questions of equal employment opportunity with those of child care, acknowledged in the federal policy arena.[42] Despite their efforts to forge these links through two major royal commissions and other government inquiries, problems of gender inequality in employment are still primarily defined as issues located *within* the public sphere of employment.

Without doubt, over the past thirty years there have been clear improvements in the position of women in the federally regulated section of the Canadian labour force. Nonetheless, women continue to cluster in the lower echelons of companies and organizations and remain under-represented in more senior positions. While this persistent pattern of inequality has many causes, this book shows how it reflects a federal policy process that concentrates on ensuring the comparable treatment of male and female employees once they have entered the labour market, yet, for complex reasons, repeatedly stalls on developing a more expansive approach to child care. As a result, federal policies to promote gender equality in the sphere of employment neglect the inequalities of access and participation that many women experience as they continue or resume employment once they have dependent children.

2
Citizenship, Motherhood, and Employment in the Wartime and Welfare States

While considerable attention has been paid to the sociopolitical forces in the late 1950s and early 1960s that encouraged the second wave of feminism in Canada, there has been little discussion of the longer-term factors that influenced women's growing concerns about the gendered nature of their employment opportunities.[1] Yet early second-wave feminist demands for gender equality in the workplace were shaped not only by the fluctuations in women's employment opportunities during and immediately after the Second World War, but also by the new discourse on worker-citizenship that accompanied the construction of Canada's postwar welfare state. However, while the new paradigm of worker-citizenship encouraged women's demands for equal employment opportunities with men, it did not prove easy for women to gain recognition of the way their participation in the labour force was shaped by the caring responsibilities that accompanied motherhood.

Fluctuations in Women's Employment during and after the War
The Second World War fundamentally disrupted established patterns of women's work. Although some women had worked for pay long before the war, their employment outside the home had typically been regarded as an activity that was undertaken either by young single women at "a stage in the life cycle between two stages of dependency" or by spinsters, divorcées, and married working-class women who had restricted means of financial support.[2] However, with the onset of war, female labour force participation rates began to escalate as more and more women, regardless of their class, race, religion, or marital status, took up employment outside their homes.[3] When hostilities broke out in 1939, just under a quarter of Canadian women were in paid employment. Six years later, when the war ended in 1945, a third of adult women in Canada had joined the labour force.[4] Indeed, when women's wartime employment peaked in the autumn of 1944, one million women were working full-time.[5]

Historical research on this period has revealed the extent to which women not only took up military and civilian employment but also engaged in extensive voluntary labour in urban and rural areas. Even though women were treated as a reserve army of labour, they conducted work that was crucial to the war effort. Moreover, because women made bombs, built ships, trained air crews, staffed the public service, and met farm production schedules on time, they debunked the long-established myth that such jobs could be done only by men.[6]

Although the war did not herald an era of major debate about equal employment opportunities for men and women, it did create the conditions in which the socially structured and culturally patterned behaviour of both men and women changed with respect to employment. Significant changes in the patterns of women's employment meant that the "cult of true womanhood," which had long correlated feminine fulfilment with domesticity, lost some of its ideological hold as the gendered demarcation between the public and private spheres weakened and women took on work that had, until then, typically been carried out by men.[7] Indeed, as they did so in increasing numbers, the possibility that women could assume a status in the labour force that was equal to that of men began to emerge.

This climate of change intensified as women's participation in the labour force increased and the idea that they were only suited to the full-time care of their children was called into question. Although married women without children were encouraged to join the civilian war effort during the early part of the war, it took longer for traditional assumptions about women with young children not working outside the home to change. However, as hostilities intensified and the demand for female labour increased, the labour force participation of mothers with young children was sanctioned officially. On 20 July 1942, the federal government signed an Order in Council authorizing the minister of Labour to assist provincial governments with the "cost of organizing and operating, where necessary, day nurseries, creches, recreation centres and like facilities" for the children of "mother or foster mothers" who were "employed in war industries in Canada."[8] Under this fiscal initiative, the federal and provincial governments split the operating costs of new child care units and ensured that 75 percent of the newly funded child care spaces were allocated to women who were working in high-priority industries.[9]

Designed to facilitate the employment of women with young children in the major war industries, this agreement demonstrated how in a period of global hostility the civic responsibilities of women with young children could be broadened beyond the domestic sphere.[10] Indeed, the initiative challenged prevailing assumptions that women's roles as full-time mothers and homemakers were natural and unchangeable. Moreover, it set important precedents that influenced the shape of child care politics in the 1970s and 1980s. The agreement legitimized federal government involvement in the provision of a service that constitutionally was deemed to be an area of provincial jurisdiction. Moreover, it highlighted how the federal government could use its spending powers to work with the provinces to finance the provision of child care. Above all, the agreement established a precedent for federal involvement in the development of child care provision to facilitate women's entry into the paid labour force.

Wartime Employment and Female Citizenship

Although historians have analyzed the Second World War as a major turning point in the history of women's work, the impact of this period on women's sense of themselves as citizens has not been fully explored. This is surprising because there has been considerable discussion of the extent to which women's assumption of civic duties during the First World War led to their being awarded the federal franchise.[11] Yet wartime propaganda during the Second World War reinforced the idea that women, like men, were assuming civic responsibilities. As Susan Bland has observed, between 1941 and 1944 "ads directed to working women (particularly to war workers) applaud[ed] these women for their 'sacrifice' and contribution to the war effort."[12]

It is interesting to note how this propaganda repeatedly emphasized women's participation in paramilitary work. For example, advertisements calling women to participate in war industries and voluntary programs frequently depicted slim, neatly dressed women in a back-up civilian army.[13] Moreover, the mottoes of the women's divisions in the military – "We Serve That Men May Fly," "We Serve That Men May Fight," and "We Are the Women Behind the Men Behind the Guns," – reinforced the idea that women, like men, were showing their worth as citizens.[14] As Carole Pateman has argued, until the end of the Second World War the dominant perception of civic duty was still framed in terms of a man being prepared to participate in armed conflict in order to defend his country.[15] Given that women were absorbed into this paradigm during the war, it was perhaps inevitable that questions about their being able to enjoy the benefits of citizenship, in a way similar to men, would emerge once the war was over.

Women's active participation in the war effort was eventually acknowledged by the Advisory Committee on Reconstruction when, two years into its existence, it established a subcommittee to examine problems that women might face in the period of postwar adjustment. Set up in June 1943, after repeated lobbying from women's organizations, the subcommittee was asked "to examine the problems relating to the re-establishment of women after the war and to make recommendations to the Committee on Reconstruction as to the procedure to deal with the problems and other matters relating to the welfare of women in the period of reconstruction."[16]

The 1944 report of the subcommittee, entitled *Post-War Problems of Women*, reflected how the concept of worker-citizenship was about to supersede previous ideas about fighter-citizenship. It held that women should be allowed to make a clear choice either to return to the domestic sphere or to continue in paid employment. While the report assumed that "the normal urge towards marriage, and home and family life ... can be relied upon to reduce largely the number of women now listed as gainfully employed," it also argued that because "in the work and sacrifice of the war years women have played their full part as responsible citizens, [they] ... expect to be treated as such in the coming years."[17] Indeed, the report concluded that women's war work entitled them to the same possibilities as men for postwar training and employment and that each woman should have "the right to choose her work and obtain the same remuneration, working conditions and opportunities for advancement" as those of men.[18] As a result, the subcommittee called for "immediate preparations to increase employment opportunities for women" once the war was over.[19]

Women's Employment Immediately after the War
Despite the subcommittee's recommendations, the female labour force declined in the immediate postwar period, as the women's divisions of the military were disbanded and the civilian women's labour force was cut by 9 percent.[20] In part, this dip signalled the conscious choices of some women to turn or return to the domestic sphere. However, it also reflected the fact that the final report of the Advisory Committee on Reconstruction did not address the issues raised by the subcommittee on the postwar problems of women. Indeed, it is well known that after the war, women were laid off from the war industries, demobilized from the military, and, if they were married, barred from certain areas of employment.[21] In the immediate postwar period, 80,000 women were laid off from the war industries in order to open up jobs for men who were returning to the civilian labour market in search of work.[22] Even though women leaving the military were offered further education and training, they typically failed to qualify for the veterans' preference scheme in the public service because they had rarely served overseas.[23] Moreover, married women who had been employed by the federal government during the war found it difficult to maintain their posts when marriage bars were re-introduced and not completely removed until 1955.[24]

The dramatic changes in women's employment opportunities immediately after the war signalled the reassertion of male economic primacy and a new discourse about men needing to earn a "family wage."[25] Although men and women had engaged in civic duties during the war, their roles as citizens became more distinct once the hostilities ceased. While men were deemed to be worker-citizens, supporting their dependants and paying tax to underwrite the emergent welfare state, women were encouraged to resume their roles as carer-citizens, nurturing male workers and tending to the young. This division was encouraged not only by a resurgence of family-centred ideology emphasizing the importance of mothers' work at home but also by a dramatic reduction in state-subsidized child care. The Quebec government discontinued its participation in the wartime agreement on day nurseries in October 1945, and despite protest, the federal government rescinded the agreement in June 1946.[26] Cost-sharing arrangements with the governments of Ontario and Alberta were terminated, as was the federal government's brief recognition of the link between child care and women's employment. Inevitably, therefore, the demarcations between the domestic and public spheres became clearer, and the reassertion of links between femininity and domesticity more pronounced.[27]

The central importance of mothers caring for children at home was reinforced by the recommendations of the 1943 Marsh Report on Social Security for Canada. These called for, among other things, the introduction of cash-based family allowances, made payable to the mothers of dependent children.[28] Interestingly, the members of the subcommittee examining the postwar problems of women supported the Marsh Report's recommendation, a decision they may well have taken to ensure that women were given a choice about whether to work inside or outside the home.[29] Nonetheless, as Pierson has noted, while Marsh proposed that children's allowances "be paid to mothers as a way of promoting motherhood and mothers' individual rights," he also assumed that the introduction of social security benefits for wives would depend on "recognition of the husband as the chief wage-earner."[30]

The postwar reduction in women's opportunities for employment generated concern that women had been treated as a reserve army of labour to be lured into and then pushed out of the workforce as the need arose. Having crossed the threshold of the public workplace and been employed in occupations that until then had only been deemed suitable for men, significant contradictions arose when women were encouraged to return to their home fires in order to release jobs for men who had been away on active military service. Articles in Canadian magazines pointed to the double standards of hiring women for temporary wartime work, only to replace them with men once the fighting had ceased.[31] Critics also questioned the legitimacy of reinforcing a marriage bar for women in the public service once the war was over.[32] Moreover, the decline in women's employment was problematic in an era when a new discourse on citizenship, built around concepts of full employment, was taking root in Canada and in other liberal democracies engaged in the creation of welfare states.

Postwar Reconstruction: Social Citizenship and the Welfare State
It is now well established that the duties and rights attached to citizenship changed fundamentally in many Western democracies as the concept of social citizenship took root in the era of postwar reconstruction. At the core of this concept was the idea that the rights of citizenship should be extended beyond the legal and political domain, so that all members of a political community could enjoy an equal set of social and economic rights.[33] In Canada, this change became manifest in the decision to construct a postwar welfare state designed to free citizens from the threat of poverty that had gripped the country during the Depression of the 1930s.

In Canada, as elsewhere, the creation of a welfare state led to a fundamental change in both the duties and rights attached to citizenship. As Pateman has noted, it was because the contributory principle formed the link between work and welfare that "paid employment became the key to citizenship in the democratic welfare state."[34] The status of the male citizen was therefore transformed from that of *citizen-fighter* into that of *citizen-worker*, who, on the grounds of participating in the labour force, was entitled to reap the benefits of social citizenship entrenched in the new welfare state. Indeed, the hope embodied in the Keynesian vision that inspired the development of welfare states was that full employment would be maintained so that citizens could ensure their own economic security, with that of their dependants, and at the same time create the wealth to underwrite the development of new universal social policies.[35] As David Wolfe has noted, "The expansion of welfare services and the commitment to full employment became the basis of the postwar settlement between capital and labour."[36] This new model of citizenship assured citizens that in return for working to underwrite the provision of welfare services, they would be guaranteed a minimum income throughout their lives.

Women and the Federal Welfare State
Two contradictions emerged in the process of constructing a welfare state based on the principle of worker-citizenship. First, although the duties and entitlements of citizenship became strongly linked to an individual's participation in the labour force, the opportunities for women to work for pay actually went down as men returned from the battlefields of Europe. Women found that although they had contributed to the war effort by working in military, civilian, and voluntary capacities during the period of global hostility, they were not being built into the postwar equation of

worker-citizenship on similar terms to men. Indeed, women found that having fulfilled their duties as citizens by working in the public sphere throughout the war, they were then forced back into a state of domestic dependency once the war was over.[37] As this process did not grant them the same social rights or economic power as men, it substantially undermined the legitimacy of the new model of social citizenship that was embedded in the Canadian welfare state.

This contradiction remained latent until married women started to enter the workforce in the 1950s. The percentage of working women who were married rose by two-thirds in that decade, from 30 percent in 1951 to 49.8 percent in 1961.[38] Indeed by 1958 (when the proportion of working women who were married stood at 40 percent) there were, for the first time in Canadian history, more married women than single women employed in the paid workforce.[39] It is hardly surprising, therefore, that when the Women's Bureau was established within the Department of Labour in 1954 to ensure that the federal government had enough information about women's employment to guide the development of labour market policy, the first big project that it commissioned surveyed married women working for pay in eight Canadian cities.[40] Though designed to establish whether married women had the necessary skills and training to take advantage of the burgeoning employment opportunities in the expanding service sector, this survey produced much broader information. As Catherine Briggs and Sandra Burt have noted, it not only examined the "characteristics of married working women, their reasons for working, the types of jobs they held ... and their long term employment plans," but also asked women "how they balanced work with home responsibilities."[41]

Marion Royce, the first director of the Women's Bureau, was clearly committed to exploring the concept of motherhood at work. In the 1960s, the bureau organized a number of conferences, including meetings about the problems faced by working women with family responsibilities.[42] In addition, in 1964 it published the results of a specific study entitled "Day Care Services for Children of Working Mothers."[43] However, although Royce and her colleagues understood how women's employment opportunities were shaped by the broader context in which they assumed paid work, it did not prove easy to gain recognition of this fact within federal government circles.[44] As Burt notes, although the establishment of the Women's Bureau indicated the federal government's wish to gather information about the potential development of married women's participation in the paid labour force, federal bureaucrats resisted policies that would "focus on the personal and family problems of married women employees."[45] Moreover, as Rianne Mahon argues – in a way that reflects subsequent limitations in federal approaches to women's employment and child care – although Royce was clearly concerned about the question of child care services for working women, she feared that "day care lay out-side her jurisdiction ('women and work' rather than 'family and social services')."[46] As a result, "she quietly urged the Family and Child Welfare Division to use its channels to probe the need for day care," a strategy that undoubtedly reinforced the definition of child care as a welfare issue in federal public policy.[47] In short, while femocrats within the Women's Bureau clearly tried to ensure that the issue of child care remained on the federal agenda, the emergent concept of worker-citizenship did not take account of the different contexts in which men and women assumed employment. Nonetheless, the new paradigm encouraged awareness about the importance of eradicating discrimination at work.

Worker-Citizenship, Anti-Discrimination, and the Postwar Social Movements

The significance of worker-citizenship in the postwar welfare state placed increased pressure on the federal government to develop measures to erad-icate employment discrimination. After all, this was an era when new dis-courses about universal human rights, the need to eradicate official racism, and the importance of men being able to earn a family wage were ascen-dant. It is hardly surprising, therefore, to find that human rights and labour movement activists worked together to ensure that all men returning to civilian employment had access to work in order to support themselves and their families.

The Canadian human rights movement had been catalyzed into exis-tence by the double standard of Canada's engagement in the war against fascism at a time when blatant discrimination continued against Jews and Japanese people within its own borders. As Brian Howe and David Johnson have noted, "The Second World War was a pivotal event in the evolution of human rights legislation ... The war, by mobilizing Canadians against state-sanctioned racism, by illustrating the evil consequences to which racism can lead, and by demonstrating – through the mistreatment of Japanese Canadians – the shortcomings of Canadian society itself, served as a catalyst for human rights awareness and for legislation against discrimination."[48]

The emergent Canadian human rights movement had two distinct wings. On the one hand, there were those like John Diefenbaker, Arthur Lower, and John Bracken, who were concerned that the state should not restrict the liberties of an individual, particularly as it had done during the war, through conscription, deportation, detention, and internment. Activ-ists in this wing of the movement campaigned for a bill of rights to protect individuals against any abuse of government power.[49] Such an instrument, they thought, would enhance national unity and ensure that individuals had recourse to the courts if they found themselves receiving unequal treatment before the law. As Diefenbaker argued in the House of Commons in 1947, "A bill of rights would be a contract between the individuals of Canada and the government of Canada. It would assert the rights of individuals; it would assert the rights of a minority to be protected in the exercise of its rights, against the majority. It would, above all, assure that each of us would have a legal right to be heard in the courts of this country."[50]

However, for others, like David Lewis and Frank Scott, on the left of the human rights movement, Diefenbaker's proposals did not go far enough. These activists were particularly concerned to stop the persistent (employment) discrimination against members of ethnic minorities.[51] They argued that the state should not simply protect the rights and freedoms of citizens but also encourage equality of opportunity in public life, particularly in the sphere of employment because it was so crucial to the realization of worker-citizenship.[52] In addition, they brought into public debate the possibility of eradicating discrimination through positive state action. In particular, they drew attention to the need for a comprehensive human rights policy, backed by a strong administrative structure to oversee and enforce its implementation.[53] Indeed, they believed that such a policy would ensure that citizens were "protected against private conduct or governmental action that distinguishes people for different treatment according to their national origins, race, sex or other unjustifiable characteristic."[54]

Links between those on the left of the human rights movement and activists in the labour movement reinforced the importance of the workplace as a site in which to tackle discrimination.[55] These connections became established shortly after the Second World War, when human rights committees were created within the Canadian Congress of Labour and when mutually supportive links were formed between Jewish community organizations and sections of the labour movement.[56] They were sustained by a mutual interest in the elimination of anti-Semitism in Canada.[57] As Howe notes, the Jewish Labour Committee and the Labour Committee for Human Rights, both under the leadership of Kalmen Kaplansky (1946-58), proved essential in mobilizing popular support for human rights.[58] Similarly, both the Canadian Congress of Labour and the Trades and Labour Congress linked together to form a Committee against Racial Intolerance, thereby formalizing their commitment to the eradication of racial discrimination in the workplace.[59]

The Canadian human rights and labour movements did not operate in isolation. Their campaigns were strengthened by the institutionalization of the international postwar movement for human rights, which promoted the question of nondiscrimination and equal opportunity on the political agendas of several Western democracies and emphasized the importance of ensuring that the benefits of social citizenship were realized within the sphere of employment.[60] As Kaplansky notes, conventions passed in both the United Nations (UN) and the International Labour Organization (ILO) not only provided benchmarks against which human rights activists could assess the incremental development of anti-discrimination legislation in Canada, but also helped to "translate the concepts of traditional basic freedoms and constitutional rights into the present-day language of our industrial society by emphasizing a wide range of social and economic rights."[61]

The Impact of Human Rights Campaigns on the Federal Government
At the federal level, the impact of the human rights movement first became apparent in parliamentary debate and in Diefenbaker's early demands for a Canadian Bill of Rights.[62] It was also evident in the establishment of a joint committee of the Senate and House of Commons on Human Rights and Fundamental Freedoms (1947-8) and a Special Senate Committee on Human Rights and Fundamental Freedoms (1950), which, as Howe has argued, "put into doubt the notion that discrimination could only be dealt with by friendly persuasion rather than legislation."[63] The movement also had some impact on federal employment legislation. The 1953 Fair Employment Practices Act outlawed employment discrimination on the grounds of race, national origin, colour, or religion.[64] Furthermore, the 1955 Unemployment Insurance Act extended these causes to prohibit discrimination on the grounds of political affiliation.[65]

However, even though the 1956 Female Employees Equal Pay Act established the principle of equal pay for equal work, it was not until the introduction of the Canadian Bill of Rights in 1960 that a more extensive approach to the question of sex discrimination developed.[66] Once the Bill of Rights required that individuals working in the federal domain be guaranteed "equality before the law and the equal protection of the law," regardless of race, national origin, colour, religion, or sex, the need to eradicate sex discrimination in the federal workplace was recognized.[67] For example, the 1967 Public Service Employment Act required that the Public Service Commission should "not discriminate against any person by reason of sex, race, national origin, colour or religion" in setting its selection standards for appointment to the federal public service.[68] Indeed, as Cook and Eberts have noted, "Enactment of equal opportunity legislation for women in Canada was accomplished by broadening the provisions of existing human rights legislation so that sex and, in some cases, marital status became 'prohibited grounds of discrimination,' along with the older grounds of race, religion [and] national origin."[69] However, while this assertion is accurate, it masks the extent to which prevailing assumptions about the best way to promote gender equality in the paid workforce were contested by women who became active in the early stages of second-wave feminism.

The Growing Awareness of Sex Discrimination in Employment

It was against the background of human rights and labour movement activism that the feminist movement took root in the 1960s, "to respond to the conditions of women's post-war lives" and "reinvigorate the long-held goals of the Canadian women's movement."[70] It is hardly surprising that in an era when the dominant paradigm was one of worker-citizenship, where "the extension of citizens' entitlements and participation rights ... largely occurred in relation to the individual's status in the labour market," that women's goal of achieving equal civic status with men focused on questions of gender equality in the sphere of employment.[71] However, while some women espoused the human rights paradigm that gender equality in employment could be achieved by extending to women the rights of worker-citizenship currently enjoyed by men, those who were active in the labour movement and in new socialist feminist organizations emphasized the importance of pursuing a more complex approach to gender equality in the workplace.

Women in the Human Rights Movement

While the Canadian human rights movement in the 1950s had been primarily concerned with combatting race discrimination, international organizations like the UN and the ILO began to extend this agenda to address the problem of sex discrimination. The relationship between human rights and women's rights was first acknowledged in 1946, when the United Nations Commission on the Status of Women was established. It was reinforced when the eradication of sex discrimination was declared as an objective of the 1948 Universal Declaration of Human Rights. Subsequent declarations by the ILO called not only for the fuller protection of individuals against discrimination but for the extension of these social rights into the field of employment.[72] For example, its 1958 Convention 111 on Discrimination in Respect of Employment and Occupation required signatories to "declare and pursue a national policy designed to promote by methods appropriate to national conditions and practice, equality of opportunity and treatment in respect of employment and occupation with a view to eliminating any discrimination in respect thereof."[73]

International concern with women's rights as human rights had an impact on established women's organizations in Canada. Indeed, once Canada joined the UN Status of Women Commission in 1958, established Canadian women's groups that had international affiliations became more actively involved in debates concerning women's status. As a result, their members began to urge the Canadian government to comply with international labour codes and ensure that legislation to prevent sex discrimination in the workplace was introduced.[74] In this respect, the resurgent feminist movement in Canada reinforced the way in which the dominant discourse on human rights shaped early debates about gender equality in the workplace. However, even though Canada ratified the ILO's Convention 111 in 1964, it was not until November 1967, when Canada participated in the unanimous adoption of the UN Declaration on the Elimination of Discrimination against Women, that the federal government fully acknowledged the importance of eradicating discrimination on the grounds of sex.[75] Interestingly, as we shall see in Chapter 3, this was the same year it appointed the Royal Commission on the Status of Women.

Women in the Labour Movement and the New Socialist-Feminist Movement

Although women who engaged in international human rights campaigns had an established history of working to eradicate sex discrimination, it was not until 1968, when the Canadian Labour Congress (CLC) included the eradication of sex discrimination within its constitution, that this issue began to have a higher profile on union agendas.[76] Undoubtedly, the involvement of union activists in campaigns to eliminate race discrimination gradually prompted awareness about the double standards of sex discrimination as well. At the same time, however, the newly formed public service unions, which served strong female constituencies, raised the profile of gender-based issues within the Canadian labour movement.[77]

The formation of women's committees within unions certainly increased the collective impact of women's demands.[78] While activists in women's committees in the 1960s were supportive of campaigns to ensure that workplaces were free from discrimination, they did not assume that anti-discrimination measures alone would promote equality of employment opportunity for all Canadian citizens. Indeed, socialist feminists called not only for anti-discrimination legislation but also for recognition of the particular barriers that different groups of citizens experienced in gaining employment and in developing their careers. In the case of women, it was argued that such barriers could only be dismantled if anti-discrimination legislation was accompanied by a more comprehensive set of policies, designed to address the way that so many women's careers were shaped by the biological demands of maternity and the social construction of motherhood. In an article printed in *Canadian Labour* in 1967, Thelma Cartwright insisted that "the whole idea of women's equality is a myth when it is based on the premise that they are the same as men. Of course we need and are entitled to equal job opportunities with men. But we need more than that. We need to be recognized as different from men with different needs and special problems. We need adequate legislation to ensure maternity leave and benefits; we need income tax concessions to enable us to claim for the help that we might be able to find for our home; we need many creches and nurseries."[79] In short, Cartwright challenged the assumption that gender equality in the workplace could be achieved simply by ensuring that women were treated in the same way as men.

At the same time, younger women who were engaged in the student movement and New Left politics in Canada began to pursue more radical critiques of women's position, which "insisted on the primacy of gender as a basis for women's oppression" as well as their liberation.[80] While these women did not completely denounce the reforms sought by their more liberal "sisters," they called for a recognition of women's specific circumstances, particularly those relating to the areas of reproduction, maternity, and child care, which they considered were overlooked in the pursuit of policy reforms based on equal rights. Indeed, those who took up this interpretation out of a concern for women's rights at work argued that gender equality in employment could only be secured if equal rights and anti-discrimination laws were accompanied by a more comprehensive set of policies that took into account the ways in which so many women's careers were affected by the biological demands of maternity and the social construction of motherhood. By the late 1960s, therefore, the question of whether gender equality in employment could best be realized by treating women in the same way as men, or by recognizing differences between them, was being aired in political debate.

Interestingly, it was the liberal feminist decision to lobby for the establishment of a royal commission on the status of women that finally brought human rights and labour movement feminists together. The decision to begin lobbying for a royal commission came from within the Canadian Federation of University Women, an organization that clearly supported the expansion of human rights. However, because its president, Laura Sabia, had recognized the importance of involving some labour movement activists in the campaign, the committee that was formed to lobby for a royal commission on the status of women brought together women from across the political spectrum.[81] These women were astute enough to frame their demand for a royal commission within the dominant human rights paradigm, but what they really wanted was to create a public forum in which women could articulate their visions of the best way to improve their status in Canadian society.[82] Without doubt, they achieved this goal. Indeed, the commission became a forum in which women's double-edged critique about including child care in the development of policies to promote the equality of male and female worker-citizens was fully articulated in the federal political arena.

3
The Royal Commission on the Status of Women

The Royal Commission on the Status of Women (RCSW) was a watershed in Canadian women's history.[1] Its establishment marked "the first publicly recognized success" of second-wave feminism in Canada, and its inquiries transformed a growing awareness among women about the inequalities and discrimination they experienced into a body of oral and written testimony about the changes they sought.[2] However, while the mobilization of women during and immediately after the RCSW has been widely noted, very little attention has been paid to the nature of the testimony they presented to the commissioners.[3] Moreover, even though the issue of women's employment – and particularly married women's employment – was central to the RCSW, no one has yet examined how women used the commission to link questions about their employment with those of child care provision.[4]

A significant number of women participated in the RCSW's inquiries. A total of 454 nonconfidential briefs were submitted to the commission from established organizations, individual citizens, and informal groups of women meeting together to formulate their concerns.[5] In addition, the commissioners received extensive correspondence from women and heard a fascinating range of oral testimony as they travelled throughout the country.[6] The level of public engagement in the RCSW not only indicates the commission's significance as a forum in which women were able to air their concerns but also reflects the proactive manner in which the commissioners set about their inquiries. Working at the outset from freezing, temporary offices that also housed the Royal Commission on Farm Machinery, the commissioners thought carefully about how to encourage women to submit written evidence. They made extensive efforts to publicize the commission in the media.[7] Indeed, as the chief commissioner, Florence Bird, noted in her autobiography, the commissioners cast their consultative net wide as they wanted to encourage women's participation in their inquiries:

Unlike the other commissions, we prepared a folder which contained our terms of reference ... as well as a description of the way to prepare a brief, where to send it, and the final date for delivery. We distributed the folders in supermarkets and libraries, and sent them to women's associations ... We believed in participatory democracy and were determined to hear the opinions of people in all income groups and with all levels of education, not just those of large organizations that had the resources to prepare well-researched submissions.[8]

By publicizing the RCSW in this way and making the consultations as broad as their budget would allow, the commissioners provided women around the country with the opportunity to talk about the discrimination they experienced in many different spheres of their lives. However, as the evidence in this chapter shows, the RCSW also became a forum in which women were able to expose the limitations of the dominant human rights approach to questions of employment discrimination. Indeed, the RCSW opened up a space in which women expressed both their desire for equal employment opportunities with men and their need for support with child care, as well as the double impetus in these concerns.[9] Moreover, by formally recognizing how women's demands for gender equality in the sphere of employment were intrinsically linked to their demands for recognition of the different responsibilities that men and women had for child care, the report of the RCSW broadened the federal policy agenda in a way that had not been fully anticipated when the commission was established.

In order to appreciate the full impact of this challenge, it is useful to examine the politics of establishing the RCSW and its terms of reference. These demonstrate that even though the RCSW was established within a human rights paradigm that required the commissioners to consider what steps the federal government might take to ensure that women enjoyed "equal opportunities with men in all aspects of Canadian society," the commissioners' consultations with Canadian women led them to write a report that had policy implications reaching well beyond the equal treatment framework in which the terms of reference were cast.[10]

The Politics of Establishing the RCSW

Although the politics surrounding the RCSW's establishment have been discussed by activists and scholars, relatively little attention has been paid to the way that the women who lobbied for the RCSW framed their demands within the dominant human rights paradigm.[11] Yet it is clear that the idea of a royal commission was conceived as a mechanism not only to get the federal government to address the discrimination that women experienced but also to ensure that women were able to enjoy equal civic rights with men. Early in 1966, when Laura Sabia, as president of the Canadian Federation of University Women (CFUW), called women from thirty-two women's organizations "together again," it was to an "exploratory meeting on human rights and a commission on the status of women."[12] Indeed, it is symbolic of the tradition in which these women were working – to equalize the status of men and women as citizens – that they formed the Committee for the *Equality of Women* in Canada (CEW) to push for a royal commission that would investigate ways of improving the status of women in Canadian society.[13]

The human rights framework ensured that questions about women's status and rights were seen as credible political issues.[14] It also provided an ideological framework in which women from a range of business, professional, church, and labour organizations could operate together to formulate demands. While the women who attended that meeting were not used to working together, the common denominator running through the resolutions they produced was that Canada should mark both its centenary (1967) and International Human Rights Year (1968) by establishing a royal commission on the status of women.[15] They immediately created a nine-member steering committee, chaired by Sabia. On 27 May 1966 it decided that the CEW should approach the federal government and demand that such an inquiry be established.[16]

The brief that the CEW presented to the federal government on 19 November 1966 demonstrated just how important the human rights framework proved to be in justifying their demands. The CEW requested "the appointment of a royal commission on the status of women in Canada today, to inquire into, to report on and to make recommendations which will enable women to achieve such excellence in public and private life as meets the standards set by the Universal Declaration of Human Rights."[17] It is worth noting that in an era when concepts of worker-citizenship were dominant, two of the seven areas identified by the CEW for consideration by the commission focused on questions of women's access to employment. One more called for a review of the International Labour Organization (ILO) conventions that had not yet been ratified by the federal government.[18]

Although these liberal feminists adopted the language of human rights to articulate their demands, it is clear from their reference to "public and private life" that they sought to expand the conventional notion of human rights as a set of objectives to be realized in the public domain. In particular, they wanted to get beyond the idea of lobbying simply for a human rights commission and persuade the federal government to establish a forum in which women could articulate concerns about the discrimination they experienced in both the public and domestic spheres of their lives. Reflecting on the process some years later, Margaret Hyndman, a past-president of the Canadian Federation of Business and Professional Women's Clubs (CFBPWC), explained that "a human rights commission would be appointed by the government and the head would be a man. What we wanted was a way of giving the majority of women a forum to make their needs and wants known."[19] The CEW did realize this objective. The RCSW was the first royal commission in Canada to be chaired by a woman.[20] Moreover, although individual women had been appointed to royal commissions on previous occasions, the fact that five of the seven commissioners were women was novel in Canadian history.[21]

The Federal Government's Rationale for Establishing the RCSW

It is part of feminist folklore in Canada that while the government's decision to establish the RCSW was the result of exhaustive cabinet lobbying by Judy LaMarsh, the final announcement was triggered by Laura Sabia's headline-grabbing remark that she would march three million women onto Parliament Hill – Duke of York style – if a commission was not established.[22] Academic accounts, however, suggest that while the federal government was keen to avoid such a confrontation, Pearson's eventual decision to establish the RCSW was driven by a need to placate the New Democratic Party (NDP), in order to keep his minority government in power, and court the votes of an increasingly active female electorate in the next federal election.[23] In addition, Pearson had a sense that although a royal commission would receive representations from radical feminists, it might contain their demands and keep the feminist agenda for policy change within a human rights framework.[24]

Pearson was also under broader national and international pressures to promote equality of opportunity among Canadian men and women. At the national level, it was difficult for him to back away from demands for a royal commission to equalize the status of men and women in Canada when his own government had promoted the equality of francophones and anglophones through the establishment of the Royal Commission on Bilingualism and Biculturalism.[25] International pressure arose in part because Canada had ratified ILO Convention 111 in 1964, thereby committing the federal government to develop national policies that would promote "equality of opportunity and treatment in respect of employment and occupation, with a view to eliminating any discrimination in [these areas of civic life]."[26] Moreover, as the governments of several other liberal democracies had recently appointed commissions to investigate the status of women, there was pressure on Pearson to follow suit.[27]

At the same time, however, Pearson's decision to establish the RCSW was not motivated by human rights issues alone. Rather, in a pattern that recurred in the subsequent establishment of the 1983 Royal Commission on Equality in Employment, the appointment of the RCSW also reflected his government's desire to improve the Canadian economy. After all, the economic implications of underutilizing the employment potential of half the adult population were being aired in the press and brought to the government's attention by senior bureaucrats in Ottawa. When Doris Anderson launched her public appeal for a royal commission on the status of women in the July 1966 edition of *Chatelaine,* she argued that "although Canada ranks near the top in the number of women with higher education, we rank near the bottom of all western nations in the percentage of women in the professions or in managerial jobs."[28] Similarly, in 1969, Sylva Gelber, as director of the Women's Bureau, noted, "The failure to utilize our human resources to their full capacity denies the nation the productivity essential for the maintenance of a high standard of living."[29]

The emphasis on promoting women's employment opportunities in the RCSW's mandate reflects the federal government's concern that the increasing numbers of women who were entering the labour force received the necessary training to take up skilled employment.[30] While the labour force participation rate of women increased in the early 1960s – from 30.1 percent in 1960 to 35.4 percent in 1966 – women were still being subject to vertical and horizontal segregation as they clustered in low-status clerical, sales, and secretarial positions and, as a result, earned significantly less than men.[31] Indeed, as Naomi Black has noted, "From the perspective of the government, women's lesser rewards and lesser opportunities to participate in the expanding economy translated into a lesser contribution to national growth."[32] These economic concerns also explain why the RCSW's mandate called on the commissioners to investigate the particular problems faced by married women returning to paid employment. After all, married women were the growth point in the female labour force. While the labour force participation rate of single women hovered around 55 percent for most of the 1960s, the proportion of married women entering paid employment rose dramatically from 20.8 percent in 1961 to 33 percent in 1971.[33]

The RCSW and Its Mandate

While the RCSW's terms of reference were framed quite directly in relation to the pulls of equity and efficiency that lie at the heart of Canadian liberalism, they also demonstrated that the commission had been established to consider how women could be more effectively included within the paradigm of worker-citizenship.[34] Although the commissioners were instructed to "inquire into and report upon the status of women in Canada, and to recommend what steps may be taken by the Federal Government to ensure for women equal opportunities with men in all aspects of Canadian society," four of the nine areas that were singled out for particular attention focused on women's employment.[35]

First, the commissioners were required to inquire into and report on "the present and potential role of women in the Canadian Labour force, including the special problems of married women in employment and measures that might be taken under federal jurisdiction to help in meeting them."[36] Second, they were asked to investigate how women's human capital might be put to better use, by considering what measures "might be taken by the federal government to permit the better use of the skills and education of women, including the special re-training requirements of married women who wish to re-enter professional or skilled employment."[37] Third, the commissioners were asked to review "federal labour laws and regulations in their application to women."[38] Finally, they were directed to consider the development of employment opportunities within the government's own bureaucracy by examining "laws, practices and policies concerning the employment and promotion of women in the Federal Public Service, by Federal Crown Corporations and by Federal Agencies."[39]

The remaining terms of reference required the RCSW to investigate "laws and practices under federal jurisdiction concerning the political rights of women," "federal taxation pertaining to women," "marriage and divorce," "the position of women in criminal law," "immigration and citizenship laws, policies and practices with respect to women," and "such other matters in relation to the status of women in Canada as may appear to the Commissioners to be relevant."[40]

Although the RCSW's mandate acknowledged the particular problems facing married women returning to work, it is noticeable that the commissioners were *not* asked to consider how women's employment opportunities might be affected by their primary responsibilities for the care of young children. At some level this was surprising, particularly as increasing numbers of women with young children were going out to work. When the royal commission was established in 1967, 19 percent of working mothers had children under the age of six. This proportion had increased to 27 percent by 1971, and continued to rise after that.[41] However, even though femocrats within the Women's Bureau at the Department of Labour had long recognized how child care responsibilities might affect the careers of working mothers, the question of further federal involvement in the field of child care was not raised in the RCSW's terms of reference.[42]

Two factors help to explain this omission. First, the RCSW was established shortly after the federal-provincial conferences in the fall of 1966, at which the federal government "marked the end of co-operative federalism" by informing the provinces of its intention to terminate the long era of shared-cost programs.[43] It was perhaps inevitable therefore that social policy questions like child care, which would engage federal and provincial governments in cost-sharing arrangements, were not specified in the commission's terms of reference. In addition, although the RCSW was established at a time when "nearly every aspect of Canadian life was in ferment," its mandate avoided questions about child care that could lead the commissioners into highly contested territory about the extent to which women's full assumption of worker-citizenship would negate their more established roles as mother-citizens.[44] As Monique Bégin reflected many years later, "The public discourse in the years immediately preceding the royal commission was done in moral terms, often rationalized with new research in psychology, and it was about whether it was good or bad or right or wrong to have mothers working in paid employment. It was only done in moral terms, focusing on the alleged consequences for their children, and it was highly controversial."[45]

Women's Written Submissions to the RCSW

The women who participated in the public inquiries of the RCSW were, however, quite happy to engage in this area of controversy. Even though women used the RCSW as a forum in which to re-assert longer-standing demands for equal employment opportunities with men, the vast majority of those who made formal written submissions to the commission went beyond the issues specified in its terms of reference by raising concerns about the problems women faced in reconciling paid work with child care. Of the 350 written briefs submitted to the commission by individual and organized women, 78 percent raised concerns about women's employment *or* child care.[46] Closer reading of these 273 documents reveals that while 21.6 percent kept within the confines of the commission's mandate and focused solely on questions of women's employment opportunities, 74 percent raised concerns about women's employment *and* the care of young children (Table 3.1).

Women used very different frameworks to present their arguments about employment opportunities and child care. When they addressed questions

Table 3.1

RCSW briefs from individual and organized women who raised issues about women's employment and child care

	Number	Percentage
Briefs focusing solely on women's employment without raising issues of child care	59	21.6
Briefs raising issues about women's employment and provision for child care	202	74.0
Briefs expressing clear opposition to mothers of young children working outside the home	12	4.4
Total	273	100.0

about the promotion of equal employment opportunities for men and women and the eradication of sex discrimination in employment, their briefs frequently drew on discourses of human rights and economic development. By contrast, when they raised concerns about the link between women's employment opportunities and child care, they not only drew directly on their own experience but in many respects challenged some key tenets of liberal feminism.

Women's Arguments about Eradicating Sex Discrimination in Employment

As one might expect in an era when human rights discourse was ascendant, many of the briefs that took up issues of sex discrimination in the workplace justified their claims by appealing to international codes of human rights. The Manitoba Volunteer Committee on the Status of Women recommended that "Canada should sign and attempt to adhere to the international conventions and declarations on the economic rights of women."[47] Similarly, the Voice of Women in Montreal argued that the RCSW should ensure that the federal government adhere to commitments made when Canada signed the United Nations 1967 Declaration on the Elimination of Discrimination against Women: "There could be no goal higher for this Royal Commission on the Status of Women than the implementation of this Declaration, which asks for changes not only in the laws but also in customs and practices, for as the preamble says: 'The full and complete development of a country, the welfare of the world and the cause of peace require the *maximum participation of women* as well as men in all fields.'"[48]

Canada's obligations to the ILO also shaped the demands that women made for the eradication of sex discrimination in employment. As the CFUW of New Brunswick argued, "In ratifying the International Labour Organization Convention 111 (The Discrimination in Employment and Occupation Law), Canada undertakes to promote equality of employment opportunity. The Convention specifically includes 'sex' as an area requiring protection against discrimination. None the less neither the Canada Fair Employment Practices Act nor the Federal Civil Service Act includes 'sex' in its anti-discrimination provisions."[49]

Women argued that the eradication of sex discrimination in employment would improve the Canadian economy and not waste the educational training that many women had already received. The Manitoba Volunteer Committee on the Status of Women recommended that "this commission study the cost to the Canadian economy of our massive inefficient use of woman-power resources."[50] Similarly, the Canadian Dietetic Association called on the federal government to "take more positive steps to educate Canadian employers on the potential source of productive personnel represented by the competent, trained female allowed to use her abilities and training to the fullest, not stifled by practices and attitudes that amount to discrimination."[51] Interestingly, the association justified this claim not only in broad economic terms but in relation to the harm such restrictions inflicted on women themselves:

> We must recognize that by limiting opportunities for females to move freely into and around in all areas of business, social and political life, serious harm is done to the women of the country. In addition, and quite separate in consideration, is the harm done to the economic stability of the country. Any country that allows one half of its most valuable resources (human resources) to be arbitrarily restricted from performing at an optimum level of productivity puts unnecessary and artificial limitations on its own economic growth by limiting the supply of trained, competent, productive individuals available to Canadian employers and Canadian development.[52]

There was a strong theme running through the briefs that the inequalities of employment opportunity that women experienced were not only wasteful of their increasing education but indicated a lack of social progress in Canada. In making these claims, the CFUW of New Brunswick almost reiterated the argument that Doris Anderson had made when she called for the establishment of the RCSW in her 1966 editorial in *Chatelaine*.[53] Indeed, the organization argued, "The underutilization of women workers in relation to their educational achievements is a matter of serious concern. It is a disgrace to Canada as a nation and a sad sign of her lack of progress that she should be so neglectful of the great loss in the potential of her women. The failure to grant women an equal or more creditable status with men is a glaring example of this neglect."[54]

Policies Advocated by Women Concerned about Eradicating Sex Discrimination in Employment

Women made a number of suggestions about how the federal government should tackle the problem of sex discrimination in employment. They argued that sex discrimination should be outlawed and a human rights agency established to oversee the implementation of such legislation. They also called on the federal government to review its own employment practices and develop public awareness about the problem of sex discrimination at work. In addition, some women argued that a substantive approach to equal employment opportunities could only come about if due recognition was given to the way that women's maternal labour affected their participation in paid employment.

Outlaw Sex Discrimination in Employment

There was clear concern in the submissions that sex discrimination should be outlawed by all governments in Canada and that the federal government should take a lead in developing mechanisms to ensure that such laws were put into practice. In some cases, women took up well-established arguments in the human rights movement that anti-discrimination legislation would be ineffective without mechanisms to ensure its implementation. The CFBPWC in Ottawa urged all governments in Canada to "adopt the principles in the Declaration of Human Rights of the United Nations Organization and the ILO Convention 111 by inclusion in every anti-discrimination act and declaration provisions providing that there shall be no discrimination on the basis of sex."[55] It also called for "effective measures [to be] built into the legislation" in order to "shift complaints away from the individual" and "allow a realistic enforcement of anti-discrimination principles."[56] In addition, the Women's Group of the London and Middlesex Ridings Association of the NDP argued that the office of "ombudsdame" should be established, headed by a woman, to investigate allegations of sex discrimination in both the federal and provincial spheres:

> Since important legislation which affects women is difficult to enforce, we recommend that the federal and provincial governments create the position of "ombudsdame." This office should be held by a woman whose function will be to investigate complaints from women about (a) alleged injustices perpetrated by the state and (b) alleged injustices by others where no legal case exists and hence the complainant cannot have recourse to the courts. The ombudsdame would also be able to recompense the complainant for injustices suffered and to give advice to the government concerned where the law is clearly being circumvented, when it requires clarification or when it should be changed.[57]

Review Employment Practices and Promote Attitudinal Change

Many submissions called on the federal government to review its employment procedures and ensure that women had the same opportunities as men for promotion to all levels of the federal public service.[58] The CFUW in New Brunswick pointed out how such provisions would encourage women to assume their roles as worker-citizens: "The Federal Government should take the lead and eliminate discrimination on the grounds of 'sex' in its own hiring and promotion practices and pass legislation to this effect. Once such legislation becomes law and giving access to equal opportunity becomes government policy, private business will follow. Only then will women be motivated to make their national contribution to the economy and national welfare of Canada."[59]

Women were also concerned that the "practices restricting the access of women to professional fields should be explored" and that the "predominance of men in senior posts in the fields of social service and teaching, particularly at university level," should be addressed.[60] They also argued that people should stop making inaccurate assumptions about the type of work to which women were most suited. Indeed, the Canadian Dietetic Association noted that the "subtle or overt practices which inhibit the opportunities of women to enter or practice in certain so-called male fields of endeavour be stopped, if need be, by regulations."[61] Similarly, Joan Hayes, a woman from Halifax, noted, "Personnel Officers and Employers pre-judge their positions as being 'suitable' or 'unsuitable' for women. 'Suitable' usually indicates that the position does not lead anywhere, or that a man would not find it challenging or rewarding. 'Unsuitable' usually means that women have not previously been employed in the position offered and there is no reason to start now."[62]

Women also argued that legislative and attitudinal changes were necessary to ensure the development of equal employment opportunities for women. The Provincial Women's Committee of the Saskatchewan NDP argued that "new legislation must be accompanied by significant changes in social attitudes."[63] The Canadian Dietetic Association expressed the problem this way:

> There continues to exist at all levels of Canadian society an acceptance of a core of practices and attitudes towards the female half of the society which are based on entirely false and illogical assumptions ... We recognize that the continued existence of these practices and attitudes is based on the fact that they are an accepted part of our mores and cultural patterns and to change this will require more than exposure of their falseness, more than concerted effort and endeavour and good intentions on the part of individuals convinced of their falseness. It will require education, legal support and a complete change of attitude. This will not happen overnight, nor will it be the result of any one single action but will be brought about by both men and women realizing that sexual differences do not imply status differences, that an individual should be evaluated with another purely on their ability to perform, to fulfil certain requirements, to meet certain demands and standards.[64]

Develop Equal Opportunity Policies That Recognize Women's Maternal Labour
The specific claims that women advanced about ways in which their opportunities for employment could be equalized with those of men were notably imbued with an understanding that the achievement of full equality of opportunity could only be realized through the recognition of gender

differences. While many of the briefs called for increased opportunities for training and retraining in order to bring women up to a level playing field with men, they also argued that issues relating to gender difference should be built into government policies to develop equality of opportunity.[65] For example, the brief from the Commission on Women's Work in the Anglican Church of Canada argued that "federal labour laws [should] ensure full status for women workers within the labour force, there should be assurance of equality of opportunity in employment, remuneration and promotion with special legislation applicable to women restricted to the protection of their health and welfare in respect to the maternal function."[66]

While some of the briefs focused on issues of maternity leave, others considered how the inequalities of employment opportunity were related to the inadequate provision of child care. Women did not, however, advance a uniform set of demands about the best way for "young mothers" to reconcile the demands of paid and caring work. Just over half of the 202 submissions that raised issues about working women *and* child care called for policies to facilitate nonmaternal care. By contrast, just under half of these submissions revealed that their authors were ambivalent about young mothers entering the paid labour force full-time (Table 3.2).

Table 3.2

Positions taken in RCSW briefs from individual and organized women who raised issues about women's employment and child care

	Number	Percentage
Briefs that favoured nonmaternal child care for working women by:		
Advocating policies to provide child care for working women	26	12.8
Advocating policies to promote women's employment and nonmaternal child care	81	40.1
Total	107	52.9
Briefs that linked calls to promote women's employment and/or nonmaternal child care with calls for:		
Employers to allow women with young children to work flexible hours or part-time	40	19.8
Cultural/fiscal measures to encourage women with young children to stay home	55	27.2
Total	95	47.0
Combined totals	202	99.9

Women's Arguments about the Need for Child Care to Support Working Women

Women who called for nonmaternal child care to support working women framed their arguments directly in relation to the government's objectives of using the RCSW to ascertain how best to root out sex discrimination and ensure that women could make a full contribution to the Canadian economy. They resisted the narrowness of the commission's mandate by arguing that women's increased contribution to the Canadian economy could only come about with the provision of child care. They also developed a more expansive concept of women's rights than that embedded in the ideology of equal treatment which underscored the commission's terms of reference. While these women were determined to assume the status of worker-citizens, they also emphasized that this would not be possible unless the different contexts in which men and women assumed employment were built into discussions about the promotion of gender equality in the workplace.

Economic Arguments for Promoting Child Care

Women approached the link between child care provision and women's economic activity by arguing that affordable child care was not only a prerequisite for women to enter the labour force but essential given their own economic need to work for pay. In making these arguments, women were concerned to dispel the myth that married women worked for pin money, and encourage the federal government to consider how women's economic contribution to society was constrained by the high costs of child care. The brief submitted by the Business and Professional Women's Clubs of British Columbia and the Yukon took up the first of these two points: "Many women need to work, thus creating a desperate need for Day Care Centres ... Many are concerned that an increase in Day Care services only serves to encourage women to abandon their parental responsibilities and seek employment just to purchase unnecessary frills and extras such as a second car or a colour television for the rumpus room. This is largely a myth. Department of Labour reports indicate that most mothers work out of economic necessity."[67]

Women were deeply concerned about the expense of day care, not least because they invariably assumed that they should contribute to the costs of substitute care. As the brief submitted by the CFBPWC in Ottawa noted, "It is only reasonable that the working mother should contribute to the cost of the day care in relation to her economic potential ... Those who benefit directly should bear the lion's share of the cost while society, which benefits indirectly from happy, well cared-for children, should be prepared to contribute to the cost."[68] Nonetheless, as Vera Alback argued, "The cost of individual baby-sitters is beyond the reach of the average young woman trying to raise children on a small income."[69] Worries about the cost of child care were particularly apparent in briefs that rejected the implication in the RCSW's terms of reference that it was only *married* women who had to juggle the demands of employment and child care. The Junior League of Toronto noted, "The person who can afford full-time live-in help must be in a high income bracket, which eliminates the single working mother who would have neither the income nor the space to accommodate such a person."[70] Similarly, Sherrie Tutt – a single mother with three children, living in rural Saskatchewan – noted how "the costs of day care, when available, are currently prohibitive to one-income families."[71]

While many briefs asserted that affordable child care was necessary because women had to work for financial reasons, others turned this argument on its head and noted how the provision of adequate child care could enhance the Canadian economy. Some women argued that the provision of child care would increase the productivity of mothers who were already employed outside the home and encourage women with needed skills back into the labour force.[72] As Betty Cooper, a CBC broadcaster from Calgary, noted, "If all married women [stayed home to look after their children] the country would come to a standstill and there would be a scarcity of teachers, factory workers, bank clerks and so on."[73] Drawing on a personal survey of the limited child care available in Regina, Zenny Burton warned that "legislators at all levels of government had better take heed of the requests of working mothers with children in regards to child care services ... as were all these women to remain home tomorrow due to child-care difficulties, the wheels of society would be slowed down considerably."[74]

Other women argued that in addition to encouraging mothers back into the labour force, the provision of child care would stimulate the economy by creating jobs for child care workers. Suzel Perron, a Québécoise living in Westmount, noted how the provision of child care enhanced women's employment opportunities, not least because it boosted the local economy, "créant ainsi des postes pour d'autres mères de la région, compétentes ou aptes à s'occuper des enfants."[75] Similarly, Bonita Bridge, a Winnipeg woman in her late twenties, argued, "We need all the trained and professional people we have, and it is a waste for them to be at home washing diapers when others need jobs and could be doing the housework for professional women. Thus we could create jobs and stimulate the economy."[76]

Clearly these women were arguing that it was futile for the government to consider strategies to enhance the labour force participation of women in order to boost the Canadian economy without addressing questions of child care. While they were not seeking to challenge the idea that women's increased participation in the labour force could enhance the Canadian economy, they were resisting the narrowness of the federal government's view that this objective could be achieved simply by ensuring that women were given the same training and employment opportunities as men.[77] Moreover, these women were challenging the notion that the Canadian economy could be wholly located in the public sphere and overlook the labour and expenses involved in caring for children.[78]

Rights-Based Arguments for Promoting Child Care
Women expanded the federal government's concerns to promote equal employment opportunities for men and women and reduce sex discrimination in the sphere of employment. However, they did so not just by focusing on the workplace but by broadening the remit of this question to include issues of child care. While some women argued that the provision of child care in the community was a prerequisite for women to enjoy their rights as worker-citizens, others approached the question of federal support for child care from the vantage point of taxation.

Many submissions framed their claims about child care provision by referring to women's right to fulfil their destinies "economically and biologically."[79] For example, Bonita Bridge noted, "the fact that women must bear children does not presuppose that they *must* take most of the responsibility of rearing children."[80] The brief from the Victoria Day Care Services argued that while women's "decision about this choice is their own, to be made with regard to the over-all well being of their families ... the community's concern for children must be expressed from a base which acknowledges the rights of mothers to free choice in this matter."[81]

Women who called for public policies to promote child care for working women were clearly concerned that without this provision, the combined responsibilities of motherhood and paid work would lead to different forms of sex discrimination. For example, Eleanor Dunn, an Ottawa newspaper editor and mother of five, wrote that "many employers tend to realize that the working woman with small children has worries and often cannot perform her function as an employee to her fullest capacity. It is my opinion that this tends to lead towards discrimination against women in hiring practices, salaries and promotion."[82] Similarly, the Toronto branch of the Young Women's Christian Association argued that the federal government should adhere to its international obligations to support working women and children by facilitating "the development of policies and services which would enable women with family responsibilities who need or choose to work outside their homes to do so without fear of discrimination."[83]

However, women's strongest sense that limited public policies on child care caused sex discrimination emerged in their pleas for tax relief to offset the costs of substitute care. As the brief from mature women students at the University of British Columbia emphasized, "The working mother who must pay her housekeeper out of her wages, yet pay income tax on those wages without deducting that expense, is in effect paying tax on money she is unable to use."[84] While this grievance arose, in part, because the RCSW's mandate required the commissioners to report on federal taxation pertaining to women, it seems to have been fuelled by the 1966 report of the Royal Commission on Taxation, which was made public just three weeks after the RCSW was established.[85] The Carter Report (as it was known) had argued that "such things as commuting expenses, the costs of child care, and recreational club memberships should be explicitly denied as deductions from income," thereby reinforcing the idea that the federal state should not assume responsibility for the costs of caring for young children whose mothers choose to go out to work.[86]

Women addressed the issue of tax discrimination from two perspectives. First, they argued that the existing tax system denied the extent of their caring work and signalled that "the work of a married woman is peripheral and not in the same category as work of other members of society."[87] Women also saw the absence of tax relief as a form of financial discrimination. Although this was clearly a class-based grievance, women who hired in-home child care were incensed that they were denied federal tax relief to offset the costs of employing such help, but typically required "to pay Canada Pension Plan contributions in respect of [their] housekeeper or babysitter."[88] After describing herself as "an ordinary housewife" who felt very strongly about the restrictions that had been placed on her because of her gender, Alice James detailed this double layer of discrimination and identified the confused assumptions about child care as work that were built into it:

> I am a university graduate, who, in spite of not having worked for seventeen years could probably make $400 a month. I believe I could obtain a good housekeeper for $300 a month. The prospect of using my training and having a $100 a month profit is very appealing until we look at the income tax picture. Instead of taxing me on my profit as they would in any other business, they say that I am not a regular employer and tax all $400. The Federal government is rather inconsistent because under the Canada Pension Act I would be an employer and would have to pay the employer's portion into the Canada Pension Fund. Of course they would still tax my housekeeper on her $300. This looks like double taxation to me. The net result of this situation would be that my husband and I would pay $98.66 of my $100 profit to the federal government, at 1966 rates. My net profit would be $1.34 ... At the new 1967 rates of tax I expect there would be a net loss.[89]

Women's submissions to the RCSW challenged the federal government on this form of discrimination and highlighted its broader social and economic implications. To Alice James, "the most tragic result" of these policies was "that many women make no arrangement for the care of their children and we all pay the costs in increased health, welfare and education costs."[90] Other women argued that the introduction of tax relief would boost the economy of child care provision, be it inside or outside the home. The Committee of Mature Students at the University of British Columbia noted that "were their employers, the working mothers, able to pay a higher, tax deductible wage, the domestic workers would benefit, the economy of many lower income groups would improve, and domestic work would achieve a badly needed boost in status."[91] Similarly, the Junior League of Toronto noted, "Tax relief for the working mother would allow her to contribute more for day-nursery care and so help to make it possible for day-nurseries to improve their care, provide more day-nurseries and some after-school care."[92]

Although women's strongest grievance was that the absence of tax relief disregarded the caring work they had always carried out at home, their submissions also expressed grievances about the sex discrimination involved. In a number of briefs, women argued that just as the taxable income of businessmen is arrived at after expenses have been claimed, "so should the woman who works a 40 hour week (minimums would have to be set up) be able to show receipts or proof in some way that she is ... paying for child care."[93] The submissions also conveyed a sense of injustice that while "single, divorced, separated, or widowed men" could claim tax relief for child care, women could not.[94] As the Women's Section of the United Nations Association of Canada commented, "An obvious case of discrimination for your commission is the provision in the Income Tax Act which provides for a deduction for child care in the case of a male single parent but none for a female single parent ... We urge that the Income Tax provisions be changed to allow both men and women a realistic figure for deductions when they have to leave their children in day care to seek employment."[95]

These submissions indicate how women who supported the liberal feminist project of increasing women's opportunities in the public sphere paid heed to the government's concerns to reduce sex discrimination in Canada and enhance women's opportunities to contribute to the Canadian economy. In so doing, they reinforced the standard liberal feminist claim that "sex discrimination is unjust primarily because it deprives women of equal rights to pursue their own self-interest."[96] At the same time, however, they called on the government to recognize that women's economic activities spanned the public and private spheres. Indeed they emphasized that women's full assumption of worker-citizenship could not be achieved unless the state acknowledged and made provision to replace women's existing unpaid work in caring for young children.

**Policies Advocated by Women Who Called for
Nonmaternal Child Care**

Women who favoured nonmaternal child care made three principal recommendations about the development of public policies to support working women. First, they demanded a rapid expansion in child care services, including the availability of trained carers. Second, they argued that the federal government should develop a system to ensure that women were adequately subsidized for the child care services they needed in order to participate in the labour force. Finally, they called on the federal government to work with the provinces across the jurisdictional boundaries that constrained the development of a national system of child care.

Increase the Provision of Child Care

There were repeated calls on the federal government to investigate the shortage of child care spaces in both urban and rural areas.[97] Many briefs expressed the need for more pre-school and after-school care that was properly regulated and staffed by trained child care workers.[98] Some bemoaned the inadequate supply of household help, arguing, as in the case of l'Association féminine d'éducation et d'action sociale, that while "le budget de la femme mariée qui droit travailler lui permet rarement de s'assurer les services d'aides-familiales compétentes ... il existe actuellement, une pénurie de ces personnes parce que leur rôle dans la société est dévalorisé."[99] Others called for the public education system to be expanded to include kindergarten for three- to five-year-old children.[100] However, even though radical feminists at the time were calling for round-the-clock child care, very few briefs called for a twenty-four-hour nursery system.[101]

Financing of Child Care

While many of the briefs – particularly those from individual women – criticized the current cost of nursery provision, very few asserted the demand for free universal day care that would become the hallmark of Canadian child care campaigns in the 1970s and 1980s.[102] The Voice of Women in Edmonton called on all levels of government to ensure that "properly supervised day care for the children of working mothers be established as a public service."[103] However, most briefs called either for child care places to be subsidized with the mother paying according to her income, or for the mother herself to be subsidized through tax deductions that offset the cost of child care.[104] Indeed, calls for tax relief for child care outstripped all other policy demands. As the Junior League of Toronto claimed in a statement that criticized the federal government's limited welfare-based involvement in the field of child care, "Although special consideration seems indicated for the single parent, the two parent working mother also should be eligible for some financial relief in regards to child care during her working hours."[105]

Nonetheless, there was a strong sense in a number of the briefs that free state child care should be available for the children of low-income parents. Louyse Oulet-Savoie argued, "Chaque municipalité devrait compter un nombre suffisant de garderies pour [subvenir] aux besoins des déshérités."[106] Similarly, Eleanor Dunn stated that she was "not sure about subsidization by any level of government unless it was in the form of assistance to mothers who were needy and the sole support of their families."[107] A few argued that child care should be financed by parents, employers, and the state. For example, Suzanne Pelletier looked forward to the day when "les garderies de jour [seront] intégrées aux services déjà fournis par le ministère de la Famille et du Bien-Être," and envisaged that, like health insurance, "ces services seraient payés au tiers, par les parents, le Gouvernment, et l'employeur."[108]

A National System of Child Care

Although many briefs called for the provision of more day care services, it was the submissions from women heading up day care organizations that most directly criticized the jurisdictional constraints imposed on the inquiry. The Day Care Section of the Ottawa Citizens' Committee on Children acknowledged that "day care for young children is primarily a matter pertaining to provincial jurisdiction and therefore of questionable relevance within the framework of reference of a Federal Royal Commission."[109] However, its members then argued that "as with many other areas of development, we feel strongly that the division of powers set out in the British North America Act should not be allowed to inhibit serious consideration of our problem and effective progress towards our goals."[110] Indeed, the committee proposed that federal, provincial, and municipal governments should work together on child care, recognizing that it is "multidimensional and does not readily fit into the traditional frameworks of education, welfare or health."[111] Moreover, it urged the commissioners to address "the practical and jurisdictional difficulties that occur at various levels of *implementation*."[112]

The Victoria Day Care Services in Toronto called on "the Government of Canada to direct the Minister of National Health and Welfare to explore in detail the development of day care programmes for children of working mothers across Canada and ... explore with the provinces the enacting of legislation governing the establishment and operation of such services and facilities."[113] In addition, the authors of this brief argued that a special federal department should be established for this purpose.[114] Indeed, they thought that unless the "efforts of Federal Departments concerned with family, employment, economic and national productivity, and other related issues [were] coordinated in action programmes aimed at Provincial Governments," the chances of developing an effective national strategy on child care would be limited.[115]

Although these women all called for nonmaternal child care to support working women, they were by no means unified in their specific policy demands. Some called for an expansion of the Canadian welfare state, arguing that federal and provincial governments should work together across jurisdictional divides to increase the provision of care for children whose mothers went out to work. Others, by contrast, argued that the state should support child care through tax redistribution by directly subsidizing mothers who paid for child care while they were out at work. Although women in the first group had a greater sense that child care should be community-based rather than an individual responsibility, there was a strong undertone in all these briefs that even though women wanted to assume the status of worker-citizens, they remained primarily responsible for ensuring their children received proper care. Not surprisingly, the desire to maintain this responsibility was even stronger among women who were ambivalent about young mothers working full-time outside the home.

Arguments Made by Women Who Were Ambivalent about Mothers Working outside the Home

While the majority of women's submissions to the RCSW called for policies to promote women's employment and develop child care, a significant proportion argued that the commissioners should pay heed to the importance of the caring work mothers undertake at home (recall Table 3.2). While the women writing these briefs clearly recognized the economic necessity of women working for pay, they also called on the commissioners to acknowledge the value of women caring for their children at home. The brief from the women of St. Andrew's United Church in Beloeil acknowledged that "it is desirable and necessary for women to work outside the home where a woman, divorced, separated or widowed, must support her children, where the family needs added income, where the woman has special skills and education needed in the labour force, or where she is temperamentally unsuited to being a homemaker."[116] Nonetheless, although this group claimed that it "would endorse every effort made to assist [these women] to train [and] make satisfactory arrangements for the care of [their] children," it clearly regretted the broader societal tendency to downgrade the role of women as citizen-carers.[117] As the authors of its submission noted, "We feel there is a growing tendency today to downgrade the role of the woman in the home, to overlook the value of her contribution, both financial and social to the home and the community, and to create an atmosphere where young women feel that it is only by getting out of the home into a paid job that they can fulfil themselves or make a contribution to society."[118]

While the women writing in this way were clearly ambivalent about the role of women as workers and carers, they were willing to contemplate the participation of mothers in the paid labour force. Others, however, took a more contradictory position, arguing that the federal government should promote women's employment and child care but at the same time discourage mothers of young children from working outside the home. For example, the brief from the Ontario Jaycettes called both for improved training and employment opportunities for women and tax relief for child care. At the same time, it not only claimed that a membership survey had shown "one hundred per cent agreeing that women with small children should not work unless it is essential," but also produced suggestions that "re-educating women to their role as wife and mother" would encourage such women not to go out to work.[119]

The general concern of women who expressed ambivalence about mothers of young children working full-time was that although policies to achieve this objective might enhance women's economic standing in Canadian society, they could well downgrade the significance of women's caring work within the home. The brief from l'Ordre des Dames Hélène de Champlain argued that the RCSW might not in fact provide a comprehensive analysis of women in Canadian society because it was measuring their status against male-defined concepts of work:

> Dans l'énumération des items suggérés par la Commission, on insiste beaucoup sur l'acquisition de droits supplémentaires pour la femme mariée ou la célibataire au travail. Il est juste et raisonnable de demander certaines mesures nécessaires pour aider à résoudre les problèmes des femmes qui travaillent à l'extérieur. À notre avis, il est nécessaire d'attacher une importance prépondérante au rôle de la femme mariée, gardienne du foyer et des valeurs familiales ... Au cours des études que l'on fera, il est à souhaiter que l'on aborde le problème de la dévalorisation de la femme au foyer, au profit de celle qui a décidé de retourner sur le marché du travail.[120]

Clearly, these women were trying to make sure that the liberal feminist agenda of the RCSW did not ignore the concerns of maternal feminists. Indeed, they wanted to ensure that women had the opportunity, if circumstances permitted, to balance their roles as workers and carers. While these women were challenging the thrust of liberal feminism, they were also developing arguments that later in the twentieth century would be revisited by feminist theorists concerned with the ethics of care.[121] In short, it was the value of the care work attached to women's role as mother-citizens that informed the arguments developed by women writing this set of briefs.

Policies Advocated by Women Who Were Ambivalent about Mothers Working outside the Home

Two principal policy recommendations were advanced in the briefs submitted by women who were concerned about balancing their working and caring lives. These briefs emphasized how flexible and part-time work could allow women to combine paid work with child care. In addition, they called for financial measures to enable women, if they so chose, to spread their time between paid and caring work.

Flexible or Part-Time Employment

Women who called for an increase in flexible or part-time work were concerned that whatever the limitations of this form of employment, the commissioners assess its potential to allow women to combine paid work with the care of their children. While the Imperial Order Daughters of the Empire in Toronto acknowledged that "such labour ... should receive due recognition and compensation," it also lauded the "Housewife Shift" because it "adjusted to the needs of housewives and mothers," provided "additional income to families," and ensured that "the skills of women willing to participate in part-time work ... [were] not lost to the Canadian economy."[122] Similarly, the National Council of Women of Canada argued that "efforts must be made by government and industry to adjust working hours for women with family responsibilities to permit them to make their maximum contribution to the economy with the minimum disadvantage to their families."[123] In addition, the Alberta Association of Registered Nurses argued that "the availability of part-time work, with appropriate personnel policies, could effect a reasonable compromise by providing time for a woman to be with her family while permitting her to use her skills and meet the needs of society."[124] In short, these submissions emphasized how part-time employment enabled women to contribute to their household and national economies without completely curtailing responsibility for the care of their children.

Measures to Encourage Mothers of Young Children to Stay Home

Briefs advocating measures to promote women's employment opportunities and encourage mothers to stay home argued, first, that greater cultural value should be placed on the maternal care of young children and, second, that the federal government should back this up with fiscal rewards. While l'Ordre des Dames Hélène de Champlain called for equal pay for equal work and state subsidies to private day care centres, it also suggested that increased family allowances would enhance the status of mothers caring for their children at home.[125] Similarly, while the Montreal Council of Women acknowledged that some women may have to work for financial or professional reasons, they expressed a firm belief that "the place of a mother of pre-school children is in the home."[126] Its members called for a study into "the advisability of granting a mother's allowance to mothers of children under the age of five in order to encourage them to stay home and watch over the psychological and physical development of their children."[127]

Appeals for greater financial support to low-income women were also apparent in briefs submitted by those who were more ambivalent about mothers working full-time outside the home. For example, the brief from the Salvation Army Women's Organization expressed opposition to the federal government's cost-sharing moves to encourage welfare mothers into the workforce. Its authors argued that "it would be ideal if mothers of low income families could be provided with adequate means of supporting their families while they remained at home to train and care for them."[128] Similarly, Margaret Gaudreau called for "stay-home wives of low-income workers [to] receive an allowance according to income and members of family," arguing that only if this scheme proved too costly, should governments establish "a nation-wide system of federally and/or provincially supported day-nurseries *solely* for the benefit of mothers who can prove that through circumstances of life they have to go to work."[129]

As with the briefs that called for nonmaternal child care, those prepared by women who were more ambivalent about mothers of young children working outside the home were by no means unified in their policy proposals. While they all called for some measures to promote women's employment, those advocating greater recognition of part-time work seemed more at ease with this objective than those calling for fiscal and educational measures to make it easier for women with young children, who so wished, to spend more time caring for them at home. Despite these variations, the women who submitted these briefs were all concerned that the RCSW's emphasis on developing public policies to promote women's paid employment could lead to a devaluation of motherhood. In this respect, they were resisting the anti-maternalist thrust of the early stages of second-wave liberal feminism.[130]

Looking back over all these arguments, it is clear that women presented the commissioners with a range of proposals that would enable working mothers to choose how to manage their offspring's care. Nonetheless, there was a clear difference in the policies proposed by those who favoured nonmaternal child care and those who questioned its value. The submissions from women who called for nonmaternal child care, in order that women could assume the rights and duties of worker-citizenship, argued that the federal government had to include child care within the remit of public policy and, if necessary, work across jurisdictional boundaries to achieve this goal. By contrast, the submissions from women who were ambivalent about mothers working outside the home asked the commissioners to be more cautious in the policies they recommended. Indeed, these women argued that any measures to promote women's employment opportunities, in the public sphere, should not undermine the legitimacy of women continuing their caring work at home. How then did the commissioners respond to these different concerns in writing their report?

How the Commissioners Reset the RCSW's Agenda

The report of the RCSW opened with a classic statement of social citizenship, emphasizing that since "everyone is entitled to the rights and freedoms proclaimed in the Universal Declaration of Human Rights," the commissioners had examined the "status of women to learn whether or not they really have these positive rights and freedoms both in principle and in practice."[131] However, even in the introduction to the report, the commissioners indicated that it would not be a document that operated simply within this paradigm. Indeed the principles that underscored the report recognized the double-edged nature of women's demands by emphasizing how the gendered context of men's and women's lives had to be acknowledged in discussions of women's employment.

The four key principles that the commissioners developed to guide their writing of the report reflected their recognition of the way that childbearing meant that, in general, women were differently situated from men with respect to assuming the rights and obligations of worker-citizenship. These were, first, that "women should be free to choose whether or not to take employment outside their homes"; second, that "the care of children is to be a responsibility shared by the mother, the father and society"; third, that differences between men and women should be recognized as "society has a responsibility for women because of pregnancy and childbirth and special treatment related to maternity will always be necessary"; and, finally, that "in certain areas women will for an interim period require special treatment to overcome the adverse effects of discriminatory practices."[132]

Equality of Employment Opportunity

The commissioners addressed the issue of equality of employment opportunity directly in the chapter entitled "Women in the Canadian Economy."[133] In so doing, they met the requirements of the terms of reference and addressed the concerns that women had raised in their submissions.

The commissioners noted that women experienced inequalities of employment opportunity on entering the workforce not only because they found themselves blocked from jobs that had traditionally been held by men but also because they then found it difficult to advance through to senior management levels in their chosen field.[134] They also noted how "opportunity is limited by occupational segregation. The traditionally female occupations seldom lead to the upper echelons of management. Nor do they often provide the kind of challenge that can earmark an employee as a prospective occupant of the executive suite."[135] However, the commissioners emphasized that while employment discrimination against women was often conspicuous and should therefore be corrected through public policies, traditional practices and assumptions that tended to keep women in low-paying, ghettoized jobs also needed to be addressed. Indeed, they noted that "the most serious obstacle to women's advancement is probably the fact that many employers think senior positions are for men. Consciously or unconsciously, these employers attribute to women as a group characteristics that result in their elimination from consideration [for promotion]."[136]

The objective of the commissioners in their proposals for change was to ensure that worker-citizenship was a viable option for women. Their principal concern was to "eliminate immediate and specific injustices" while keeping "an ultimate objective in mind, [that] our recommendations should also lead to a future in which women and men will be recognized as contributing to the economy on an equal footing."[137] In order to achieve this, they emphasized how the federal government should ensure that its own employment laws, policies, and practices reflect its declared commitment to the principles of equal opportunity and nondiscrimination. Indeed, the commissioners argued that the federal public service was a key site in which to develop women's employment opportunities not only because the federal government was the major employer of women in the country but also because it should make its own adherence to principles conspicuous to other employers.[138]

The report recommended that "a Women's Programme Secretariat be established in the Privy Council Office for promoting a programme for equality of opportunity for women in the federal Government Service."[139] It also called on the federal government to make greater efforts to ensure that "women candidates get full consideration" for posts throughout the federal public service and that women's experiences of working in the domestic and voluntary sectors be recognized as part of the work experience they bring with them when entering the labour market.[140] Indeed, the commissioners argued that "the relationship of their unpaid housework to the economy should be clarified. Perhaps it would help if a way could be found to include their unpaid production of goods and services in the

Gross National Product."[141] In addition, the report noted that "the federal Public Service Commission and federal government departments should have as an objective the elimination of the imbalance in the proportion of women and men in senior positions."[142] Indeed, it called for more general attention to be paid to the way in which women experience inequality of opportunity with men, not only at the point of recruitment but also in the subsequent stages of employment: "Inequality of opportunity does not disappear when women enter the labour force."[143]

Child Care

Two of the four key principles that guided the commissioners in writing the report of the RCSW recognized how women's responsibilities for child-rearing meant they were differently situated from men with respect to enjoying the rights and assuming the responsibilities of worker-citizenship. The first principle – "Women should be free to choose whether or not to take employment outside their homes" – not only played to arguments about maternal self-fulfilment but addressed (albeit briefly) the reservations of those who were more ambivalent about mothers working full-time outside their homes.[144] The second principle – "The care of children is to be a responsibility shared by the mother, the father, and society" – was a radical move on the commissioners' part, not only because it went beyond the maternalist assumptions in most of the briefs but also because it signalled, at the outset, that the report would recommend federal involvement in the field of child care.[145] Although the call for national child care legislation was opposed by the two male commissioners, Jacques Henripin and John Humphrey, the commissioners all agreed that questions about child care to support working women required urgent attention.[146]

The report of the RCSW emphasized that "the time is past when society can refuse to provide community child care services in the hope of dissuading mothers from leaving their children and going out to work."[147] It argued not only that "change is needed in the most central function of the family – the care of children," but that "women cannot be accorded true equality" until the joint parental-societal responsibility for the care of children is fully acknowledged.[148] Nonetheless, although the bias of the report favoured the public provision of child care as a way of promoting women's entry into the workforce, it also acknowledged the concerns of women who wanted to balance their paid work with care of their own children. The report pointed to the fact that part-time work "helps women achieve equality of opportunity in employment" by maintaining their skills while raising a family.[149] It also recommended that "a federal annual taxable cash allowance in the order of $500 be provided for each child under 16 to be paid in instalments to the mother under the present Family Allowance system."[150] Indeed, the report argued strongly in favour of a child tax credit rather than a tax exemption for child care expenses, claiming that "tax credits [were] preferable to tax exemptions [because they were] independent of the size of income and do not benefit the rich ... more than the poor."[151] In so doing, the commissioners appeared to be giving mothers of young children maximum choice about working inside or outside the home.

While the report's recommendations on family allowances fell within the federal domain, the decision to link this recommendation with calls for a national child care system challenged the jurisdictional constraints that had shaped the RCSW's terms of reference. The report asserted that "for the federal government to fail to proceed with a specific child care programme, removed from welfare legislation of a more general nature, would be to deny the claim that Canadian women have made for concrete assistance in the burden of responsibility which they have been compelled to carry."[152] As a result it called on the federal government to "immediately take steps to enter into an agreement with the provinces leading to the adoption of a national Day-Care Act under which federal funds would be made available on a cost sharing basis for the building and running of day-care centres meeting specified national standards."[153] Moreover, by acknowledging that child care did not simply concern parents with preschool children but was an issue affecting working parents with child dependants, the commissioners linked the question of school-age child care with that of educational provision.[154]

The report clearly acknowledged the demands of women who defined child care as the ramp to worker-citizenship and those who wanted to balance their roles as worker-carer-citizens. Nonetheless, while the commissioners sought to forge a middle ground between these two positions, they ultimately moved beyond them by emphasizing *society's* responsibility for child care. In part, this reflects the predispositions of the commission's staff, who, Monique Bégin remembers, were "biased in favour of day care."[155] Nonetheless, it shows how the commissioners who signed the main report also contested the narrowness of the ideological and jurisdictional framework in which questions about women's employment opportunities had been framed. Moreover, although the report's authors insisted that women should be under no obligation to enter paid employment, they effectively argued that if women were to assume more responsibility as worker-citizens, the welfare state they would help to underwrite should include extensive provision for child care.

Women used the RCSW not simply as a forum in which to challenge dominant paradigms and jurisdictional constraints on policy development but as a means to engender policy discourse. They did so by drawing directly on their own experiences and inserting their varied concerns about women's employment and child care into public debate. In the process, women not only brought to public attention questions about care that were being sidelined in the pursuit of equal employment opportunities for men and women but highlighted both the potential and the limitations of liberal feminism. Nonetheless, the commissioners writing the main report found it easier than most women submitting briefs to question cultural assumptions about maternal responsibility for children and emphasize the need for *societal* engagement with child care.

The report of the RCSW placed the concept of equal employment opportunity for men and women squarely on the federal policy agenda. Indeed, the commissioners responded to the government's request for information about "the present and potential role of women in the Canadian labour force" by legitimizing women's right to worker-citizenship. They argued that "the full use of human resources [was] in the national interest" and that women and men should have "equality of opportunity to share the responsibilities of society as well as its privileges and prerogatives."[156] However, while the commissioners responded to their terms of reference in this way, they also moved beyond them in writing their report. Indeed, they used the evidence and arguments that women had presented to challenge the idea that gender equality in employment could be achieved simply by ensuring that men and women were treated in an identical fashion. Although the commissioners rooted their recommendations for the development of equal employment opportunity policies in well-established arguments about the promotion of human rights and the encouragement of economic growth, they also emphasized that policies to promote gender equality in employment would only be effective if they acknowledged the different ways in which parenthood tended to shape men's and women's employment careers. In short, the report of the RCSW developed a contextual approach to gender equality that linked together issues of women's paid and caring work. As a result, it placed a double-edged analysis of women's restricted employment opportunities squarely on the federal policy agenda.

4

A Just Society? The Trudeau Government's Response to the Royal Commission on the Status of Women

When Florence Bird and her colleagues handed Prime Minister Trudeau the report of the Royal Commission on the Status of Women (RCSW), they presented his government with a mammoth agenda for policy change. Two years earlier, when Trudeau secured the Liberal leadership, he had declared that "this beautiful, rich and energetic country of ours can become a model in which every citizen will enjoy his fundamental rights, in which two great linguistic communities and people of many cultures will live in harmony and in which every individual will find fulfilment."[1] Constitutional rights for men and equal opportunities for French and English Canadians were clearly part of Trudeau's just society. But how would a government headed by Canada's sexiest prime minister deal with a report on the status of women? And how would a Liberal prime minister who had encouraged his predecessor to tone down federal involvement in shared-cost programs respond to a report that called for increased federal-provincial cooperation in the field of child care?

Federal Government Strategy to Promote
Equal Employment Opportunities for Men and Women
The federal government's immediate response to the report of the RCSW was in keeping with the recommendation that federal, provincial, and municipal governments should establish implementation committees, composed of senior bureaucrats, to plan and coordinate their government's response to the recommendations in the report.[2] Shortly after the report was published, an Interdepartmental Committee on the Status of Women (IDC) was established for this purpose within the Privy Council Office. Freda Paltiel, a senior bureaucrat in the Department of Health and Welfare, was asked to coordinate its work. Many years later she recalled the process of her appointment:

I was summoned to the Privy Council Office and handed the newly tabled report by the RCSW. I took the historic document home for the week-end and realized the values it contained were far ahead of prevailing views in Canadian society and that implementation would result in a trans-formed Canada. I also realized that timely implementation would require a pragmatic approach to policy development rather than a full-scale debate on principles. Subsequently, one of my conditions for undertaking the role of Canada's first coordinator, Status of Women was that not only public servants but also citizens be invited and remunerated for sitting on working groups.[3]

Paltiel's insistence that bureaucrats and citizens work together in design-ing the federal government's response to the report of the RCSW was a radical interpretation of the commission's recommendation on this issue. In a recent collection by Judith Finlayson, Paltiel clarified how this process worked:

> In addition to the conventional interdepartmental committee of senior public servants, we establish[ed] a working group for each policy cluster, resourced with citizens as well as public servants ... I also requested an interdepartmental committee constituted mainly of women. That was a little difficult to achieve. When I started, only one or two women had reached the assistant deputy minister level – none was yet a deputy. I compiled a "crib sheet" of all the over-qualified women who were train-ing their bosses at the time and asked their surprised deputies if these women could represent their departments. Fortunately, I was able to achieve my objectives.[4]

Paltiel set up five different working groups of the IDC to examine the RCSW's recommendations. The minutes of their meetings suggest that despite Paltiel's good intentions to engage citizens in these deliberations, these working groups were, in fact, dominated by public servants.[5] The various groups examined the economic participation of women, the par-ticipation of women in public life and the judicial process, the education and training of Canadian women, family life and community services, and disadvantaged women. Paltiel's decision to divide up the groups in this way suggests that she was concerned the IDC should not only respond to the RCSW's recommendations but also keep the commission's terms of reference in mind. However, her decision to have the working group on women's economic participation deal with questions of employment, while that on family life and community services considered recommenda-tions on child care, reinforced a distinction between these two issues that had beleaguered previous attempts by the Women's Bureau to have the link between women's labour force participation and family commitments recognized in federal policy.[6] Moreover, it maintained a distinction between these issues in the process of federal policy development that has never been reversed.

Equal Employment Opportunity Programs for Women in the Federal Public Service

The federal government responded to RCSW concerns about women's employment inequality by putting its own house in order and promoting women's employment opportunities within the federal public service (FPS). This response meshed well with the prevailing ethos of an expanding federal bureaucracy in the early 1970s. It was a time of growing interest in the idea of representative bureaucracies and a point when the merit system had come under scrutiny for reinforcing the employment opportunities of certain groups of citizens at the expense of others.[7] In particular, it was an era in which the first Trudeau government had decided to use the FPS as a key site in which to "transform the linguistic face of Canada" by ensuring that the federal bureaucracy reflected the population it served.[8]

The Trudeau government's decision to improve the employment and promotion opportunities of francophones within the federal public service was a direct response to the growth of state-centred nationalism in Quebec. Nonetheless, the 1969 Official Languages Act set a precedent that federal employment initiatives could be used to redress historic discrimination against disaffected citizens and adjust the symbolic order of Canadian society.[9] However, even though the initiative to francize the federal bureaucracy had an impact on debates about feminizing the FPS, the process set in train by the Official Languages Act differed fundamentally from subsequent policies to improve women's employment opportunities within the public service.[10] The Official Languages Act legitimized the use of French and English in the federal workplace and linked this process to the creation of jobs for francophones at all levels of the public service.[11] However, while recognition of language difference was intrinsic to the promotion of employment opportunities for francophones within the FPS, a similar level of respect for gender difference did not characterize the development of federal policies to promote women's employment opportunities within its own bureaucracy.

The federal government's initial response to the question of promoting women's employment opportunities within the FPS was clarified in the 1971 report of the Public Service Commission of Canada (PSC). This declared that "the merit system, though originally designed to eliminate patronage, had failed to meet changing values and conditions," not least because "women's presence in the higher ranks of the public service was virtually non-existent."[12] Although the RCSW had called for temporary special programs to compensate women for historic employment discrimination and promote their employment opportunities, the report of the PSC advocated that it should create an Office of Equal Opportunity to promote equal employment opportunities within the federal bureaucracy. This office was established in 1971. However, because its mandate was to encourage rather than implement an equal opportunities program within the FPS, measures to address the extent of women's under-representation proved slow to develop.

An attempt to speed up the process occurred in April 1972 when Cabinet Directive 44 was issued to all deputy ministers, encouraging them "to take steps to assign and advance more women into middle and upper echelon positions" within their organizations.[13] However, like the Office of Equal Opportunity, the directive carried no instructions for compliance. Inevitably, therefore, it was inconsistently implemented across agencies and departments. The result, as Nicole Morgan has noted, was "a remarkable demonstration of the grip of bureaucratic culture and ideology ... islands of enthusiasm adrift in a sea of indifference, inertia and resistance."[14]

It was not until October 1975, during International Women's Year, that Jean Chrétien, as president of the Treasury Board, announced the Equal Opportunities for Women (EOW) program. This became the backbone of the federal government's strategy to promote women's employment opportunities during the second half of the 1970s. Although Chrétien's announcement indicated that the federal government was developing a more systematic approach to the issue of equal employment opportunities within the federal bureaucracy, it was a policy rooted in employment norms that had been established by employing men. Even though the policy sought "to ensure that women were accorded equal access to employment and career opportunities in the public service of Canada" by removing employment practices that "militated against the participation of women in all levels of any occupational group," such practices were deemed to be rooted in the discriminatory attitudes of employers rather than in systemic factors within the institutions that might restrict women's employment opportunities.[15] The concept of equal opportunity that was embedded in the program was one that emphasized the need to recruit, promote, and accelerate qualified women within the FPS, by encouraging managers to overcome their prejudices and recognize that these women were just as capable as similarly qualified men.[16]

It is hardly surprising, given its emphasis on the need to promote and accelerate the careers of qualified applicants of both sexes, that the program was criticized by women's organizations for its failure to address the patriarchal assumptions underlying the merit system and deal with the "legacy of discrimination" that women faced.[17] The slight adjustments that were made to hiring and promotion criteria when the EOW program was introduced did not legitimize the experience that women could bring to public service employment. In particular, they failed to respond to the RCSW's recommendation that employers should recognize the skills that women had developed through voluntary work outside the labour force.[18]

While the program reflected how ideas about representative bureaucracy were in vogue in the mid-1970s, it did not, as in the case of the francophone initiative, restructure employment practices in a way that fully acknowledged the particular circumstances in which many women took up employment. Although it declared that "within a reasonable period of time, the representation of male and female employees within the public service should approximate the proportion of qualified and interested persons of both sexes, available by department, occupational group and level," bureaus were encouraged to conduct a general review of departmental regulations and practices rather than think about how the organization of the workplace failed to recognize the specific issues that women workers faced.[19] In keeping with the rational style of administration for which Trudeau's government was well known, it implemented a review of departmental regulations and practices.[20] It also established a five-year plan of action "based on measurable objectives and annual numerical targets" that did not challenge the established merit system on which public service employment was based.[21]

Although the EOW program encouraged the hiring of women within the federal bureaucracy, it made little impact on the proportion of male and female bureaucrats employed within the FPS. Data published by the Treasury Board Secretariat for the period between 1973 and 1979 reveal that a far larger number of women (22,965) than men (6,742) were appointed to the federal public service.[22] However, the overall proportion of women employed in the FPS increased by only 4.8 percent over this period, so that women accounted for 36.2 percent of the total public service staff in 1979.[23] Moreover, the increased feminization of the federal workforce did little to break the pattern of women's under-representation in senior management and their concentration in traditional female-dominated occupational groups.[24]

Employment Training and Job Creation Schemes

Questions of equity and efficiency were intricately linked in the federal government's decision to promote women's employment opportunities. Indeed, the government recognized that attempts to promote the concept of equal employment opportunities for men and women would fail if there was an inadequate supply of skilled female labour to fill positions. It assumed that if retraining programs and equal opportunity initiatives were introduced in tandem there would be no reason for those who had previously been excluded from employment to remain outside the work-force. Thus, while the Treasury Board Secretariat was engaged in the sym-bolic politics of managing the EOW program within the FPS, the Canadian Employment and Immigration Commission (CEIC) focused on broader questions about the supply of skilled female labour.

In the 1970s, the CEIC began to formulate policies to "promote the development of labour market conditions in which the economic poten-tial of the female labour force [would be] fully tapped" and "support women workers in their pursuit of economically viable and self-fulfilling employment."[25] It established a Women's Employment Division, staffed by a small coterie of advisors in Ottawa and twelve coordinators in the regions, to develop its employment initiatives.[26] In addition, it created annual plans of action to improve women's participation in federal train-ing programs that had been set up under the 1967 Adult Occupational Training Act.[27]

There were, however, significant problems with these initiatives. Women were encouraged to engage in repeated periods of low-level and segregated job experience training, which did little to improve their employment opportunities in the longer term.[28] The programs placed too great an em-phasis on institutional and classroom training and engaged women only minimally in industrial training and apprenticeships. In addition, failure to link women's retraining with the specific nature of market demand meant that the CEIC's ability to engage women in these programs never matched the female unemployment rate.[29] Even though women constituted 45 per-cent of the unemployed in Canada in 1978, female representation in most federal labour market programs never rose above 40 percent.[30]

Statistics on the participation of women in federal training schemes during the 1970s reveal how poorly women were represented in programs other than those of the most basic or language-related nature. While female participation in language courses, basic skills development, and job readi-ness training was well over 50 percent, women's participation in specific skills training, work adjustment training, or industrial apprenticeships was lower, hovering around 30 to 40 percent and consistently plummeting to 3 percent on the apprenticeship scheme.[31] Very few women received train-ing in nontraditional occupations. Although women's participation in the "skills training program" increased from 37 percent in 1975 to 42 percent by the end of the decade, women were still concentrated in training pro-grams for sex-typed occupations.[32] In 1978, over 50 percent of women were trained in skills for stenographic/typing occupations or clerical and related occupations, despite the fact that only 14 percent of female trainees cited these as their usual occupations.[33]

The emphasis on full-time training courses and male career/job models exacerbated the problem of women's under-recruitment.[34] Problems of access were addressed to a very limited extent when an allowance of $10 per week for each dependant, up to a weekly maximum of $40, was introduced in August 1979, under the federal government's Plan of Action on the Status of Women.[35] However, despite the acknowledgement of the difficulty that many women faced in coping with dependants while seeking the necessary training to enter or re-enter the labour force, this allowance was at best a token because it could not begin to cover the costs of child or dependant care in the late 1970s. Moreover, as the introduction of this allowance was preceded by a reduction in training allowances from $45 to $10 per week for those living with a parent or working spouse, it is clear that they were targeted at single mothers or women with an unemployed husband. This reflected a developing pattern of the federal government focusing child care subsidies on the working poor rather than at women in general. In addition, even though part-time courses were available in some areas, all federal training allowances were only available to full-time trainees.[36]

Government involvement in the direct creation of jobs, typically on a temporary basis, was one other way in which the federal government sought to improve the employment opportunities of disadvantaged groups, including women. Policies such as Canada Works, the Local Initiatives Project, Young Canada Works, and the Summer Job Corps all proved integral to federal employment policy during the 1970s.[37] These public works initiatives were designed to provide unemployed people with bridging employment that would lead to permanent employment in the private sector and encourage community development in certain areas of the country. However, although women accounted for around 45 percent of those unemployed during the 1970s, their recruitment into such programs, with the exception of those aimed at young people, tended to account for only about 30 percent of the places offered.[38] Nonetheless, the Local Initiatives Project (LIP) encouraged the development of some community-based child care projects that engaged female trainees. As Martha Friendly has noted, "In Québec about seventy child care centres were established through LIP (and Perspectives Jeunesse) and when federal funding was withdrawn, public protests eventually forced the Québec government to develop its first child care policy, Plan Bacon, in 1974."[39] Similarly, in Ontario, "the Day Care Organizing Committee was funded as a Local Initiatives Project in 1970 ... which eventually helped establish the Day Care Reform Action Alliance."[40]

It is clear that although attempts were made to create training and employment opportunities for women in both the public and private sectors during the 1970s, these programs did not keep pace with the female unemployment rate. In addition, they left older women in a more precarious position than younger ones, did very little to address the problems that women with dependants faced in seeking training, and more often than not trained women for low-paying, sex-typed occupations that tended to lead to short-term rather than more permanent absorption of women into the labour force.

Ironically, while job creation programs were needed in some areas, other jobs could not be filled, suggesting an "increasing mismatch between the skills and expectations of job seekers and the kind of jobs offered."[41] One of the paradoxes of the 1970s was that the creation of new job openings was no longer reducing unemployment, because an increasing proportion of new jobs remained unfilled. Nonetheless, the absence of demand for workers who had been trained or had engaged in a job creation project remained. It is interesting to note that while this was viewed as a weakness of both the job creation and training strategies that had been developed, the federal government also began to see the problem as one perpetuated by the discriminatory attitudes of employers. Indeed, it was the latter perspective that encouraged the development of more stringent legislation to outlaw sex discrimination in federally regulated workplaces.

Anti-Discrimination Legislation and the Development of a Federal Human Rights Policy

The third facet of the federal government's employment opportunity strategy focused on eradicating sex discrimination in the federally regulated workplace. The report of the RCSW reminded the federal government that since it had embraced the principle of equality of opportunity for men and women in its 1960 Bill of Rights, it should "ensure that its employment laws, policies and practices reflect and implement these principles."[42] The RCSW also recommended that the federal government amend its Fair Employment Practices Act so that the legislation applied throughout the federal sphere and included both "sex" and "marital status" as prohibited grounds for discrimination.[43]

Between 1970 and 1972, amendments outlawing discrimination on the grounds of sex and marital status were added to both the Public Service Employment Act and the Unemployment Insurance Act.[44] While these legislative adjustments were significant, they did not address the deeper concern among feminists about the need for the federal government to develop a more sustained approach to eradicating sex discrimination in the federal sphere. Indeed, the RCSW argued that the federal government should follow the initiatives of some provincial governments and develop a comprehensive human rights policy, including the establishment of a Human Rights Commission that "for a period of seven to 10 years" included "a division dealing specifically with the protection of women's rights."[45]

This recommendation was part of a much longer process to try to get adequate anti-discrimination encoded in Canadian law and fully implemented in practice.[46] The culmination of this pressure saw the introduction of the Canadian Human Rights Act (CHRA) in 1977 and the establishment of the Canadian Human Rights Commission (CHRC) in 1978 to oversee its implementation. However, even though the chief commissioner of the CHRC was given powers under the Act to "establish divisions of the Commission," as appropriate, the legislation did not specify the establishment of a special women's division.[47]

The immediate objective of the CHRA was to outlaw any identifiable act of discrimination – on the grounds of race and ethnicity, religion, age, sex, marital and family status, disability, and pardoned conviction – that occurred in the provision of federal government services or in the hiring, training, promotion, and remuneration of federal employees.[48] However, the CHRA also contained the seeds of a more systemic approach to the problem of workplace discrimination. It introduced the concept of equal pay for work of equal value into federal law.[49] It also provided the CHRC with powers to demand both the implementation of "special programs to prevent future disadvantage" and contract compliance as methods for promoting women's employment opportunities.[50] Indeed, it was the proactive emphasis of these two powers that heralded the development of a more institutionalized approach to questions of employment discrimination in the 1980s.

The Policy Strands Compared

While the goal of the three strands in this phase of federal policy development was the equalization of men's and women's employment opportunities, they varied in the degree to which they began to realize this objective. The EOW program ensured that women were included within broader attempts to improve the representativeness of federal bureaucracies. However, it failed to have any significant impact on the overall proportion of male and female employees within the FPS, the under-representation of women in its higher echelons, or the disproportionate concentration of women in the clerical and service sectors at the bottom end of the public service hierarchy.[51] The explanation for this may lie in the fact that despite the RCSW's pleas for the recognition of differences in men's and women's career paths, the program incorrectly assumed that women would slot into a career pattern that was identical to that of men. Moreover, these assumptions may well have been reinforced by the fact that the EOW directives were generally issued to male managers, who would not have experienced the same complexities as women in developing their careers and would therefore have been less aware of the institutional dimensions of employment discrimination.[52]

The training programs for women, though designed to encourage the development of a pool of skilled female labour that could then be channelled into the labour market, were not particularly successful. They failed to break down the sex-typing in occupational training and to assess the nature of employment demand.[53] As a result, federal government hopes that the development of new equal employment opportunity policies for women would encourage efficient use of the female labour pool were not fully realized.

The element within this policy phase that had the most sustained impact on the development of policies to promote women's employment was that of addressing employment discrimination through the introduction of the CHRA and the establishment of the CHRC. Nevertheless, while both these developments institutionalized a mandatory strategy to tackle employment discrimination within the federal sphere, the approach to the problem that was adopted assumed that such discrimination was overt and identifiable and should therefore be addressed as and when it occurred. It was only at the end of the 1970s, as the CHRC became established and a group of professionals committed to the development of effective anti-discrimination strategies evolved, that the idea of developing a proactive approach to eradicating the less obvious but more ingrained causes of workplace discrimination began to emerge in Canada.

It is clear that the three strands of federal policy, discussed in the first part of this chapter, all reflect the federal government's desire to create policies that would link the development of equal employment opportunities for worker-citizens with the goal of enhancing Canada's economic productivity. As I turn now to consider how the federal government responded to the RCSW's recommendations on child care, it is worth noting how these responses were completely split off from those concerned with improving women's employment opportunities and eradicating sex discrimination in the public sphere.

Federal Government Strategy on Child Care

As we saw in Chapter 3, the RCSW's terms of reference did not include the question of child care. Nonetheless, the commissioners used their mandate to examine "the special problems of married women in employment" and "federal taxation pertaining to women" to address women's varied concerns about child care.[54] Specifically, the report of the RCSW urged the federal government to move child care beyond its existing welfare mould by introducing a national Day-Care Act that would make new federal funds available to the provinces to share the costs of building and running day care centres, in line with specified national standards.[55] It also argued strongly in favour of the federal government introducing tax credits rather than tax exemptions to assist parents with the costs of child care. Indeed, it recommended that "a federal annual taxable cash allowance in the order of $500 be provided for each child under 16 to be paid in instalments to the mother under the present Family Allowance system."[56]

In order to appreciate the significance of both these proposals, it is necessary to understand that the federal government's sole involvement in the field of child care came through fiscal transfers to the provinces, made as a result of the 1966 Canada Assistance Plan (CAP). This was a welfare measure, *par excellence*, through which the federal government split the costs of child care (and other support services) with the provinces when services were provided to "persons in need or those who are likely to become persons in need" if such services were not already provided.[57] Child care was included in CAP to "provide services that lessen, remove or prevent the causes and effects of poverty, child neglect or dependence on public assistance."[58] It was designed to subsidize the child care costs of low-income families and ensure that the children of these parents were kept in publicly regulated child care centres. In short, it was a workfare measure to keep parents of low-income families in the labour force rather than dependent on welfare.

By recommending the creation of new legislation to promote a national system of child care, the report of the RCSW was trying to achieve two things. First, the commissioners were attempting to reframe the provision of child care for working women so that the service was not simply delivered within a welfare context. Second, they were trying to promote a more even pattern of service delivery that did not depend, as CAP had done, on provincial initiatives for the fifty-fifty federal-provincial cost share. Despite the RCSW's recommendations, no new national child care legislation was developed, and the federal-provincial cost sharing of welfare-related child care remained in place through CAP.

In fact, the federal government only developed two main policies in response to the RCSW's recommendations on child care. In 1973, it amended the National Housing Act to permit the construction of child care centres in federally financed housing developments, and in 1978 it introduced the Child Tax Credit as compensation for reducing family allowances. This latter development is interesting because it was introduced when Monique Bégin, the former executive secretary to the RCSW, became the minister for National Health and Welfare. As Rodney Haddow has noted, Monique Bégin's significant influence in writing the report of the RCSW meant that its recommendations on introducing a child tax credit came to have an important influence on federal policy making once she joined the government.[59] Interestingly, as he explained, the child tax credit was a political paradox because it was introduced "in conjunction with a severe spending restraint exercise launched by Trudeau."[60] In other words, it was targeted at those families with children whose income was below the national average and introduced to divert public attention away from the significant cuts being made in family allowances and other social programs. The maximum annual tax credit of $200 per child was made available to families with annual incomes under $18,000. It was financed from the $690 million annual saving made by cutting family allowances from $25.68 to $20 a month.[61]

While the federal government responded to the RCSW's recommendations in these two ways, it also went against the spirit of the report when it introduced the Child Care Expense Deduction (CCED) in 1971 as a provision of the Income Tax Act. Section 63 of the Act permitted single parents and the lower-income-earning parent in a dual-parent household to deduct up to $1,000 from taxable income for child care expenses that were incurred because they were working, undergoing training, or conducting research.[62] Although the CCED accounted for almost half of all federal spending on child care, it proved to be discriminatory in class terms because it benefited those at the higher end of the income scale. Moreover, the requirement that those claiming the deduction produce receipts failed to tackle parents' continued dependence on informal child care and the reality that such services were often provided by women with low incomes who preferred nonreceipted payments in cash.

The continuation of CAP and the introduction of the CCED reinforced a pattern of provision that directed subsidies for child care primarily towards parents in the highest and lowest income groups. In the case of CAP, this took the form of a displaced welfare payment that ensured children of low-income families were placed in public child care while their parents sought employment. CAP was slightly amended in November 1972. As a result, although the federal government still did not share the capital costs of child care centres with the provinces, it did begin to share their total operating costs, including the costs of repairing depreciating facilities.[63] However, the emphasis on federal-provincial cost sharing of a *welfare* service remained. In the case of the CCED, the subsidy was designed to encourage parental choice of child care and to offload the supply side of these services onto the commercial and nonprofit sectors.

Interpreting the Federal Response to the RCSW Recommendations on Child Care

There are three principal reasons why the federal government limited its response to the RCSW in the way described. First and foremost, although the Interdepartmental Committee and the PSC addressed questions about developing child care within the federal public service, the climate of federal-provincial relations in the early 1970s meant that the federal government was reluctant to re-enter negotiations with the provinces about funding a national child care program. While the federal government recognized the link between women's employment opportunities and the provision of child care, its 1976 Speech from the Throne emphasized provincial responsibilities for this service: "In response to the need for good day-care services everywhere in Canada, the Government will help to provide more and better day-care services by encouraging the provincial governments to adopt a new system of fees related to incomes. A great many more Canadian mothers who seek employment outside the home will thereby be free to do so, because partially subsidized day-care will be more widely available."[64]

Martha Hynna, who had represented the Department of Finance on the IDC before replacing Freda Paltiel as its coordinator in 1973, clarified why the federal government was reluctant to engage in new negotiations with the provinces:

> The government had just been through a period where there had been quite a few new federal-provincial programs – in the area of post-secondary education and with the introduction of CAP. They'd had a lot of trouble because the provinces resented the interference of the federal government, so they had announced in effect that there weren't going to be any more programs for a while. Then we got these recommendations from the royal commission report and from women's groups, to the extent that they existed then, which said that the federal government must set up a day care program. And even back then, working in federal-provincial relations in Finance, I said, "I don't think this is the way to approach this thing because the federal government has said we're not going to do a new federal-provincial program, why aren't you pushing the provinces more, because it is a provincial responsibility and you've got this reluctance in Ottawa to get involved in something new?" We looked at what we could do through the Canada Assistance Plan to at least get something, because that was an existing program ... but I knew we were not going to get a new day care program.[65]

The tensions in federal-provincial relations that characterized so much of the Trudeau era undoubtedly shaped the federal government's decision not to engage in the development of new national child care legislation. Nevertheless, there are other explanations for the Trudeau government's refusal to address this aspect of the RCSW's recommendations on child care. After all, at the time, the government's own opinion polls showed that even though the RCSW had generated clear demands for policies to promote women's employment, Canadians remained ambivalent about the public provision of child care.[66] Polls conducted in 1970, the year the report of the RCSW was released, found that while 77 percent of respondents agreed that "married women should take a job outside the home if they have no young children," 80 percent thought that they should not do so if they had young children.[67] In a sense, therefore, by relying on tax relief, which fell within federal jurisdiction and gave parents a choice about whether to claim relief for child care expenses, the federal government was pursuing the least contentious course of action.

Interestingly, however, it was not just the general public (or the male commissioners on the RCSW) that had reservations about the development of a national child care policy. Ironically, the emergent National Action Committee on the Status of Women (NAC) – which came into being in 1972 in order to ensure that the federal government implemented recommendations made in the RCSW's report – also proved ambivalent about this issue. When the first edition of NAC's newsletter, *Status of Women News,* was published in the summer of 1973, it indicated that a special meeting of the NAC Steering Committee, held on 27 June, had recommended that "a federal-provincial conference on child care be held as soon as it can be thoroughly prepared."[68] Yet a year earlier, a submission from NAC's predecessor, the National Ad Hoc Action Committee on the Status of Women in Canada (NAHAC), to the federal government had been less clear about the appropriate course of action.

The submission that NAHAC presented to the federal government in February 1972 supported almost all the RCSW's recommendations on child care. Nonetheless, it expressed some reservations about Recommendation No. 118, which suggested that "the federal government immediately take steps to enter into an agreement with the provinces leading to the adoption of a national Day-Care Act."[69] The brief from NAHAC argued that "there is a need for federal guidelines and national federal leadership."[70] However, it also raised concerns about provincial jurisdiction and the absence of a federal department with "broad enough terms of reference to encompass the many levels of society and life styles to which the day care issue relates."[71] Moreover, the brief indicated that some, though by no means all, members of NAHAC believed that the "most important focus [of child care provision was] not the mother and her needs but the child and its needs."[72]

Earlier in the submission, NAC quoted child care specialist Barbara Chisholm, who was concerned that while the provision of child care necessarily affected women, the guiding principle of the RCSW's report had been that this responsibility was to be shared by the mother, the father, and society. As a result, she argued that "further consideration of day-care should not be undertaken within the context of the Report ... This is because the focus of the Report is, rightly, on women. Day-care, while inseparable from that focus as one of its aspects, has many more. Perhaps its most important focus is not the mother and her needs but the child and his needs. And perhaps all of those needs can only be planned effectively in terms of the Canadian family and its needs."[73]

As Adamson, Briskin, and McPhail noted, although "NAC, other feminist organizations, and many individuals remained supportive of and active in the day care movement," this submission reflected an ambiguity about child care "on the part of the women's liberation movement."[74] On the one hand, feminists had insisted from the outset of the contemporary women's movement that universal child care provision was a prerequisite for their enjoyment of equal employment opportunities with men. On the other hand, it appears that by the early 1970s, some feminists were becoming a little concerned that women's repeated demands for better child care provision might serve to reinforce society's assumptions about maternal responsibility for the care of young children. Indeed, as the next chapter shows, this debate encouraged the emergence of an autonomous child care movement, concerned first and foremost with the delivery of a quality service to children rather than with questions about the relationship between women, work, and child care.

Assessing the Liberals' Response to the RCSW

Although the federal government sought to encourage economic growth in the 1970s by including women within the redrawn boundaries of worker-citizenship, it failed to respond to the very real connections between equal employment opportunity and child care that had been articulated by women in their submissions to the RCSW and emphasized in the commission's report. Linking the two issues did not fit within the dominant concept of equal opportunity that focused on treating male and female workers in the same way, rather than recognizing the different context in which they assumed employment. Instead, the concept of equal employment opportunity that underscored the emergent federal strategy focused on maintaining the link between equity and efficiency. As a result, questions about promoting women's employment opportunities to encourage economic growth took precedence over the more expensive project of enhancing women's employment opportunities through the increased provision of child care. Moreover, even though the RCSW had argued that equal employment opportunities for men and women could only be brought about through increased federal-provincial cooperation in the provision of child care, the federal government maintained a narrow definition of its constitutional capacity to engage in this area of policy development. In short, although the 1970s witnessed significant improvements in the development of federal policies to promote women's employment opportunities and reduce employment discrimination against them, the issue of how women were supposed to enjoy these opportunities while maintaining primary responsibility for the care of their children was deflected away from the federal agenda in the early stages of the Trudeau government.

5

Redefining the Issues: Systemic Discrimination and National Child Care Policies in Trudeau's Final Term

In the late 1970s, concern about the persistent employment discrimination that women experienced intensified in both feminist and federal government circles. Activists in the organized women's movement and femocrats in the federal bureaucracy became increasingly aware that although a decade had passed since the publication of the report of the Royal Commission on the Status of Women (RCSW), the gendered nature of employment discrimination remained starkly evident in Canada. Sociological studies confirmed that even though female labour force participation rates had continued to increase in the 1970s, women were still concentrated in the lowest echelons of companies and organizations.[1] In addition, research commissioned by the Canadian Advisory Council on the Status of Women (CACSW) revealed that although the government's equal opportunity initiatives in the mid-1970s had improved the representation of women in the middle management of the federal public service (FPS), very few women staffed its senior ranks.[2]

There was a sense, therefore, not only in feminist organizations but also within the federal government, that the equal opportunity, training, and anti-discrimination initiatives of the 1970s had not yet tackled the root causes of the employment discrimination experienced by women. In both communities there was an increasing recognition that the sources of employment inequality and discrimination had been inadequately defined in the 1970s because they were deemed to result either from the underdevelopment of women's technical skills or from the prejudiced and bigoted actions of individual employers. As David Dodge observed in his 1981 report of the Task Force on Labour Market Development in the 1980s, the assumption underscoring employment opportunity policies in the previous decade was that "'ownership' of the employment problem rested with the individuals or groups rather than with their circumstances and with barriers in society and in the labour market."[3] He went on to analyze the problems with this method of tackling employment inequality:

This approach, which forms the backbone of most past policies, failed to consider the barriers in the employment system itself and concentrated on the perceived skill deficiencies of the individual as defined by market requirements. With the problem defined primarily in these terms, remedial measures have aimed at expanding the individual's or group's store of "human capital" and have not sought to alter demand. For target group members this approach has too often been reduced to providing repeated periods of low-level training, temporary job creation and segregated job-experience training ... While the skills of some individuals have been improved, programs for target groups have lacked long-term employment and development goals.[4]

However, while there was a growing sense that the systemic – or institutionalized – nature of employment discrimination had to be addressed, there was no clear consensus in Canada about the most appropriate way to tackle the problem. Indeed, the lack of consensus was heightened by divergent reactions – both inside and outside government – to the development of target-based affirmative action programs and contract compliance schemes that had been developed in the United States.[5] In federal government circles, left-of-centre Liberals and bureaucrats concerned with the eradication of discrimination tended to favour the development of mandatory affirmative action policies. By contrast, right-of-centre Liberals and bureaucrats concerned with promoting good relations between government and the private sector were either deeply opposed to such initiatives or only prepared to pursue a voluntary model. Outside government, while many feminists called for mandatory affirmative action, members of the business community were, at best, in favour of a voluntary model and, at worst, opposed to any policy development of this kind.[6]

As debates about affirmative action intensified in Canada in the early 1980s, two clear patterns of policy development evolved. On the one hand, women became just one of a number of target groups to be included in catch-all affirmative action policies. As a result, concerns about the particular sources of employment discrimination that women (or for that matter any other target group) experienced became lost in a search for systematic ways of embracing a variety of groups in a single, anti-discriminatory policy. On the other hand, policy makers became more and more concerned about identifying the root causes of discrimination *within* employment systems. As a result, broader social questions about the way that women's employment opportunities were shaped by their primary responsibility for the care of young children slipped further down the federal policy agenda.

The weakening of the link between women's employment opportunities and child care provision was encouraged not only by the federal government's decision to maintain a separation between these two issues but also by the way that women's campaigns on employment equality and child care became more specialized during the Liberal government of 1980-4. In the early 1980s, the established women's movement put an enormous amount of energy into entrenching gender equality in the Canadian Charter of Rights and Freedoms. While this campaign focused feminists' attention on the complexities of substantive equality and the importance of affirmative action, it detracted their energy away from debates about broader issues of social policy. Moreover, in September 1982, just five months after the Charter was entrenched in the Constitution, an autonomous, national, child care movement was formed to lobby the federal government for a national, publicly funded, child care service.

Gender Equality, Affirmative Action, and the Charter of Rights and Freedoms

From 1980 to 1982, Canadian feminists became very concerned about eradicating sex discrimination and promoting gender equality in the public sphere. The intensification of feminist concern about these issues can be explained not only by the publication of a number of studies documenting the persistence of gender inequalities, but also by women's increasing concern to ensure that strong anti-discrimination measures were entrenched in the Charter of Rights and Freedoms when the Canadian Constitution was patriated from the United Kingdom in 1982.[7] Arguably, the institutionalized women's movement became so focused on constitutional issues relating to gender equality in the early 1980s that questions about social policies relating to gender difference received less attention within the feminist community than they had at earlier stages in the second wave of Canadian feminism. As Lise Gotell has noted, the drive to achieve constitutional equality encouraged many feminists to see "gender oppression in terms of legal discrimination while ignoring underlying structures such as family reproductive relations and capitalist productive relations in which they are embedded."[8]

Women's concern to ensure that strong anti-discrimination clauses and full gender equality rights were entrenched in the Charter stemmed primarily from their awareness about how badly women had fared under the anti-discrimination clause in the 1960 Bill of Rights. As Burt has observed, "The Canadian Bill of Rights ... guaranteed women and men equal treatment before the law, in cases where they were in equal situations ... [Nevertheless,] litigation based on the Bill of Rights demonstrated quickly how few instances there might be in which such equal situations could be judged to exist."[9] Indeed, as Gotell noted, "The most important variable drawing the Canadian women's movement into the constitutional fray was the weakness of the draft Charter proposed by the federal Liberals, [which] contained essentially the same equality clause as that found in the ineffectual Canadian Bill of Rights."[10]

The intensity of feeling was reinforced by two sex-equality cases that had been brought before the Supreme Court in the 1970s and in each case led to rulings that perpetuated discrimination against women. The first case, brought by Jeanette Lavell and Yvonne Bedard, concerned two Indian women who claimed that they suffered sex discrimination because section 12(1)b of the Indian Act denied status to Indian women who married non-Indian men. In this case, the court ruled that because the regulation was encoded in the Indian Act and related solely to the organization of reserves, the appellants were not subject to the denial of equality before the law and were not therefore victims of sex discrimination, as defined in the Bill of Rights.[11] In the second case, brought by Sandra Bliss, the appellant claimed that she had suffered sex discrimination under the Unemployment Insurance Act because she had been required to work longer to earn maternity benefits than she would have been to earn sickness benefits. In its decision, the court deemed the provisions of the Act legitimate, arguing that because the lesser benefits were allocated to women on the basis of pregnancy, rather than their sex, they did not constitute a form of sex discrimination per se.[12] Both these cases raised concerns about the development of a comprehensive anti-discrimination clause that would prevent blatant sex discrimination within the law or in its application. In addition, the Bliss case encouraged active feminists to ensure that the Charter would overcome the ideology of sexual difference that had been clearly demonstrated in that decision.

While the limitations of the Bill of Rights had long concerned some feminists, the mass mobilization of women around the Charter stemmed from Lloyd Axworthy's attempts, as minister responsible for the Status of Women, to stop the 1981 conference "Women and the Constitution," being organized by the CACSW.[13] Although the CACSW's conference was cancelled, Axworthy's attempts to block debate on gender equality and the Charter sparked such anger in the women's movement that a substitute conference, organized by the newly formed Ad Hoc Committee on the Constitution, was held in Ottawa on 14 February 1981 and attended by over 1,400 women.[14]

The resolutions passed at that conference demonstrate the strength of women's concern to give constitutional legitimacy to their campaigns to eradicate sex discrimination in all spheres of public life, and particularly in the sphere of employment. These called, first, for section 7 of the Charter to include the right to reproductive freedom and the right to equality of economic opportunity and, second, for section 15 to be strengthened so that, in addition to there being no discrimination on the basis of sex, there also be a compelling reason for any distinction made on this basis.[15] Furthermore, the resolutions called for the proposed three-year moratorium on the implementation of section 15 to be lifted so that governments would be forced to address anti-discrimination issues as soon as the Charter came into effect.[16]

By all accounts, the work of the Ad Hoc Committee on the Constitution was successful. Its campaign to include equal rights and anti-discrimination clauses in the reformulated Constitution proved significant, not only because it was a landmark of feminist effectiveness in the face of both federal and provincial government resistance but also because it reinforced the legitimacy of gender equality as a goal of Canadian public policy.[17] The campaigners got the gender equality clause (section 28) entrenched in the Charter, and managed to save it from inclusion within the remit of section 33, the notwithstanding clause.[18] In addition, the Ad Hoc Committee lobbied successfully for sections 15(1) and 15(2), thereby helping to create two of the most innovative anti-discrimination clauses in liberal democratic constitutions.[19] Section 15(1) not only proclaimed that "every individual is equal before and under the law and has the right to the equal protection and equal benefit of the law," but also outlawed discrimination on the grounds of "race, national or ethnic origin, colour, religion, sex, age or mental or physical disability."[20] At the same time, section 15(2) ensured that this approach to equality did not preclude the use of affirmative action to "ameliorate conditions of disadvantaged individuals or groups."[21] Indeed, women's success in getting section 15(2) included in the Charter reinforced the validity of initiatives that were already under way in Ottawa to introduce affirmative action measures in the federal sphere.

The Liberal Government's Approach to Affirmative Action

By the end of the 1970s, American innovations had clearly begun to influence federal bureaucrats in both the Canadian Employment and Immigration Commission (CEIC) and the Canadian Human Rights Commission (CHRC). However, it was the re-election of a Liberal government, in February 1980, that marked a clear shift in government policy, away from the equal opportunity programs of the 1970s, towards the adoption of affirmative action models in the 1980s. In its Throne Speech of 14 April 1980, the new government declared its intention to tackle the systemic roots of employment inequality within the context of a broader set of policies to promote economic productivity and growth. While the government emphasized that "the state cannot meet every demand or satisfy every group," women were given a high priority. A clear commitment was made both to promoting "equality for women" and to ensuring "that there [was] no room in Canada for sexual discrimination of any kind." Moreover, the government declared that in responding to the "economic challenges of the 1980s" it would expand training and employment opportunities for women and implement affirmative action programs in the FPS.[22]

The Throne Speech had been drafted by Tom Axworthy (the assistant principal secretary in the Prime Minister's Office), who, as Christina McCall and Stephen Clarkson note, saw this as the culmination of a longer effort to get the Liberal Party back into power in Ottawa by returning it to a left-of-centre, neo-Keynesian agenda.[23] However, the references in the speech to ensuring women's equality and their economic productivity also reflected the more fundamental tension in contemporary Canadian liberalism between the pursuit of human rights, on the one hand, and economic progress, on the other.[24] Indeed, because this tension is so endemic to Canadian liberalism, it fundamentally shaped most of the debate about the development of affirmative action in the 1980s.

Human Rights Forces Propelling Affirmative Action Policy in the Federal Sphere

Two significant forces on the human rights side of the equation encouraged the federal government to develop and implement affirmative action policies in the early 1980s. First, as we have already seen, Canadian feminists secured both the constitutional equality for men and women that had evaded their American "sisters" and the entrenchment of affirmative action in the Canadian Charter of Rights and Freedoms as a method for eradicating sex discrimination.[25] Second, the CHRC adopted a policy position that increasingly favoured affirmative action as a method for rooting out systemic discrimination against the target groups it had been established to protect.

The CHRC's Increasing Advocacy of Affirmative Action Policies

In the early 1980s, the CHRC proved to be one of the key agencies within the federal policy system that propelled the government towards the adoption of a proactive affirmative action policy. Early on in its mandate, the commission recognized that most of the complaints it was receiving were not simply the result of bigoted or prejudiced actions by one individual against another, but rather a reflection of the way that employment systems impacted on the groups it was there to protect from discrimination.

The commission's commitment to the eradication of systemic discrimination in the federal sphere was evident early on in its mandate. Its 1980 annual report noted: "We cannot define discrimination purely in terms of behaviour motivated by evil intentions; the definition has to include the impact of whole systems on the lives of individuals – what is called structural or systemic discrimination. As well as offering redress in isolated cases of discrimination against specific individuals, therefore, the Commission must study employment systems and social programs from the point of view of their effect on certain groups."[26]

The CHRC's rapid recognition of the systemic nature of much employment discrimination was encouraged not only by the complaints it received but also by professional links that its newly appointed bureaucrats established with their counterparts in longer-established institutions in provinces and in the United States.[27] Despite this, the CHRC's ability to act in a way that could take account of the impact of whole systems on the lives of women workers was restricted by the legislation under which it was established. Nonetheless, there were a number of different ways in which the CHRC raised the profile of affirmative action in the federal sphere.

The CHRC initiated this process by arguing that the systematic collection of workforce statistics would ensure its bureaucrats had a database from which to identify patterns of institutional discrimination against the target groups it was mandated to protect. While the CHRC was concerned to ensure that such data "could not be used in a negative way against a particular group or individual," it argued that this information would make it possible to "help establish the rate of change taking place" and "identify problem areas so that appropriate special programs could be developed."[28] The following extract from the CHRC's 1981 annual report clarifies why the commission was so concerned to establish this database:

> At the present time planning to improve the representation of women and members of minorities at all levels of the work force is hampered by a lack of adequate data. Those concerned are unable to find out enough about the numbers of women, disabled persons, native people, and other minority group members available for different kinds of work in different areas; we do not know the make-up of the employed labour force in general. Without this information it is often impossible to determine whether there are basic problems in the policies and practices of an employer affecting the overall position of minorities or women, and it is extremely difficult for employers to make realistic plans for the future. We therefore suggest that consideration be given to requiring employers under federal jurisdiction to report the breakdown of their work force regularly by sex and minority status.[29]

The CHRC's lobbying for systematic data collection about the employment of women and minority groups marked the beginning of a process that came to fruition with the introduction of the 1986 Employment Equity Act (EEA). It was an important means of establishing a database from which to assess the degree of systemic discrimination experienced by different target groups employed in the federal sphere. At the same time, however, this emphasis encouraged the idea that the labour force profiles of various target groups could be compared quantitatively, an approach that blocked awareness about the need to recognize the different contexts in which members of each group enter the labour market.

The CHRC also played a crucial role in advancing the concept of affirmative action within the federal sphere by lobbying for its entrenchment in the Charter of Rights and Freedoms. Indeed, on 7 September 1978 the commission submitted a brief to the Joint Senate and House of Commons Committee set up to examine the Constitutional Amendment Bill, recommending that "the Charter be amended to permit special programs, which, under the Canadian Human Rights Act, may differentiate in favour of certain groups who have suffered or are likely to suffer discrimination."[30] Such lobbying was, in part, driven by self-interest because the CHRC wanted to ensure that in the event of the Charter being entrenched in the Constitution, its own powers to implement special programs would have constitutional backing. The CHRC noted in its 1981 annual report:

> The CHRC strongly favours the use of special employment programs (affirmative action) ... A number of organizations, including the federal government, have already experimented with voluntary affirmative action programs. Although their efforts have not yet resulted in significant changes in the labour market, they are nonetheless important as first steps which recognize that special measures are necessary and justifiable if labour market conditions are to be improved ... The time has come for us to consider a wider and more effective use of affirmative action in both the public and private sectors, to improve conditions for those groups in the Canadian labour force who most need it – the disabled, women, native people, older workers, and racial minorities. We will strongly support such programs and will aid and abet their implementation in any way we can.[31]

As it turned out, the inclusion of section 15(2) in the Charter proved crucial in a subsequent appeal to the Supreme Court of Canada over a case that evolved from a complaint to the CHRC by the Quebec labour organization Action travail des femmes.

Action travail des femmes v. *Canadian National Railway*
Action travail des femmes (ATF) lodged its complaint with the CHRC on 6 November 1979, arguing that women employees at Canadian National Railway (CNR) experienced systemic discrimination because they found it difficult to secure more highly paid jobs within the company, particularly those in nontraditional sectors in the car-maintenance yards.[32] The CHRC substantiated the complaint, noting that "ATF has reasonable grounds to

believe that CNR in the St Lawrence Region has established or pursued a policy or practice that deprives or tends to deprive a class of individuals of employment opportunities because they are female."[33] However, as the CHRC then failed to establish any conciliation between ATF and CNR, a tribunal was established in July 1981.

Tribunal hearings began on 7 December 1981 to adjudicate the case and consider whether CNR should be required to implement an affirmative action program to ensure that women were hired in those sections of the company that were not traditionally considered to be areas of women's work.[34] On 22 August 1984 the tribunal substantiated ATF's complaint. It found CNR guilty of contravening section 10 of the Canadian Human Rights Act (CHRA) because it was pursuing an employment practice that "deprives or tends to deprive an individual or class of individuals of any employment opportunities on a prohibited ground of discrimination."[35] In this case, CNR was found to be denying employment opportunities to women in certain unskilled blue-collar jobs.

The tribunal's ruling was heavily influenced by the landmark decision made by the Supreme Court of the United States in 1971, in the case of *Griggs* v. *Duke Power Company*.[36] This case had demonstrated how seemingly neutral hiring policies could reinforce systemic discrimination. The US Supreme Court had found the Duke Power Company guilty of systemic discrimination on the grounds that it required applicants to have a high school diploma or obtain satisfactory scores on two aptitude tests, neither of which could be proven to be directly related to the type of work that would be undertaken at the power company. Both practices were found to exclude African Americans at a substantially higher rate than white applicants and, in fact, proved to be unnecessary prerequisites for the job in hand.

Even though the precedent set by the *Griggs* case has been weakened by subsequent US Supreme Court decisions, the ruling was a turning point in American law because it found that an employer could be held responsible for discrimination, even when there was no evidence of a conscious decision to discriminate.[37] Indeed, as McDermott has noted, "The most important finding in the *Griggs* case ... was that, for the first time ever, a senior court in a common-law jurisdiction found that the employer did not have to engage consciously in wilful discrimination to be held accountable. Even when discriminatory behaviour was deemed unintentional, the outcomes of any action could still be discrimination. Thus the legal stage was set for the fundamental and critical legal concept of 'systemic discrimination.'"[38]

As in the *Griggs* case, the CHRC tribunal ruled that CNR was discriminating against a group of employees because its criteria for selecting applicants went beyond the *bona fide* occupational qualifications required for purposes of the job at hand. Using its powers under section 41(2a) of the CHRA, the tribunal ordered CNR to curtail its discriminatory hiring practices. Specifically, CNR was to ensure that women applicants did not have to take physical tests that were not required of male candidates or prove that they had welding experience for entry-level positions.[39] Special temporary measures that indicated the adoption of affirmative action were also required. To quote directly from the tribunal, "Within the period of one year and until the percentage of women in non-traditional jobs has reached 13, CN shall undertake an information and publicity campaign inviting women in particular to apply for non-traditional positions [and] hire at least one woman for every four non-traditional positions filled in the future ... over a quarterly period."[40]

CNR was instructed to implement these measures within a year, and to ensure that employees who had been laid off subject to recall were, in fact, recalled. In addition, CNR was required to appoint a specific, named person to oversee the implementation of the special temporary measures and to submit quarterly progress reports to the CHRC. The company was also instructed to overhaul its advertising of posts, its processes for disseminating information about vacancies, and its interviewing and internal promotion processes. In addition, it was required to set in place measures to eliminate all forms of discrimination, including sexual harassment.[41]

In May 1985, CNR appealed to the Federal Court, arguing that the CHRC tribunal had not made a decision on the basis of the facts before it and had exceeded its jurisdiction by mandating quotas to redress the alleged discriminatory hiring practices without referring the case back to the CHRC. While CNR won the case on appeal to the Federal Court, a subsequent appeal by ATF to the Supreme Court of Canada led to a final decision in its favour. On 25 June 1987, the Supreme Court ruled that the actions of the CHRC tribunal had been legitimate and upheld its decision to implement the first mandatory affirmative action program in the federal domain.

There were a number of reasons why this case proved to be so significant. It was the first time that section 15(2) of the Charter had been used to justify mandatory affirmative action as a way of countering discrimination. As a result, the decision was lauded by the feminist community and received with some trepidation in business circles.[42] However, beyond this, the case was significant because it was a class action that reinforced the idea that women workers could secure important victories in the Supreme Court when they wanted to be treated in the same way as male workers. The ATF case was, after all, one in which women sought entrance into a male bastion of CNR. The case was important because it recognized that women could do the work as well as men and should therefore be compensated for past discrimination. However, it did little to raise public awareness about the different circumstances in which men and women would take on that work, and certainly not with respect to the care of children. Moreover, it reinforced the notion that the different treatment of

women in the pursuit of equality actually involved temporary, special programs to bring their participation up to a level with men, rather than the
development of policies that continuously reconcile issues of equality and
issues of difference, as questions about employment equality and child
care inevitably do.[43]

Although the CHRC's proactive approach to the problem of systemic
employment discrimination indicated that it was clearly concerned about
the "impact of whole systems on the lives of individuals," its ability to
acknowledge how issues of gender difference might impact on women's
employment was limited by the legislation under which it operated.[44] This
became particularly clear in the way the commission acted on questions
of discrimination relating to pregnancy, childbirth, and child care.

*The CHRC on Questions of Gender Difference: Pregnancy, Childbirth,
and Child Care*

Annual reports from the CHRC indicate that the commission was highly
conscious of the fact that men and women were often differently situated
with respect to employment. In its 1978 annual report, the commission
noted that it had dealt with a number of "cases involv[ing] policies and
practices which differentiate adversely against women who combine the
roles of working and childbearing. A variety of issues surrounding maternity – leave, benefits, questions asked of prospective employees, working
conditions, and so on – were brought to our attention as hindering the
equality of opportunity for women."[45] However, the nature of the CHRA
meant that the commission could only focus on questions relating to
childbirth and child care to the extent that these created situations that
specifically discriminated against women or men. Inevitably, therefore,
the CHRC's ability to address problems of systemic discrimination tended
to encourage a government perspective that emphasized gender equality,
rather than recognizing gender difference.

Nonetheless, the CHRC clearly wanted to consider how parenting could
affect women's employment opportunities. In its early years, the commission sought to improve the clarity of sex discrimination in section 20 of
the CHRA so that "discriminatory practices based on pregnancy or childbirth" were included within the remit of this clause.[46] Additional concerns
about child care emerged in 1979 and 1980 when the commission's
annual reports recommended that "provision be made permitting special
or preferential arrangements for leave to permit parents to care for a
child."[47] Bill C-141, the Act to amend the CHRA, was passed in 1983 and
ensured that it was no longer discriminatory for employers to provide
special leave or benefits to employees of either sex in connection with
child care. However, as this amendment focused on the provision of temporary leave, usually around childbirth, it was not designed to enable the

commission to address the way that long-term demands of child care might restrict either parent's participation in the labour force.[48]

Ironically, questions about child care found their way onto the commission's agenda as a result of complaints from men that they confronted more stringent conditions than did women when claiming child care expense deductions against federal income tax.[49] Early in its existence, the CHRC received a complaint from Mr. Pellerin and Mr. McCaffrey that the Income Tax Act allowed mothers, but not all fathers, to deduct child care expenses in the calculation of their income tax. Even though discrimination was deemed to have occurred, the complaint was dismissed on 14 October 1980 because the CHRA could not be used to amend federal legislation (in this case the Income Tax Act).[50]

The CHRC's frustration at not being able to put a stop to this form of discrimination was clearly reflected in its 1979 annual report:

> The CHRC considers that the claiming of child care expenses should not be more restrictive for men than for women. This policy harks back to a vision of the family which is no longer solidly based in reality. It is not fair to either men or women to assume that a man's wife will inevitably be tending their children at no cost to him unless she is in an institution or has legally surrendered custody of the children. This premise is discriminatory, and perpetuates negative attitudes to women who are working or completing their education, as well as penalizing men who are unable to claim a substantial deduction.[51]

The commission lobbied Parliament to remove the differential treatment of men and women from the legislation, an action that eventually proved successful with the 1983 amendments to the Income Tax Act.[52] However, the fact that the CHRC's sole action on questions of child care during the early 1980s was one concerned with the discriminatory effects of child care expense deductions on men, suggests that the commission's ability to influence broader social policy debates about the link between women's employment opportunities and the provision of child care was limited.

While the CHRC was unable to push debates about child care beyond its anti-discrimination remit, this new federal agency clearly had a powerful impact on debates about using affirmative action to eradicate employment discrimination. Had the CHRC been in control of the policy agenda in Ottawa, it is very likely that mandatory affirmative action programs would have been introduced throughout the federally regulated sphere. However, as we turn now and look at how questions of economic productivity also influenced the development of policies concerned with women's employment, we can begin to understand why the Liberals developed a more ambiguous set of policy proposals that fluctuated between the implementation of voluntary and of mandatory affirmative action programs.

Economic Imperatives Propelling Affirmative Action Policies in the Federal Sphere

Almost at the same time as the new human rights professionals were arguing about the need to identify the systemic roots of employment discrimination, politicians and professionals within the CEIC were becoming increasingly concerned about the under-representation of women in key sectors of the federally regulated labour force. However, while the CHRC's concern to eradicate systemic employment discrimination against women was part of its broader project to root out discrimination in the federal sphere, the concern to eradicate systemic employment discrimination in the CEIC stemmed from questions about how the underutilization of workers, affected by this form of prejudice, reduced Canada's economic productivity.

Growing awareness of the economic rationale for pursuing affirmative action stemmed from the recognition that women constituted an increasingly crucial part of the labour supply. As Harish Jain noted in a paper prepared for the CEIC's Affirmative Action Directorate in 1981, "Over the past several decades the labour force participation rate of women has significantly increased, from 21.8 per cent in 1931 to 47.8 per cent in 1978, while that of men declined from 87.2 to 77.9 per cent over the same period. These trends are expected to continue in the future, so that the female labour force will constitute an increasingly critical source of labour supply. It is imperative therefore that employers develop non-discriminatory pay and staffing systems to attract, retain and motivate female employees."[53]

Interestingly, recognition of women's economic significance stemmed, first, from the knowledge that more and more women were seeking paid employment outside their homes and, second, from the realization that a recent dip in the number of immigrants admitted to Canada made it important to encourage women (and other groups of Canadians) into critical sectors of the labour force.[54] As Sue Findlay has noted, this was a marked change as, historically, "labour market policies had tended to rely on the manipulation of immigration policy, rather than on investment, in developing the full potential of Canadian workers regardless of sex, race or physical handicaps."[55] However, while these general demographic patterns certainly impacted on the CEIC's decision to encourage the federal government to develop a clear affirmative action policy, the difficulties that the commission's bureaucrats experienced when trying to introduce voluntary affirmative action measures into the private sector added impetus to their campaign.

The CEIC's Voluntary Affirmative Action Initiative
In 1979, before the Liberals were temporarily voted out of office, the CEIC set up a voluntary affirmative action program to try to persuade key organizations within the private sector to adopt a proactive approach to hiring women and other target groups. This initiative aimed to encourage crown corporations and companies in the private sector, particularly those under contract to the federal government, to develop and maintain affirmative action programs in order to increase the representation of women and minority groups in their workforces. In return, the CEIC offered to support corporations by providing data on relevant labour markets, analyzing their employment practices, and supplying information on federal training and wage-subsidy programs.[56]

The program sought to extend the federal government's equal opportunity initiatives into the private sector and encourage private sector employers to reassess their human resource planning systems by setting clearly defined employment goals.[57] It was designed to encourage employers to draw more extensively on the pool of qualified female labour that was emerging from federal government training programs. It was also set up to assess the effectiveness of adopting a voluntary affirmative action model, in the hope that this would encourage the employment of women (and other target groups), while preventing the federal government from being criticized for over-regulating the private sector.[58]

The initiative was not, however, successful. Between 1979 and 1982, only twenty-seven of the 700 companies approached by the CEIC agreed to implement affirmative action programs.[59] By 1983 a total of 900 had been approached, with only thirty-four affirmative action agreements secured.[60] In part, the initiative failed because there was a mismatch between the desire of bureaucrats in Ottawa to diffuse American innovations into Canada and the resources their colleagues in regional offices had to promote these programs. As the coordinator of Justice and Public Services in the Northwest Territories noted in her 1983 submission to the Royal Commission on Equality in Employment, "CEIC has a voluntary affirmative action program which has been available to NWT employers for nearly three years. There is no person here assigned to promote it, rather it was added to the already heavy program load presently carried by CEIC employees and therefore the concept is not being promoted."[61] In addition, employers proved resistant to the concept of affirmative action. They viewed it as an unpalatable American import that would increase corporate running costs and lessen productivity.[62] They also resented federal intrusion on questions of corporate hiring policy, particularly at a time when the government's own record on promoting gender equality was generally considered to be less than exemplary.[63] Indeed, it was for the latter reason that the minister of Employment and Immigration galvanized the federal government into developing an affirmative action program in the early 1980s.

Affirmative Action in the Federal Public Service

The cautious introduction of an affirmative action program within the federal public service (FPS) began in August 1980 and put the first pound of flesh on the bones of the Liberals' Throne Speech.[64] A pilot scheme established in the offices of the CEIC, the Treasury Board Secretariat, and the Secretary of State was extended in 1982 to include the Public Service Commission of Canada and Environment Canada.[65] Finally, in 1983 the affirmative action program was extended throughout the FPS.[66]

The program had three components: neutralized employment practices, the establishment of goals and timetables to improve the representation of women at all levels in the federal bureaucracy, and reports on their realization.[67] Under the program each deputy minister had to produce an analysis of the status of women, Aboriginals, the disabled, and (after July 1985) visible minorities employed in their ministries. They were also required to set annual targets for the hiring and promotion of qualified employees in each of these target groups.[68]

The implementation of affirmative action within the FPS served the double function of creating a flexible employment equality strategy within the federal bureaucracy and an affirmative action model that might prove palatable to the corporate sector. The significance of this point was clarified in the 1980 annual report of the Treasury Board: "It was for reasons of equity that Cabinet set out its Equal Opportunities for Women (EOW) policy in 1975, but today it is for efficiency and the smooth operation of the national economic system that the government must ensure that women take part in all fields of economic activity, particularly where there are still few women, such as in the business, administration, industrial and operational sectors."[69]

Even though the introduction of an affirmative action policy within the FPS was hailed as a significant and necessary expansion of the EOW policy, in effect it was an incremental change. The objectives of the policy – neutralized employment practices, the setting of flexible goals and timetables, and reporting on the realization of these objectives – were not, in essence, any different from those that had characterized the EOW program. While the inclusion of a larger number of target groups within the policy remit was laudable in the way it gradually improved the anti-discriminatory objectives of federal employment policy, this process marked the beginning of a much longer development of policies designed to treat very different target groups in a similar – "neutralized" – fashion.

Economic Arguments and the Task Forces

The recognition that policies to eradicate systemic discrimination against women might enhance labour market development was clarified in the reports of two separate task forces that were established shortly after the 1980 Throne Speech. The Task Force on Employment Opportunities for the '80s was established on 23 May 1980 to examine the paradox of high unemployment and critical shortages of skilled labour existing side by side in different communities and to seek "the views of industrial labour, voluntary, human resource and educational specialists on the matter."[70] Created primarily to engage the public in discussions about how best to improve the employment opportunities of Canadians in different regions, the task force also helped to build awareness about systemic discrimination.[71] Its report recommended that the federal government "encourage affirmative action in the private sector and [adopt] a contract compliance policy to open up more training and employment opportunities for women, Natives, minorities and the handicapped."[72]

Two months later, in July 1980, a more intensive, academic study of labour market development was commissioned by Lloyd Axworthy as minister of Employment and Immigration. The Task Force on Labour Market Development was designed to provide the minister with an analysis of labour demand and supply conditions in the 1980s, an assessment of the adequacy and cost-effectiveness of training programs in meeting the projected demand for trained workers, a review of existing government programs to promote employment, and finally, an analysis of the special needs of particular groups of workers, including women.[73]

Reporting to Axworthy in 1981, the task force director, David Dodge, highlighted the urgent necessity of restructuring the declining labour force in order to ensure economic growth in an era of rapid technological change. His report argued that key men and women within the existing labour force should be retrained with the skills necessary to meet changing technological demands. Given the declining availability of skilled immigrant labour, it also recommended that growth points in the labour force be identified, so that new personnel could be trained in essential skills and channelled into the productive sectors of the economy. Noting that women and young Native people were "projected to account for 75 to 80 per cent of labour force growth in the 1980s," Dodge emphasized that "failure to utilize these groups fully will unnecessarily inhibit economic growth by restricting potential labour force growth. In addition, continued under-utilization of already developed skills and abilities, particularly those of women, will act as a drag on improvement in productivity."[74]

The reasons that Dodge's recommendation seemed to be so influential within the CEIC is that he argued that if groups that had been historically excluded from the goods-producing sectors of the labour force could be absorbed into these areas of work, the goals of economic productivity and equal opportunity could be achieved at the same time: "This is most clearly the case with measures designed to better integrate women and Native people into the labour force. To the extent that these groups acquire a greater diversity of skills and experience, equity will be increased, labour market adjustment processes will occur more smoothly and the economy will be able to adapt more easily to change in the industrial and geographic structure of economic activity."[75]

In order to achieve the goal of gender equity, Dodge argued that it was necessary, first, to remove the systemic barriers to women's employment, particularly in the manufacturing areas that had traditionally been dominated by men, and second, to divert women out of their traditional ghetto in the service sector and into manufacturing. If this did not occur, Dodge predicted that the "continued high concentration of women in service sector occupations, combined with high labour force growth will result in a growing problem of unemployment among women, while simultaneously labour markets in occupations and industries which primarily employ men will become increasingly tight."[76]

While Dodge's primary concern was with labour market training, he recognized that "an effective labour market planning approach must be based on an accurate assessment of those elements which operate to exclude certain groups from full participation."[77] Indeed, he went on to argue that "a comprehensive approach ... based on the need to develop required skills, change unacceptable behaviours and remove unnecessary systemic demand barriers ... [against] target groups will contribute to the government's goals of improving equity and economic productivity, as efficiency in the labour market is enhanced by efforts to assure all workers the opportunity to develop and participate as fully as possible."[78]

The task force recommended that the integration of women and Native peoples into productive employment would be brought about by "improved market information, enriched counselling, employment support measures, training, wage subsidies, employment development measures, flexible arrangements of work and legislated measures to ensure employers adopt employment practices which encourage the hiring and promotion of target group members."[79] In other words, although Dodge recommended the development of affirmative action, he argued that it should be voluntary and combined with other strategies that would open up the labour market to members of economically disadvantaged groups currently excluded from it.[80]

Although the task force was asked to recommend training and labour market measures that could apply to all target groups, its report emphasized that it was "critical that [individuals from target groups] receive additional program support tailored to the specific needs and problems of each group and that these problems be operated as mainline programs of the CEIC."[81] Moreover, even though it made no specific recommendations on the subject, the report noted that "support for child-care programs cannot be over-emphasized."[82] Moreover, the task force acknowledged that women's labour market activity is often detrimentally affected by child care responsibilities:

> Many women have had to adjust their labour market commitments to accommodate family responsibilities by dropping out of the work force for significant periods, by taking part-time work and jobs with no overtime demands. These decisions often involve serious penalties in terms of career progress and future earnings, a particularly serious problem for women who may have become sole supporting. Women also generally have the responsibility for finding substitute care for their children when they enter the labour force. The double burden of family and work responsibilities often provides significant barriers to women entering or reentering the labour force.[83]

Dodge's recommendations on the importance of addressing the special employment needs of women and minority groups fell on receptive ground within the CEIC, in part because they coincided with increased demands on Axworthy from women's groups and disabled people's organizations for policies that addressed the systemic nature of employment discrimination.[84] However, what is less recognized is that the publication of his report also coincided with the CEIC being subject to the first employment systems review of a federal government department to be carried out by the new Complaints and Compliance Branch of the CHRC.[85] Clearly, therefore, the motivation for Axworthy to develop and implement programs that would address the problem of systemic employment discrimination within, and well beyond, the CEIC was very strong. Indeed, his decision to do so reflected the deep-rooted pattern of bureaucratic competition between the CEIC and the CHRC that clearly shaped the development of federal policies to eradicate systemic employment discrimination in this period.

While both the CHRA and the Charter legitimized affirmative action as a tool for remedying previous discrimination, the federal government's experience with developing these programs remained very tenuous. Despite the fact that concerns about labour market expansion and improved antidiscrimination measures could be realized by the extension of affirmative action policies throughout the federal sphere, the Liberal government was reluctant to develop a comprehensive policy at a time when it was being heavily criticized for over-regulating the private sector and encouraging fiscal restraint.[86] As a result, Axworthy decided that his only option was to forge a middle path between the economic and human rights imperatives facing the government. Indeed, as Chapter 6 shows, he did so by persuading the cabinet to establish a royal commission that would investigate the federal government's varied policy options more closely.

The Reactivation and Federalization of Child Care

It was as a result of a rather less complex combination of factors that questions about the limited provision of child care in Canada gained increasing prominence on the federal agenda during the final Trudeau government. Although, as the previous chapter demonstrated, the federal government's response to the report of the RCSW had been to deflect the question of developing a national child care system away from its policy agenda, the provincial child care lobbies that had come into being in the 1970s brought the issue back into the federal arena in the early 1980s.

The opportunity to do so arose as a result of a decision by the Canadian Council for Social Development (CCSD) to hold its second national child care conference in Winnipeg in September 1982.[87] Although the idea of creating a national child care campaign had taken root among child care activists before the Winnipeg conference, once the meeting was announced they seized the opportunity to "go federal."[88] It was to the government in Ottawa that activists now began to address their demands for the "development of an affordable, comprehensive, high quality, not-for-profit child care system ... supported by public funds and accessible to every Canadian family who wishes to use it."[89]

Pat Schulz, the founder of Action Day Care in Toronto, was pivotal in ensuring that the Winnipeg conference led to the creation of a national child care movement. She set up an ad hoc committee to coordinate a national day care campaign and to strategize ahead of the Winnipeg conference. Schulz recognized that the conference presented "an enormous opportunity for the day care community in Canada to further its efforts to expand and improve the service ... [to develop both] a national day care policy with recommendations to the federal government for changes in legislation [and] a national campaign to publicize and educate around the issue of day care."[90] As Laurel Rothman, a key activist in the Ontario child care movement, reflected many years later,

> Pat was phenomenal because she said, "If we're going to [the conference], well, two things have to happen. We have to have a bit more than a tea party and we have to get one of us, meaning the activists, on the platform." And she got herself to be one of the main speakers. She also said that we have to organize on the floor, so I can remember getting on the plane with Sue Colley and Gord Cleveland, her husband ... Gord had *Roberts' Rules of Order* and a whole bunch of other things, and I remember, as is often the case in these big assembly type meetings, the teachers

were handling the formal running of the meeting. I forget who it was, whether it was the Canadian Teachers' Federation or whether it was [the] Winnipeg or Manitoba [association], but Gord was quite clear that he would know what to do, and he would work with us. We had meetings before about motions and we had this Universal Access Caucus booklet saying what we wanted ... universal access to quality child care ... and we went to the meeting with the intent of ensuring that our viewpoint would be heard and taken seriously.[91]

As they went into that conference, the key concern of the activists in the Universal Access Caucus was that the Winnipeg meeting be used to launch their demand that child care should become a universal social program. Indeed, the members of the caucus wanted to prevent the Winnipeg conference leading solely to the redefinition of child care as an issue of early childhood education. Prior to the conference, activists in the caucus had become aware that there was some interest within the CCSD in founding a federally funded national child care organization that would link together early childhood educators across the country and push the subject of child care beyond its existing welfare realm. Indeed, the Universal Access Caucus wanted to ensure that if a national organization was created as a result of the conference, it would not simply become "an organization where people were talking about what was good for kids in the playroom," but one that recognized how child care was "a big political issue that had to be taken forward in an activist kind of way, if anything was going to happen."[92]

Given the different political priorities of the various provincial delegates attending the Winnipeg conference, it had in fact seemed unlikely that the meeting would lead to the creation of a national child care movement. Reports of the conference in the *Winnipeg Free Press* noted that although delegates from Manitoba, Saskatchewan, and Ontario were pressing for a national system of publicly funded child care, those from Quebec and Alberta were resisting this idea.[93] However, despite the divisions among provincial delegates, the conference voted to lobby the federal government for the provision of nonprofit, universally accessible, community-based child care, available for children between the ages of zero and twelve. A resolution declaring that "there should be recognition of the right of every parent and child to universal access to high quality non-profit day care, notwithstanding their right to choose other existing options," was carried by 75 percent of the delegates voting in its favour.[94] In order to bring this about, the conference called for "the immediate appointment of a Parliamentary Standing Committee in order to make recommendations to a National Day Care Act."[95] In addition, it resolved not only that "the federal government establish, under a new Child Care Act, an equitable cost-shared program to provide for universal access to quality day care," but also that a new federal department, separate from Health and Welfare, be established to administer it.[96]

It is notable that not one of the thirty resolutions passed at this conference made a reference to the relationship between the provision of child care and the promotion of women's employment. The thrust of the resolutions was that parents and children should enjoy their rights to "high quality non-profit day care."[97] Given that it was this conference that led to the creation of a national child care movement, it was perhaps inevitable that questions about child care and women's employment opportunities would become even more distinct in federal policy circles.

In fact, the Winnipeg conference led to the creation of two national child care organizations. The Canadian Child Care Federation was formed as a network for early childhood educators, and the Canadian Day Care Advocacy Association (CDCAA) was formed to lobby the federal government on child care and ensure that child care was recognized as a crucial social policy issue in the next general election campaign.[98] It was also created to raise public awareness about child care and help coordinate local, provincial, and territorial campaigns for improved services.[99] Initially formed as an interim committee, with two representatives from each province and territory, the CDCAA set up an office in Ottawa in 1983, with financial support from the Secretary of State, Women's Program. It was then that the CDCAA, acting on the recommendation of the Winnipeg conference, began to pressure the federal government to establish a national task force on child care and examine the possibility of developing national child care legislation to support a universally accessible nonprofit day care service.

Distinctions between Questions of Child Care and Questions of Women's Employment

Although the creation of a national child care movement with an office in Ottawa brought the issue of child care to national attention, the process reinforced the division between questions about women's employment opportunities and the provision of child care services. Child care advocates were supportive of feminist concerns to ensure that the link between women's employment opportunities and the provision of child care was recognized in Canadian public policy.[100] However, their *primary concern* was not to lobby for child care in order to promote gender equality in the workplace but rather to pressure governments to develop a *universal public service for children,* with decent employment conditions for child care workers.

These priorities can be explained by looking briefly at the period just before the birth of the national child care movement, when some provincial child care activists chose to build support through the labour movement rather than the women's movement. The case of Ontario is instructive not only because key child care organizations were based in Toronto at the time but also because the city was the centre of operations for the National Action Committee on the Status of Women (NAC). However, even though the women involved in the provincial child care movement were members of both the Ontario Federation of Labour (OFL) and NAC, they chose the OFL as the base from which to build support for their campaign.

The Ontario Child Care Lobby and the Ontario Federation of Labour
The link between the Ontario child care lobby and the provincial unions was forged not only because key activists like Pat Schulz and Sue Colley were involved in both movements but also because in the 1970s the nascent child care lobbies focused their energy entirely on the provincial domain.[101] As a result, it made much more sense to build institutional support for their claims through the provincially oriented labour movement than through the federally oriented NAC. Moreover, the principal concerns of the child care lobby – to turn child care from a welfare service for impoverished parents to an educational right for Ontario's children, to improve the working conditions of child care workers, to encourage their unionization and to extend the idea that day care provision should be entrenched in the collective bargaining process – were demands that had a broad appeal within the labour movement.[102] Indeed, labour movement activists contended that "the unionization of day care workers would be the first step towards a common front to deal with such problems as the lack of universal access to day care, inadequate funding for centres, and workers' concerns such as low pay, few benefits, lack of job security and high staff turnover."[103]

Ironically, the process of securing union support, although organized by working women, slightly obscured feminist concerns about the link between child care and women's employment opportunities.[104] The OFL's 1980 Statement on Day Care shows that although the federation was clearly concerned to support its women members with regard to child care, it was also concerned to see child care as a social service developed to assist all working parents with the care of their children:

We must ensure that day care is made a priority issue for it underpins the home and working lives of both men and women ... The demands of the work place and the policies of governments have never seriously taken into consideration the needs of families. It was assumed that women were in the home with the children and that childrearing was a private responsibility that belonged to individual parents alone. Somehow the two exceptions to this rule were always overlooked: working class women, who had to work and could not raise their own children ... and the aristocracy, who never raised their own children ... Working people today, both women and men, are still plagued by the long-lasting results of these class assumptions. We are victims of the government dictum that your children are yours, you take care of them.[105]

The Child Care Movement and the Women's Movement

Very little attention has been paid in the literature on child care politics in the 1980s to the difference between the priorities of the national child care movement and those of the organized women's movement. Yet as Adamson, Briskin, and Macphail have suggested, activists in the two movements have not always focused on the same issues. Indeed, in their discussion of child care politics in the 1970s, these authors note how "in later years some day-care activists remarked that the women's movement had more or less ignored day-care in favour of other issues."[106] It is therefore important to consider how the dynamics of these social movements have influenced the extent to which debates about women's employment equality and child care have been driven apart.

One of the ironies of the early 1980s was that the intensification of activist campaigns on issues of child care and women's employment equality meant that the concerns emerging from these two arenas began to be identified as distinct policy issues. After all, the priority of the child care movement was the development of a universally accessible child care service driven by educational rather than welfare objectives. As a result, its members focused on the right of children to receive quality care and the right of day care workers to good employment standards. By contrast, although the institutionalized women's movement was clearly concerned about the rights of children and the nature of the service itself, its key motivation for becoming involved in debates about child care was to encourage the development of a nonwelfare service that would relieve working women of the burden of child care.[107]

The priorities of the institutionalized women's movement were made particularly clear in NAC's 1984 submission to the Royal Commission on Economic Union and Development Prospects for Canada. The Macdonald Commission (as it was called) proved to be an important forum for NAC to reinforce the link between child care and women's employment opportunities. At the forefront of NAC's demands was a concern to get child care out of the welfare ghetto of the Canada Assistance Plan (CAP) so that it could be redefined as a support service to enhance women's employment. As Chaviva Hošek, then vice-president of NAC, argued in her presentation to the Macdonald Commission:

At the moment we have a system, created under the CAP, in order to take care of people in need or likely to be in need. In other words, the basic social service cost sharing system we now have is for people in poverty or close to the poverty line. What has become clear since 1966, when that particular arrangement was worked out, is that there are a lot of services that women in particular do require, but they do not require them because they are in financial need. They require them because they are in other sorts of need. *The biggest one here is childcare, and it seems to us that one of the most important connections between women's economic equality and the social service sector is adequate child care funding.*[108]

Indeed, Hošek emphasized that women could not enjoy economic equality with men without adequate child care:

It makes no sense to say to women "enter the economy as equal partners" if they do not have access to affordable and accessible child care all over the country. It is simply a meaningless promise or invitation. It becomes to us a basic social service that needs to be provided so that it is not so expensive that only very few people can take advantage of it. Otherwise women's participation in the economy in the year 2000 is meaningless. As long as we have the assumption that the children that exist in the world are primarily the responsibility of women, we must have some adequate funding for the care of those children so that women can enter the labour force or make other kinds of contributions to the economic and social structure of the country.[109]

Hošek also maintained that instead of focusing solely on the costs of child care provision, the federal government should consider how jobs were created through child care and other social services. In addition, she reminded the commissioners how the potential to develop a child care policy that would support working women in Canada was constantly blocked by jurisdictional struggles over this issue: "It seems to us that essential social services for women get lost at the moment in the power struggle and jurisdictional struggles between the federal government and the provinces, and it seems clear to us also that this commission has an opportunity to say something about how this kind of problem can be addressed in the future."[110] As we shall see in subsequent chapters on policy development in both the Mulroney and Chrétien governments, this observation went to the core of child care politics in the late twentieth century.

The Final Trudeau Government's Response to Affirmative Action and Child Care
Looking back over the period of the final Trudeau government, we can see that although debates about affirmative action and child care intensified,

there were very few major policy developments in either field. Mandatory affirmative action was introduced in the federal public service. However, even the government's attempts to put its own house in order in this way did not make private sector companies embrace voluntary affirmative action programs to the extent that the CEIC had hoped. In the area of child care, no new federal policy developments occurred. The CHRC did succeed in getting discriminatory tax exemption laws changed in the Income Tax Act, but beyond this the only policy initiative on child care was the federal government's decision, in 1981, to establish pilot day care centres in buildings that were federally owned or leased.[111] The pattern of nondevelopment in this policy field was very indicative of Trudeau's strong position that child care was a provincial responsibility. As he wrote in a letter to Doris Anderson when she was president of NAC, "The delivery of social services is a provincial jurisdiction, with the federal government having no authority to deliver child care services directly, except in its own very limited jurisdiction."[112]

Although a number of attempts were made to address systemic employment discrimination and child care in the early 1980s, during the period the two issues, which had long been linked in feminist analysis, were driven apart. The ascendance of a discourse on constitutional equality reinforced the idea that difference could best be absorbed into equal opportunity policies through special temporary programs to remedy past discrimination rather than through policies that sought to reconcile the more deeply rooted dimensions of gender equality and gender difference. The bureaucratic competition between the CHRC and the CEIC to devise the best approach to remedying employment discrimination within the federal sphere encouraged the development of anti-discrimination and affirmative action policies that were applicable to a large number of target groups. Inevitably, this process limited the federal government's ability to recognize the specific barriers to employment that any one group experienced. Once again, the pursuit of equal opportunity in Canadian public policy was based on the identical treatment of the target groups rather than a recognition of differences among them.

In keeping with its history of failing to build a recognition of group differences into the design of policies to promote equality of employment opportunity, the federal government was much more reluctant to engage with questions about the development of child care policy than with those concerning the eradication of gender discrimination in the workplace. The two issues were driven further apart by Trudeau's insistence that while employment equality was a legitimate area for federal policy development, child care, in his opinion, remained a matter of provincial jurisdiction. Moreover, the creation of a national child care movement, whose members were committed first and foremost to the development of child care as a universal social service, deflected some activists' attention away from considering how women's employment opportunities could be enhanced by the public provision of child care.

Towards the end of its term of office, however, the Trudeau government appointed a royal commission to examine equality in employment and a task force to look at child care. The Royal Commission on Equality in Employment (RCEE) was set up on 23 June 1983, under a sole commissioner, Judge Rosalie Silberman Abella. She was instructed "to inquire into the opportunities for employment of women, native peoples, disabled persons and visible minorities in certain crown corporations and corporations wholly owned by the Government of Canada" and to report on "the most efficient, effective and equitable means of promoting employment opportunities, eliminating systemic discrimination and assisting all individuals to compete for employment opportunities on an equal basis."[113] It is indicative of the purpose of this commission that Abella was instructed to "inquire into means to respond to deficiencies in employment practices, including without limiting the generality of the foregoing means, such as an enhanced voluntary program, possibly linked with mandatory reporting requirements and a mandatory affirmative action program."[114]

In May 1984, one month before Trudeau's (second) retirement from federal politics, Minister Responsible for the Status of Women Judy Erola announced the establishment of a special task force on child care, subsequently known as the Katie Cooke Task Force.[115] This task force was set up "to examine and assess the need for child care services and paid parental leave as well as the adequacy of the current system in meeting this need ... and ... to make recommendations to the minister responsible for the Status of Women concerning the federal government's role in the development of a system of quality child care in Canada."[116] Although Erola managed to extract this concession from a cabinet that had been categorical about the federal government's not intervening in an area of provincial jurisdiction, the establishment of the task force, at a point when the Liberal government was pessimistic about re-election, did not indicate its firm commitment to policy development in this area. Arguably, the decision to establish the task force was a last-ditch attempt by the Liberal government to pacify the child care lobby and improve its own electoral credibility by taking action on an issue that had gained increasing prominence in debates about social policy.

The fact that two separate inquiries were established on these two issues, within a year of each other, indicates not only how distinct the lobbying on employment equality and child care had become but also how separate these two issues were on the federal government's agenda. Moreover, while the two investigations demonstrated that the federal government recognized the need to address problems of employment inequality and child care, their creation reflected the federal government's unwillingness to act decisively on either policy issue.

Although both the Royal Commission on Equality in Employment and the Task Force on Child Care had been established to carry out their separate inquiries, the report of the first effectively trumped that of the second. Inevitably, the RCEE's status as a royal commission meant that its report was likely to have a broader impact on the federal government than that of a departmental task force. Moreover, as is discussed in Chapter 7, the Conservative government that was in office when each report was published proved more willing to address the recommendations of the RCEE than those of the task force. However, the real significance of the RCEE lay in Abella's decision to consider how "the history of discrimination in Canada" had shaped the employment opportunities of the four target groups, but in the case of women to do so by linking issues of employment equality with those of child care.[117] It is therefore to an analysis of the RCEE – its mandate, proceedings, and recommendations – that I now turn.

6

The Royal Commission on Equality in Employment

The Royal Commission on Equality in Employment (RCEE) was set up on 23 June 1983 to identify "the most efficient, effective and equitable means of promoting employment opportunities, eliminating systemic discrimination and assisting all individuals to compete for employment opportunities on an equal basis."[1] Its establishment highlighted the federal government's concern to eradicate employment discrimination within its own jurisdiction and ensure that employment equality policies were integrated into a broader labour market strategy to encourage economic growth. Indeed, the commission's terms of reference opened with a declaration that "the government of Canada is dedicated to the principle of equality in the world of work."[2] They went on to note that as "women will constitute the majority of new entrants into the Canadian labour force in the 1980s," it was "imperative from an economic point of view to ensure that women are employed to the full extent of their productive potential and from a social point of view to ensure that women receive an equitable share of the benefits of productive work."[3]

The terms of reference indicated that the RCEE was established within a tradition of federal policy making that assumed that the solution to employment discrimination lay in the development of policies that encouraged the equal, nondiscriminatory treatment of all worker-citizens. Nonetheless, it was the first public inquiry in Canada to focus on the employment discrimination experienced by women, Native people, disabled persons, and visible minorities – the four target groups considered most at risk from employment discrimination.[4] The focus on these four target groups was in part a reflection of the fact that the RCEE was established shortly after the Charter of Rights and Freedoms was entrenched in the Canadian Constitution, at a time when a new group politics was developing in Canada.[5] However, it also reflected an established pattern of federal government concern about developing representative bureaucracies. As former Liberal senator Lorna Marsden noted, for her "the most important objective [of the commission] was to ensure that when the Report was finished Canadians (both as workers and employers) could see themselves and their own society reflected in the recommendations."[6]

The RCEE was also established with a remit to bridge the public-corporate divide by considering what kind of equal employment opportunity policies could be developed in crown corporations. The sole commissioner, Judge Rosalie Abella, was instructed to examine the employment practices of eleven crown corporations and asked to recommend what measures the federal government might take to "respond to deficiencies in employment practices" she identified.[7] Although instructed to do so "without limiting the generality of the foregoing means," it was clear from the suggestion that she consider options like "an enhanced voluntary program, possibly linked with mandatory reporting requirements, and a mandatory affirmative action program" that the RCEE also marked an important turning point in the development of federal employment policy.[8] In short, the commission was established to explore what type of affirmative action policies the federal government could demand from state-funded and corporate organizations within its jurisdiction.

There were, it seems, two reasons for the decision to focus on crown corporations. First, as Abella herself noted, "Even where the tasks of Crown Corporations directly parallel those of private sector enterprises ... they are engaged in something more than a business venture. Most are created as instruments of national purpose and that purpose, as expressed in their mandates, extends beyond the business at hand."[9] In addition, the crown corporations provided a compromise between those in the cabinet and parliamentary caucus who wanted to expand affirmative action programs beyond the federal bureaucracy and those who were concerned to protect the business sector from further government regulation.

Although the RCEE was created to establish a policy framework that would equalize the employment opportunities of four different groups of worker-citizens, questions about the specific forms of employment discrimination that women, Native people, disabled persons, or visible minorities experienced were *not* included in its terms of reference. This reflects the fact that the RCEE was established to develop a policy mechanism that could be systematically applied to any target group, rather than develop remedies for the specific forms of employment discrimination experienced by each of them. Given that the political saliency of target groups changes over time, this was in many respects an astute approach to the development of public policy. After all, concerns about employment discrimination against war veterans, francophones, senior citizens, gays, and lesbians have also gained political prominence at different times since the Second World War.

The commission's mandate encouraged a search for policy solutions that would ensure the equal treatment of target groups, rather than a recognition of differences among them. Despite this, Abella not only considered the specific circumstances in which members of the different target groups entered the labour market but inquired about the various forms of discrimination they experienced within the workforce. She analyzed how women's employment opportunities were structured in different ways from those of men. In the process, she linked questions about the promotion of equal employment opportunities for men and women with questions about the provision of child care. As a result, Abella re-established the link between the promotion of gender equality in the workplace and the provision of child care that was first articulated in the federal policy arena in the report of the Royal Commission on the Status of Women (RCSW).

The Politics of Establishing the RCEE

Although the RCEE drew questions about women's employment opportunities and the provision of child care back together again on the federal policy agenda, the politics behind its establishment indicate that this was not the objective of its creators. As Lloyd Axworthy – the minister who devised the RCEE – noted, the commission was "an expedient ... a technique to get the concept of employment equity or affirmative action into the legislative process" by building some public consensus around the issue.[10] Such a consensus was needed because although the minister of Employment and Immigration was being lobbied to develop more effective affirmative action policies throughout the federal sphere, he was also confronting significant resistance to this idea both inside and outside the government.

Pressure on Axworthy to develop more effective affirmative action policies came from a number of sources. Organizations representing those groups of worker-citizens who experienced the most persistent forms of employment discrimination were lobbying him to address the problem through stringent policy measures. As he noted later, "There was a pretty strong case being made by women's organizations, disabled organizations, and others that in order for affirmative action to work you had to have a legislative base primarily attached to some form of sanctions."[11] Moreover, federal government reports, both inside and outside his own department, highlighted the need for new policy initiatives to address the persistent discrimination experienced by a range of target groups.[12] In addition, Axworthy was highly influenced by the prognosis of the report of the Task Force on Labour Market Development in the 1980s that if women and Aboriginal peoples were not encouraged to develop crucial skills they could, in little more than a decade, become "a kind of [deskilled] lumpen proletariat."[13] Moreover, as the minister responsible for immigration as well as employment, Axworthy was acutely conscious of the discrimination faced by many new Canadians who could be identified as visible minorities. Finally, like other legislators in both federal and provincial governments, he was well aware that when section 15 of the Charter came into force in 1985, the employment practices of all Canadian governments would come under greater scrutiny for evidence of discrimination.[14] Indeed, it was for this reason that female parliamentarians who had campaigned to secure gender equality in the Charter, lobbied Axworthy to develop policies that would eradicate employment discrimination in the federal sphere.[15] In short, the combined impact of questions about expanding human rights and diversifying the labour supply for economic reasons encouraged Axworthy to think about developing policies to combat the employment discrimination experienced by different groups of citizens.

While Axworthy was under pressure to address the systemic and persistent nature of employment discrimination in areas of federal employment, he also feared strong resistance to mandatory affirmative action programs. Although the federal government had implemented a voluntary affirmative action program within its own bureaucracy in 1983, as we saw in Chapter 5, attempts by the Canadian Employment and Immigration Commission (CEIC) to extend this model into the private sector during the late 1970s and early 1980s had been unsuccessful. In the end, only seventy-one of the 1,400 companies contacted by the Affirmative Action Directorate of the CEIC between 1979 and 1984 agreed to undertake voluntary affirmative action measures.[16] The resistance from company managers reflected their fear of hiring quotas creeping up from the south and their irritation that the federal government was seeking to diffuse this American idea into Canada at a time of intense economic restraint.[17]

In 1982, the Liberals had imposed heavy controls on the private sector through their introduction of a two-year program to keep inflation below 6 percent in the first year and 5 percent in the second.[18] Indeed, the government had established the Six and Five Committee – chaired by Ian Sinclair, then president of Canadian Pacific – to monitor the program and review all proposed regulations of the corporate sector in its light. When Axworthy sought the committee's approval to extend the federal government's own voluntary affirmative action program into the private sector, he was "given the thumbs down" because the corporate sector was already under severe recessionary constraints and, in the view of the committee, could not be expected to take on further employment regulations at this stage.[19] After all, as one of his policy advisors remarked, "Things were tough ... People were being laid off, profits were down and the general view in the business community was that this would be a costly initiative at a time when the economy was in bad shape."[20] Moreover, in January 1983, when Axworthy presented his proposals to the Federal-Provincial Committee on Human Rights, "some of the Conservative provinces like Alberta told

[him] to butt out" because his proposals to extend affirmative action policies into the private sector encroached on provincial jurisdiction.[21]

The Decision to Establish a Royal Commission and
Appoint Abella as Its Commissioner

It was the lack of consensus about affirmative action that led Axworthy to
consider establishing a royal commission. As he reflected later, "The conclusion that I came to was that the only way, in effect, to get affirmative
action programs out of the voluntary system and into the other sectors
was to appoint the royal commission. [I also thought] that the mandate of
that commission should not just be fact finding and research, which was
already done, but in fact to put forward a formula for implementation. It
was really a question that if you get your nose in the tent, after that you
can move right in."[22]

However, although Axworthy was supported in cabinet by colleagues
like Francis Fox, Herb Gray, and Don Johnson, he still had a battle to get
the royal commission approved. Even after he secured cabinet approval to
establish the RCEE, he encountered huge resistance from the senior man-
darins within the Department of Finance, the Treasury Board, and the
Privy Council Office.[23] Though manifest in persistent questioning of the
terms of reference, and in concerns about Axworthy's wish to appoint a
provincial court judge to carry out the inquiry, this bureaucratic harassment reflected deep-rooted concerns about maintaining the support of the
business community during the recession. In the end it took ten months
of intense negotiations before the commission's terms of reference were
finally agreed.[24]

In the fall of 1982, when Axworthy first thought of establishing the
RCEE, he decided that Judge Rosalie Abella would be "the perfect person"
to carry it out.[25] His choice was astute because she was well known not
only in Liberal, human rights, and feminist circles but also among those
active in disability politics. Through previous involvement in the women's
movement, Abella was known personally to both Lorna Marsden, Axworthy's close ally in the Senate, and to his press officer, Pat Preston.[26] In addition, in the fall of 1982 when Axworthy decided he wanted Abella to direct
the inquiry, she was in active consultation with disability groups while
conducting a study of disabled people's access to legal services for the
attorney general of Ontario.[27] Moreover, as Axworthy's senior advisor –
Ron Collett – noted later, Abella "had a good understanding of the issues
and, given that background, had both the knowledge and the force of
personality [to] encourage the cooperation [that was] obviously needed in
the private sector."[28] After all, this royal commission was designed to
achieve consensus about the best way to promote diversity in the Canadian workforce.

The Methodology of the RCEE

Abella's own history – as a Jewish refugee to Canada and as a well-known human rights activist – suggested that she would take a tough stance on questions of discrimination.[29] However, while her predisposition to the human rights side of her mandate might have been anticipated, her decision to treat the crown corporations "as illustrative models of the issues under study" was not so predictable.[30] Even though Abella was instructed to focus on the employment practices of the designated corporations, she sought to identify policy approaches that would be acceptable to public and commercial employers and ensure that the varied concerns of her four target groups were addressed as fully as possible.

Conscious, no doubt, of the tight time constraints under which she had to operate, Abella initiated a broad process of public consultation within four days of receiving the terms of reference for the RCEE. On 27 June 1983, she sent a letter to "a thousand individuals and organizations enclosing the Terms of Reference and inviting the participation of as many people as possible."[31] This stated that the RCEE would "examine ways in which access to equal employment opportunities is available to women, native people, disabled individuals and visible minorities," and noted that "by concentrating on 11 Crown Corporations the study would be able to explore these broad issues in a defined context."[32] While this initial letter served to publicize the commission, it also indicated that Abella would inquire as fully into the discrimination experienced by the four target groups as she would into the employment practices of the designated crown corporations.

Advertisements placed in sixty Canadian newspapers, magazines, and journals during September 1983 reinforced Abella's decision to focus extensively on the employment discrimination experienced by the four target groups. These issued a broad appeal for submissions but made *no reference at all* to the eleven crown corporations. They simply noted that the RCEE had been established "to study discrimination in the workplace against women, native people, disabled persons, and visible minorities," and was required to report on "the most efficient, effective, and equitable ways to promote equal employment opportunities, eliminate systemic discrimination, and assist all individuals to compete for employment opportunities on an equal basis."[33]

Abella followed her initial letter with a more detailed missive, dispatched to nearly 3,000 individuals and organizations. Mailed first on 5 August 1983 and "throughout the fall to additional interested groups and representatives," it was further evidence of Abella's determination to push her inquiry to the margins – even beyond the boundaries – of her mandate.[34] Although the letter solicited responses to the commission's terms of reference, Abella also asked about a broad range of issues that could affect people's employment apportunities. Significantly, she invited comments on both affirmative action *and* child care:

1 Affirmative action
   • relative merits of voluntary and mandatory equality programs
   • advantages or disadvantages of various kinds of mandatory programs
   • determination of appropriate goals and timetables in each target group
   • use of economic incentives to encourage equality measures
   • monitoring and enforcement of voluntary or mandatory schemes
   • collection, use, and analysis of statistical data on employees
   • possible conflict between seniority and affirmative action targets
2 Flexible work patterns and child care
   • desirability of flexible work patterns
   • desirability of parental and maternity leave
   • desirability of child benefits and child care
   • financing of child care facilities
3 Training, recruitment, promotion, equal opportunity, and pay
   • importance, duration, and effectiveness of training
   • responsibility for training programs
   • problems in recruiting, hiring, and promoting employees
   • existing schemes to eliminate or minimize barriers to employment equality
   • problems with arbitrary differences in income, pensions, and other benefits
4 General issues
   • impact of technology on the promotion of equality in employment
   • impact of a restrictive economic climate on employment equality
   • any other perceived or actual barriers to equality in employment.

While Abella invited all those submitting briefs to comment on each of the issues she specified, her letter acknowledged that the list was "by no means exhaustive" but designed to give respondents "some idea of the kind of issues the Commission [would] be examining."[35] Indeed, Abella encouraged respondents to comment on any other factors they considered "barriers to equality in employment."[36] Moreover, by signalling that "the approach and emphasis [would] necessarily differ with each target group and that the remedies proposed [would] have to reflect these differences," Abella indicated early in the inquiry that her report would not simply recommend the identical treatment of all worker-citizens.[37]

In constructing this list of issues and circulating it widely, Abella broadened the spectrum of her inquiry. Her letter actively encouraged individuals and organizations concerned with women's employment to consider the forms and causes of gender-based discrimination in the workplace. In addition, it encouraged those submitting briefs to consider how women's roles as the bearers and carers of children shaped their opportunities for employment.[38] Indeed, data on the extent to which those submitting testimony on women's employment raised issues of affirmative action, flexible work, and child care reveal how the majority linked issues of affirmative action and child care (Table 6.1). Although the proportion of women using the RCEE to link these two issues was not quite as high as those linking concerns about employment opportunity and child care in submissions to the Royal Commission on the Status of Women (recall Table 3.1), the parallels in the way women expanded the limits of each commission's mandate are striking.

RCEE Briefs Concerned with Women's Employment

The RCEE received a total of sixty-two briefs concerned with women's employment. Of these submissions, fifty-five were from organizations and seven were from individuals.[39] Although Abella encouraged respondents to raise issues in addition to those she had identified, most submissions focused directly on the points she had outlined in her letter publicizing the commission. As a result, the briefs were shorter and less impassioned than those women had submitted to the Royal Commission on the Status of Women in the late 1960s.

These briefs were written not by women participating in one of the first royal commissions concerned with women's employment but primarily by representatives of established voluntary and professional organizations who had become somewhat routinized in their response to federal inquiries about the status of women. Indeed, there was an undertone in many of the briefs that these organizations had been "royal commissioned to death."[40] Abella noted in her report:

> There is much cynicism and frustration among members of the designated groups. Many with whom the Commission met have been presenting the same arguments to governments for years. They feel their views are frequently sought but rarely accommodated. Within months,

Table 6.1

Support for affirmative action and child care in RCEE submissions concerned with women's employment

	Number	Percentage
Address affirmative action only	15	24.2
Address flexible work and child care only	7	11.3
Address affirmative action and child care	34	54.8
Address none of the above	6	9.7
Total	62	100.0

and sometimes days, of meeting with this Commission, these individuals said that they had or would be presenting identical facts and positions to a Parliamentary Task Force on Participation of Visible Minorities in Canadian Society, a Royal Commission on the Economic Union and Development Prospects for Canada, a Parliamentary Task Force on Pension Reform, a Commission of Inquiry into Part-Time Work, and a Parliamentary Task Force on Indian Self-Government. In addition, women pointed out that since the 1970 Royal Commission on the Status of Women little substantial improvement had taken place.[41]

Evidence of this cynicism and frustration was also evident in the way that some organizations simply resubmitted briefs that had already been prepared for another recent public inquiry. Their authors clearly felt that although they had continuously contributed to agenda-setting debates, the federal government had made no sustained policy response to the issues they had raised.

What the Briefs Indicated about Affirmative Action

Of the submissions concerned with women's employment, 79 percent called for some kind of affirmative action policy (Table 6.2). Nonetheless, although there was a general consensus that "what was needed ... was a comprehensive approach that would end an era of tinkering with systemic discrimination and introduce one that confronts it," the briefs presented different methods for dealing with the problem.[42]

It is often assumed that in the 1980s all feminist organizations were calling for mandatory affirmative action policies, while businesses were constantly resisting the idea. An analysis of the briefs concerned with women's employment reveals that the picture was in fact more complex. Most submissions acknowledged that an affirmative action policy would only be effective if some form of monitoring were built into the process either through reports to an enforcement agency or through the systematic monitoring of labour force data, or both. Interestingly, however, there was also a clear preference in these submissions for policies to be built around flexible goals and timetables rather than fixed quotas. Although a number of the briefs made reference to American affirmative action programs, the dominant opinion was that an equal employment opportunity policy based on goals and timetables was preferable to one relying on quotas. While 27.4 percent of the submissions argued that mandatory policies would be most effectively developed through the use of flexible goals and timetables, only 6.5 percent supported fixed employment quotas (Table 6.2).

Those favouring a flexible, goal-oriented approach to employment opportunity argued that this method would be most palatable to employers. For example, the brief from the Canadian Psychological Association noted:

Table 6.2

Positions on affirmative action in RCEE submissions concerned with women's employment

	Number	Percentage
Total making comment on affirmative action, out of sixty-two briefs	49	79.0
Total of the sixty-two that supported:		
Mandatory affirmative action	23	37.1
Mandatory affirmative action with flexible goals and timetables	17	27.4
Mandatory affirmative action with fixed quotas	4	6.5
Voluntary affirmative action	17	27.4
Mandatory affirmative action in public sector/voluntary in corporate sector	5	8.1
No affirmative action	1	1.6
Financial incentives to secure compliance in corporate sector	11	17.7
Contract compliance to secure compliance in corporate sector	12	19.4
Financial incentives and contract compliance	2	3.2
Compulsory reporting and monitoring schemes	18	29.0
Systematic collection of carefully protected workforce data	11	17.7
Creation of a special enforcement agency	3	4.8

Fully cognizant of the difficulties inherent in either type of programme, the Canadian Psychological Association suggests that, with respect to women, the advantages of adopting a mandatory programme would, in the long run, outweigh those of a voluntary programme. The Association maintains that, to maximize the benefits for the recipients, the policies governing a mandatory programme should be reward-oriented rather than punitive in nature. More specifically, it is suggested that each Crown Corporation be required (a) to set goals and specify an appropriate time-table within which to achieve these goals, and (b) to report, at specified intervals, on its progress toward completion and maintenance of criteria of fair employment practices.[43]

By contrast, those favouring a mandatory approach had a much stronger sense of the systemic nature of employment discrimination. For example, the Congress of Canadian Women, a Toronto-based pressure group estab-lished to fight racism and sexism, called for "immediate legislation of mandatory affirmative action programs with precisely stated time sched-ules and quotas, linked to an equal pay policy."[44] It went on to argue that "if one is serious in effectively ridding our society of sexism and racism then illegalities, such as sexual discrimination, can only be dealt with by the force of legal sanctions. This necessarily means that there must be universal measurability, that is, standard criteria that can be operationalized and implemented on the basis of objective specifications right across the board."[45]

Twenty-nine percent of the briefs conveyed a fairly strong sense that for affirmative action to be effective in either the public or private sectors, a reporting or monitoring scheme had to be built into the policy process. Moreover, 17.7 percent argued that the systematic collection of carefully protected data on employees was essential. The Ottawa Valley chapter of Women in Science and Engineering (WISE) took a strong position in favour of mandatory affirmative action and argued that "the proper collection, use and analysis of relevant statistical information/data on employees are required for mandatory programs."[46]

Relatively few submissions that advocated a reporting requirement called for a special enforcement agency to oversee the process. However, the submission from the National Action Committee on the Status of Women (NAC) argued strongly that the role of the CHRC should be strengthened to ensure that it could make full use of its powers to require affirmative action and contract compliance.[47] Moreover, the Canadian Congress on Learning Opportunities for Women argued that "an agency mandated to deal with and rectify complaints" be set up.[48] The Ottawa Women's Lobby drew parallels with the implementation of official bilingualism, arguing that "serious thought should be given to the establishment of an Affirmative Action Commissioner with responsibilities similar to those of the Official Languages Commissioner."[49]

The only submission that was completely opposed to the idea of affirmative action was that of the Federal Progressive Conservative Women's Caucus of Peel-Halton. This group stated that "we are not in favour of affirmative action as it always carries a buried insult to the target group ... We are confident that women's natural abilities will win them all the recognition they deserve."[50] Moreover, almost foreshadowing the kind of rhetoric that became familiar in the 1984 Mulroney government, the Federal Progressive Conservative Women's Caucus of Calgary argued strongly that "not one new civil servant need be hired to gather the requisite statistics. The country cannot afford anything short of a guarantee that the civil service will not be increased."[51]

Although the federal government set up the RCEE with a view to developing affirmative action policies across the public and corporate sectors, some submissions maintained a distinction between the type of program applicable in each case. Only 8.1 percent of the submissions indicated that while organizations in the public sector should be required to implement affirmative action, companies in the private sector should be given a choice about whether to develop such schemes. For example, while the Ontario Native Women's Association favoured the implementation of mandatory affirmative action policies in "all federal [and] provincial government departments and crown corporations," it argued that "voluntary affirmative action could be promoted in the private sector by offering wage subsidies to those employing natives."[52]

Among those arguing that private companies should be required to develop affirmative action programs, opinion was fairly evenly divided on the question of using financial incentives or contract compliance. While 17.7 percent of the briefs advocated the use of tax incentives, wage subsidies, or other financial measures, 19.4 percent advocated the use of contract compliance. Only 3.2 percent of the briefs advocated the use of both mechanisms at the same time (Table 6.2).

What the Briefs Said about Flexible Employment, Child Benefits, and Child Care

Abella called for comments on the desirability of flexible work patterns, child care benefits, and child care facilities and also on methods to finance child care. The fact that 61.3 percent of women's submissions argued that child care facilities were a prerequisite for them to enjoy equal employment opportunities with men indicates how much this issue shaped women's perceptions of employment equality in the early 1980s (Table 6.3). In addition, it is noticeable that while 16.1 percent of the sixty-two submissions on women's employment argued that flexible work patterns would enhance the employment opportunities of women, and 8.1 percent mentioned child benefits or tax relief, only 1.6 percent argued that working women should be responsible for the care of their children. Thus although women were revisiting questions about the link between child care provision and employment equality that had been raised in the inquiries of the RCSW, general perceptions about the extent to which women should be responsible for the care of their children had clearly shifted since Florence Bird and her colleagues addressed this issue in the late 1960s.

Flexible Employment

Some of the briefs advocated the use of flexible work patterns in order that women could combine their mothering roles with paid employment. However, it is important to note that with the exception of the Federated Women's Institutes of Canada, which argued for flexible employment patterns specifically to enable women to spend more time with their children, all submissions advocating the adoption of flexible work patterns also called for working women to have full access to child care facilities.[53] Once again, this was in marked contrast to the way that women had approached the question of flexible employment in their briefs to the 1967 Royal Commission on the Status of Women.

The principal argument advanced in the briefs where women commented on this issue was that although more flexible work patterns would enhance the employment opportunities of women with dependants, it was essential that women did not experience further discrimination as a result. The Ottawa Women's Lobby expressed the rationale for flexible working patterns in the following way: "Given society's present expectation that women will be responsible for the care of children, at least in their early years, and given the very real desire of many women to perform this, the most valuable of all society's tasks, it is not possible to envision truly fair access to jobs, training and promotion for women unless more flexible work patterns become the norm rather than the exception."[54] Similarly, the Ottawa Valley chapter of WISE argued that "it is very important

Table 6.3

Positions on child care in RCEE submissions concerned with women's employment

	Number	Percentage
Total making comment on child care, out of sixty-two briefs	41	66.1
Total of the sixty-two that argued:		
Child care prerequisite for gender equality at work	38	61.3
Flexible employment and child care prerequisite for gender equality	10	16.1
Child care benefits/tax relief necessary	5	8.1
Working women should be responsible for own child care	1	1.6
Child care should be provided at or near woman's workplace	16	25.8
Government should subsidize employer for child care	3	4.8
Costs of child care should be shared between employer, employee, and state	4	6.5
Workplace child care should be subsidized only for low-income parents	2	3.2
In favour of free twenty-four-hour child care	3	4.8
In favour of free universal daytime child care	3	4.8
In favour of publicly or privately funded twenty-four-hour child care	2	3.2
Child care is a means of educating young children	2	3.2
National child care legislation needed	1	1.6

for women to have the option of flexible work patterns, in particular, part-time, flexi-time and improved maternity leave, with proportional benefits being paid by employers and employees."[55] In addition, the Battlefords Interval House Society of Saskatchewan and the BC Native Women's Society both stressed the value of flexible work for single mothers.[56]

Only the Ottawa Women's Lobby saw the development of flexible employment as a route to encouraging women and men to share child care responsibilities. As its brief noted, "Flexible work patterns such as job sharing, drop out provisions for periods of up to five years, [and] negotiated shorter working hours would also recognize the process of social change which would encourage men and women to adopt a division of remunerated jobs, housework and family responsibilities."[57]

Concern that women should not face greater employment discrimination if flexible work patterns were introduced was expressed in a number of the briefs. The submission from the Business and Professional Women's Clubs of British Columbia and the Yukon noted that "part-time workers should receive the same hourly pay, protection and fringe benefits as full-time workers on a pro-rated basis."[58] Similarly, the University Women's Club of Ottawa argued that "there must be a greater attempt to accommodate women within the employment system so they are not unnecessarily disadvantaged [either] in choosing to work part-time, [or because of] shift-work, job-sharing, leave provisions and/or decentralization of their work place. Many of these women may be primary caretakers within their families so require flexibility in time and place of employment."[59]

Some of the briefs emphasized that flexible work patterns would allow women to pursue education and training. The Federation of Women Teachers' Associations of Ontario noted that "all training opportunities available to workers should allow for such flexible work times."[60] Similarly the BC Native Women's Society noted that "flexible work patterns, work sharing and part-time work all allow the woman to find more time for herself and her family, [and] to take advantage of education and training."[61]

Only one of the briefs advocating flexible employment considered the economic implications of its position. The Nova Scotia Advisory Council on the Status of Women noted that flexibility was reasonable, providing "it [did] not impact negatively on productivity."[62] It also cautioned that "while at first glance the concept may be desirable between people who are satisfied with income sharing, let us not be forced into accepting that our Canadian society should not be able to anticipate what is termed full employment."[63]

Child Benefits and Tax Relief for Child Care
Women's concerns about the financing of child care did not feature as strongly in the briefs to the RCEE as they had in those submitted to the

RCSW. Just 8.1 percent of the submissions called specifically for child benefits or tax relief for child care. The Federation of Junior Leagues of Canada linked these with maternity benefits, noting that "in order to assist women in their dual careers as homemakers and work force employees, better maternity and child care benefits [were] required."[64] The Federation of Women Teachers' Associations of Ontario endorsed "appropriate child care leaves and either benefits to support child care or workplace child care," arguing that these should be the cooperative responsibility of the individual, the employer, and the government through subsidies, union negotiations, and cooperation.[65] The brief from the Battlefords Interval House Society argued that "child care benefits should be legislated."[66] Similarly, the Ottawa Valley chapter of WISE argued that "child care benefits and facilities are not a responsibility of the employer but of the government."[67] Only the Federal Progressive Conservative Women's Caucus of Calgary called for "better tax deductions for child care expenses."[68]

Child Care
Of the briefs concerned with women's employment, 25.8 percent argued that child care facilities should be available at or near the woman's place of work. While 4.8 percent of the submissions argued that the government should subsidize the employer for the service, 6.5 percent argued that the costs of the service should be shared between the government, the employer, and the employee. Interestingly, given the thrust of federal government policy, only 3.2 percent of the briefs argued that subsidies for workplace child care should be reserved for low-income parents (Table 6.3).[69]

Some submissions made specific points about the way that employers should develop child care provision. Infant Formula Action's entire brief focused on the need for employers to ensure adequate facilities for nursing mothers.[70] The Ontario Native Women's Association argued that in order "to ensure full participation by women, support services such as child care should be part of an affirmative action program."[71] The Battlefords Interval House Society argued that "employers should be compelled to provide quality day care at or near the place of work when a certain number of parents are employed."[72]

Only 9.6 percent of the submissions called for free universal child care. Half of these argued that such care should be available round the clock.[73] Moreover, the idea of twenty-four-hour child care was supported in a further 3.2 percent of the submissions, which indicated that this type of care could be publicly or privately funded.[74]

Interestingly, the small proportion of the briefs that emphasized the pivotal role of child care in educating young children – 3.2 percent – came from Aboriginal women's associations. While the Quesnel Tillicum Society argued that "we should be looking at personal growth of children as an investment in the future," members of the Native Women's Association of the Northwest Territories argued that child care would ensure that their children did not "lose their language or culture as a result of more women entering the labour force."[75]

Only one brief called for the introduction of a national child care act. Yet Abella included this proposal in her recommendations. The nascent Canadian Day Care Advocacy Association (CDCAA) began its brief by stating, "We believe the ready availability of high quality, affordable day care to be a necessary prerequisite for the equality of women in employment, given the economic structure of Canadian society."[76] However, it then used the brief to advance its calls for the federal government to recognize the child care crisis and provide leadership towards its resolution.[77] It called on the government to "undertake specific actions within the next year in order to facilitate a nation-wide dialogue on the multifaceted issue of how we, as a people, will manage to practice sexual equality, raise the next generation and have a growing economy."[78] It also urged the government to "develop a comprehensive plan, with long-term and short-term goals, for the implementation of universally accessible, publicly funded, high quality, affordable day care for every Canadian child in need."[79]

An Overview of the Briefs Concerned with Women's Employment
Like the RCSW before it, the RCEE provided women with an important opportunity to voice the connection between equal employment opportunity policies and child care provision that federal policy making structures tend to drive apart. Although this indicates how important the links between these two issues remained for women's enjoyment of worker-citizenship, women's submissions to the RCEE also reveal how perceptions about the link between these two issues had changed since women testified before the RCSW in the late 1960s. Those voicing concerns about women's employment opportunities were much less reliant on justifying their demands by reference to broad international codes of human rights than women had been when submitting evidence to the RCSW. By the early 1980s, some time after equal opportunity programs had been developed in the federal sphere, women were more specific than they had been in the late 1960s about how governments should act to promote women's employment.

The other important difference between the submissions women made to the RCSW and the RCEE is that even though women still articulated a clear sense of responsibility for the care of their children, there was virtually no evidence in the RCEE of women contesting the legitimacy of child care outside the home. Although opinions varied about the appropriate level of state involvement in the provision of child care services, there was an assumption running through these submissions that women had entered the workforce and needed child care support. Indeed, as Abella herself noted, "The urgency ... of the submissions made by women in all groups on this issue impel the Commission to give it special attention."[80]

Even though most of the submissions addressed questions about affirmative action and child care, the two organizations at the centre of the Canadian women's movement and the Canadian child care movement did not develop an analysis of the links between these two issues in their briefs. Although both organizations made fleeting reference to the link between gender equality in the workplace and the provision of child care, the brief from NAC focused almost exclusively on the question of affirmative action, while that submitted by the CDCAA advanced claims about the importance of federal involvement in child care.[81]

In part, this pattern reflects the priorities of the women who wrote each organization's brief. The brief from NAC was written by Carole Wallace, a key actor in the employment discrimination case that Action travail des femmes initiated against the Canadian National Railway in 1979.[82] The brief from the CDCAA was written by Judith Martin, a well-known child care activist from Saskatchewan who was heavily involved in the province's child care movement and active in the creation of the CDCAA.[83] The specific focus of NAC's brief reflects not only how this large umbrella organization is run by volunteers from a wide variety of organizations who have particular concerns that they might wish to prioritize, but also how different constituencies of interest dominate NAC at different points in time. The focus of the brief submitted by the CDCAA reflects how Abella specifically called for comments on child care and indicates the desire of activists in a nascent national organization to get their concerns about child care placed on the federal policy agenda. Nonetheless, the difference of emphasis in these two briefs also reflects how the institutionalization of national organizations concerned with the status of women and child care had themselves been affected by the way that questions about employment equality and child care were separated out in federal policy structures.

By contrast, organizations and individuals that were less routinely involved in lobbying on employment equality and child care not only responded more frequently to Abella's questions on these two issues but also seemed more at ease in linking them together in a way that had, historically, characterized Canadian feminist thought on women's employment. Indeed, as with the RCSW, a more general pattern emerged whereby women used the opportunity of submitting briefs to the RCEE to argue that the provision of government-subsidized child care in the community or the workplace was a prerequisite for women enjoying equal employment opportunities with men. Moreover, although Abella drew heavily on specific recommendations made by NAC and the CDCAA, it was the connection between equal employment opportunities and child care that dominated the recommendations she made in the report of the RCEE.

The Survey of Crown Corporations

The RCEE's inquiries into eleven designated corporations examined each company's data on hirings, promotions, terminations, and part-time positions, as well as employee breakdowns by income, job classification, and geographic distribution. It also analyzed information about systems within each corporation that dealt with human resource planning, measures to increase the participation of any of the four designated groups, the number of employee groups subject to collective agreements, and details of those agreements. In addition, the RCEE examined the corporations' policies and practices respecting education and training, and also assessed their plans to change any of these procedures.

The results of both inquiries certainly provided good cause for the development of new legislation to promote gender equality in this sphere of federal employment. The questionnaire that officials within the RCEE designed "to elicit a picture of each corporation's workforce and human resource systems" revealed that although they could "provide relatively reliable data on the numerical distribution and participation rates" of women, they had no systematic evidence about the employment of Aboriginal peoples, disabled persons, and visible minorities within their corporations.[84] Moreover, as Abella noted, "It was clear from the meetings with senior representatives ... that native people, visible minorities and disabled persons were not employed in significant numbers by any of the corporations."[85]

The data on the corporations' workforces revealed that only 21 percent of their employees were women, a figure that was well below that of the Canadian workforce as a whole.[86] It also highlighted the virtual absence of part-time employment in ten of the eleven crown corporations, thereby raising questions about the validity of focusing on crown corporations to develop policies to promote equality in employment, when "one in every four women working in Canada works part-time."[87] In addition, data on women's representation across occupational categories revealed their concentration in clerical and service occupations, their minimal presence in upper-level managerial positions, and their significant under-representation in middle management and semi-professional positions.[88] It also showed that although women had experienced fewer job terminations than men in the year prior to the inquiry, they remained at a significant disadvantage to their male colleagues in regard to hirings, pay, and promotion.

The conclusion that Abella drew from this survey was that while the levels of female employment in the eleven crown corporations had improved over the previous five years, the rate of change was so slow that it could "take several generations to reach even a 30-per-cent level of female representation in most occupational groupings."[89] In view of these data, it is not surprising Abella recommended that the federal government should develop policies whereby employers were required to set goals and timetables to increase the representation of target group members at different *levels* in their workforces.

In addition to considering the setting of goals and timetables, the chief executives of each corporation "acknowledged that legislated mandatory requirements were the most effective path to widespread equitable participation by the designated groups."[90] In view of the legislation that followed Abella's report, it is worth noting that while "all agreed that, at the very least, a public reporting requirement was essential ... they also felt that reporting alone, without further legislation, would likely not operate as a sufficient incentive to deal intensely with the issue, particularly in a depressed economy."[91]

The chief executives of all the corporations agreed that the employment opportunity initiatives that were already in place in their companies had been developed in response to the report of the RCSW, the provisions in the Canadian Human Rights Act, or in response to requests from government "for information on employment opportunities for women."[92] These directors were not averse to the setting of goals and timetables to achieve employment equity, though they were concerned "that the actual practices used to achieve equitable participation be left to each corporation."[93] Interestingly, they also thought that the achievement of these equality objectives needed to "be part of a manager's performance appraisal, which in turn should be tied to a manager's benefits, such as income and promotion."[94]

Despite the under-representation of women in crown corporations, Abella's inquiry into their employment practices revealed that in each case "it was one of their corporate objectives to have equal employment opportunities available particularly for women."[95] Indeed, her report noted that while most of the corporations' equal employment opportunity statements were "expressed as a prohibition against discrimination on specified grounds in much the same language as is found in human rights legislation," four of them had begun to develop "more meaningful strategies" and "allocated resources to carry these out."[96] Indeed, Abella found that it was corporations like the Canada Mortgage and Housing Corporation, "with human resource programs implemented specifically to counteract inequities ... that [had] been most successful in increasing the participation of women."[97] Though impressed by "the diversity of [equal opportunity initiatives] among the corporations," she was also concerned about two patterns.[98] First, the strong emphasis on promotion from within the corporations made it less likely that members of the already under-represented target groups would benefit from this process.[99] Second, it was noticeable that although some corporations had taken measures to develop awareness about the problems of employment discrimination and encouraged the appointment of women in nontraditional jobs, none of the corporations provided their employees with child care facilities.[100]

Corporate executives did, however, have some concerns about prospective legislation. They argued that it would be difficult for them to increase the representation of any of the target groups dramatically during a period of economic recession.[101] They also believed that the crown corporations should not be singled out as the focus for new federal legislation in the hope that this would then create a demonstration effect on the private sector.[102] Though sympathetic to the second concern, Abella was less well disposed to the first, noting that "where there was a corporate commitment to the increased participation of women, significant improvements in their participation continued throughout recessionary periods."[103] Indeed, Abella's response marked her clear wish to prioritize issues of human rights and anti-discrimination over questions of economic productivity.

The Report of the RCEE

In the introductory chapter of the report of the RCEE, Abella set out the three main principles that informed her analysis. First, she argued that employment equality could only be realized if the equal, nondiscriminatory treatment of disadvantaged groups was linked to a recognition of differences among them. Second, she indicated that the remedies for gender discrimination in employment had to focus on the broader societal factors that shaped women's access to the labour market, as well as on practices in the workplace. Finally, she situated her analysis within the human rights strain of Canadian liberalism, signalling that her priority was to recommend policies that sought to eradicate employment discrimination against the target groups, rather than simply increase their labour force participation in order to encourage economic efficiency and growth.

Near the outset of the report, Abella asserted that "equality in employment is access to the fullest opportunity to exercise individual potential [so that] no one is denied opportunities for reasons that have nothing to do with inherent ability."[104] Clearly, this statement situated the report within the developmental strand of Canadian liberalism, a fact that elicited criticism from commentators like Carole Geller.[105] Nonetheless, it is important to recognize that Abella's approach disrupted established assumptions in Canadian liberalism that equality of employment opportunity could be achieved by treating all workers in an identical fashion. Early on in the report, Abella noted that "sometimes equality means treating people the same, despite their differences, and sometimes it means treating them as equals by accommodating their differences ... ignoring differences and refusing to accommodate them is a denial of equal access and opportunity. It is discrimination."[106] Indeed, she went on to reflect that the "paradox at the core of any question for employment equality [is that] differences exist and must be respected, equality in the workplace does not, and cannot be allowed to, mean the same treatment for all."[107]

It was Abella's *in camera* consultations with the various target groups that made her realize the need to link the promotion of equal employment opportunities with the recognition of difference.[108] Many of the target groups she met argued that because "their economic histories are different, their social and cultural contexts are different, their concerns are different and the particular solutions required by each group are widely disparate ... it minimized the significance of each of their unique concerns to be combined analytically with three other groups."[109] Thus, although Abella upheld the importance of implementing effective affirmative action policies, her report emphasized that these should be supplemented by policies that recognized the specific – and different – problems faced by members of each target group.

Abella asserted that "the achievement of equality in employment depends on a double-edged approach. The first concerns those pre-employment conditions that affect access to employment. The second concerns those conditions in the workplace that militate against participation in employment."[110] In the case of women, Abella made clear that pre-employment equality with men would only come about if two conditions were met. First, society needed to accommodate "the changing role of women in the care of the family by helping both them and their male partners to function effectively both as labour force participants and as parents."[111] Second, it was essential to provide "the education and training to permit women the chance to compete for the widest possible range of job options."[112]

While the federal government's concern to link the pursuit of human rights and economic efficiency was evident in the commission's terms of reference, Abella's concern to promote human rights through equal employment opportunities was clearly the guiding principle of her report. Though conscious of the economic circumstances in which she was writing, Abella's primary concern was that "the members of the four designated groups [who, together] represent about 60 per cent of Canada's total population" should enjoy their "right, whatever the economic conditions, to compete equally for their fair share of employment opportunities."[113]

There were a number of ways in which Abella clarified how her analysis would be rooted primarily in the promotion of an agenda concerned with human rights rather than economic efficiency. She emphasized the importance of shifting policy away from a case-by-case approach that focused on intentional discrimination, developing instead employment equity programs that sought to eradicate systemic discrimination. Moreover, she

stressed the importance of bringing federal policy in line with the principles enunciated in the Charter of Rights and Freedoms by arguing that
"section 15 protects every individual's right to equality without discrimination ... section 28 reinforces gender equality ... [and] section 36 reiter-
ates Canada's commitment to the promotion of equality of opportunity
and the reduction of economic disparity."[114] Indeed, Abella reinforced her
commitment to developmental rather than economic liberalism in the
concluding statement of her introductory chapter by stating simply that
"section 15 of the Canadian Charter of Rights and Freedoms cancels the
debate over whether the country's economic conditions should be permitted to dictate the timing of the implementation of equality."[115]

Policy Proposals to Tackle Systemic Discrimination and Promote Equality in Employment

Abella's understanding of gender equality within employment was comprehensive. It included "active recruitment of women into the fullest
range of employment opportunities, equal pay for work of equal value, fair
consideration for promotions into more responsible positions, participation in corporate policy decision-making through corporate task forces
and committees, accessible childcare of adequate quality, paid parental
leaves for either parent, and equal pensions and benefits."[116] Moreover,
Abella made two distinctive contributions to a broader international debate about addressing systemic discrimination in the workplace. First, she
devised a new term – employment equity – to describe policy measures
designed to promote the employment opportunities of the four target
groups. Second, she produced a report that did not locate employment discrimination solely in the workplace but linked the manifestations of employment inequality with broader societal factors that restricted women's
opportunities for employment.

Employment Equity

The term "employment equity" was created by Abella as a Canadian vari-
ant of the American concept of affirmative action. It sought to distinguish this Canadian policy initiative from popular misconceptions about
American affirmative action policies and, in particular, to coin a term that
disassociated government regulation of employment opportunities from
the implementation of employment quotas.[117] Abella considered that "no
great principle [was] sacrificed in exchanging phrases of disputed definition for newer ones that may be more accurate and less destructive of
reasoned debate."[118] As she noted in her report, "Ultimately it matters little
whether in Canada we call this process employment equity or affirmative
action, so long as we understand that what we mean by both terms are
employment practices designed to eliminate discriminatory barriers and

to provide in a meaningful way equitable opportunities in employment."[119] In fact, the subsequent decision by the Harris government in Ontario to repeal the province's 1993 Employment Equity Act and introduce the 1995 Act to Repeal Job Quotas and Restore Merit-Based Employment in Ontario suggests that Abella was overly optimistic.[120]

Abella defined employment equity as a method for obliging "all federally regulated employers to develop and maintain employment practices designed to eliminate discriminatory barriers in the workplace and improve, where necessary, the participation, occupational distribution, and income levels" of the target groups.[121] In her report, Abella dismissed the idea of voluntary affirmative action programs and argued that equality in employment could only be achieved if federally regulated employers were required, first, to set goals and timetables for developing equitable employment practices and, second, to report their annual progress in achieving these objectives to a designated enforcement agency.[122] The ingenuity of this recommendation was that although it advocated a mandatory reporting requirement, it found a link between the views of the four different target groups and the crown corporations with regard to the establishment of goals and timetables.

Abella's policy recommendations on employment equity differed from the American model of affirmative action because they did not, at the initial stage, involve the imposition of quotas. Indeed, it was because employment equity required employers to collect data that would enable them to identify and eliminate discriminatory employment practices within their own organizations that Abella considered it preferable to the quota-based model of affirmative action.[123] She conceded that "if the collection, filing and reporting of data and the statutory requirement to improve practices produce inadequate results, consideration may be given to the use of quotas."[124] In general, however, Abella was opposed to quotas because she found them to be "inflexible and arbitrary" instruments that could not take account of an employer's circumstances or the regional composition of the available labour force.[125] She also believed that quotas set sights for improvement too low and could "foster resistance, condescension, and resentment in the workplace and [could] be gratuitously insulting to, and undermining of the individuals so hired or promoted."[126] Above all, she maintained that "quotas as arbitrary objectives represent short term solutions. The elimination of barriers, on the other hand, is a long term approach to the pursuit of equality."[127] Indeed, Abella envisaged this to be a flexible approach that measured "successful compliance by whether the results are reasonable in the circumstances regardless of the system used by an employer to improve employment practices."[128]

By defying quotas and recommending that employers be given considerable flexibility in designing their own employment equity strategies,

Abella not only encouraged employers to think about how they might tackle systemic employment discrimination within their own organizations but acknowledged that different remedies could well be required to address the various forms of discrimination experienced by the four target groups. Moreover, by recommending that the federal government would simply monitor the results of corporate employment equity schemes while assuming responsibility for both training and child care, the report allayed corporate fears of over-regulation and a substantial rise in company costs.

While Abella was concerned to avoid the level of regulation associated with the imposition of quotas, she was clear that employment equity legislation would only be effective if an enforcement mechanism was set in place to monitor employers' reports. She believed that simple reliance on the pressure of public opinion was inadequate because although "public reporting may result in public pressure on a company to revise its systems ... it is unrealistic to rely on public opinion as an effective monitoring agent. It results in a speculative and scattered approach and creates the perception, in the absence of enforcement, that the issue is deserving of only casual attention."[129] Abella was particularly concerned that her recommendations should move beyond the voluntary employment opportunity programs recommended in the RCSW, primarily because their impact had been minimal.[130] Moreover, she maintained that "the seriousness and apparent intractability of employment discrimination [meant] it [was] unrealistic and somewhat ingenuous to rely on there being sufficient public goodwill to fuel a voluntary program."[131] Furthermore, she noted that "the sense of urgency expressed by individuals in the designated groups across Canada and validated by the evidence of their economic disadvantage [was] irreconcilable with the voluntary and gradual introduction of measures to generate more equitable participation."[132]

Contract Compliance
Interestingly, although Abella's recommendations on employment equity were made in an attempt to distance Canadian policy development from the American experience, her recommendations on extending employment equity into the corporate sector, through the use of contract compliance, drew directly on American policy innovations: "Contract compliance is a method of encouraging employment equity in the private sector by using government purchasing power as leverage. It has proven to be an effective incentive for changing discriminatory practices in the United States. It means in practice that government will agree to purchase goods and services only from businesses that agree to implement employment equity ... Contract compliance in Canada should apply to subcontractors, as it does in the United States."[133]

Abella recommended that as "the federal government has the authority to require contract compliance pursuant to section 91(1A) of the Constitution," all companies under contract to the federal government should "by the terms of their contracts, be expected to comply with the same statutory requirements as those binding federally regulated employers, including the implementation of employment equity and the collection and filing of data."[134] The "spending power" to which Abella refers permits the federal government to "spend money and impose conditions on the disposition of such funds while they are still in its hands."[135] It is ironic that while Abella's recommendation that the federal government should use its spending power to pursue contract compliance was taken up in Ottawa, the suggestion that this same constitutional power be used to develop national child care legislation was not.

Although Abella emphasized the value of adopting this American innovation to broaden the implementation of employment equity, the report of the RCEE recommended that the methods for implementing and monitoring the process should be distinct from those developed in the United States. Abella argued that "a legislative, rather than an administrative, base seems preferable given the uncertain life span of cabinet directives."[136] She also noted that "ideally, the same Canadian agency enforcing employment equity in the federally regulated sector should enforce contract compliance in the private sector."[137] However, as we shall see in Chapter 7, although the federal government took up the RCEE's general recommendations on contract compliance, neither of these specific suggestions were observed.

Monitoring and Enforcing Employment Equity
Abella developed four different models for enforcement, all of which assumed that "the statutory requirement to implement employment equity and to collect data would be imposed by legislation."[138] These were, first, to make the CHRC form a liaison with a new, independent agency designed "to facilitate the implementation by employers of employment equity"; second, to create a "new independent agency to deal exclusively with the monitoring and enforcement of employment equity"; third, to rely on the CHRC and the Canadian Labour Market Productivity Centre to implement employment equity; and finally, to rely on the CHRC working together with inspectors appointed under the Canada Labour Code.[139] Although the name and nature of the enforcement agency varied from model to model, they all assumed that it "should be independent from government and should have an ongoing consultative relationship in the development of employment equity guidelines with national and regional representatives from business, labour and the designated groups."[140] In addition, Abella recommended that to make the model effective, the support of Statistics Canada would be necessary to provide regional labour force data to employers and those analyzing their reports.[141]

Child Care

In addressing the question of pre-employment opportunities, the RCEE (like the RCSW before it) stressed that "for women who are mothers, a major barrier to equality in the workplace is the absence of affordable childcare of adequate quality."[142] While Abella argued that "the care of children needs to be a parental rather than a maternal responsibility," she recognized that "because responsibility for childcare used to be an exclusively maternal one, the greatest psychological pressure for the care of children is still felt by women."[143] Indeed, she argued that unless child care was "provided in adequate quality and quantity, the debate about the right to equal employment opportunity is academic for most women."[144]

While Abella saw the provision of child care as "the ramp that provides equal access to the workforce for mothers," she did not frame her recommendations on this subject solely in relation to women's participation in the labour force, but rather in relation to the responsibilities of worker-parents.[145] Indeed, she emphasized how Canada's ratification of the United Nations Convention on the Elimination of All Forms of Discrimination against Women, in 1981, required the federal government "to encourage the provision of the necessary supporting social services to enable parents to combine family obligations with work responsibilities and participation in public life, in particular through promoting a network of child care facilities."[146]

Abella also argued, as one would expect from a human rights activist, that the development of good child care policies would not only ensure full recognition of women's rights as worker-citizens but, in addition, guarantee the rights of children to decent care. Indeed, she viewed child care in terms of the "fruitful partnership between state and parent with the child as beneficiary," that characterized the public education system.[147] "Childcare," she claimed, "should be seen as a public service to which every child has a right."[148] Indeed, Abella's recommendation that where possible child care facilities should be attached to public schools, reinforced her claim that child care "is a logical extension" of the partnership between parents and the state inherent in the public school system.[149] It also reflected her concerns that workplace child care could "tie a parent to an unsatisfactory job."[150]

The ideal system of child care recommended by Abella was situated very clearly within the context of arguments presented to her by the CDCAA and taken up by child care advocacy groups in the early 1980s. Abella recommended the development of a system of universally accessible, affordable, noncompulsory, quality child care, designed to provide "care for children whenever the absence of the parent(s) requires an alternative form of care."[151] The report argued that ideally a child care system should be publicly funded and of acceptable quality, so that no child would be permitted to remain at home unattended by an adult.[152] Moreover, reflecting the demands for twenty-four-hour care that were noted in a few of the submissions, Abella argued that "the term 'childcare' is preferable to 'daycare' because it describes a more comprehensive system intended to provide care for children whenever the absence of a parent requires this alternative."[153]

Abella was very clear about the need to integrate child care into a policy process designed to promote gender equality in employment. Thus, she not only recommended that the federal government introduce employment equity legislation to ensure employers set goals and timetables to improve the representation of target group members in their workforces but also called for national child care legislation to improve the provision of child care for working women. Indeed, just as the commissioners who headed up the RCSW had done fourteen years before, Abella recommended that the federal government, "in cooperation with the provinces and territories, develop an appropriate funding mechanism for childcare" and introduce "a National Childcare Act" that would guarantee consistent national standards in the provision of child care services.[154] In addition, she recommended that revisions to the existing Child Care Expense Deduction should ensure that it reflected the cost of child care, recognize both men's and women's responsibilities for the care of their children, and be made available to those in training or seeking employment.[155] Furthermore, Abella argued that the deduction should be set at a level that would encourage better rates of pay for child care workers.[156]

Reflections on the Report of the RCEE

Without doubt, Abella expanded the mandate she was handed in the RCEE's terms of reference. She did so by inserting into her remit a clear recognition that equality in employment could only come about if the specific conditions in which any group of worker-citizens entered the labour market were taken into account. In the case of women, Abella emphasized the importance of linking policies that improved pre-employment access through training and child care with mechanisms to ensure employment equity in the workplace.

All this was done within the context of a mandate that had required Abella to consider not only the plausibility of implementing voluntary or mandatory forms of affirmative action within public and corporate institutions, but also how these procedures might reduce employment discrimination experienced by four very different target groups. Reflecting on her experience some years later, Abella noted that "the trick was to come up with a report that was going to be relevant to all of the groups, unique where the uniqueness was necessary, but still a master strategy that would be equally useful for each one of them."[157]

In my opinion, Abella did more than this. She not only made a set of policy recommendations that linked the promotion of equality with the recognition of group differences, but produced a "master strategy" that reflected, as closely as possible, the points of consensus between the corporations and the target group organizations she had been instructed to consult. Their common ground was evident in Abella's proposal that federally regulated organizations and companies under federal contract set goals and timetables to improve target group representation in their workforces and use this process, together with the routine collection and reporting of workforce data, to identify discriminatory employment practices within their organizations. Furthermore, her recommendations that the federal government allow women the fullest opportunity to exercise their potential for worker-citizenship, by linking the implementation of employment equity with the development of an accessible and affordable system of quality child care, directly reflected one of the dominant concerns voiced by those who submitted testimony on women's employment to the RCEE.

In developing models of public policy that took women's pre-employment conditions as well as within-employment conditions into account, Abella extended the boundaries of her mandate well beyond its initial remit. It is not surprising that someone who found herself "writing the history of discrimination in Canada" also went well beyond the six-month time-frame she had originally been granted.[158] In fact, Abella secured two extensions to complete her inquiry. The first, granted on 22 December 1983, extended the inquiry for six months, through 30 April 1984.[159] The second, granted on 18 April 1984, gave Abella until 31 October that year to complete this work.[160] Interestingly, the correspondence between John Roberts – who by then was the minister of Employment and Immigration – and Rosalie Abella indicated his reluctance to seek cabinet approval for this second extension. In a letter dated 21 March 1984, Roberts told Abella, "I do not feel that I should be going back to my Cabinet colleagues to seek a further extension ... In all frankness, I am anxious, as are I know many others, to have the debate begin on your findings and recommendations."[161] A personal note at the bottom of the letter indicated the reasons for his concern. It simply said, "Rosalie – We've got to get this out for public discussion or otherwise we risk losing the whole momentum after the election – John."[162]

John Roberts was one of the seven male contenders for the crown of the post-Trudeau Liberal Party, all of whom had to declare their position on women's issues.[163] Certainly, he and his competitors would not have wished that the government in power after the next general election would be led by a Conservative prime minister. In September 1984, however, the Conservatives won a landslide election victory and the new prime minister, Brian Mulroney, appointed Flora MacDonald as minister of Employment and Immigration.[164] MacDonald was well known both as a "red Tory" and as a promoter of gender equality in Canadian society. Nonetheless, when the report of the Royal Commission on Equality in Employment rolled off the presses that autumn, it was not clear how the government in which she served would respond to Abella's recommendations on employment equity and child care.

7

Breaking the Links: The Mulroney Government's Response to the Royal Commission on Equality in Employment

The new Conservative government, to which Abella presented the report of the Royal Commission on Equality in Employment (RCEE) in October 1984, did not, at first sight, appear to be predisposed to questions of employment equity or child care. Its leader, Brian Mulroney, wanted to reduce the federal bureaucracy, create jobs in the private sector, and ensure that Canada was "open for business again."[1] Moreover, both his cabinet and the Conservative caucus contained significant pro-family lobbies that were reluctant to develop legislation that might encourage the mothers of young children to work outside their homes.[2]

Nonetheless, by the end of the first Mulroney government both issues had been absorbed onto the federal policy agenda. Although the new Employment Equity Act (EEA) was proclaimed as law on 13 August 1986, the Conservatives' National Strategy on Child Care was only implemented in part. Its proposals to increase tax relief on child care and child tax credits came into effect on 1 April 1988, as did the new Child Care Initiatives Fund, created to support special projects in the field. However, the new government's attempts to introduce legislation that would overhaul the federal-provincial mechanisms for subsidizing child care spaces across the country never reached the statute books. They came close, but the proposed Canada Child Care Act – Bill C-144 – died on the Senate's order papers when the 1988 general election was called on 1 October that year.[3]

This legislative pattern indicates that although the Conservative government took up the questions about employment equity and child care that Abella had raised in the RCEE, it dealt with them as completely separate policy issues, and at very different points in its first four-year term of office. In so doing, it broke the link that Abella had re-established between the enhancement of women's employment opportunities and the provision of child care. Moreover, in order to placate different factions within the Conservative Party, it devised policy instruments that drew on neo-conservative views of the economy and the family, while addressing some traditional red-Tory concerns about welfare support.[4]

The Conservatives' Approach to Employment Equity

Though Flora MacDonald, the new Conservative minister of Employment and Immigration, was committed to women's equality, it was by no means easy for her to secure a legislative response to the RCEE. Given that she was a member of a government that wanted to deregulate the private sector and downsize the federal bureaucracy, it is amazing that the issue of employment equity was taken up at all. Some time after she had left office, Flora MacDonald indicated just how difficult it had been to get the proposed legislation accepted within her own party, particularly in an era when the neo-conservative ideas associated with Reaganism and Thatcherism were in vogue:

> The problem was that I couldn't argue to the extent that I would have liked to have done, either in cabinet or in caucus, about the value of this bill and what it could accomplish if it were strongly implemented ... because it would be seen, at a time when every other conservative government was going in the opposite direction, that what we were advocating was a much stronger regulatory power than had been introduced elsewhere ... So I wouldn't talk about it that much for fear it would stir up a backlash, or more of a backlash than it had already created, and that meant in cabinet as well. I mean, if I really got into explaining how I thought this should work, people would say, "Gee ... those businesses just can't afford all that extra paperwork and reporting."[5]

However, although the Conservative caucus contained anti-regulation and pro-family lobbies that would resist such legislation, the prime minister was clearly committed to improving the political and economic status of women in public life – and doing so in a measurable, quantifiable form that would prove he had acted on campaign promises. Conscious, no doubt, of the need to appeal to "the female vote," Mulroney had promised to increase the number of women appointed to senior political office during the leaders' debate on women's issues that was organized by the National Action Committee on the Status of Women (NAC) during the 1984 election campaign.[6] Moreover, in March 1984 he had pledged that a Conservative government would implement contract compliance measures to ensure that private-sector firms seeking federal government contracts proved they would hire increasing numbers of women to do the work.[7] Both promises were kept. On entering government, Mulroney appointed more women to cabinet than any previous prime minister.[8] In addition, contract compliance regulations were introduced alongside the EEA.

Mulroney's speeches about the need to improve women's representation in public office not only distinguished him from Reagan and Thatcher but predisposed him to support the promotion of their employment opportunities in federally regulated organizations.[9] As Michael Sabia – MacDonald's senior policy advisor at the time – pointed out, the prime minister's view was that "I, Brian Mulroney, made these commitments during the campaign and we've got to live up to them and if we don't we're going to get saddled."[10] Indeed, it was because of this personal commitment that the prime minister actively supported MacDonald in her efforts to get the employment equity legislation past the pro-family and anti-regulation lobbies, which were strong in both caucus and cabinet and opposed to its introduction. As Sabia reflected shortly after the legislation was introduced, "Probably with the exception of Mr. Epp and Mr. Clark, I think she would have got clobbered. Now obviously the dynamic changes when this item comes up at P[riorities] and P[lanning] and the PM says, 'Well we've got to do something and this is a reasonable package. Any comments?' ... People don't tend to go, 'Well I think it's bullshit' ... they tend to go 'Yes ... well ... right Prime Minister!'"[11]

Although reminiscent of a well-known British comedy, this remark reflects a second important point about Mulroney's style of governing that helped the employment equity legislation on its course, namely, that he liked "to cut a deal."[12] As Aucoin has argued, "Mulroney's philosophy assume[d] that political leadership is about the accommodation of interests and not the interplay of ideas."[13] Renowned throughout his premiership as a brokerage politician rather than an ideological heavyweight, Mulroney was intent on building consensus not just among different factions in his cabinet and caucus but, as he demonstrated in the initial development of the Meech Lake Accord, among the provincial premiers as well. As Robert Fulford noted, "Compromise has been the specialty of Canadian prime ministers for 120 years – without it they couldn't have kept the country in one piece – but none of them has compromised with the breathtaking audacity of Mulroney."[14]

Mulroney's brokerage style clearly shaped MacDonald's approach to her colleagues in cabinet and in the Conservative Party caucus. As she commented,

> If you're going into cabinet it's all about brokerage politics and consensus. That's really what it's all about. You cannot purport to be an ideologue. The ideologues exist in caucus. So a person who is heavily oriented to family values, to the place of women in the home, pro-life, all of those things, of whom there were a number in the caucus, were not going to

be supportive of a bill like this. I had difficulty even though I went round and explained it individually to people, trying to bend their ears. It certainly wasn't as difficult in cabinet as in caucus ... there may have been cabinet ministers who didn't take it very seriously, who were not its chief crusaders, but they were sensible enough and political enough to understand that moves had to be taken to shore up the support of the Conservative Party among women's groups. So they wouldn't try to stop something like that.[15]

However, while MacDonald's comments point to the rationale behind Mulroney's support, it was not simply brokerage politics that got the legislation accepted. In caucus, where resistance to the legislation was even stronger than in cabinet, it appears that a small but significant group of new female MPs played a crucial role in countering the pro-family lobby. To quote MacDonald again: "We had come into the House in 1984 with a fairly sizeable group of women ... more than ever before in any party ... and I didn't know many of them ... and one way of getting to know them was to explain the Bill to them, in more detail than I would to others in the caucus, and then use them as emissaries to say 'now this is something I feel very strongly about.' They were a great help to me in caucus because the caucus was not used to having that many women around."[16]

It was in this context, having trod a very careful path through cabinet and caucus, with Mulroney's support, that MacDonald announced the government's decision to develop employment equity legislation. It is clear, however, that despite her success in getting the proposed legislation accepted in both cabinet and caucus, it was not an easy process. Many Conservatives in the governing party did not want the state intervening in the commercial sector. Nor did they want to pass legislation that would encourage mothers with young children to work outside the home. These undercurrents of resistance were always there in the process of devising a legislative response to the RCEE's recommendations. Indeed, they help to explain why the Conservative government was less interventionist than Abella would have wished.

Formal Federal Response to the RCEE: Launching the Policy Initiative
It is indicative of the extent to which the concept of employment equity became linked in the mid-1980s with the promotion of women's employment opportunities that the formal federal response to the report of the RCEE was made on International Women's Day: 8 March 1985. However, it is also clear that the government's decision to pursue employment equity legislation was motivated by a desire to build concepts of equity into its strategies for creating jobs and making a leaner federal bureaucracy more efficient. As MacDonald reflected some years later, "I was trying to

come up with a different kind of jobs strategy, but in doing that I wanted to incorporate equity all the way."[17]

The Conservatives' decision to conflate their response to Abella's recommendations on equity with a strategy to stimulate job creation and encourage economic growth was explicit in MacDonald's speech tabling the government's formal response to the RCEE in the House of Commons. This stressed that because employment equity was linked to a broader strategy for economic renewal, it would encourage Canadians to take up the jobs that Mulroney had promised them: "As a country, we cannot afford to exclude these [target group] Canadians from full participation in working life. We need their contribution to the economic renewal and growth of this nation ... Our economic development demands the full participation of all. Give Canadians real opportunities and they'll get jobs. Give them jobs, and they will create wealth. Generate wealth and there will be economic growth – and growth means more jobs."[18]

The government's background paper, published on the same day as MacDonald's speech, reinforced the link between employment opportunity and economic expansion. Appropriately entitled *Employment Equity and Economic Growth,* it declared that "equity in the workplace is not only just in a democratic society but is a key to economic growth. A priority on jobs and economic renewal must therefore involve an attack on barriers to equity, just as it involves an attack on obstacles to economic growth."[19]

A simultaneous announcement from Robert de Cotret, then president of the Treasury Board, declared that his department would analyze the existing affirmative action programs set in place by the previous Liberal government, "in an effort to make the Public Service more conducive to the employment of women and other target groups."[20] He also noted that the Treasury Board would be "playing a lead role in the implementation of employment equity by Crown corporations."[21] Nevertheless, while de Cotret's announcement showed that the Conservatives recognized they had to put their own house in order if they were to make demands on federally regulated companies, it also signalled that changes in the government's own employment practices would be incremental rather than radical in nature.

Although lip service was paid to the question of child care in the ministerial statements of 8 March 1985, the Conservative government sent clear indications that their concept of employment equity would be narrower in scope than Abella had envisaged. De Cotret made passing mention that he would be "evaluating the pilot daycare centres project [in the federal public service] with a view to establishing future policy directions in this area."[22] Similarly, Walter McLean, the minister responsible for the Status of Women, noted that employment equity "includes supportive measures in the areas of child care and training [which] have been identified as being particularly significant to the full participation of women in the Canadian economy."[23] Nonetheless, references to the question of child care were completely absent from any of the speeches or press releases issued by the minister of Employment and Immigration, despite the fact that it was she who had promised the establishment of a parliamentary task force on child care during an election campaign speech to the Professional Secretaries International.[24]

Above all, the ministerial statements on 8 March 1985 indicated that the Conservatives wanted to place minimal constraints on federally regulated organizations and private companies under contract to the federal government, so that they would be able to create the jobs that Mulroney had promised and recruit more extensively than before from the four target groups. As Flora MacDonald noted later, "The employment equity legislation was designed as enabling legislation to allow a new concept to work."[25] It would simply require these employers to report on the goals they set themselves for achieving employment equity and would not compel them to undertake specific initiatives to improve the representation of women and other target groups within their workforce, or identify the multidimensional causes of employment inequality that might vary for the four different groups. As McLean noted in his statement, although the Conservatives wanted "to tackle the systemic problems facing women in employment ... help debunk outdated myths about working women [and] ... alert employers to the cost incurred by overlooking equally qualified women," this legislation was designed "to ensure that employers recognize the benefits to be gained by training, hiring and promoting women *on the same basis as men.*"[26]

Comparisons of the Report of the RCEE and the EEA

A comparison of the RCEE and the EEA reveals how the concept of employment equity was narrowed between the publication of Abella's report and the implementation of federal legislation (Table 7.1). The Conservatives adopted Abella's terminology of "employment equity" in the legislation, thereby distinguishing the new initiatives from existing affirmative action measures within the federal public service. They also adopted her recommendations that employers be given the flexibility to set their own goals and timetables for improving the participation of target group members throughout their organizations (Table 7.1.a). Beyond this, however, the legislation departed from the recommendations of the RCEE in a number of different ways.

Key Discrepancies between the RCEE and the EEA: Its Scope and Enforcement
The most significant differences between the RCEE and the EEA were in the range of employers included in the Act and in the processes designed to enforce the legislation. Instead of covering all federally regulated and

contracted employers, as Abella had recommended, the legislation focused solely on federally regulated employers with 100 or more employees (Table 7.1.b). This category was clearly intended to show that the government was responding to the RCEE without, at the same time, alienating the small business lobby or its supporters in Parliament. However, in an era that had seen the first stages of a now-familiar pattern of outsourcing, the decision to use this threshold prompted questions about the government's commitment to the full eradication of systemic discrimination within the federally regulated sphere.

One of the most noticeable differences between the recommendations of the RCEE and the clauses in the EEA was the institutional structure for developing, monitoring, and enforcing employment equity in the federal sphere. The report of the RCEE had recommended that the implementation of employment equity should be subject to enforcement by a designated enforcement agency, staffed by personnel qualified in human rights and labour issues (Table 7.1.e). Moreover, while three of the four alternative enforcement models that Abella proposed gave the Canadian Human Rights Commission (CHRC) prime responsibility for the development and enforcement of employment equity, the fourth recommended that a new independent enforcement agency be established.[27]

None of these recommendations was adopted by MacDonald. While the CHRC was expected to play an important role in evaluating the results of employers' reports, key responsibility for implementing the Act was given to the Canadian Employment and Immigration Commission (CEIC). Moreover, the EEA only mandated the annual reporting of goals and timetables. While employers were required to identify and eliminate discriminatory employment practices within their organization and institute positive policies and practices to improve the representation of target group members, no measures were introduced to ensure that such policies were actually implemented (Table 7.1.a).[28] Nonetheless, the annual reports at least provided the CHRC with enough data to begin to identify cases where systemic discrimination appeared to be persistent in federally regulated organizations.[29]

A system was devised whereby the mandated reports from employers were analyzed by the minister of Employment and Immigration, passed to the CHRC, reported to Parliament and made available, at cost, for public scrutiny.[30] Indeed, MacDonald set considerable store by the role that public accountability would play in holding employers' accountable for their actions: "The employment practices and policies of federally regulated businesses will go on public record, and these companies will have to answer to the people of Canada if they fail to achieve equity in employment. And, of course, this legislation will mean that the Canadian Human

Rights Commission has the information it needs to exercise fully its powers and authorities."[31]

The discrepancies between Abella's recommendations and the legislative instrument that MacDonald and her colleagues devised reflects the Conservatives' reluctance to increase the size of the federal bureaucracy, particularly if this expansion would impose further constraints on the private sector. As Michael Sabia emphasized, "It was simply *not on* that the government was going to set up an enforcement agency; a separate, identifiable, employment equity enforcement agency ... because we weren't going to have a government which, at the time, was trying very hard to send deregulatory signals to the business community that we are going to get government out of the boardrooms of the nation, now say we're going to set up a new bureaucratic agency and tell you how to run your businesses."[32] This was particularly true at a point when MacDonald's prime concern as a Conservative government minister was to ensure that the new policy instrument did nothing to harm the government's broader strategy to create jobs in the private sector.

Other Discrepancies between the RCEE and the EEA
There were several other discrepancies between Abella's recommendations and the Conservative government's employment equity legislation. One of the most apparent was the way the legislation ignored the important role Abella had earmarked for Statistics Canada in the development of federal employment equity policies (Table 7.1.e). Abella considered that Statistics Canada should not only advise employers about targets they might set themselves, given the composition of the regional workforce, but also encourage the enforcement agency to develop reporting categories that matched those used in the Canadian census.[33] Indeed, she argued that additional labour force questions should be included in the census and that Statistics Canada should undertake more longitudinal studies to measure the integration of the designated groups into the labour force.[34] Moreover, she thought, first, that "the performance of each employer should be compared with the performance of other employers in the same industry or region and with each employer's previous performance," and, second, that a database should be developed to permit comparisons between an employer's workforce and the local labour supply.[35] This kind of rational statistical planning was not, however, part of the Tory game plan of allowing employers maximum flexibility in setting goals that suited their business ends. Thus, although the CEIC could issue guidelines, employers were left to create their own employment equity goals and timetables.

It is also clear that Abella had envisaged a more expansive set of reporting categories than those encoded in the legislation (Table 7.1.a and d).

Table 7.1

RCEE employment equality recommendations implemented in the 1986 Employment Equity Act

RCEE recommendations	EEA clause
a. Meaning of employment equity (1, 2, 3, 4)* Employment equity should be used rather than affirmative action.	a. Meaning of employment equity (1, 4) Employment equity used in EEA. Affirmative action kept in FPS.
All federally regulated employers must: • eliminate discriminatory employment barriers/practices in their workplaces in consultation with representatives from management, labour, and target groups • improve target group participation, where necessary, by redesigning employment practices, without using quotas • collect and annually file data of target group: participation rates, occupational distribution, income levels • be subject to enforcement.	Designated employers must: • identify and eliminate illegal discriminatory employment practices, in consultation with bargaining agent or designated employees • institute positive policies/practices, and make reasonable accommodation, to ensure target group members' participation throughout organization is proportionate to their representation in the workforce or segments of the qualified, eligible, regional workforce from which employer can draw.
b. Employers to be covered (1, 27, 28) • all federally regulated employers • companies under contract to the federal government.	b. Employers covered by legislation (3) • employers of federally regulated industries employing 100 or more • Federal Contractors Program introduced separately.
c. Employment equity guidelines and regulations (8, 9, 13) Employment equity guidelines should be prepared by the enforcement agency with relevant data analysis from Statistics Canada.	c. Employment equity guidelines and regulations (11, 12) Minister may issue guidelines to assist employers with implementation.

An employee's self-identification as target group member should be voluntary.

d. Implementing employment equity (2, 6, 10, 19)
Requirement to implement employment equity should take effect immediately Act is passed. Employers should be given flexibility in redesigning employment practices.

All federally regulated employers must collect standardized, confidential data on target group members'
• participation rates
• occupational distribution
• salary quartile/range
and proportion of their
• hirings
• promotions
• terminations
• lay-offs
• part-time/contract work
• committee work
• training and educational leaves
and after three years file this data annually with the enforcement agency.

Governor-in-Council may regulate:
• meaning of reporting categories
• target group membership
• anything prescribed under the Act
• measures for carrying out the Act.

d. Implementing employment equity (5, 6)
Employers required to prepare an annual plan of goals and a timetable for implementation and retain plans for three years after last year covered by plan.

Two years after Act comes into effect, employers must submit certified annual report to minister for Employment and Immigration, in form prescribed, showing their industrial sector and target group members' proportional
• participation rates
• occupational distribution
• salary range
• hirings
• promotions
• terminations
and retain these reports for three years.

Employers who fail to submit records would be guilty of an offence and liable to a maximum fine of $50,000 (7).

▼ *Table 7.1*

RCEE recommendations	EEA clause
e. Enforcement of employment equity (2, 7, 18, 23) All federally regulated employers must be subject to an enforcement mechanism.	e. Enforcement of employment equity (8, 9, 10) Minister for Employment must send copies of employers' reports to CHRC.
The enforcement agency should be independent; have qualified staff familiar with labour issues, employment systems, and human rights issues; be sufficiently resourced to discharge its mandate; and engage in consultation with national and regional representatives of business, labour, and the target groups.	
Enforcement agency will publicize employers' data, Statistics Canada's analysis, and their report to Parliament.	Minister must submit annual consolidated report and analysis to Parliament.
Results rather than procedures should be reviewed initially. If these are unreasonably low, enforcement agency can advise employers to amend practices.	Minister must ensure that copies of all reports are available for public scrutiny/purchase.

Note: Only those recommendations of direct relevance to women's employment have been included.

* Figures in parentheses indicate the recommendation numbers or legislative clause.

Sources: Royal Commission on Equality in Employment, *Report* (Ottawa: Supply and Services, 1984), 255-88; *Employment Equity Act*, S.C. 1986, c. 31.

While the EEA reflected Abella's recommendations about reporting participation rates, occupational distribution, salary range, hirings, promotions, and terminations, it did not include the recommended sections on part-time and contract work (in which women are over-represented), or on committee work, training, and educational leaves (in which they tend to be under-represented).

The EEA further narrowed Abella's interpretation of employment equity by failing to include pay equity within its remit.[36] In addition, the Conservative government's response overlooked her suggestions that measures be introduced to protect part-time and domestic workers, ensure that homemaking and volunteer work were seen as legitimate aspects of women's employment experience, address the problem of sexual harassment in the workplace, and develop training programs to recognize women's particular needs – especially those of women re-entering the labour market.[37] Indeed, the Act was not designed to address any of the broader societal factors that affect women's access to employment.

Finally, and by contrast, there were only three relatively minor ways in which the Act went beyond the recommendations that Abella had made. First, it mandated employers to keep their employment equity plans for three years after they had been reported (Table 7.1.d). Second, it introduced a $50,000 fine for companies that failed to submit annual reports to the CEIC. Finally, it introduced a sunset clause declaring that the effectiveness of the legislation should be reviewed five years after it had come into effect, a process, as Chapter 8 describes, that was carried out by the Conservatives in 1991.[38]

The Federal Contractors Program

Contrary to the recommendations in the RCEE, the Federal Contractors Program (FCP) was implemented by means of a separate cabinet directive, rather than as an integral part of the EEA. It was also restricted to companies with over 100 employees that were bidding for government contracts over $200,000. In short, the program was a symbolic gesture to fulfil promises made by the prime minister in his 1984 election campaign, rather than a substantive policy to restructure women's employment opportunities across a wide range of companies.

A comparison of the EEA and the FCP reveals not only that different regulations were developed for federally regulated industries and companies under contract to the federal government, but also that the FCP was a much weaker policy instrument than Abella had envisaged (Table 7.2). The requirements for monitoring the development of employment equity in companies under contract to the government were not as stringent as those for federally regulated companies. Although federally regulated companies were given specific guidelines about how they should quantify their workforce data, companies under contract to the federal government were given discretion about the specific format for presenting this type of information. Moreover, while companies that fell within the gamut of the EEA were required to report *annually* to the minister for Employment and Immigration on the effectiveness of their employment equity schedules, in reports that would be presented to Parliament, companies engaged on federal contracts were simply required to have their employment equity plans available for on-site inspection by CEIC officials. Finally, while federally regulated companies would be subject to investigation by the CHRC if their annual reports suggested evidence of systemic discrimination, employers under contract would be given twelve months by the CEIC to amend their employment practices, risking the ultimate sanction of no renewed contract if this process was not implemented.[39]

These differences indicate how the federal government clearly developed one set of rules for federally regulated corporations and a different set of rules for private sector companies under contract. Although MacDonald's press release of 27 June 1986 claimed that "this program affects more than 800 employers, 700,000 employees and will involve about $6 billion in government business," the Conservatives' contract compliance program was a limited form of regulation.[40] While a more interventionist program would have been out of line with the Conservatives' promises about deregulating the commercial sector, it is unfortunate that one was not developed. After all, this policy instrument could shape the employment opportunities of a far wider range of employees than the 300,000 covered by the EEA.

Interpreting the Federal Policy Response to the RCEE

The EEA and the FCP were clearly designed as policy instruments that would encourage employers to think about employment equity, without over-regulating either the public or private sectors. As Mona Kornberg notes, they were instruments that not only relied on employers to identify discrimination within their own organizations and implement measures to eradicate the problem but also assumed that they would emulate the federal government's approach in the process.[41] Moreover, while these policy instruments gave the federal government a clear role in monitoring systemic employment discrimination, they also emphasized that target group activists would have to continue to pressure the government for further change. Shortly before Bill C-62 became law, MacDonald made this explicit in a speech to the Institute for Research on Public Policy: "The legislation sets forth a framework within which interest groups and government can work together in achieving social and economic equality ... the Bill presents a challenge – to women, to Native people, to disabled persons and to visible minorities ... a challenge, to be vigilant, and to find flexible solutions to surmount barriers to an equitable society ... and it allows

Table 7.2

Comparison of RCEE recommendations on contract compliance and Federal Contractors Program

RCEE	FCP
Contract compliance should be imposed by legislation (27).*	Contract compliance would be implemented through a cabinet directive rather than through legislation.
Government should only purchase goods and services from employers who agree to implement employment equity (27).	Contract compliance would be limited to employers with 100 or more employees, bidding on contracts of $200,000 or more; these employers would be required to develop employment equity plans.
Contracts may include additional clauses to reflect specific goals and timetables, provision of training, transportation, or accommodation (28).	Accommodation could include assistance with child care.
Enforcement of contract compliance should be carried out by the agency established to enforce employment equity in the federally regulated sphere (29).	Organizations would be subject to on-site compliance reviews by the CEIC; sanctions for noncompliance would include eventual exclusion from future government contracts.

* Figures in parentheses indicate the recommendation number.

Sources: Royal Commission on Equality in Employment, *Report* (Ottawa: Supply and Services, 1984), 260; Employment and Immigration Canada, *Federal Contractors Program: Criteria for Implementation*, Internal document, 1986.

groups to seize the opportunity of this legislation in advancing their own agendas and defining their own goals ... without relying on government."[42]

It is hardly surprising, given the limited responsibility that government was prepared or able to take for developing effective employment equity legislation, that feminists were clearly ambivalent about the passage of this legislation.[43] Although pleased that legislation had followed from the RCEE, their criticisms of the Act itself were widespread. Some feared that the Act failed to clarify what was expected of employers, either in terms of the kind of goals and timetables they should try to create, or the standards they should create for themselves. Others were concerned that the enforcement procedures failed to separate out the standard-setting and enforcement agencies. Despite the fact that most of the submissions women had made to the RCEE argued against the use of quotas, when the legislation was introduced many feminists criticized the government for not developing affirmative action measures that would compel federal employers to hire and promote more women. In addition, they were critical of the government's failure to build training and child care into the design of employment equity policies.[44]

Flora MacDonald was well aware of Abella's calls for policies that recognized the link between child care provision and women's participation in the labour force. However, despite her declarations of support for such provision prior to the 1984 election, the divisions of responsibility within cabinet and the spending constraints imposed on her ministry made it impossible to realize this link in practice: "I would have been in real conflict with the minister for Health and Welfare. The employment minister couldn't do it. So I could support proposals for day care in cabinet but I couldn't originate them. And besides, people didn't see employment equity as a big spending item that was going to involve the provincial governments and the minister of Finance and so on and so forth."[45]

Given these constraints, it was perhaps inevitable that questions of employment equity and child care would get driven apart in the federal government's response to the RCEE. Indeed, as I turn now to consider the National Strategy on Child Care, developed by the Conservatives, we can see how this was shaped not just by institutional and fiscal forces at work within the federal government but also by broader ideological and jurisdictional factors. These included the party's concern to emphasize the central role of the family in the provision of child care, its ambivalence about encouraging women to relinquish the care of their children in order to take up employment outside the home, its broader agenda of promoting the delivery of social services through public and commercial means and, finally, the dynamics of federal-provincial relations during a period in which Mulroney sought to restructure Canadian federalism through the constitutional entrenchment of the Meech Lake Accord.

The Conservative Approach to Questions of Child Care
While the Conservative government moved swiftly on the question of employment equity, its response to Abella's recommendations on child care took much longer to emerge. In November 1985, well into the period in which the Conservatives were developing new employment equity legislation, the federal government established the Special Parliamentary Committee on Child Care (SPCCC), chaired by Shirley Martin, the MP for Lincoln, Ontario. The terms of reference for the committee required it to explore "the needs of children being cared for inside or outside the family," to examine "parents' views on the kinds of care they would like for their children," and to consider the appropriate "role for the federal government in child care," given the existing responsibilities for child care of "parents, the voluntary sector, the private sector, and provincial and territorial governments."[46]

The mandate of the SPCCC indicated that even though the new Conservative government was prepared to address the question of child care, it was unwilling to pursue this issue simply as part of a broader policy to promote equal employment opportunities for women and men. In fact, while the committee was instructed to consider the needs of children being cared for inside and outside their homes, its key objectives were to focus on the child "in the context of the family," and to emphasize the "primary responsibility" of parents to choose the best care for their children.[47] In short, the SPCCC was established to send a signal to child care activists that the Conservative government would only pursue the question of child care on its own terms. Moreover, the timing of its creation pre-empted the possibility that Abella's calls for a national system of child care would be reinforced when the Liberal-appointed Task Force on Child Care, chaired by Katie Cooke, reported the following spring. As Derek Hum noted, by establishing the SPCCC "the Conservative government could safely remain silent on the Cooke Report's recommendations upon its release. By waiting for the House of Commons Committee to conclude its examination of the same questions, the government could chart its course in private while appearing appropriately judicious in public."[48]

Comparing the RCEE, the Cooke Task Force, and the SPCCC
Although the discrepancies between the Cooke Task Force and the Special Parliamentary Committee on Child Care have been well documented, virtually no attention has been paid to the way that the SPCCC report recast the proposals for child care that both Abella and Cooke had developed.[49] A three-way analysis – comparing the recommendations of the RCEE, the Cooke Task Force, and the SPCCC – shows how the SPCCC shifted the policy agenda away from Abella and Cooke's proposals for a national, publicly funded system of child care (Table 7.3).[50]

Table 7.3

Comparison of RCEE, Cooke Task Force, and SPCCC recommendations on child care

	RCEE	Cooke Task Force	SPCCC
Nature of provision	Publicly funded; universal access	Publicly funded; universal access	Public/private funding
Canada Assistance Plan	Inappropriate method of funding child care	Subsume under new cost-sharing arrangement for universal service.	Keep current system; encourage take-up by provinces/territories; publicize the scheme.
Child care legislation	National Childcare Act to guarantee consistent national standards and meet special group needs.	No recommendations	Family and Child Care Act to complement CAP and ensure tax credits to parents and subsidies to public and commercial child care centres.
Child care funding	Federal government should develop appropriate funding mechanism with provinces/territories.	Federal government should initiate new nation-wide system to cost-share capital and operating costs of licensed centres with provinces/territories.	Federal government should develop system to complement CAP by cost-sharing capital and operating costs of new child care spaces with provinces/territories.
			Establish Child Care Development Program for single mothers.

Tax deductions/credits	Child care expenses should be fully deductible by either parent.	Tax relief for child care cannot provide the basis for a new child care system.	Child Care Expense Credit should replace Child Care Expense Deduction; new Child Care Tax Credit for infants.
Child benefits	No recommendations	No recommendations	Keep current system.
Tax breaks for employers	No recommendations	Capital costs of employer-provided child care should be tax deductible. Employers should not be taxed for child care benefits for employees.	Employers should have a 100 percent Capital Cost Allowance for new child care spaces they provide for employees.
Child care services for federal employees	No recommendations	Federal government should provide child care services in federal buildings where numbers warrant. Department of National Defence should provide child care on military bases.	Treasury Board should encourage provision of child care in federal buildings where numbers warrant. Department of National Defence should promote family resource programs on military bases.
Family responsibility leave	Either parent should be allowed five days leave per year for child care.	Either parent should be allowed five days leave per year for family-related reasons.	No recommendations

▲

▲ *Table 7.3*

	RCEE	Cooke Task Force	SPCCC
Child care workers	Adequate training and pay should be provided for workers of both genders and from minority groups.	Revenue Canada should issue expense-claim guidelines for self-employed carers.	No recommendations
Disabled children	Special needs should be considered and given priority until universal child care system established.	Federal government should cost-share any special costs in providing disabled child care.	Health and Welfare should make prevention of disability a major goal and fund voluntary groups to develop such programs.
Native children	National Child Care Act should recognize special needs of Native children.	No recommendations	Federal government should develop support services to strengthen families, promote health in Native communities, and train Native carers.
Visible minority children	National Child Care Act should recognize special needs of children from minority groups.	No recommendations	Re-examine provision of child care services under Immigrant Settlement and Adaptation program. Promote multicultural awareness in child care.

Policy review	No recommendations	Fund research on child care.	Fund research on child care.
	No recommendations	Set up National Day Care Information Centre.	Set up National Day Care Information Centre.
	No recommendations	Review child care system after ten years.	Establish Secretariat within Health and Welfare Canada to implement Family and Child Care Act and review government response to SPCCC recommendations.
	No recommendations	Appoint minister for children.	No recommendations

Note: Excludes the Cooke Task Force and Special Committee on Child Care recommendations on birth/adoption leave and auxiliary services. For a detailed comparison of the recommendations in each report see Annis May Timpson, "Driven Apart: The Construction of Women as Worker-Citizens and Mother-Citizens in Canadian Employment and Child Care Policies, 1940-1988," PhD diss., University of Toronto, 1997, 373-81.

Sources: Royal Commission on Equality in Employment, *Report* (Ottawa: Supply and Services, 1984), 267-8; Status of Women Canada, *Report of the Task Force on Child Care* (Ottawa: Supply and Services, 1986), 373-8; House of Commons, *Sharing the Responsibility: Report of the Special Committee on Child Care* (Ottawa: Queen's Printer, 1987), 85-92.

A National System of Child Care

Although Abella and Cooke had addressed the question of child care from the perspective of workers (in the first case) and parents (in the second), they both recommended that a national system of child care should be developed. Specifically, they argued that child care should be a universally accessible, noncompulsory extension of the public school system, designed to ensure the quality care of infants and school-aged children when their parents cannot look after them.[51] In addition, Abella and Cooke both called on the federal government to remove child care from its existing welfare mould within the Canada Assistance Plan (CAP) and work with the provinces and territories to develop a national, publicly funded system of child care.[52] By contrast, the report of the SPCCC argued that although CAP should be maintained, a child care system based on public and private funding should be developed. As a result, it emphasized the distinction between child care as a remedial form of welfare support for the children of impoverished parents and child care as an optional, subsidized service to be purchased by parents who chose to do so.[53]

Abella argued that her proposals for a national system of child care would best be realized through the enactment of a "National Childcare Act." Such legislation, she thought, should be "based on consultation with the provinces, territories and interest groups, to guarantee consistent national standards ... [and] ... take into account an appropriate child/staff ratio, urban and rural needs, and special needs of children who are native, members of minority groups or disabled."[54] Her proposals were clearly designed to ensure quality child care across the country in a system that catered to the needs of children in the RCEE's target groups.

Although the report of the SPCCC was careful to consider the particular needs of children from Native, disabled, and minority groups, the prime objective of its proposals was to recommend a "Family and Child Care Act" (note the emphasis on family) that set out federal funding mechanisms for child care to *complement* rather than replace the provisions of CAP. Moreover, instead of setting out guidelines for the development of a national system of publicly funded child care, it sought to enhance the public, commercial, and domestic provision of child care through a complex process of subsidizing nonprofit and commercial child care centres, offering tax relief to parents who purchased child care, and providing tax credits for parents who looked after their children at home.

The report of the SPCCC substantially changed the proposals that Abella and Cooke had made for federal, provincial, and territorial governments to subsidize a national child care system. Abella and Cooke had called for the development of new federal-provincial/territorial mechanisms to fund a system of universally accessible, licensed, nonprofit child care. Indeed, to the delight of child care activists, the Cooke Task Force argued that capital and operating grants for new child care spaces should go only to "services that are licensed and monitored by provincial or territorial governments."[55] The SPCCC report mirrored Cooke's recommendations on federal-provincial/territorial mechanisms for sharing the costs of new child care spaces.[56] However, not only did it recommend that the per capita rate for federal subsidies should be lower than that advocated by Cooke but it avoided specifying the kinds of child care that could be subsidized.[57] As a result, the report opened up a route for the Conservative government to negotiate cost-sharing agreements with the provinces and territories to subsidize the provision of both commercial and nonprofit child care.

Tax Relief and Tax Credits
Although Abella and Cooke both recognized that the current system of subsidizing parents' child care costs through tax relief could not be abandoned overnight, they maintained that this was not an appropriate mechanism for funding a universal child care system. Abella asserted that child care was "a public expense that should ultimately be borne by all taxpayers."[58] Similarly, Cooke argued that "new child care financing should *not* take the form of tax relief since ... tax measures, in whatever form, cannot provide the basis for development of a new child care system."[59]

While Abella and Cooke were adamant about the inappropriateness of using tax relief to underwrite child care, the Conservatives were equally convinced of its value. The report of the SPCCC recommended that the "existing Child Care Expense Deduction [CCED] be replaced by a renamed Child Care Expense Credit to cover up to 30% of expenses, but not to exceed $3,000 per child under 14 and $12,000 per family."[60] In addition, it recommended that a refundable Child Care Tax Credit (CCTC) of $200 for the first child, $100 for the second, and $50 for each subsequent child be introduced concurrently with the Child Care Expense Credit. Designed, no doubt, to placate both the pro-family and red-Tory elements within the Conservative caucus, this tax credit sought to "provide financial recognition where a spouse stays home to care for children" and "assist other families who may, for whatever reason, have child care expenses not eligible for the Child Care Expense Credit."[61] Furthermore, although neither Abella nor Cooke made recommendations on the subject, the SPCCC report recommended that "the existing elements of the child benefit system should be retained."[62]

Although the RCEE had examined methods of promoting women's employment opportunities, Abella's concern that workplace child care could tie parents to unsatisfactory jobs may well explain why, unlike the Cooke Task Force and the SPCCC, she made no specific recommendations on this subject. By contrast, both the Cooke Task Force and the SPCCC argued that employers providing new child care spaces should be able to claim these expenses against tax including, in the case of Cooke, the costs of providing child care benefits to employees.[63] Similarly, both Cooke and the SPCCC recommended the development of child care services, where needed, in federal government buildings and on Canadian military bases.[64]

The report of the SPCCC, entitled *Sharing the Responsibility,* was published in March 1987. It shifted the policy agenda away from the creation of a national, publicly funded system of child care towards one that linked the existing system of welfare-based public provision with the expansion of child care in the commercial sphere. Its key emphasis was on the role the federal government should play in subsidizing commercial and nonprofit child care to complement the central role of parental care in families.[65] Thus while the report emphasized the importance of subsidizing the individual purchaser of child care, it also placated the pro-family lobby within the Conservative Party by arguing that stay-at-home parents should be subsidized through child-tax credits.[66]

The report of the SPCCC did acknowledge the link between parental employment and the provision of child care. It recommended that the federal government should create child care centres in government buildings and that employers should be given tax breaks to create new child care spaces. However, while Abella and Cooke had emphasized the rights of parents and children to be assured quality child care in the community, *Sharing the Responsibility* redefined the relationship between parents, children, and the state. It emphasized both the importance of parental child care and the idea that when children were cared for outside the home it should, wherever possible, be in centres that parents select and pay for, albeit with the help of state subsidies.[67]

National Strategy on Child Care
On 3 December 1987, Jake Epp, the minister of Health and Welfare, unveiled the government's National Strategy on Child Care. This new child care initiative was presented as "a progressive, responsible step forward on behalf of Canadian families" that would "dramatically increase the number of quality child care spaces for children in Canada."[68] Moreover, the government noted that the strategy would be realized through "a balanced package of federal tax assistance to families and a new federal-provincial cost-sharing partnership."[69]

The National Strategy was based on a three-pronged approach to child care provision, costed at a total of $6.4 billion over a seven-year period.[70] The first element recognized "the right and the responsibility of Canadian parents to choose how they want to raise their children" through tax assistance with child care expenses.[71] It announced that the CCED would be doubled from $2,000 to $4,000 a year for children who were under six or had special needs as a result of disability. While it remained at $2,000 a year for children aged seven to fourteen, the existing limit of $8,000 per family was abolished.[72] In addition, and in an effort to assist "lower and middle income parents who care for their children at home or who may have non-receipted child care expenses," the refundable CCTC was increased by $200 a year for children under six.[73] The cost to the federal government of these subsidies was estimated at $2.3 billion over seven years.[74]

The second element of the National Strategy was the creation of a research and special projects fund, which later became known as the Child Care Initiatives Fund, funded at $100 million over seven years and administered by the Department of National Health and Welfare. The range of projects for which this fund was intended included "child care problems related to shift-work, part-time employment and entry or re-entry into the labour force," as well as those concerning services to Native children, "headstart" programs for children with special needs, and the development of "non-profit, community based child care services," including parent resource centres.[75]

Despite the SPCCC's recommendation that the CAP-based system of funding child care for low-income families should be maintained, the third component of the National Strategy seemed, at first, to be more akin to the RCEE's recommendations on this subject. It announced the introduction of a new Canada Child Care Act to "replace the existing 'day care' provisions in the CAP" and "establish a new legislative framework for treating child care as a basic social and economic priority."[76] This legislation, it declared, would commit the federal government to spend $3 billion over the next seven years "to increase the number of quality child care spaces in Canada by 200,000 and to maintain the system at the expanded level."[77]

The National Strategy document noted that "the federal government recognizes its responsibility to work with the provinces to ensure the development and implementation of the necessary standards for quality in a jointly funded child care system."[78] To this end it stipulated that over a seven-year period the federal government would not only provide 75 percent of the capital costs of creating child care spaces in the nonprofit sector but share the operational costs equally.[79] Such a system might well have been encouraged by Abella and Cooke. However, the National Strategy document also announced that because "the federal government recognizes the important role played by the private sector in a number of provinces" – one it claimed accounted for 40 percent of existing licensed child care spaces – it would use the cost-sharing mechanisms in the Canada Child Care Act to provide "greater flexibility for the provinces in accommodating both non-profit and commercial child care services."[80] Clearly, therefore, if the National Strategy had been implemented, it would have led to a mixed economy of child care services very different from the system envisaged by Abella or Cooke.

Child Care and Women's Employment Opportunities in the National Strategy on Child Care

The National Strategy on Child Care was a far cry from the proposals for a publicly funded system of child care put forth by Abella and Cooke. Nonetheless, the Conservative government demonstrated some recognition of Abella's concerns about the link between child care provision and the promotion of gender equality in employment. These statements were so enmeshed in rhetoric about the government's commitment to strengthening the family, however, that they seemed to be a form of lip service to the idea of women's equality, rather than declarations of intent to realize this objective.

The contradiction was clearly apparent in the National Strategy document itself. It indicated that the strategy was being implemented not only because "major improvements and new resources are required to enhance and sustain quality child care in Canada" but also because "the economic equality of Canadian women must be promoted."[81] On the same page, however, the document stated that "the federal government is committed to strengthening Canadian families as the foundation of our society and so creating the potential for Canadians to fulfil their aspirations. It is to these goals that the federal government, in partnership with parents, caregivers, and provincial governments, commits itself."[82]

Although the ministerial statements that accompanied the government's unveiling of the National Strategy demonstrated some recognition of the link between women's employment opportunities and the provision of child care, they constantly reinforced the centrality of the family in Canadian society and the idea that participation in the paid labour force was an option women could choose to take, if they so wished. While Benoît Bouchard, who had by that time replaced Flora MacDonald as minister of Employment and Immigration, commented that "the strategy will assist many Canadian families: those headed by single parents as well as those with two parents," he also added that "it will be particularly important to women, whether they work in the labour force or stay home to care for their children."[83] Similarly, Barbara McDougall, the minister responsible for the Status of Women, hailed the National Strategy as "a landmark commitment to the economic equality of women" and then went on to say that it was "vital to the government's recognition of the important role women play in the economy of their individual families and of Canada as a whole."[84] Even though she emphasized that the National Strategy would assist women "whether they choose to work inside or outside the home," she also stressed that its central purpose was to ensure "the well-being of Canadian children."[85]

Most telling about the National Strategy, however, was that the statement issued by Jake Epp as minister of Health and Welfare chose to ignore the connection between child care and women's employment altogether. He described the government's program as one characterized by "fiscally responsible measures that will assist families in making choices about the care their children receive," and assured parents that "in partnership with them, the federal government will continue to work to strengthen Canadian families and to help provide good quality care for their children."[86]

Considered together, these statements suggest that although the Conservatives paid lip service to the connection between women's employment and child care when announcing the National Strategy, their prime objective was to emphasize the place of child care in the Conservative government's *family* policies. The point is reinforced by the fact that even though women have historically taken primary responsibility for child care, the language in which the National Strategy was framed generally neutered the parent who did the caring or purchased the care. Indeed, as Hum has argued, the National Strategy was not designed to promote the employment of either parent outside the home but to place the interests of stay-at-home carers on a more even footing with those demanding child care support when they were working outside the home.[87] Moreover, it is clear that the National Strategy was much more concerned with creating a financial formula to subsidize the individual purchaser of child care and the delivery of this service in both the commercial and nonprofit sectors than it was with addressing the normative questions that Abella had raised about the provision of child care for working women.

Three elements of the National Strategy were enacted shortly after it was unveiled. The CCED, the new CCTC, and the Child Care Initiatives Fund came into force on 1 April 1988, in the form specified in the strategy document.[88] In July of that year, an additional $1 billion was added to the child care budget, bringing the total budget to $7.3 billion. Of this additional money, $60 million was guaranteed, over six years, "to determine child care requirements of on-reserve Indians, train child care workers, and build and operate accredited child care services in Indian communities."[89] The remaining $940 million was added to the budget for the new cost-sharing mechanisms introduced under Bill C-144, after preliminary negotiations with Ontario revealed that the costs of funding a further 200,000 places had been underestimated.[90]

Bill C-144: The Canada Child Care Act

While the National Strategy paid lip service to the link between child care provision and women's employment opportunities, the proposed Canada

Child Care Act (Bill C-144) made no reference to it at all. The preamble to the Bill simply stated that the government recognized the "need to improve the availability, affordability, quality and accessibility of child care spaces throughout Canada" by helping to finance the creation and maintenance of at least 200,000 spaces over the following seven years.[91]

The Bill proposed a new system of federal-provincial/territorial cost-sharing that enabled the provinces to remain within the child care provisions of CAP or negotiate agreements consistent with the National Strategy. In the latter case, the federal government declared it would pay 75 percent of the capital costs for nonprofit spaces and subsidize the operating costs of child care spaces in commercial or nonprofit centres on a fifty-fifty basis with the provinces.[92]

The important distinction between this new system and the one linked to CAP was that although it appeared more generous, it was not an open-ended, cost-sharing program in which the federal government matched the provincial output. Instead it placed a ceiling on federal child care spending of $4 billion over seven years. As Phillips has noted, "This ceiling convert[ed] the open-ended cost-sharing arrangement of CAP into the equivalent of negotiated block funding grants."[93] Moreover, although the Bill would have placed quite strong reporting requirements on the provinces, in terms of accounting for the way in which the federal block grant was spent, it left the process of licensing child care spaces clearly in provincial hands.[94]

When the Bill received its second reading in the House of Commons on 11 August 1988, the minister of National Health and Welfare outlined the fiscal and jurisdictional imperatives that had shaped the legislation. He emphasized that "in contributing to the resolution of a social issue, government must always find the proper balance between direct intervention and a laissez-faire approach."[95] Moreover, he explained that the government's decision to match the "operating funds to both the 'not-for-profit' and commercial sectors" had been made in recognition of "the fact that about 40 per cent of the existing number of [child care] spaces are in the commercial sector."[96] Indeed, he went on to say that "we would have a great deal of trouble meeting our twin goals of improved quality and availability if we were to ignore almost half of the existing system."[97] What he failed to point out, as Phillips makes clear, is that the new funding formula was designed to "spur expansion of child care spaces and ... remove funding from the open-ended CAP before costs sky-rocketed under greatly increased spending by Ontario and Quebec."[98]

On the jurisdictional front, the minister stressed that if federal social policies were to be effective, "they had to be flexible and involve provincial co-operation."[99] Indeed, the federal government's decision not to interfere with provincial licensing arrangements and only hold the provinces accountable for their use of federal child care grants reflected the concessions that the federal government had to make to the provinces to ensure this cooperation.[100]

The Activists' Response to Bill C-144

Child care advocates and activists in NAC were enraged by the Bill because it enhanced the role of the commercial sector in the provision of child care and relied on the system of tax relief that Cooke had condemned in the report of the Task Force on Child Care.[101] For both groups, the Bill was a travesty. It would finally produce national child care legislation, for which women had been lobbying since the 1967 Royal Commission on the Status of Women. At the same time, it would create a new national system of funding child care that was a far cry from the system of publicly funded, universally accessible child care for which activists in NAC and the CDCAA had fought for so long.

It is interesting to note that at this point in the history of Canadian child care politics, activists in NAC and the CDCAA worked closely together. Although NAC and the CDCAA continued to pursue their distinct strategies of lobbying for child care services to support working women, in the first case, and children in the second, child care advocates worked to promote child care in both organizations. For example, Martha Friendly, a founding member of the CDCAA, prepared NAC's brief to the Special Parliamentary Committee on Child Care – the "last thing [she] ever wrote on a typewriter."[102] Similarly, Tricia Willis, an activist in the child care movement, co-authored and presented NAC's brief to the legislative committee on Bill C-144.[103] Furthermore, Sue Colley, a key activist in the Ontario child care movement, served as treasurer of NAC and co-chair of its child care committee.[104] Moreover, the links between activists in the two movements were reinforced by their shared concern to challenge both the privatization policies of the Conservative government and the potential harmonization of social programs under the proposed Free Trade Agreement with the United States.[105]

Nonetheless, despite these common political concerns, the statements issued by each organization during their campaigns to block Bill C-144 reflected their specific priorities. For example, NAC's brief to the legislative committee on Bill C-144 emphasized, at the outset, how "women's social and economic opportunities are determined by good access to child care."[106] By contrast, a critique of the Bill issued by the CDCAA indicated that it would "be a major step back for children and families in Canada."[107] Beyond this rhetoric, however, it is clear that both organizations shared a number of concerns about the proposed legislation. They recognized that it would not ensure the creation of sufficient child care spaces in Canada. They feared that far from facilitating a national system of universally accessible child care, the Act would put at risk the existing welfare-based provision under CAP and encourage the growth of nonprofit child care. Moreover, both organizations were concerned that the federal government's fear of invading provincial jurisdiction meant that the proposed legislation evaded the important issue of ensuring the delivery of quality child care services.[108] Indeed, in the period before the 1988 general election, when the debate about Bill C-144 was at its height, activists in NAC and the CDCAA wanted not simply to protect child care from commercialization through individual tax relief and subsidies to the profit-led sector but also to stop the replacement of open-ended cost-sharing with the introduction of federal block grants, allocated for a seven-year period.[109]

During the 1988 election campaign, activists in both movements became completely absorbed with the impact that the proposed Free Trade Agreement with the United States might have on Canada's social programs. The fear they shared with many activists on the Left was that social programs would be increasingly privatized in order to ensure harmonization with the United States.[110] Indeed, their concern during the election campaign was that if the Conservatives were returned to power and child care legislation reintroduced, it could be the first social program in Canada to fall victim to the harmonization of Canadian social policies with those of the United States.

Assessing the Conservative Government's Response to the RCEE

Shortly after being elected to office, the 1984 Conservative government was presented with royal commission recommendations that argued very strongly for the need to link the development of employment equity measures with the provision of publicly funded child care. The Conservatives did not maintain this link in the development of public policies on either issue. Indeed, in addressing the RCEE's recommendations they not only reverted to the narrow idea of employment equality that the Liberal government had originally encoded in the mandate of the RCEE but recast the policy options on child care in Conservative rhetoric about the relationship between the family, the market, and the state.

In certain respects, however, the Conservatives perpetuated an approach to developing public policies on women's employment that was similar to that pursued by previous Liberal governments. Despite the fact that women had, once again, used a royal commission to reinforce the links between the development of gender equality in the workplace and the provision of child care, the Conservatives, like the Liberals, failed to develop this link in the subsequent design of public policies. Indeed, just as their predecessors had done, the Conservatives claimed that institutional, jurisdictional, and fiscal imperatives made it impossible for them to do so.

In short, and like the Liberals before them, the Conservatives found it altogether easier to develop and implement policies concerned with employment equity than those relating to child care. In constitutional terms, it remained much easier for the federal government to address issues about introducing employment equity into a federally regulated workforce, than to act in any way that might seem *ultra vires* by invading provincial jurisdiction on questions of child care. In institutional terms, the familiar pattern of the linked recommendations on women's employment and child care from a royal commission being addressed by different government departments recurred and helped drive the federal response to Abella's twin concerns further apart. In fiscal terms, particularly taking into account the Conservatives' attempt to put a lid on the spiralling costs of child care, there was a clear recognition that employment equity, particularly in its report-based form, was altogether cheaper than policies concerned with financing the full- or part-time care of Canada's youngest citizens.

Beyond this series of pattern repeats, the Conservative government responded to the RCEE with a framework rooted in neo-conservative ideas about the economy and the family. Deregulation, rather than more regulation, was the order of the day and it was this philosophy that in many respects shaped the Conservatives' response to employment equity and child care. In the case of employment equity, concerns about deregulating the private sector meant that flexibility in designing employment equity plans to meet the business objectives of federally regulated companies was given a higher priority than the development of policies to eradicate employment discrimination within these organizations. In the case of child care, deregulation took on both a federal-provincial and a state-citizen dynamic. In the first case, the Conservative government ensured that the provinces were given complete freedom to set their own conditions for licensing nonprofit and commercial child care. In the second, the government subsidized individual parents through tax relief, so that they were given the "choice" to purchase child care or stay home and care for their children themselves.

While the patterns of deregulation appear to be consistent across these two areas of public policy, the Conservatives' approach to questions about women's employment seems to have been contradictory in some respects. On the one hand, they enacted employment equity programs to reduce employment discrimination against women and encourage federally regulated employers to think about the goals and timetables they could reasonably set themselves to increase the representation of women in their organizations' workforces. On the other hand, they developed a National Strategy on Child Care that was rooted in rhetoric about the value of the family as the centre-piece of child care and, despite ministerial lip service to the contrary, ambivalent about developing policies that would encourage women to abandon the care of their children and take up employment outside their homes.

8

Tiny Timid Steps: Employment Equity and Child Care in Mulroney's Second Term

When Prime Minister Mulroney sought re-election in 1988, he went into that famous free-trade campaign knowing that although the Conservatives had introduced Canada's first employment equity act, the businesses it covered resented that the legislation did not apply to the government's own bureaucracy. Despite signs of a backlash against employment equity, however, the Mulroney government's image was far more tarnished by the pre-election débâcle over its proposed Canada Child Care Act.[1] Given this context, it was perhaps inevitable that the development of employment equity and child care policies in the second Mulroney government would proceed at very different rates. Although the Conservatives went into the 1988 election promising to re-introduce child care legislation if they were returned to power, they backed away from this promise on resuming office. They did, however, proceed in an incremental manner with questions of employment equity.

Employment Equity in the Second Mulroney Government

During its second term in office, the Mulroney government took two principal initiatives in the field of employment equity. In accordance with section 13(1) of the 1986 Employment Equity Act (EEA), it ensured that the review of its own legislation was carried out in 1991, five years after the Act came into force. Moreover, in 1992, the government brought employment equity regulations within the government's own bureaucracy in line with those of other federally regulated organizations.

1991 Review of the Employment Equity Act

The special committee of the House of Commons responsible for the statutory review of the EEA carried out its evaluation between 25 November 1991 and 2 April 1992, under the chairmanship of John Redway. During its inquiries, the Redway Committee drew on evidence submitted by 104 witnesses.[2] It is perhaps indicative of the "very significant valley" into which feminist organizing had descended by the early 1990s that only sixteen women's organizations submitted evidence.[3] Moreover, in contrast to the submissions received by Rosalie Abella during the inquiries of the 1983 Royal Commission on Equality in Employment (RCEE), *no* submissions or presentations were made by child care organizations. This indicates how distinct questions about federal employment equity and child care policies had become by this time. It also suggests that by the early 1990s the campaign strategies of the women's movement and the child care movement were not as closely linked as they had been in the run-up to the 1988 election.

Nonetheless, the testimony from women's organizations highlighted a number of important factors about the working of the 1986 EEA.[4] First and foremost it brought out a shared concern that while employment equity was a good idea in principle, the implementation of the EEA had done little to alleviate the systemic employment discrimination that women experienced in the federal sphere. Indeed, a number of organizations pointed out how the government's annual reports on the workings of the EEA revealed only a marginal improvement in women's employment opportunities over the previous six years.[5] This point was writ large in the submission from the National Action Committee on the Status of Women (NAC), whose in-house research showed that employment opportunities for women in the Bank of Nova Scotia, Air Canada, and the Canadian Broadcasting Corporation had hardly improved since the introduction of the EEA in 1986.[6]

While the number of organizations presenting testimony to the Redway Committee points to a decline in feminist activity by the early 1990s, their testimony reveals a more complex understanding of gender that had taken root in the movement by this time. In contrast to the submissions that women made to the RCEE in the mid-1980s, the authors of these documents no longer viewed women as a unified target group. Reflecting the growing awareness of diversity issues within the Canadian women's movement in the late 1980s and early 1990s, these submissions repeatedly emphasized the complex nature of discrimination experienced by women belonging to the three other target groups.[7] As the Canadian Advisory Council on the Status of Women (CACSW) noted, "The evidence has shown that women have not progressed significantly in the employment equity work force during the first years of the [EEA]; occupational segregation and lower earnings still plague the occupational profile of women. Aboriginal women, disabled women, and visible minority women remain doubly disadvantaged in this respect. At this rate of progress, it will take decades before women achieve freedom from systemic discrimination in the work force covered by the Act."[8]

Women's organizations had a number of different suggestions about the way that the discrimination experienced by women in the three other target groups should be addressed. NAC argued that distinct goals and timetables for women in each of these groups should be established, "otherwise women who belong to one of the other designated groups disappear into the category of 'woman' or the other category, and the double discrimination they face is not addressed."[9] The Native Women's Association of Canada argued that the Employment Equity Branch of the Canadian Employment and Immigration Commission (CEIC) should continue its initiative to tabulate employment data relating specifically to Native women.[10] The National Organization of Immigrant and Visible Minority Women and the Congress of Black Women of Canada both argued that policy makers needed to be more aware of huge variation in the forms of employment discrimination faced by women from different ethnic groups.[11] In addition, women argued that systemic discrimination against women in the other target groups was reinforced by the current methods of measuring their workforce availability.[12] As the Congress argued, because the statistical data used to develop employment equity programs "capture those employees already in the stated occupation," they tend to underrepresent the availability of visible minority and Aboriginal women.[13]

Women's organizations were also concerned that systemic employment discrimination against women was reinforced by the limited span of the 1986 EEA. Although women made various suggestions about how the legislation might be improved, four key concerns stood out. First, women argued that the thresholds for organizations that were subject to employment equity regulations should be lowered so that small to medium-sized organizations falling within the federal jurisdiction were covered by the legislation.[14] Second, women regarded it as "ridiculous that the Federal Public Service with employment of 215,000 people, 43 per cent of whom are women, was not included in the Employment Equity Act."[15] The National Association of Women and the Law (NAWAL) questioned the exclusion of the federal public service "on the grounds that it had been implementing its own employment equity programs for some time."[16] Similarly, NAC expressed outrage that "the federal government [did] not require its own departments to implement employment equity through legislation as it [did] those in the private sector."[17] Third, there was a clear concern that employment equity regulations cover part-time as well as full-time employees, particularly, as the CACSW pointed out, because women remain overrepresented in part-time employment.[18] Finally, some organizations urged that the regulations on contract compliance be brought within the remit of the legislation and expanded to cover a wider range of organizations. Women also believed that contract compliance measures should ensure that companies and organizations accumulating a series of small government grants or contracts were not able to circumvent the regulations.[19]

The only issue on which women's organizations were not united was union involvement in developing employment equity measures. For example, the authors of the brief from NAC argued that in their experience it was rarely true that unions block employers' attempts to introduce employment equity measures.[20] By contrast, the Toronto Women in Film and Television argued that "broadcasters willing to implement employment equity soon discover subtle and inflexible union opposition."[21] However, while most women's groups commenting on this issue argued that unions should be involved in the development of employment equity measures, there was also a clear concern that target group representatives should be involved in these consultations.[22]

Women's desire for a more proactive approach to employment equity was also reflected in their concerns about the cumbersome, reactive way in which the Canadian Human Rights Commission (CHRC) currently reviewed complaints filed under the EEA.[23] As NAWAL argued, "Enforcement of the Act currently depends on individual complaints and verification of employer records by the Human Rights Commission. This reactive mechanism is largely ineffective, particularly since the role of the CHRC is not well defined, and it is underfunded."[24] Organizations called either for a more proactive role for the CHRC or for the creation of a new, independent enforcement agency that would report directly to Parliament.[25] Some organizations also argued that such an enforcement agency should be dominated by target group members and armed with sufficient resources to enable "one arm to do the enforcement and the other arm to do the education."[26]

Many women's organizations asserted that the major weakness in the existing employment equity legislation lay not with the methods of securing compliance but with the quantitative emphasis on reporting numeric results. Women were particularly concerned that employers remained unaccountable for the ways they sought to achieve their declared goals by adjusting employment practices within their workplaces.[27] Several women's organizations argued that "employment equity was more than a question of numbers," and called for the Act to be revised so that employers had to account for the plans implemented to realize goals and timetables.[28] This reflected a broader concern among women's organizations that one of the principal weaknesses of the current employment equity legislation was that it failed to encourage employers to consider how the culture of a workplace might inhibit women's employment opportunities.[29] As NAC argued, "While we believe that mandatory goals and timetables are the centre of an employment equity plan, fifteen years of international experience with affirmative action have shown that numbers are not enough. The atmosphere and culture in the workplace must be accommodating to the designated groups or they will not stay and certainly will not be encouraged to develop new skills or move up in the enterprise."[30]

Although women's reflections on the way that the culture of workplaces might be improved varied, it was noticeable that half of the women's organizations submitting briefs to the House of Commons Committee argued that employers needed to do more to facilitate the integration of employees' work and family responsibilities. As the CACSW argued, these questions remained important in discussion of gender equality in the sphere of employment:

> The labour force participation of women is strongly linked to family responsibilities. In spite of their increased employment levels, women continue to have primary responsibility for the care of children and the management of household duties. Because of the failure of the workplace to accommodate these responsibilities, they continue to have a significant impact on the employment that women are able to secure and on the capacity to earn an adequate level of income in the labour market. The social and economic institutions interact to produce an effect on women which can hardly be qualified as "neutral." For these reasons, employment equity for women will have a greater chance of success if the external conditions facilitate the integration of work and family responsibilities. Such favourable conditions include affordable child-care facilities, increased parental supports, and other education and social programs.[31]

Recommendations about the most appropriate way for women to achieve this integration included the provision for child care, the development of flexible working practices, family and parental leave provisions and, in the case of the Toronto Women in Film and Television, a call for "significant income tax deductions for child care."[32] Interestingly, in contrast to the brief that NAC submitted to the Royal Commission on Equality in Employment, the document its members prepared for the Redway Committee contained a substantial section on child care. As its authors Judy Rebick, and Phebe Poole reflected, "Over the past thirty years we have witnessed a revolution in women's participation in the workplace but few of our institutions have changed accordingly. Growth in child care spaces has remained stagnant since the early 1970s; the school day is still short and there is no public provision for caring for children during the summer; parental and family leave provisions are woefully inadequate. While employment equity plans cannot deal with all of these issues, they can address them and in larger corporations significant changes can be made."[33]

While the women's organizations that submitted evidence to the Redway Committee clearly had a number of different concerns, their testimony was characterized by calls to expand the remit of the current employment equity legislation and fine-tune the reporting process so that the barriers to women's employment equity were more easily identified. In addition, women called for a much more qualitative understanding of employment equity, one that forced employers to think about alleviating the barriers to employment equity rather than just setting themselves numeric goals and targets. Furthermore, although questions about child care had been hived off from those of employment equity when the 1986 EEA was introduced, half of the women's organizations submitting evidence to the Redway Committee used the opportunity, once again, to link together questions about women's employment opportunities and the provision of child care.

Report of the Special Committee on the Review of the Employment Equity Act

As anticipated, the 1992 report of the Redway Committee put a fairly positive spin on the way in which employment equity regulations had been developed and implemented during the Conservatives' term in office. Although it argued that the existing employment equity regulations needed to apply to a wider range of organizations, include qualitative as well as quantitative measures, and be monitored more effectively, the report did not launch a fundamental critique of the 1986 EEA. As a result, the Liberal and New Democrat members of the committee filed separate minority reports calling for the remit of the Act to be broadened and its regulatory mechanisms improved.[34]

Even though the Redway Report took note of many of the concerns that women had raised in their testimony, those it did accept were more often adopted in part than in whole. The report agreed with women's proposals that the federal public service should be covered by the EEA.[35] It also recognized women's wish that Statistics Canada refine labour force availability data.[36] The report acknowledged women's general concern that employment equity measures should have both qualitative and quantitative dimensions.[37] In addition, it recommended, as women had done, that federally regulated unions as well as employers should be covered by the legislation.[38]

Beyond these specific points, however, where agreement did exist it was most often in principle rather than in detail. Thus while the Redway Report concurred with women's organizations that the threshold for companies to be regulated by the EEA should be lowered, it did not recommend that it should be lowered as far as women had suggested (Table 8.1.a).[39] In addition, though the report acknowledged that the employment equity regulations for companies under contract to the federal government should be improved, it did not agree, for jurisdictional reasons, that contract compliance regulations should be written into the EEA (Table 8.1.b).[40] Moreover, while the report agreed with women that employers should develop qualitative and quantitative employment equity measures, in consultation with target group representatives, it also recommended that employers should be allowed some flexibility to modify these goals and objectives if necessary (Table 8.1.c and d).[41] Furthermore, although the Redway Report acknowledged the need to improve the roles played by the Department of Employment and Immigration (EIC), Labour Canada, and the CHRC in monitoring and enforcing the Act, it did not contemplate the establishment of a new, independent enforcement agency, dominated by target groups (Tables 8.1.e).[42] Finally, though it reflected women's concerns that employment equity procedures be extended to federally funded training programs, the report emphasized setting quantitative goals and targets rather than developing qualitative and quantitative procedures (Table 8.1.f).[43]

At the same time, the Redway Report did not recognize a number of issues raised by women in their submissions. Women's calls for employment equity plans to incorporate measures that would enable employees to integrate work and family responsibilities were not included in its recommendations (Table 8.2.a). Although women's emphasis on the way in which workplace cultures can create barriers to employment was mentioned in the report, the only recommendation in this regard was that the federal government develop a national employment equity strategy to deal with broader issues raised by the various target groups (Table 8.2.b).[44] Recommendations that greater attention be paid to the complex nature of discrimination experienced by women in the three other target groups were not taken up (Table 8.2.c). Moreover, the challenges advanced by gay and lesbian organizations about discrimination on the grounds of sexual orientation were completely overlooked, as the report recommended that the existing target group categories be maintained (Table 8.2.d).[45] Women's concerns that the career trajectories of part-time and contract employees be monitored in the development of employment equity data were disregarded in favour of maintaining the existing method of reporting workforce data (Table 8.2.e).[46] In addition, women's recommendations that the sanctions for noncompliance be made more severe were not taken up (Table 8.2.f).

The Redway Report recommended some marginal improvements in the EEA. It called both for an expansion of the Act's legislative remit and for mechanisms to ensure that employment equity regulations focused more effectively on employment procedures. It also acknowledged the need to enhance the powers of the EIC and the CHRC, so that the EIC could implement the legislation and the CHRC enforce it. Indeed, as Chapter 9 discusses, the Redway Report did set a number of reforms on course. Its recommendations that the remit of the EEA be expanded to cover more federal employees were eventually addressed when the Act was revised by

Table 8.1

Points of partial agreement between women's organizations' submissions to Redway Committee and recommendations of Redway Report

Women's organizations' submissions to Redway Committee	Redway Report recommendations
a. Act should apply to federally regulated organizations with fifty or more employees.	a. Act should apply to federally regulated organizations with seventy-five or more employees.
b. Contract compliance should be expanded to small and medium-sized companies and program brought under EEA.	b. Contract compliance should be expanded to companies of seventy-five employees with contracts of $200,000. Contract compliance should not be brought under EEA.
c. Implementation of qualitative measures, developed in consultation with target groups, should be an intrinsic part of an employment equity plan.	c. Compliance agency should confer with employers, employee organizations, and target groups to improve assessment of qualitative measures developed by employers to achieve employment equity.
d. Employers should be required to (a) specify quantitative and qualitative goals in employment equity plans, and (b) ensure their realization.	d. All employment equity plans should contain quantitative and qualitative goals that are achievable. Plans should be inspected by the monitoring agency and become binding on employers, with some flexibility for modification.
e. Enforcement powers of the CHRC should be enhanced or a new independent enforcement agency set up.	e. Department of Employment and Immigration (EIC) should monitor and CHRC oversee enforcement with adequate resources. Labour Canada should monitor EIC.
f. Employment equity should be applied to designated federal government training programs.	f. Federal training programs should allocate funds to train target groups. Statistics on and goals for target group participation should be included in annual Employment Equity Act reports.

Sources: Submissions to the Special Committee on the Review of the Employment Equity Act, Archives of the Committees and Parliamentary Associations Directorate (ACPAD), House of Commons, 5700-343-E2; House of Commons, *A Matter of Fairness*, Report of the Special Committee on the Review of the Employment Equity Act (Ottawa: Queen's Printer, 1992).

Table 8.2

Points of disagreement between women's organizations' submissions to Redway Committee and recommendations of Redway Report

Women's organizations' submissions to Redway Committee	Redway Report recommendations
a. Employment equity plans should include measures to promote the integration of work and family responsibilities, including child care, flexible work, and family care leave.	a. No recommendations
b. Employment equity plans should pay more attention to work-place culture and removal of subtle barriers to equity.	b. Federal government should develop a National Employment Equity Strategy to address broader employment equity issues.
c. Employment Equity Act should recognize complex discrimination against women in three other target groups.	c. Current target group categories should be maintained.
d. Employment Equity Act should be broadened to stop discrimination against lesbians.	d. Current target group categories should be maintained.
e. Employers should provide career progress data on part-time and contract employees.	e. Annual reporting procedures and numerical reporting system should not be changed.
f. Government should tighten financial/contract sanctions for noncompliance.	f. Employers who fail to submit plan, consult employees, or file annual reports should be fined $50,000.

Sources: Submissions to the Special Committee on the Review of the Employment Equity Act, Archives of the Committees and Parliamentary Associations Directorate (ACPAD), House of Commons, 5700-343-E2; House of Commons, *A Matter of Fairness*, Report of the Special Committee on the Review of the Employment Equity Act (Ottawa: Queen's Printer, 1992).

the new Liberal government in 1995. In addition, its proposals to clarify the monitoring and enforcement roles of the EIC and the CHRC were addressed in the revised legislation. Furthermore, the report laid the groundwork for the eventual introduction of a process whereby employers would be required to report not just their goals and timetables for implementing employment equity but also the procedures they were developing to make those targets a reality.[47] However, while the parliamentary review process was set up by a Conservative government in accordance with the stipulations it had encoded in the EEA, "the politically charged atmosphere in which the Committee's recommendations [were] received" meant that the government did not act on its own committee's recommendations.[48] Although the government planned to do so, the last thing that Brian Mulroney's increasingly unpopular Conservative government needed by 1992 was for the emergent right-wing Reform Party to mount a massive backlash against employment equity. As a result, although Monique Vezina as Conservative minister of Employment and Immigration discussed the Redway Report's recommendations with officials in her department, the Conservative government backed away from revising the EEA.

Employment Equity in the Public Service

While the second Mulroney government proved reluctant to pursue the recommendations of the 1992 Redway Report, it did initiate reforms in the federal public service (FPS). These were triggered not simply by corporate criticism of the government for failing to include the public service within the gamut of the 1986 EEA but also by the 1990 report of the Task Force on Barriers to Women in the Public Service.

The task force had been established in 1988 by Pat Carney, as president of the Treasury Board, shortly after the Conservatives were re-elected to government. In the foreword to its final report, she explained the rationale for her decision: "The impetus for the Task Force on Barriers to Women in the Public Service came from my own experience as a cabinet minister in Prime Minister Brian Mulroney's government. I served in three different portfolios – Energy, Mines and Resources, International Trade, and Treasury Board. In all three I noticed very few women at the senior levels of the bureaucracy. When officials gathered in my ministerial office, they were normally men. The few women who did attend were often there in an 'acting' capacity."[49]

Carney was encouraged to set up the task force by a small group of senior women in the FPS who were also conscious that although equal employment opportunity policies had been in place for more than a decade, women were still compressed in the lower and middle echelons of the federal bureaucracy. As Kay Stanley, who was coordinator of Status of Women Canada at the time, explained a decade later,

It was basically an attempt to move to the empirical from the emotive. You know you could talk women's equality to a lot of senior managers in this town [Ottawa], but their reaction was, "Oh what's your problem, Kay? There are lots of women in my organization." [The task force] was designed to focus on the issue of compression and part of that I think is still to this day a spirited attempt by women leaders in the public service to effect change from within. The women's movement and the advocacy groups were out there banging on the doors and we were people who were in these organizations, in these departments, and in these agencies and [had formed] a sort of a collegial network.[50]

The task force was asked to assess the principal barriers to women's entry into the public service and career progress through its ranks. Specifically, it was asked to identify and rank the barriers to women's employment "in occupational groups where the labour force availability significantly exceeds the proportion of women employed in those occupational groups," and to women's promotion within occupational groups where they were "significantly skewed towards the lower levels."[51] It was also asked to identify "attitudinal and other barriers that women face as they move into positions where the working environment is male dominated."[52] Nonetheless, it was a sign of the times that the task force was instructed to make recommendations to overcome these barriers within a framework that recognized "the Government's objectives of fiscal responsibility and control of the growth of the public service."[53]

Although members of the task force were concerned "to avoid reinventing the wheel," their statistical findings were depressingly familiar.[54] These showed that even though women's participation in the federal public service mirrored that of the Canadian labour force, they were concentrated in clerical and secretarial occupations and "in almost all occupational groups" compressed into low-status occupations.[55] In addition, the task force found repeated evidence of women and men providing very different accounts of the way responsibilities for dependent children shaped their careers within the public service. Indeed, a survey of current employees, carried out for the task force by Statistics Canada, found that while just 18.6 percent of male respondents believed that they had "missed out on promotion over the past three years" because they "had children or other dependents at home," 81.4 percent of the female respondents cited this as a reason for their limited career progress.[56] Similarly, while only 28.7 percent of the male respondents thought that they had missed career development opportunities in the past three years because of family responsibilities, 71.3 percent of the female respondents cited this as a reason.[57] In addition, the survey showed huge discrepancies in workers' ideas about who should be responsible for their offsprings' care. While 70.6 percent of the male respondents felt that "raising children should be a woman's responsibility," only 29.5 percent of the female respondents agreed with them.[58]

Given these findings, it is not surprising that the task force uncovered substantial qualitative evidence about the difficulties women faced in balancing their work and family responsibilities. *Beneath the Veneer* (as the report was entitled) noted that "recent progress notwithstanding, most of the women addressing their concerns on this issue to the task force felt that child care, elder care and domestic chores are still overwhelmingly the responsibility of women."[59] One woman quoted in the report remarked how "women are still the primary caregivers. I still don't think there are enough support systems to allow women to get ahead."[60] Another commented on how "the amounts allowed for child care while mothers travel on business are inadequate and would not meet, for example, minimum pay requirements set out by Ontario legislation for domestic employees."[61] Two other women summed up the need for workplaces that were more family-friendly. While the first argued that "we have a very long way to go before the caring dimensions of life is legitimate in business," the second emphasized a point that women made frequently in their evidence to the Redway Committee: "Right now we've got mechanical solutions coming out of our ears. We've got action programs, we've got this, we've got that. But nothing is being done about the real problems in the so-called 'softer' areas. Can we underestimate the importance of childbearing and child-rearing to women? Women endure increasing stress from conflicts between their jobs and their family responsibilities, and society still requires women to accept those responsibilities."[62]

In short, the task force produced both quantitative evidence of a fundamental difference in attitude between men and women about responsibilities for the care of children and qualitative reflections about how the corporate culture within the FPS made it difficult for women to integrate their work and family responsibilities. It also recognized that "increased flexibility in accommodating family responsibilities is key to integrating the changing work force and ensuring the maximum return on the investment of time and money."[63] The report concluded by recommending that the Treasury Board should "take gender balance seriously [and] make a commitment to achieve it" by addressing gender balance "as a management problem," taking "action on system improvements that have been recommended in the past," and tackling "attitudes and the corporate culture."[64]

Immediately after making these recommendations, the report noted that "it is clear from the evidence we have presented that adequate provision for the care of children and pay equity are both essential to a better balance of gender in the public service."[65] However, the authors of the report then noted that these were "two issues on which we are not making specific recommendations, because they have been well-documented else-where and highly credible recommendations have been made by others."[66] Their accompanying comment that "it should not be assumed that because we make no recommendations we consider these issues less important than the matters on which we do recommend," suggests that beneath the veneer of another glossy government report lay all sorts of politics about not making policy recommendations on child care provision in the middle of the Conservatives' second term.[67] Nonetheless, the evidence that women presented both to this task force and the Redway Committee reveals, once again, that women's vision of employment equality took account not simply of their paid labour but also their caring work at home.

The issue of integrating work and family responsibilities remained on the Treasury Board's agenda after the publication of *Beneath the Veneer*. In part, this was the result of pressure placed on the Treasury Board Secretariat by the Consultation Group on Employment Equity for Women, which was set up in the wake of the task force to address issues identified in its report. The first report of the Consultation Group, published in May 1992, recommended not only that "deputy ministers should demonstrate their willingness to implement flexible work arrangements," but also that there should be a centralized referral service within the FPS to "provide employees with information on child care services, particularly when emergency child care is required."[68] Nonetheless, it was policies on employment equity rather than those concerned with the integration of work and family responsibilities that became mandatory in the FPS when the 1992 Public Service Reform Act required the Treasury Board to develop regulatory procedures "comparable to those of the 1986 Employment Equity Act," and, after 1994, to report its progress annually to Parliament.[69]

Throughout the second Mulroney government, women kept articulating the need for employment equality policies that moved beyond their existing quantitative focus. Indeed, they called for an approach to employment equity that recognized how women's burden of responsibility for the care of young children could impede their career development. However, all women got back from the Conservative government was incremental policy change within the federal public service, modelled on existing employment equity legislation. Child care, as far as the Conservative government was concerned, was a completely separate policy issue.

The Conservative Shift from Child Care to Child Poverty

The second Mulroney government beat a gradual retreat from its 1988 election promises to implement the National Strategy on Child Care. The deficit-reduction priorities of its 1989 budget meant that the Conservatives never kept their pre-election promise to proceed with the strategy.[70]

Moreover, in March 1990, the federal government "put a cap on CAP" by limiting the extent to which the three wealthiest provinces of Ontario, Alberta, and British Columbia were reimbursed with cost-sharing funds from the federal government.[71] In fact, the federal government informed these three provinces that it would not increase its contribution to CAP-based provision by more than 5 percent per annum. As a result, if any of these provinces increased their CAP-based spending by more than 5 percent, they would not have their additional expenditures matched by the federal government. Finally, in February 1992, Benoît Bouchard as minister of Health announced that on grounds of fiscal restraint the Tories had no option but to abandon the National Strategy.[72] Ron Yzerman, a former director of Child Care Programs in Ottawa, described the Conservatives' change of course in the following way:

> They began to claim that the fiscal picture had changed dramatically [and] that the money that was going to be there – that was intended to be earmarked for the original bill – wasn't there any more because there was a drastic downturn in federal revenues ... And then on top of that, some more spin was put on, saying, "Oh times have changed, the polls show that child care isn't the number one concern, the people are saying that we should take a more shotgun approach, there are other social issues – child abuse, child poverty, child health nutrition." These were all the key phrases that were used when the Brighter Futures program was introduced as a replacement about three years later.[73]

The Conservatives' decision to shift their focus away from questions of child care to those of child poverty and child development took root when the House of Commons unanimously passed a resolution in 1989 "to seek to achieve the goal of eliminating poverty among Canadian children by the year 2000."[74] The motion had been introduced by Ed Broadbent as his "swansong" when retiring from the leadership of the New Democratic Party.[75] However, the idea of joining an international offensive on child poverty rather than sinking back into a controversial debate on child care appealed to the Conservatives part way through their second term. As one policy researcher on child care noted, "It's a lot easier to swallow having your tax dollars spent on feeding poor children than it is to swallow having your tax dollars spent on providing child care for middle-class two-income parents."[76] Nonetheless, what the Conservatives failed to notice was that behind every poverty-stricken child there was typically an impoverished mother experiencing employment inequality because of lack of training, employment discrimination, or the limited provision of child care.

Mulroney's focus on the rights of children rather than those of their working mothers was reinforced after he co-hosted the 1990 World Summit for Children at the United Nations, while Canadian child care activists issued communications to ensure that the prime minister "did not get away with telling the world how great child care [was] in Canada."[77] In December 1991, Canada ratified the United Nations 1989 Convention on the Rights of the Child – a document that interestingly included a clause stating that the signatories "shall take all appropriate measures to ensure that children of working parents have the right to benefit from childcare services and facilities for which they are eligible."[78] Nevertheless, the Brighter Futures Program that the Conservatives then developed was designed to support children and families rather than focus on questions of child care provision for working women. At its core lay a new initiative called the Community Action Program for Children (CAP-C), which emphasized the centrality of parents and families in the care of children and the need to invest in the development of children at risk.[79] In addition, as part of the Brighter Futures Program, the government set up a Children's Bureau in February 1992 to "co-ordinate federal programs and activities related to the health, welfare and development of children and their families, enhance public awareness and support for children's issues and encourage all sectors of society to work together on behalf of children."[80] Then, in May 1992, it announced the Child Development Initiative, "a five-year, $500 million series of programs that claimed to address conditions of risk that threaten the health and well-being of children, especially children zero to six years of age."[81]

Significantly, the question of federal support for child care was not incorporated into the Mulroney government's new initiatives to promote the well-being of children. As a senior policy analyst on the HRDC's Children's Task Team noted subsequently, the introduction of Brighter Futures and CAP-C meant that "the focus [of federal policy] really shifted from child care to child development. [These programs] were to be early development and community based rather than [focus on] child care. There was a shift of focus there, and although it [did] include child development, child care just kind of dropped off the edge."[82] Noticeably, however, at the same time that the government shifted the agenda away from child care to child development, it also announced a new Child Tax Benefit. This came into effect in 1993, replacing the existing system of universal family allowances and tax credits for children with a targeted fiscal transfer.[83] While it was designed to channel a further $2.1 billion in federal assistance to families over the following five years, this new benefit provided tax-free monthly payments and supplements for low-income families with young children whose parents were in the labour force. Clearly, therefore, although the Mulroney government had put limits on its CAP-based contributions to the delivery of welfare-based child care services in the richest provinces, it was prepared to engage in direct, tax-based subsidies to the working poor.

The Conservatives' retreat from child care during their second term of office reflected the context in which the government was operating. In an era when recessionary forces were growing stronger, the price tag attached to the development of a policy that had proved contentious seemed too great. Moreover, the devolutionist trend in the early 1990s, expressed in the 1992 Charlottetown Accord and reinforced by the resurgence of Québécois nationalism, meant the Conservatives became increasingly reluctant to take initiatives in areas of social policy that fell into provincial jurisdiction. As a result, the Mulroney government initiated a shift in children's policy away from initiatives that relied on federal-provincial cost-sharing and towards issues that could be addressed more easily within the federal sphere. With hindsight, however, we can see that his government's initiatives to link the eradication of child poverty with moves to provide child tax benefits for the working poor, and its decision to focus on child development rather than child care, marked a fundamental shift in federal policy that would extend well beyond this era of Conservative government.

Changes at the End of the Conservatives' Second Term

Although Mulroney's increasing unpopularity in the second part of his mandate made it unlikely that he would seek a third term in office, it was not clear whether a subsequent government would continue to address the questions of child poverty, children's rights, and child development on which he had begun to focus. As it turned out, his successor, Kim Campbell, enjoyed such a brief term as Canada's only female prime minister that no substantive policy developments in child care or employment equity occurred under her summer-long premiership in 1993.

Nonetheless, a major restructuring of government departments, initiated during the second Mulroney government, was brought to fruition at that time. This included the creation of Human Resources Development Canada (HRDC), a new super-department that re-jigged the bureaucratic map of Ottawa, bringing the federal government's literacy, student finance, training, welfare, and employment programs together under one bureaucratic roof.[84] In the process, the Department of Health and Welfare and that of EIC were cut in half. The health programs stayed in the new department of Health Canada, while the immigration files from EIC were moved to the department of Citizenship and Immigration. As a result, the welfare programs from Health and Welfare and the employment programs from EIC were both relocated in the new Human Resources Development Canada.

It took a while, with this restructuring, for the officers in the former Children's Bureau at Health and Welfare to find the best bureaucratic home. Those running CAP-C, developed under the Brighter Futures Program, went to HRDC and in a matter of weeks returned to Health Canada. However, the newly created Children's Task Team at HRDC retained the files on child care and child benefits. As a result, for the first time in Canadian government history, the new minister of HRDC had the potential to regulate federal employment equity programs *and* work with the provinces to develop a national child care program.[85] The question this reconfiguration raised, as Kim Campbell headed towards that fateful 1993 election, was whether the first minister to take charge of the new bureaucratic empire at HRDC would be able to forge fresh understandings about the link between women's employment opportunities and federal involvement in the field of child care.[86]

9

Creating Opportunity? The Chrétien Government's Approach to Employment Equity and Child Care

The Liberals' return to power in October 1993 produced a sense of optimism among activists and federal bureaucrats working in the field of social policy. Although the new government had been elected primarily on a mandate to create jobs, maintain fiscal responsibility, and steer clear of any proposals for mega-constitutional change, the Liberals' election manifesto contained short, specific promises on employment equity and child care. Known as the "Red Book," this manifesto declared that the Liberals would "strengthen the Employment Equity Act" by embracing "the federal public service, federal agencies and commissions" within its remit and increasing the powers of the Canadian Human Rights Commission (CHRC) to secure compliance.[1] The manifesto also declared that "a Liberal government, working with the provinces, will implement a realistic and fiscally responsible program to increase the number of child care spaces in Canada."[2] Indeed, the Liberals' promises on child care were costed in terms of the federal, provincial, and parental contributions required to bring about this expanded provision.[3] As a result, the prospects for the development of a national child care program were good.

At the core of the Red Book was a strong argument that investment in human development and human resources were the keys to economic growth. Reducing the barriers to employment through improved employment equity legislation made sense to a political party that was promulgating a neo-Keynesian manifesto and seeking to create employment opportunities for as many citizens as possible. Moreover, the Red Book acknowledged how "Canadians with young families need a support system that enables parents to participate fully in the economic life of the country."[4] As a result, the Liberals assured Canadians that providing they secured a 3 percent annual growth rate and "the agreement of the provinces," they would allocate $720 million to a federal-provincial shared-cost program, over a specified three-year period, in order to create over 150,000 child care spaces.[5] In addition, the Liberals promised "to work with the provinces and the business community to identify appropriate incentives for the creation and funding of child care spaces in the workplace."[6]

While the Liberals' promises on child care were designed to support both single-parent and two-parent families, the manifesto suggested that at last a party elected to office would respond to Abella's claim that "child-care is the ramp that provides equal access to the workforce for mothers."[7] However, it was not just these promises that provided grounds for optimism. When the new Liberal prime minister, Jean Chrétien, formed his cabinet, he appointed Lloyd Axworthy as the first ever Liberal minister of Human Resources Development. Activists and bureaucrats concerned with employment equity and child care could not have hoped for a better ministerial appointment. Here was a veteran politician who was clearly committed to both aspects of social policy. Even though Axworthy had been vilified by feminists when he cancelled the Canadian Advisory Council on the Status of Women (CACSW) constitutional conference in 1981, activists recognized that he had fought for the 1983 Royal Commission on Equality in Employment, only to experience the political frustration of being in opposition when its report was presented to government. However, he now had the chance to improve the employment equity legislation that the Conservatives had introduced. Moreover, as someone who worked closely with him at that stage remarked, "He was quite passionately interested in issues around children, because he basically believed that if you didn't get it right with kids then other issues really couldn't be resolved."[8]

It was not simply Axworthy's grasp of employment equity and child care issues that was encouraging. It was also that the organization of Human Resources Development Canada (HRDC) at last put a minister of the Canadian government in a position to act on *both* areas of public policy. Axworthy initiated policy development in each field shortly after resuming office. Nonetheless, as the Conservatives had not acted on the recommendations of the 1992 report of the special parliamentary committee established to review the 1986 Employment Equity Act (Redway Report), and the Liberal members of that committee had filed a minority report, this was the easiest of the two areas on which to proceed with legislative reform. Indeed, when Bill C-64 received royal assent on 15 December 1995, it was the first piece of the new government's legislation to flow directly from the Red Book.

Bill C-64 and the 1995 Employment Equity Act

Even though the Liberals broadened the scope and mandates of the 1986 EEA, their reforms were not as extensive as those advocated by John Nunziata and Mary Clancy in the minority report they wrote as Liberal members of the 1992 Redway Committee.[9] In opposition, the Liberals had argued that employment equity legislation should apply to companies employing fifteen or more employees.[10] In government, however, the bureaucratic costs of reducing the threshold meant that the Liberals retained the 100-person cut-off point devised by the Conservatives (Table 9.1.a). Neil Gavigan, the senior bureaucrat responsible for employment equity programs at HRDC explained the rationale for their decision:

> It is a good cut-off point. You want to cover as many employees as possible and you want to make sure that you're not placing administrative burdens on the private sector. At the same time you have to be able to administer the program effectively. I think the decision reflected the balance of possibilities of keeping the program working effectively and government costs under control. Of course, when the Liberal Party came into power in 1993 we immediately embarked upon a program review because Canada's debt was in the region of $40 billion dollars annually ... and in that process of reductions it is not the time to expand your workload if it is not really a necessity.[11]

While the remit of the 1986 EEA had been limited to federally regulated organizations employing 100 or more people, Bill C-64 ensured that the federal public service (FPS), the Royal Canadian Mounted Police, and the Canadian armed forces were all covered by employment equity legislation. Although there was clearly some resistance within the public sector to this expansion of the legislation's remit, it reflected a clear commitment in the Red Book. Moreover, as Kay Stanley – the senior bureaucrat responsible for employment equity at the Treasury Board Secretariat – noted, "There had long been this tension that governments were demanding of the banks and the transportation sector, things they were not demanding of themselves."[12]

Fundamental to Bill C-64 was an expectation that employers would not only set and report their achievement of numerical goals for the hiring of target group members (as Bill C-62 had required) but also develop and report progress in implementing policies and practices to remove barriers to their hiring and promotion (Table 9.1.b, d, and e). While this clearly mirrored the recommendations that women had made in their submissions to the Redway Committee, the change also reflected the bureaucrats' concerns to develop measures of progress that did not rely solely on quantifiable goals. As Neil Gavigan explained, "It's really important for all equity practitioners to remember that people can work very, very hard on good solid employment equity programs and the numerical changes may in fact be quite small over the short haul."[13] However, while clearly an improvement on the EEA, in the sense that the Act linked the projection of quantifiable goals to the implementation of organizational policies, Bill

Table 9.1

Comparison of the 1986 and 1995 Employment Equity Acts

1986 Employment Equity Act (Conservative government)	1995 Employment Equity Act (Liberal government)
a. Employers covered by legislation Employers of federally regulated industries employing 100 or more	a. Employers covered by legislation Employers of federally regulated industries employing 100 or more, federal public service, Canadian Forces, Royal Canadian Mounted Police
b. Meaning of employment equity Designated employers must: • identify and eliminate illegal discriminatory employment practices, in consultation with bargaining agent or designated employees • institute positive policies/practices, and make reasonable accommodation, to ensure target group members' participation throughout organization is proportionate to their representation in the workforce or segments of the qualified, eligible, regional workforce from which employer can draw.	b. Meaning of employment equity Designated employers must: • identify and eliminate illegal discriminatory employment practices, in consultation with bargaining agent or designated employees • institute positive policies/practices, and make reasonable accommodation, to ensure target group members' participation throughout organization is proportionate to their representation in the workforce or segments of the qualified, eligible, regional workforce from which employer can draw.
No provisions outlined.	These obligations do not require an employer to: • undertake employment equity measures that would cause employer undue hardship • hire or promote unqualified persons. Seniority rights are not deemed to be employment barriers unless found to constitute discrimination under the Canadian Human Rights Act.

c. Consultation with employees

Employers must implement employment equity in consultation with bargaining agent or persons designated by employees to act as representatives.

d. Employment equity plans

Employers are required to prepare an annual plan of goals and a timetable for implementation, and retain plans for three years after last year covered by plan.

c. Consultation with employees

Employers must consult employees' representatives – the bargaining agent if present – on ways to facilitate employment equity, devise plan, and communicate plan to employees.

d. Employment equity plans

Employers are required to:

- collect information and analyze workforce to assess degree of under-representation of target group members in each occupational group
- establish short-term numerical goals for hiring and promotion of target groups to increase their representation in occupational groups where under-representation is identified. Goals to be set with consideration of availability of qualified persons and anticipated growth, reduction, and turnover of employer's workforce.
- update goals at least once in plan cycle
- conduct a review of employment systems to identify barriers against target groups
- prepare a plan and timetable for instituting positive policies and practices to improve the employment opportunities for target groups and remove systemic employment barriers
- set out long-term goals/plans for increasing representation of target group members
- make reasonable efforts to implement employment equity plans and monitor these routinely.

▲ *Table 9.1*

1986 Employment Equity Act (Conservative government)	1995 Employment Equity Act (Liberal government)
e. Filing employment equity reports Employers must submit certified annual report to the minister of Employment and Immigration, in form prescribed, showing proportional • hirings • sectoral location • occupations • salary ranges • promotions • terminations of target group members, and retain reports for three years. No provisions outlined.	e. Filing employment equity reports Employers must submit certified annual report to the minister of Human Resources Development, in the form prescribed, showing proportional • hirings • sectoral location • occupations • salary ranges • promotions • terminations of target group members. Employers must include in report a description of • measures taken during the reporting period to implement employment equity and results • consultations with employers' representatives concerning implementation of employment equity. Employer must provide copy of report to the employees' representatives.
f. Responsibilities of government Minister must file copy of reports with the CHRC. Minister must make reports available for public inspection, subject to copying fee.	f. Responsibilities of government Minister must file copy of reports with the CHRC. Minister must make reports available for public inspection unless special circumstances warrant withholding information for one year.

Minister must prepare annual consolidated report to Parliament.

No provisions outlined.

No provisions outlined.

g. Compliance with legislation
No provisions outlined.

Minister must prepare annual consolidated report to Parliament.

Minister is responsible for fostering public understanding of the legislation.

Minister is responsible for administration of the Federal Contractors Program and must ensure that requirements are equivalent to those required of employers under the Employment Equity Act.

President of Treasury Board must prepare annual consolidated report to Parliament showing total numbers of target group employees and their proportions in

• occupational groups
• salary ranges
• hirings
• promotions
• terminations.

Report must also describe principal measures taken to improve employment equity in public sector and consultation with employees' representatives.

Canadian Security Intelligence Service must file similar reports with president of Treasury Board.

President of Treasury Board must file copies of public sector reports with the CHRC and with employees' representatives.

g. Compliance with legislation
CHRC is responsible for enforcing obligations imposed on employers. Whenever possible, causes of noncompliance should be resolved through persuasion and negotiation of written undertakings.

▼ Table 9.1

1986 Employment Equity Act (Conservative government)	1995 Employment Equity Act (Liberal government)
	CHRC compliance officers may conduct audits at any reasonable time if they have grounds for so doing. Employers are required to assist in these inquiries. If officers conclude that employment equity plans are not being implemented, then they must negotiate written remedy with employer. This undertaking may be adjusted on presentation of new facts. If employer fails to carry out written agreement, an employment equity review tribunal may be established to assess non-compliance. Tribunal orders become orders of the Federal Court.
Employers who fail to submit reports will be liable to a maximum fine of $50,000.	Employers who fail to comply with legislation liable to initial fine of $10,000, thereafter $50,000.
h. Review of the Employment Equity Act Review of the EEA will be carried out five years after coming into force and every three years after that.	h. Review of the Employment Equity Act Review of the EEA will be carried out five years after coming into force and every five years after that.

Sources: *Employment Equity Act*, S.C. 1986, c. 31; *Employment Equity Act*, S.C. 1995, c. 44.

C-64 still gave employers complete flexibility in choosing how to develop and implement employment equity programs. This, however, was welcomed by the bureaucrats. As Neil Gavigan explained, "Although many employment equity practitioners believe in the importance of mandatory measures, if you make the legislation too strong, you will actually do a disservice, because you create a compliance nightmare that would probably kill more initiative than it supported."[14]

While the passing of Bill C-64 meant that federally regulated employers were required to be more self-conscious in the design, implementation, and monitoring of employment equity measures, it is also clear that the government's expectations of what employers could achieve were shaped both by the culture of restructuring and the backlash against employment equity that had taken hold since the introduction of the EEA (Table 9.1.b and d). This backlash was fuelled not only by the emergence of the Reform Party as a significant force in federal politics but also by the 1995 election of Conservative Mike Harris, who became premier of Ontario after campaigning hard against Ontario's new employment equity legislation. As Neil Gavigan reflected, "When the [EEA] was passed in 1986, the front page on the *Ottawa Citizen* the next day was that this was a toothless sham. When the Act was passed again in 1995, all journalists were talking about quotas and reverse discrimination so the whole atmosphere had changed, in part in reaction to the Ontario Employment Equity Act."[15]

The Liberal government in Ottawa – elected as it had been on the strength of winning all but one of the ninety-nine seats in Ontario – was determined to show itself to be more moderate than the provincial Conservatives. Nonetheless, the force of the anti-quota rhetoric that characterized the times in which Bill C-64 was developed clearly had an impact on the legislation. As a result, the legislation protected employers against having to introduce measures that would cause economic hardship, necessitate the hiring or promotion of unqualified people, or, in the case of the federal public service, negate the principle of appointment on the basis of qualification and merit. In addition, the legislation emphasized that employers would not be required to develop employment equity targets that were out of line with labour market projections (Table 9.1.b).

The other important way in which Bill C-64 superseded the 1986 EEA was that it clarified the regulatory and audit responsibilities roles of HRDC and the CHRC (Table 9.1.f and g). Clarification did seem to be necessary as some conflicts had begun to emerge between the CHRC and the former Canadian Employment and Immigration Commission (CEIC) in the course of developing their work in response to the EEA. As Rhys Phillips – as the Chief of Legislation and Program Development in the Employment Equity Branch at CHRC – noted, "What was missing from the 1986 Employment Equity Act was any sort of enforcement procedure and the ability, in an effective way, to ensure that employers actually did what they were supposed to do."[16] As a result the CHRC had been left with two options under the 1986 Act. It could invite companies that seemed to be demonstrating major under-representation to undergo a "voluntary joint review" (which they did in about twenty-five cases). If companies failed to comply with that process, the CHRC could initiate a complaint under section 10 of the Canadian Human Rights Act (which happened in two cases against the Canadian Broadcasting Corporation and Bell Canada).[17]

While Bill C-64 gave the minister of Human Resources Development powers to publicize the new legislation, research its impact, and oversee the Federal Contractors Program, it gave the CHRC systematic powers for reviewing reports, conducting audits, securing compliance, and, in cases where this failed, the capacity to refer the matter to a special Employment Equity Tribunal. By the end of 1998 the CHRC had initiated 109 audits, which, as Rhys Phillips reflected, showed that "in the ten years [since the EEA had been in effect], most of those employers who didn't have us knocking at their door, hadn't come close to what they should have done."[18] However, Neil Gavigan cautioned,

> I think the real test of the audit isn't right now. What [colleagues at the CHRC] are finding is similar to what we found under the contractors program, which is that companies, even though they have been obliged for some time to implement employment equity, really haven't done anything much. At this particular stage the commission is just negotiating the principles. That's a pretty straightforward step. Where it will get complicated for them is in the next phase, when they go and see what has actually been done and find that, in some cases, the employers haven't quite made it. That is when we'll see how flexible the commission is or how effective they can be in achieving the kind of compliance that is necessary.[19]

Nonetheless, by providing the CHRC and HRDC with more clearly defined roles, Bill C-64 set the context for a more constructive relationship not only between government and the federally regulated employers covered by the legislation, but also between the two agencies themselves. Indeed, the legislation distinguished the identification and redress of discrimination from the development and implementation of employment equity. As Neil Gavigan reflected, this freed officials in the Workplace Equity Branch of HRDC to pursue a no-fault approach to employment equity:

> If I accuse you – as a human resources manager at company X – of discrimination, your immediate reaction is to say "No" and get your lawyers. What we wanted to say is, "Look, let's assume that discrimination is alive

and ... well ... let's get off that, and say instead that what we have here is a situation where target group representation is low. Let's look at the positive side and think how can your company's action plan deal with that?" That's the language that business people live with and work with and that gets them off defending the status quo – "No I didn't hurt anybody, I didn't discriminate against anybody" – we can argue that till we're blue in the face and we will get nowhere.[20]

Interestingly, the Act's clarification of the roles of the CHRC and HRDC seemed to facilitate bureaucratic cooperation rather than competition between the two agencies. Undoubtedly this process was facilitated by the fact that key actors in both agencies were "old friends," having worked in the human rights and employment equity business for some time, and made a concerted effort "to share information, have regular management-style meetings, use each other's data and meet to talk about the issues."[21] At the same time, however, the CHRC's new capacity to audit the work of departments and agencies within the federal government appears to have created some strains in the relationship between the Human Rights Commission and the Treasury Board Secretariat. As Elizabeth Bertoldi, a program officer in the Employment Equity Division of the Secretariat explained, "There is a difference in the philosophy of the two organizations. While both organizations expect departments and agencies to conform to the legislation, the Treasury Board Secretariat sets frameworks, policy, and guidelines, and has emphasized creating a hospitable working environment for employees. The Canadian Human Rights Commission, on the other hand, uses a strict set of criteria based on the legislation and is auditing departments to ensure their compliance with the law."[22] Such tensions undoubtedly arose because the Treasury Board Secretariat had always controlled the development of its own employment equity programs. Some effort to address them was made in 1997, when the CHRC and the Treasury Board Secretariat signed a memorandum of understanding clarifying the relationship between these two arms of government. This memorandum established that there should be meetings "to address issues of interdepartmental significance picked up during the audit process."[23]

The Federal Contractors Program

While Bill C-64 clearly intensified the degree of accountability for employment equity procedures within the federal bureaucracy and within companies regulated by the federal government, companies under contract to the federal government were not to be subject to audits from the CHRC. As in 1986, the Federal Contractors Program (FCP) was kept distinct from the legislative program in order that the federal government not be considered to be encroaching on areas of provincial jurisdiction. Nonetheless, the status of the FCP improved with the introduction of Bill C-64 because it obtained legislative mention. As Michael Paliga, director of the FCP in HRDC explained, "That does not mean that we have a law, but we have implications from the law. And since it is mentioned in the law, the Federal Contractors Program is no longer a program that one can simply get rid of. In the past, many organizations representing designated groups felt that because we were simply nothing more than a circular that was passed around by the Treasury Board, at a moment's notice, with the strike of a pen, someone could have said, 'Well, we do not need this program around.' Now you would have to go through the House to remove it, so that is one important change."[24]

However, while those overseeing the FCP now had to ensure that the 750 companies covered by the program "maintained equivalence with the Act," the employment equity regulations imposed on companies under contract to the federal government remained less stringent than those imposed on organizations covered by the EEA.[25] Companies under contract to the government still only have to sign a certificate of compliance rather than report on their progress year by year. Moreover, although companies are still subject to a review process by officers running the FCP, the restructuring of HRDC and the downsizing of staff engaged in various aspects of the employment equity program means that companies are now reviewed every three or four years, rather than every two or three.[26] Moreover, while the 340 organizations covered by the legislative program have had to submit data annually, companies under the FCP are not required to do so. As a result it is impossible for those managing the FCP to build up a profile of the effectiveness of the program. As Michael Paliga noted, "We have no way of reporting on or measuring progress. If somebody was to say, 'Can you sit down and tell me how the program is working, can you show me some stuff that you would think would substantiate that?' Well, we can't."[27] Indeed, the fact that only eight companies have ever been removed from the contract bidding process does raise questions about the effectiveness of the FCP to ensure that proposed employment equity plans are implemented in these organizations. Given that the program covers more than twice the number of companies covered under the legislative program, the limits on its effectiveness may require closer scrutiny.

Assessing the 1995 Employment Equity Act

Bill C-64 was an improvement on the 1986 EEA, but it did not depart fundamentally from the principles of the legislation that was introduced by the Conservatives in 1986. The new Liberal government expanded the remit of the legislation to include the government's own bureaucracy, paid greater attention to the procedures for developing and monitoring employment equity, and increased the capacity of the CHRC to ensure that employers complied with the legislation. At the same time, however, the Liberals were even more explicit than the Conservatives had been in allowing employers flexibility to adjust their employment equity targets and plans in relation to the economic climate, labour force availability, and other extraneous circumstances.

When Axworthy introduced the final reading of Bill C-64, he claimed that as a result of being "on an extended sabbatical on the other side of the house" when the 1986 EEA was passed, he had not been "in a position to fully implement" the recommendations of Justice Abella's "very historic report."[28] It is true that in giving the CHRC greater powers to ensure compliance with the Act, Axworthy had honoured an important part of the spirit of the report of the Royal Commission on Equality in Employment. However, although the 1995 Employment Equity Act (Bill C-64) broadened the gamut of the legislation introduced by the Conservatives nine years earlier and tightened the procedures for ensuring compliance with its regulations, the fundamental purposes of each Act remained the same. The second clause of both Acts states that the principal objective of employment equity legislation is to "achieve equality in the work place so that no person shall be denied employment opportunities or benefits for reasons unrelated to ability."[29] In addition, both pieces of legislation were designed to "correct the conditions of disadvantage experienced by women, aboriginal peoples, persons with disabilities and persons who are, because of their race and colour, in a visible minority in Canada by giving effect to the principle that employment equity means more than treating people in the same way but also requires special measures and the accommodation of differences."[30] However, although employers were now required to submit a description of the measures taken to implement employment equity in their organizations, no specific measures to recognize the particular contexts in which women or members of the three other target groups took up and continued with paid employment were built into the legislation.[31] Moreover, as the annual employment equity reports issued by HRDC since the Act came into force contain relatively brief discussion of the qualitative measures implemented by employers, it is not clear whether any employment equity plans have included provision for child care in order to promote women's employment.[32]

Nonetheless, the fact that Lloyd Axworthy introduced the 1995 EEA just two months before he made an offer to the provinces to proceed with a new national child care initiative suggests that in his mind, at least, there may have been a symbolic link between these two areas of public policy. However, although Axworthy alluded to this initiative when he introduced the third reading of Bill C-64 in the House of Commons, he did so in the context of informing parliamentary colleagues about the rapidly declining participation of single mothers in the workforce.[33] The question this raised was whether the minister responsible for the Liberal government's human resource strategy would, in the end, only be able to think about the development of child care in the context of women's basic employability rather than their enjoyment of gender equality in the paid workplace.

Rock-a-Bye Red Book: The Liberals and Child Care

As earlier chapters in this book have shown, questions about federal involvement in child care have often been shaped by broader debates about women enjoying equal employment opportunities with men. By the early 1990s, however, there was a growing recognition within the child care movement, within the Liberal Party, and among child care experts within the federal bureaucracy that issues of women's employment did not provide the only lens on child care. Key advocates in the child care movement, influenced by discussions with their European counterparts, became increasingly conscious that they might have more success at securing a national child care program if they highlighted the important benefits that child care brought to children rather than simply focusing on how such provision could enhance gender equality in the workplace.[34] Moreover, at least one key strategist within the Liberal Party began to realize that child care questions needed to be reframed if they were going to move back up the federal government's policy agenda.

Chaviva Hošek, a former president of the National Action Committee on the Status of Women (NAC), had by this time become co-chair of the Liberal Party's Platform Committee.[35] In 1992 and 1993, she and her co-chair, Paul Martin, toured the country, "meeting and listening with thousands of Canadians" before drafting the Red Book.[36] According to one observer, during these meetings Hošek began to realize that one of the reasons parents' demands for child care provision were still unmet was that the issue was still defined primarily in relation to gender equality.[37] As a result, she recognized that it was important to place questions of child care in a broader context within the Liberal Party's election manifesto.

Hošek persuaded the Liberal Party to include child care in the Red Book by arguing that it represented an investment in Canada's youngest citizens, who, in time, would form Canada's workforce.[38] Those close to her claim that she strongly believed child care needed to be addressed not simply as an element of the government's social policy but also as a question integral to economic policy. As one observer commented, "By including child care in the Red Book, Hošek was trying to get her tough, bottom-line colleagues to recognize that it is good economic policy to put child care up front as it is not just a question of providing care for children but investing in people who will be affected by that service later on."[39] Nonetheless, while Hošek's perspective may have focused on the benefits of child care for young children, others in the Liberal Party were probably thinking that child care could be used as a mechanism to get "welfare" mothers out to work. Indeed, the competition to define child care as an issue related to child development, on the one hand, and parental employability, on the other, had also taken root among federal bureaucrats working on the "kids' file" in Health Canada and HRDC.

Once in office, the new Liberal government certainly began to address the promises on child care that it had made in the Red Book. Sandra Harder, a researcher in the Social and Political Affairs Division of the Library of Parliament, remembers getting "a lot of requests in my job for information on child care at that point. Questions about costing, issues on quality ... the components of good child care, those kind of things."[40] It was also apparent to child care bureaucrats in HRDC that the Liberals were determined to act on their election promises but were not entirely clear about the most effective way to get all the different provinces on side. As Ron Yzerman, former director of Child Care Programs in HRDC, reflected after his retirement,

> When the Liberals came into power they took the first couple of months to adjust, then the concern was "How do we now act on our Red Book commitments over all, but specific to the social policy area and more specifically to child care – what do we do folks? We have a commitment, it's only one paragraph in the [Red] Book, what the heck does it mean? It said there was going to be cost sharing – enhanced cost sharing over and above the existing program – so what do we do?" The question was put to us because there was just one little unit in the department called Child Care.[41]

In fact, Ron Yzerman and his colleague Don Ogston were dispatched to woo the provinces and assess how receptive their governments were to the idea of a new shared-cost program in the field of child care. As Yzerman explained, he and Ogston were told,

> "Well, you guys had better go out there and meet with the provinces, and see how receptive they are to the Red Book commitment on child care," meaning see what they think it means, because if we go back a bit, even in 1987 when we were developing the National Strategy on Child Care, some provinces had indicated that child care was not high on their agenda. So it couldn't be taken for granted that child care was a number one priority, or indeed a priority of any sort in some provinces, so we knew that it couldn't be assumed that all provinces were going to welcome a federal initiative on child care.[42]

The provincial tour of Yzerman and Ogston became known in the child care community as "the Ron and Don show."[43] The circuit was not entirely straightforward for HRDC's bureaucrats. After all, the richer provinces had been angered by the Mulroney government's cap on CAP. Moreover, by the time the Liberals got into power, the provinces were beginning to put pressure on Ottawa to devolve social policy and allow their governments greater flexibility in devising social programs.[44] Ron Yzerman recalled those meetings with provincial officials in the following way:

> Don and I jumped on an airplane and away we went. We visited all the provinces and territories and they said a variety of things, none of which was unexpected. They said, "Yes, we are always pleased to hear that the federal government wants to spend money, but we have a number of reservations." The first thing they said was, "Don't talk to us if there is any time limit put on your funding because the days of you coming in and creating demand and then leaving us to foot the bill long-term are over, and so if you are not talking ongoing commitment, don't come." That was at the officials' level, but I think it was true at the political level as well. They didn't want to talk unless they were sure the feds were in for the long haul. Secondly, they said, "We don't want to talk to you if there is going to be a lot of overlap and duplication. We want flexibility so that we have a role in the design of the program." Then of course every province, depending on their political stripe, had their pet little thing. Funding was an issue, variable cost-sharing rose its head, some provinces were saying, "Well, we can't do it unless we get 90 percent funding." None of these things was unexpected, but what we were looking for when we went out was whether there was a willingness to discuss an initiative, or were they going to be digging in their heels so that it would be a nonstarter from day one. That was the real intent.[45]

Interestingly, the child care bureaucrats in Ottawa decided not simply to try to get their provincial counterparts on side but also to build support for their initiative within the child care community. Indeed, in the course of their provincial tour, Yzerman and Ogston made a point of meeting with child care activists "to discuss issues of mutual concern and strategize about how to advance the case of child care."[46] In addition, in February 1994 they scheduled a meeting in Montreal "not simply because it was central, so to speak, and easily accessible by plane, but also because we wanted to include our colleagues from Quebec, because in terms of child care they're miles ahead of us – years ahead."[47] Billed as "A Vision for Child Care into the 21st Century," the Montreal meeting was designed to "identify the strengths and weaknesses of current child care policies and practices, ... elaborate a shared vision for the future of child care in Canada, ... identify core values important in guiding child care policy in Canada, ... enhance collaboration between non-governmental and governmental sectors involved in child care and ... identify key themes and areas for action to realize the shared vision during the next decade."[48] It not only created a meeting point for the different regional representatives of the child care community but – like the Winnipeg conference in 1982 – brought together "the disparate parties in the child care community ... the Advocacy Association, the Child Care Federation, the advocates, the researchers, and the federal and provincial bureaucrats."[49]

The Montreal meeting provides two important indicators about the nature of the child care community in Canada in the mid-1990s. First, in contrast to the child care consultations that the Mulroney government carried out during the hearings of the Special Committee on Child Care, there were no commercial operators present. Second, although Nadine Pinton and Pat Storey were invited to participate as representatives of the federal Women's Program and Farm Women's Program, no other representatives of women's agencies or organizations were present at the meeting.[50] Moreover, the final report of the meeting contained only one brief reference to the relationship between women and child care, when it noted a "growing recognition of [the] inter-relationship of child care with other programs e.g. women's organizations; addictions; agricultural development."[51]

While the shared vision of delegates at the Montreal meeting emphasized the importance of recognizing child care as "a collective responsibility and facilitating equity," the equitable society that the participants had in mind was more concerned with ensuring the equal treatment of Canada's children than that of male and female parents employed in the Canadian labour force.[52] Indeed, while those attending the meeting were content that the Red Book "makes a clear statement about collective responsibility for child care," they were concerned that because it "focuses solely on the needs of mothers in the labour force [it] shifts child care away from children's needs and thus threatens quality."[53] Indeed, those present at the meeting were concerned that "the employability focus [of the Red Book] loses the perspective of viewing child care as a social investment, which is primarily supportive of children."[54] The old tension about whether child care was designed to serve children or their working mothers was re-emerging, but this time it was being raised around questions of women's employability rather than their enjoyment of equal employment opportunities with men.

The fact that members of the child care community were so concerned about the Red Book's emphasis on the relationship between child care and women's employability was not simply a reflection of their long campaign to achieve quality child care as a service developed for children. It also highlighted the fact that on 31 January 1994, just days before the Montreal meeting, Lloyd Axworthy had announced the establishment of the Social Security Review (SSR).[55] This major review and accompanying public consultation on "how best to redesign and reform Canada's system of social security" was carried out by the Standing Committee on Human Resources Development, with "particular reference to the needs of families with children, youth and working age adults."[56] In the end, the three broad themes of caring for children, investing in people, and enhancing security and fairness informed the committee's final report.[57] However, at the point when the SSR was announced, it was not at all clear that the provision of child care – as a service – would be included in its remit.

Child Care and the 1994 Social Security Review

In many senses, the fact that child care proved central to the final analysis of the Standing Committee on Human Resources Development was a victory – albeit a pyrrhic victory – for the child care movement. As Martha Friendly recalled, "The Social Security Review didn't originally include child care and so I called up the clerk of the committee and said, 'What about child care?' And whoever it was said, 'What do you mean, child care?' And I said, 'How can you have a review of social programs without including child care?' So I put it on paper and my impression is that it was questions like mine that led to child care being included in the SSR."[58] As Sandra Harder, the key sociological researcher on the SSR, who was seconded for this purpose from her regular post in the Library of Parliament reflected, "Questions about child care were not front and centre of the SSR at the outset. In fact as the sociological researcher for that committee, I kept saying, 'We've got to draft child care in there.' But, you see, because of the nature of child care in Canada, you can't go to a place under the bureaucratic map and say, 'Boom, there's child care and it falls under the mandate of the SSR.' But child care got included, in a large part because the child care advocates were saying, 'You've got to include the child care sector in the review.'"[59]

The Framework for the Social Security Review

In October 1994, Lloyd Axworthy, as minister for Human Resources Development, released a discussion paper outlining the parameters for social security reform. Entitled *Agenda: Jobs and Growth, Improving Social Security in Canada,* the Green Paper (as it became known) clearly located the Social Security Review within the context of the government's economic agenda:

> The status quo is not an option. Changes in our economy, in our families, in our workplaces, in our communities, and in the financial standing of

our country are too dramatic to allow us to tinker at the edges of social policy and programming. The fact is that Canada's social security system needs to be fixed. It is an important task, something all Canadians will be asked over the coming months to consider carefully and participate in. This generation must use its ingenuity to rebuild our social programs for a new era, just as an earlier generation after the Second World War forged solutions to meet the social needs of the post-war world.[60]

However, while the Green Paper emphasized that the four key components of the federal government's agenda for jobs and growth were "reforming social security, ensuring a healthy fiscal climate, reviewing government programs and priorities, and strengthening the performance of the Canadian economy," in true Axworthian style it also noted at the outset that "our economic and social priorities are interdependent."[61] Thus it emphasized that the SSR was designed "to build a social security system that enables all Canadians, children and adults alike, to obtain a fair and equal opportunity to exploit their talents, lead fulfilling lives, and experience the dignity of work."[62] However, it is also clear that the SSR was established to develop a new model of citizenship, based on a much greater degree of self-reliance: "Providing basic support for those in need and those who cannot work is unquestioned. But for those with the potential to help themselves, improved government support must be targeted at those who demonstrate a willingness and commitment to self help."[63] Federal government involvement in the field of child care was therefore likely to be directed at women who managed to get themselves off welfare and into paid work.

While questions about creating jobs for men and women rather than ensuring their equity in the workplace drove the SSR, the Green Paper acknowledged that "for most Canadian parents ... finding and paying for child care is one of their biggest concerns. In many cases, the lack of affordable, high quality child care is an insurmountable barrier to a job."[64] Indeed, the paper emphasized that "the federal government sees child care as a priority for the reform of social security programs, lying at the heart of the three areas ... working, learning and security."[65] At the same time, it noted how child care could contribute to child development because "child care is more than an employment measure if it also provides children with a good environment in which to grow and learn. Effective child care can help to ensure the future success of children who might otherwise be at risk."[66] Moreover, it emphasized that "linking child care and child development could represent a comprehensive and preventative approach to social problems at the earliest point in life."[67] In short, the paper indicated that while questions of child care might be relevant to debates about gender equity from the federal government's perspective, they lay at the nexus of social security concerns about women's employability and child development.

The link between child care and women's employability was reinforced in the Supplementary Paper on Child Care and Development, published at the same time as Axworthy's Green Paper.[68] This emphasized the links between child care, work, and citizenship by showing how child care lay at the centre of four overlapping policy circles designed to support parental access to the labour force, enhance child development, ensure the foundations of early childhood education, and create jobs for child care workers.[69] The paper highlighted "child care as an important support for parental employment and a priority for any new social security system in Canada."[70] However, it also stressed that "although Canadians increasingly recognize that both parents have responsibility for the care of their children ... mothers bear most of the responsibility and stress in securing quality, affordable child care, and are most likely to leave their jobs if there are problems with child care."[71] Indeed, while the paper identified child care "as an important measure to promote women's economic independence," it underscored how "the lack of affordable child care helps keep lone mothers out of the labour force and dependent on social assistance."[72] Moreover, it stressed that while the "lack of affordable child care is a barrier to labour force participation" of low-income parents, its absence also impedes child development because "quality care is essential to meet child development goals."[73] In short, like the Green Paper that it accompanied, this supplementary paper reinforced the fact that child care could meet the twin goals of promoting women's employability and enhancing child development.

Public Testimony to the Social Security Review
The Social Security Review was not, however, simply an exercise conducted within the offices of HRDC. As one observer noted, "It was a three-ring circus going on in Axworthy's advisory panel, within the central agencies and in the public hearings conducted by the Standing Committee on Human Resources Development."[74] The SSR received a huge volume of oral and written testimony from the public. Over 1,200 written submissions "in printed form, on audio or video cassette or diskette" were received by the Standing Committee on Human Resources Development.[75] In addition, when the committee travelled from coast to coast to coast they heard oral testimony from an additional 637 citizens.[76] Significantly, research by Michelle Turiano reveals that 30 percent of those presenting material to the committee during its public hearings brought up the question of child care.[77] Moreover, her analysis shows that while, as one might expect in a review of social security programs, those presenting testimony

to the SSR most frequently positioned the question of child care as an anti-poverty measure, 37.6 percent of those participating in the hearings emphasized the importance of child care to women.[78]

Both NAC and the Child Care Advocacy Association of Canada (CCAAC) presented evidence to the Standing Committee on Human Resources Development. While their submissions raised questions of women's equality and those of child care, interestingly it was the brief from NAC that most explicitly linked the two issues together. This argued that "a national childcare program is fundamental to eradicating women's poverty, and to enable women to participate in the paid workforce on an equitable basis."[79] By contrast, while the CCAAC claimed that their model of social security reform would "recognize the promotion of women's equality as central," their calls for a national, universally accessible system of child care that was properly funded to ensure healthy child development focused on the needs of children more than on those of their mothers.[80]

Interestingly, key women's organizations proved to be far more critical of the SSR as an exercise in the development of social policy than national child care organizations. For example, the final report of the National Women's Consultation on the SSR emphasized women's dismay at the way "the Green Paper's proposals, in combination with the government's economic policies, represent the implementation of the neo-liberal economic restructuring in the Canadian context."[81] Similarly, the presentation from NAC noted that "it is of great concern to NAC that the Social Security Review is informed by a complete absence of gender analysis. The discussion paper is based on a conceptual framework which addressed social policy from the experience of ... youth, children and families, and working adults. Women, who are 52% of the population, are therefore made invisible in this conceptual framework."[82]

By contrast, even though briefs from the CCAAC and the Child Care Federation of Canada differed on whether child care should be publicly or privately funded, the briefs from both national organizations demonstrated far less criticism of the parameters of the SSR than those submitted by NAC and the National Women's Consultation.[83] This is not entirely surprising. As Gillian Doherty and her colleagues have noted, "For the child care community, the Social Security Review seemed to be a good opportunity to reinforce the idea of a national child care program."[84] However, while the child care community felt optimistic that the SSR had recognized how child care formed a link between questions of citizen's employability and child development, feminists active in the women's movement could see the link between questions about the provision of child care and those of gender equity in the workforce getting weaker all the time.

Report of the Standing Committee on Human Resources Development

In some respects, women's organizations need not have been so concerned about the shifting context in which questions of child care seemed to be being discussed. When the report of the Standing Committee on Human Resources Development was published in January 1995, its authors did not flinch from acknowledging the link between gender equity and child care. As they noted, "Presentations by women's groups across the country detailed the barriers faced by women that prevent their full economic participation, including high levels of poverty, greater risk of becoming poor, unequal access to training and employment opportunities, segregation into low-paying employment, primary responsibility for child and elder care, disproportionate share of work and family responsibilities, and violence in the home and in the workplace. Women with disabilities, Aboriginal women, and visible minority women face additional attitudinal and cultural barriers."[85] As a result, the committee recommended that "the reform of social security programs be subjected to gender-based analysis to ensure women's increased and equal social and economic participation in the paid labour market."[86] It also argued that in order "to alleviate the high levels of women's poverty, reforms to social programs must eliminate occupational and financial barriers to women's economic advancement and promote an equitable sharing of work and family responsibilities."[87] Moreover, the report recommended not only that the "federal government, as a major employer, provide greater opportunities for flexible work arrangements ... to help workers balance family and paid work responsibilities and ... stimulate employment," but also that "the federal government develop initiatives to measure unwaged work and estimate its economic value."[88]

The report of the Standing Committee on Human Resources Development did link questions of child care with those of gender equality. It argued that "since most of the work of caring for Canada's children is performed by women, adequate child care is absolutely essential to provide women with the choices and flexibility they need to live and work as full and equal participants in Canadian society."[89] It endorsed the public's concern that "the current patchwork nature of child care in Canada does not adequately ensure that both formal and informal child care settings are of a consistently high quality, reflective of current knowledge of early childhood development needs."[90] Moreover, it reaffirmed the Liberals' Red Book commitment to provide additional child care spaces and called on the government to confer with the provinces and territories about how best to achieve this objective.[91]

Reflecting the increased government focus on child care as a key component of healthy child development, the report noted how many people who had presented evidence to the committee "underscored the importance of preparing children for healthy development, and many saw high quality child care as a key contributor to this process."[92] Moreover, the committee reported that it had been presented with "persuasive arguments" that there was too great a variation in the costs of child care across the country and that the limited availability of subsidized child care spaces needed to be addressed.[93] Although the committee noted that it had also received testimony from "those who spoke against the implementation of a coordinated approach to child care" and argued, instead, for the retention of fiscal subsidies to parents purchasing child care, there was little doubt that the committee favoured a move towards "fundamental reforms to child care in the context of the social security review."[94]

The report also noted how many witnesses were concerned that "the Green Paper fell short of advocating and endorsing the implementation of an overall national child care program" and called for "upcoming federal-provincial-territorial negotiations to agree on a set of principles that would form the heart of a national child care program."[95] As Martha Friendly noted, "This already represented a big shift from the feds coming up with principles to suggesting that the provinces and territories should do so."[96] The report emphasized that while those concerned with child care had demonstrated "strong support for a continuing federal government leadership role in CAP to maintain national standards," they also "stressed the need to revamp the way the federal government finances child care."[97] Indeed, the report called for new funding arrangements, stressing that "the current federal financing arrangements, where child care is funded under CAP in the context of 'welfare services,' [provided] an inadequate approach."[98]

Demise of the Social Security Review
Although the SSR was designed as a comprehensive review of federal government services to ensure the social security of Canadian citizens, the review itself got out of hand. Many different factors contributed to its demise. At a practical level, the process was complicated because the different elements of the review taking place in Axworthy's advisory panel, in the public hearings conducted by the parliamentary committee and within the central agencies in Ottawa, were not coordinated. Moreover, the government placed on the standing committee expectations of a royal commission without giving its members the full support they needed to carry out extensive public consultations. At a political level, the federal government realized that it could not carry out a comprehensive review of social security without examining provincial programs and, in an era of mounting tension around Quebec's pursuit of sovereignty, this was simply not

appropriate. Finally, from an economic standpoint, although the SSR was fiscally driven from the outset, there is little doubt that once the federal government realized that the parameters of the review were expanding, the Department of Finance really stepped in.[99] As one observer noted, "It became less of Axworthy's review and more of Paul Martin's review."[100]

The impact of the government's financial agenda on the SSR became acutely apparent in the early days of 1995. In fact it was so powerful that the SSR was closed down and, as a result, the report of the Standing Committee on Human Resources Development became little more than a work in progress, redrafted by the Department of Finance before it was made public. As an HRDC policy analyst explained, fiscal and devolutionary pressures brought that closure about: "There were two factors that caused [the closure of the SSR]. One was obviously the need to chop an enormous amount, but it was also the federal/provincial dynamic that was to move to a far less conditional kind of broad transfer to the provinces. It's hard to say which of those two factors would be the biggest one, because they [were] both significant."[101]

The closure of the SSR was unfortunate for both the women's movement and for the child care movement. After all, the final report of the Standing Committee on Human Resources Development had reinforced the claims that women had made about the need to link questions of their employment with those of child care. Moreover, although the report had not recommended the adoption of a national child care act, it had emphasized the importance of federal-provincial/territorial coordination in a review of funding arrangements for child care under CAP. However, as Martha Friendly recalled, when the report was published in January 1995, there was a strong sense among social activists that "the terrain had really shifted ... rumours were flying around that the federal government was going to dump everything."[102] Indeed, as one observer reflected, when Paul Martin revealed the contents of the 1995 budget in February of that year, the initial optimism that surrounded the inclusion of child care within the SSR "went crashing."[103]

The 1995 Budget and the Introduction of the
Canada Health and Social Transfer
The introduction of the Canada Health and Social Transfer (CHST) in the Liberal's famous 1995 budget signalled a radical restructuring of the federal welfare state. The CHST replaced CAP and Established Programs Financing arrangements with "a block grant from the federal government to the provinces and territories as a contribution to their expenditures for health, social assistance and related social programs and post-secondary education"[104] As a result, even though the 1994 federal budget had made it seem that the Liberals' election promise on child care would be realized,

the restructuring of federal-provincial/territorial fiscal relations that accompanied the announcement of the CHST meant that most of the allocations were subsequently withdrawn.

The announcement of the CHST put child care advocates and, indeed, many other social activists in a tail spin. The block funding that was inherent in the CHST not only removed the specific identification of child care funding that had been present in CAP but diminished the federal government's leverage over the development of provincial social programs.[105] Moreover, under the CHST, federal transfers to the provinces declined in real terms. As Bach and Phillips note, "In 1997 the federal government [spent] approximately one-third less ($105 million) on child care services for the general population than it [did] in 1993; and roughly $274 million less than it had promised in the Red Book."[106] These enormous reductions were due to the CHST cuts that "abolished the $300 million portion of CAP directed annually to child care."[107]

Martha Friendly recalls that "it was really hard to follow what was going on in the federal government that year, because [when they introduced the CHST in February 1995] the Liberals didn't immediately dump the Red Book commitment to child care. They only dumped CAP."[108] The question then became whether Lloyd Axworthy as minister of Human Resources Development could hang on to the Red Book's proposed financial allocation for child care in a period of increasing fiscal gloom. Even if Axworthy did manage to do so, could he realistically hope to secure provincial cooperation with a federal government shared-cost initiative on child care in the wake of the federal government's announcement of the CHST?

Axworthy's National Child Care Program in the Context of Increased Devolution

After two rounds of negotiations with the provinces, the federal government did in fact announce its proposal for a national child care program. On 13 December 1995, Axworthy unveiled the government's response to its Red Book promise on child care at a press conference in which he shared the platform with Ovide Mercredi, Grand Chief of the Assembly of First Nations and Martha Flaherty, president of Pauktuutit, the Inuit Women's Association of Canada. Declaring that "child care is an important tool to the government's jobs and growth agenda," Axworthy outlined the program's three components.[109] These were, first, an allocation of $72 million, over the next five years, to provide up to 6,000 child care spaces for First Nations and Inuit infants and children; second, the establishment of Child Care Visions, a research and development program of $18 million (including a special grant of $1.6 million to the Canadian Child Care Federation "to establish a national clearing house and resource centre for child care providers and users across the country"); and, third, an offer to the provinces and territories of $630 million over the next three to five years to promote intergovernmental collaboration in the financing of additional child care spaces.[110]

Later that day, despite attempts by bureaucrats in the Department of Finance to block its dissemination, a letter from Axworthy was faxed to the provinces and territories outlining the offer and clarifying its potential significance.[111] The provinces of New Brunswick, Nova Scotia, and British Columbia had all indicated that they wished to embark on such a program. Others had expressed a clear interest. While no provinces opposed the idea, some, like Alberta, did not like it.[112]

While Axworthy's missive recognized that "child care falls under provincial jurisdiction," it also emphasized the two principal reasons why the federal government wished "to explore ways of working in concert with the provinces" to develop a national, shared-cost child care program.[113] First, "child care services contribute to achieving national employment objectives, particularly for lone parent families and for parents wishing to make the transition from social assistance to economic independence." Second, "quality child care also contributes to the employability of the next generation." Clearly, Axworthy's offer to work with the provinces on developing a national, shared-cost child care program was driven by "employability and child development objectives," not by a concern to make access to employment more equitable for men and women.

Securing the money for that offer had been complex. Axworthy had to battle in cabinet not only against those wanting to use it for other programs but also against Paul Martin's edict that there was no new money available for social programs. While Lloyd Axworthy and those supporting him "believed he had a mandate and a commitment to meet," those supporting Paul Martin maintained that the government "had been overtaken by events" and could not therefore engage in new social spending.[114] However, the battle was not simply about finances. It also reflected a debate in cabinet about whether such an offer, characterized as it was by a fifty-fifty split in funding, would "smack of the traditional way of doing business" with the provinces that was inappropriate in an era characterized by increasing pressure on the federal government to devolve responsibility for social policy to the provincial and territorial levels.[115] Moreover, these debates went on in cabinet just weeks after the 1995 Quebec referendum on sovereignty, when the federal government was shaken to its core by a result that came very, very close to legitimizing a fundamental redefinition of the Canadian state.[116]

In the run-up to the 1995 referendum, while federal politicians and bureaucrats were under a gag order not to engage in debate about the potential separation of Quebec from Canada, provincial premiers like Ralph Klein and Mike Harris were actively courting the Quebec government to stay in Canada and fight with them for the devolution of greater powers to the provinces.[117] After all, they had the backing of agreements reached at recent annual conferences of the premiers. In 1994, the premiers had agreed that "closer co-operation among Provinces and Territories, with respect to sectors within their jurisdiction, is essential in order to achieve greater efficiency and effectiveness within the federation."[118] Moreover, at their annual meeting in 1995, the premiers reaffirmed their commitment to "improve cooperation and take on a leadership role with respect to national matters that affect areas of provincial and territorial jurisdiction."[119] As a result, by the time the Quebec referendum result made it blatantly clear to the federal government that it had to rethink its relationship with Quebec, other provinces were ready to weigh in and ensure that any talk of giving Quebec greater recognition as a distinct society was part of a broader package of devolution from the federal government to the provinces.

Given this political context, it is amazing that Axworthy managed to secure cabinet approval for his new national child care program. After all, the federal government became extremely wary of new policy initiatives that might be interpreted as impinging on areas of provincial jurisdiction. In his letter to the provinces and territories, Axworthy informed the ministers responsible for child care that as he could not hang on to the money forever, he needed to hear from them by 15 January 1996 in order to take the matter back to cabinet in early February.[120] As Yzerman recalls, "We knew with the letter going out over the Christmas season that physically we were not going to get formal written responses by then. So the deadline was an impossible one to meet, but the expectation was that this would prompt [the provinces and territories] to act sooner rather than later."[121] However, looking beyond the antics of the festive season, it is clear that the big geopolitical conditions were not there to make the offer work. Axworthy's offer to the provinces simply could not work because it was made at a point when the provinces were strapped for cash and furious about the reduction in federal transfers that accompanied the CHST. Moreover, they were thinking through ways of developing a new approach to social policy that would give the subnational levels of government greater control in its development. In this regard, it is important to note that Axworthy's offer was made nine days before the premiers received the first report of the Ministerial Council for Social Policy Reform.

The Ministerial Council for Social Policy Reform had been established by the premiers in August 1995 in order to develop a common approach to the essential elements of social policy reform that would guide subsequent federal-provincial/territorial negotiations. Two strong messages lay at the core of its initial report. First, it argued that "areas of joint federal-provincial/territorial responsibility be minimized in those instances in which this would improve the effectiveness of these programs." Second, it recommended that "as responsibilities within the federation are clarified and realigned, commensurate resources also be transferred."[122] While the council argued that the federal government should "accept full responsibility for all programming for Aboriginal people, both on and off reserve, with a gradual transfer of authority to Aboriginal communities," the report signalled a radical restructuring of federal-provincial/territorial relations on questions of social policy.[123] In this context, it was very unlikely that Axworthy's call for provincial and territorial participation in an old-style shared-cost program would be acceptable.

Although eight provinces expressed an interest in the package, the possibility of any such shared-cost program being realized receded rapidly in 1996.[124] Axworthy moved on (and up) to Foreign Affairs and was replaced by Doug Young, who, despite all the groundwork done by bureaucrats in HRDC to woo their provincial counterparts, "literally jumped on a plane, went out, and met with a number of ministers and concluded that none of them wanted child care."[125] In a press release of 21 February 1996, Young declared that "it has become clear to the Government of Canada through the meetings held with provincial ministers to date, and through written responses received prior to these meetings, that there is agreement on the need to sit down and discuss child care, and to reach consensus on the appropriate use of federal funds for child care programs."[126] Moreover, the press release indicated that Young's "provincial and territorial counterparts have emphasized that any new federal-provincial-territorial child care arrangements must be consistent with efforts to clarify the respective roles and responsibilities of both orders of government and with efforts to eliminate overlap and duplication."[127]

Young's position was formalized in a more general sense on 27 February 1996, when the Speech from the Throne indicated, first, that "the Government [would] not use its spending power to create a new shared-cost jurisdiction, unless the majority of the provinces agree," and, second, that "any new program [would] be designed so that non-participating provinces will be compensated, provided they establish equivalent or comparable initiatives."[128] This speech signalled not only that the federal government was being ultra-cautious about federal-provincial relations in the wake of the 1995 Quebec referendum, but that national and subnational governments were contemplating the creation of a new social union framework in which to pursue issues of social policy.

Child Care and the New Social Union
The report of the Ministerial Council on Social Policy, endorsed by all territories and provinces except Quebec, laid the groundwork for a fundamental recasting of federal-provincial/territorial relations around provisions for

children. This was reinforced at the Edmonton first ministers meeting in June 1996, when federal, provincial, and territorial premiers agreed that as questions about child poverty were of mutual concern, the three levels of government would all address this problem. In short, while some provinces had not been prepared to let the federal government intervene in the field of child care, the first ministers agreed that they could work together on questions of child poverty. Indeed, the Edmonton meeting signalled a new stage in federal-provincial/territorial relations on social policy, one that would lead eventually to the creation of the Social Union and the National Children's Agenda.

At the heart of the Social Union lies a new federal-provincial/territorial agreement on the provision of benefits to children of low-income parents. The National Child Benefit (NCB), which came into effect on 1 July 1998, is designed to encourage poor parents to move from dependency on welfare to self-reliance on paid work.[129] Described by the federal government as "an innovative and progressive new program that invests in the well being of children," the NCB aims to ensure that the working poor do not face the problems of the past, whereby they have to give up regular welfare cheques and free benefits (like child care) once they assumed low-paid work.[130]

The NCB has been designed to meet federal concerns about getting welfare recipients back to work and provincial and territorial demands for greater autonomy in the field of social policy. In order to initiate the new policy, the federal government agreed to channel a total of $1.7 billion into the Canada Child Tax Benefit by the year 2000.[131] Under the scheme, low-income families with net incomes under $25,921, headed by a parent or parents who are in the labour force, have been allowed to keep their entire tax benefit increase. Provinces and territories may, if they wish, claw back the additional benefit from those remaining on social assistance and use this money to invest in social services that could benefit all low-income families.

The NCB clearly reflects the federal-provincial/territorial consensus on the most appropriate way to tackle the problem of child poverty. As Martha Friendly notes, "The National Child Benefit is very much in the model of the 1997-era Social Union."[132] Not only did the provinces initiate discussions about the viability of the NCB, but the scheme clearly distinguishes between the federal government's capacity to intervene in child welfare services through income transfer and the province's wish to maintain its clear jurisdictional control over service delivery. The question of course is whether the capacity the provinces and territories now have to claw back welfare monies to re-invest in services will lead to increased provision of child care.[133] Even if it does, the problem remains that there are no clear national standards about the nature of this provision. As Martha Friendly notes, "Although child care has been chosen for reinvestment by seven provinces, there are no national principles that can contribute to a national, pan-Canadian early childhood care and education program."[134]

The NCB of course gives the federal government a much higher profile in the battle against child poverty. As Ron Yzerman reflected,

> The federal government was becoming increasingly fed up with lack of recognition for the money that they spent. I'm talking right from 1966 [when CAP was introduced], but clearly in the 1980s and more so in the 1990s, and that contributed to their decision. One other aspect was the fact that it was easier for the government to use its spending powers in financial programs than it was to get in on the cost-shared support of provincial programs. [In addition,] the federal government could act much more unilaterally without having to placate provinces, [and] they got better recognition because they put their name on the cheques. Hand in hand with that was the notion that you put the benefit in the hand of the potential user and they will go out and do their thing. That's front and centre of both Conservative and Liberal government policy. It's easier to do, it empowers the individual. I think that putting the money in the hands of the people and letting them go out and do their thing, which is characteristic of social programs in the provinces as well, satisfies the federal concern about lack of visibility. It is also consistent with the commitment to the avoidance of overlap and duplication, which are going to become key features of the debate on the Social Union. However, if there was a universal day care system out there that was fully comprehensive and affordable, you wouldn't have to give people the money to go and make their units of purchase.[135]

Moreover, as Boismenu and Jenson argue, "The deal agreed to by all governments, except Quebec, is that Ottawa will individualize its relationship with poor families and their children, via tax credits."[136] Indeed, the Liberals have encouraged this process through three other policy developments, each of which involves a fiscal transfer to individual citizens. They have maintained the Child Care Expense Deduction (CCED), raising the age limit for care to sixteen in 1996.[137] They have increased the Working Income Supplement to "encourage people to move from welfare to work by offering income supplements to working-poor families."[138] In addition, they have introduced the Young Child Supplement to give "direct child care assistance [of $213 per child] to parents with children under the age of seven who have not claimed child care expenses under the CCED."[139]

At the core of the NCB is a vision of responsible citizenship in which low-income parents are encouraged to fend for themselves rather than remain dependent on state support. Indeed, the National Children's Agenda (NCA), endorsed by the premiers at their annual conference in the summer of 1997 and supported by the federal government in its Speech from the Throne the following September, seems to expand notions of responsible citizenship to include children.[140] Described as "a comprehensive strategy to improve the health and well-being of Canada's children," the NCA is not just an intergovernmental agreement but an intersectoral agreement that attempts to bridge the policy divide between those working on questions of child care in the Departments of Health and HRDC.[141] This emergent agenda aims to encourage the physical, emotional, and spiritual health of Canada's children, as well as their safety and security. It is designed to ensure that children are "ready for learning throughout their lives," having developed "the skills, knowledge and competencies they need for successful transition to adulthood," and that they "develop an understanding of the rights and responsibilities of belonging to a wider society."[142]

In the Supplementary Paper issued for public discussion in May 1999, Canadians were encouraged to air their views on the NCA and be assured that "governments [would] be sitting down with key partners to encourage dialogue about the vision, values, goals and areas for action proposed by the National Children's Agenda."[143] The Supplementary Paper also indicated that at the end of this dialogue "governments [would] incorporate the views of Canadians into a vision document and report back so that the vision can guide all of our efforts to improve the lives of Canada's children."[144]

Three questions remain to be answered. Will the Social Union Framework, announced by the prime minister on 4 February 1999 really develop the kind of consensus it seeks between governments to promote more than just a vision? Will the National Children's Agenda provide a forum in which questions about the development and provision of a national child care program re-emerge? Finally, if the NCA does create yet another forum in which the demands for a national child care agenda are articulated, will the demands be able to survive the reality of federal-provincial/territorial negotiations in an era of flexible federalism?

Assessing the Liberal Government's Record on Employment Equity and Child Care

There is no doubt that the Liberal government of Jean Chrétien has tackled questions of employment equity and child care. After all, the Liberals introduced new employment equity legislation that broadened the remit of federal regulations and strengthened the role of the CHRC to secure compliance with the Act. Moreover, they inserted questions of child care, front and centre, into a major review of social security, made moves to deliver a national shared-cost child care program as promised in the Red Book, and in recent years worked with the provinces to develop new fiscal and discursive frameworks in which to approach questions about the care, development, and financial support of Canada's children. Nonetheless, as this record reveals, it is programs to promote employment equity rather than child care that have reached the statute books under the government of Jean Chrétien.

Like previous Liberal and Conservative governments that were in power during the 1970s and 1980s, the Chrétien government has found that even in an era of more flexible federalism, it has been much easier to address questions of employment equity that are located within the federal sphere of reference than those of child care which span federal, provincial, and territorial jurisdictions. Moreover, despite recent talk of creating a National Children's Agenda, the Chrétien government has also relied principally on addressing child care through fiscal transfers to individual citizens, in particular to encourage those on welfare to return to work. However, in contrast to the governments led by Pierre Trudeau and Brian Mulroney, the Liberal government of Jean Chrétien has not had to face these questions during an era of intense feminist mobilization or in the wake of royal commission reports that have linked questions of equal employment opportunities for men and women with the provision of child care. As a result, it has been much freer than previous federal governments to reset the agenda on both policy issues. The Liberals have linked questions about women's employment and the provision of child care, but they have not done so with a view to promoting gender equality in the labour force. Instead these links have been reforged to increase the productivity of the female labour force, reduce the federal government's welfare bill, and ensure that the youngest generation of Canadians have access to facilities that will enable them to develop into healthy, responsible worker-citizens.

10
Linked Together, Yet Driven Apart

Explaining the Disconnection between Employment Equality and Child Care Policies

Why have questions about women's employment equality and child care been driven apart in the federal policy process and, despite the recommendations of two royal commissions, received such uneven treatment from the federal government? The answer is multidimensional: it has jurisdictional, fiscal, institutional, interest-based, and ideological façades.

Jurisdictional Politics

Viewed from a jurisdictional perspective, it is clear that while policies to promote women's employment opportunities within federally regulated organizations can be neatly contained within the federal sphere, questions of child care lead the federal government into the jurisdictional swamp of intergovernmental negotiations. As a result, federal governments have been reluctant to address the calls of two royal commissions for a national child care policy to support women's participation in the paid labour force. At the same time, it is evident from the development of the 1966 Canada Assistance Plan, the 1995 Canada Health and Social Transfer, and the 1998 National Child Benefit that the federal government is willing to use its constitutionally defined spending power to influence the development of provincially controlled fields of social policy. However, as these three examples demonstrate, the federal government has only been prepared to use this power to support the development of child care services for welfare recipients and, more recently, the working poor.

The governments of Trudeau, Mulroney, and Chrétien have responded in different ways to the jurisdictional context in which questions of employment equity and child care are addressed. As we saw in Chapters 4 and 5, the Trudeau government introduced measures to enhance women's employment opportunities and root out broader patterns of discrimination in the federal arena. After all, the eradication of sex discrimination in areas of federal employment fitted well with Trudeau's vision of a just society of rights-bearing citizens. Moreover, the promotion of equal employment opportunities for men and women made sense to a government concerned with the economic imperatives of developing the full potential of the Canadian labour force. However, Trudeau's insistence on the jurisdictional imperative of not crossing the federal-provincial divide on questions of child care stopped the federal government from developing a national child care policy in the way that had been recommended in the report of the Royal Commission on the Status of Women. As a result, federal intervention in the field of child care during the Trudeau era was restricted to fiscal transfers to the provinces in support of welfare-based child care under CAP and tax relief for individual parents to assist in their purchase of child care. With hindsight we can see how this two-pronged approach set the template for federal intervention in the field of child care for the next two decades.

Like the Trudeau government, the Conservative government of Brian Mulroney and the Liberal government of Jean Chrétien found it easier to develop employment equity policies than those concerning child care. As we saw in Chapters 7 and 9, both the Mulroney Conservatives and the Chrétien Liberals developed employment equity legislation that reflected their different ideological perspectives. While the 1986 Employment Equity Act (EEA), introduced by the Conservatives, put minimal constraints on federally regulated employers by asking them to report on their goals and timetables for implementing employment equity, the Liberals broadened this legislation and tightened the methods for securing compliance. Thus the 1995 EEA brought key areas of the federal bureaucracy under its legislative remit and enhanced the powers of the Canadian Human Rights Commission (CHRC) to audit employers' implementation of equity. Nonetheless, it was a sign of the fiscal and ideological times in which the Chrétien Liberals were governing during their first term of office, that the legislation also gave employers a great deal of flexibility in setting goals and developing procedures for equity.

In contrast to the Trudeau government, those led by Mulroney and Chrétien did engage provincial, territorial, and Aboriginal leaders in negotiations to improve the provision of child care. However, despite the repeated calls of child care advocates for a free, universal system of child care, both Conservative and Liberal governments used these negotiations to promote a mixed economy of child care services. Nonetheless, the plans that both governments made to develop a national child care strategy failed, in part because of difficulties in bringing all the provinces and territories on side. In the case of the Mulroney government, this failure became just one component of a broader débâcle over the demise of Bill C-144, its proposed

Canada Child Care Act. In the case of the Chrétien government, the failure reflects two distinct but related forces. First, the cost-sharing offer made to the provinces and territories in December 1995 came at a time when these subnational governments were livid about the replacement of the open-ended Canada Assistance Plan with the block-funded Canada Health and Social Transfer. Second, it was made at a point when the provinces were clearly in the process of shifting the terrain in which federal-provincial/territorial negotiations over social policy would be carried out. In short, this old-style approach to federal intervention in social policy did not mesh well with the emergent Social Union.

Fiscal Constraints

While the high politics of federal-provincial/territorial negotiations have certainly restricted the evolution of child care policy in Canada, it is important to recognize that fiscal, as well as jurisdictional, forces have made the implementation of employment equity legislation more palatable to the federal government than that of child care. The significant cutbacks endured by the Workplace Equity Program in Human Resources Development Canada (HRDC) since the Liberals took office in 1993, indicate how even this initiative was seen to be too expensive in an era of deficit reduction.[1] Nonetheless, while the development and regulation of employment equity policies requires finance to operate the Workplace Equity Program in HRDC and the Employment Equity Branch of the CHRC, most of the costs of implementing employment equity are downloaded onto federally regulated employers and those under contract to the federal government. Of course, since 1995, the federal government has carried responsibilities as an employer for implementing employment equity within the federal public service. Nonetheless, the overall costs to the federal government of developing, implementing, and regulating employment equity measures are minor when compared to the fiscal transfers made to provinces, territories, Aboriginal communities, and individual citizens to support the delivery and purchase of high-cost child care services.[2] Indeed, these financial realities, combined with jurisdictional sensitivities, explain why both Liberal and Conservative governments have relied so heavily on individual tax relief, rather than the direct subsidization of services, to finance child care provision for the majority of Canadian children. It also explains why both Liberal and Conservative governments have repeatedly backed away from developing a national, publicly funded child care policy.

Institutional Forces

Institutional forces within the federal government have also encouraged the distinct rather than related treatment of policies to promote child care and gender equality in the federally regulated workplace. While femocrats in the Women's Bureau and Status of Women Canada have tried, with varying degrees of success, to promote awareness of the link between gender equality in employment and the provision of child care, they have never had the power to shape specific developments in either policy field. Moreover, as we saw in discussions of policy developments during the Trudeau and Mulroney governments, the driving force behind the development of equal opportunity and anti-discrimination policies came from the CHRC and the Affirmative Action Unit within the CEIC, while questions about child care policy were located entirely in the Department of Health and Welfare Canada. The creation of HRDC, in 1993, did bring policy units concerned with women's employment equality and child care into one mega-department. Even then, the only way that questions about women's employment have been linked with those of child care under the Chrétien government has been in its strategies to get mothers on welfare off social assistance and into paid work. As I indicated at the outset of this book, despite the physical proximity of the offices in HRDC that oversee its programs on children and employment equity, the public servants who staff them operate in different bureaucratic worlds.

Organization of Social Movements

If we look beyond the dynamics of the federal policy process, it is fascinating to note how the key national organizations concerned with the status of women and the development of federal policies on child care have been affected by the way that questions about employment equality and child care are treated so distinctly by the federal government. Although individual and organized women have repeatedly used public inquiries to articulate the link between women's employment equality and the provision of child care, the distinction between these two issues has at times been reinforced by the way that activists in national organizations have developed their campaigns.

In the early stages of second-wave feminism, even though (as indicated in Chapter 4) there was some ambiguity within the National Ad Hoc Action Committee on the Status of Women about linking questions of women's employment opportunity with those of child care, the organized women's movement embraced both issues in their campaigns. In part, this reflects how the National Action Committee on the Status of Women (NAC) emerged as an organization committed to ensuring that the federal government acted on the recommendations of the report of the RCSW. However, it also reflects that in the 1970s the focus of the emergent Canadian child care movement was almost entirely provincial. By contrast, when a new, national child care organization – the Canadian Day Care Advocacy Association (CDCAA) – emerged in 1982 and brought provincial child care advocates together in pursuit of a national child care policy, the question about whether child care would be defined as a women's issue or a children's issue began to emerge in federal debate.

In fact, it took close to a decade for the distinction between child care and employment equity issues to come about, in part because child care advocates worked through both NAC and the CDCAA to raise their concerns. However, as Chapter 9 demonstrated, by the time the CDCAA renamed itself the Child Care Advocacy Association of Canada (CCAAC) in 1992, the campaigns of child care advocates and activists in NAC were no longer meshed together in the way they had been in the late 1980s. Indeed, at this stage it became clear that while activists in NAC and the CCAAC shared a general concern about women's employment equality, child care advocates were increasingly focused on the need to bring about a universal, quality child care service *for children*. As one well-known child care activist is reputed to have said, "I don't want my children in child care in order to work, I want to work in order to place my children in quality child care."[3]

Ideological Forces
While jurisdictional, fiscal, and institutional factors all help to explain why questions about employment equity and child care have been driven apart in the federal policy process, it is important not to allow these explanations to mask the ideological factors in Liberal and Conservative governments that have shaped the process of policy development.

Both governments have been much more willing to regulate employment equity than to engage in the development of child care. Nonetheless, they severed the connection between these two issues in different ways. Liberal government policies have been characterized, primarily, by a desire to contain questions about employment equality for men and women within the public sphere, allowing royal commission mandates and policy developments to be shaped by the tensions between developmental and economic branches of Canadian liberalism. While the forces of developmental liberalism have encouraged Liberal governments to engage in the creation of equal opportunity, anti-discrimination, and employment equity policies, the concerns of economic liberals have at times acted as an impediment to this process. Moreover, even though Liberal governments have a clear record of developing equal opportunity and anti-discrimination policies to enhance the status of women as worker-citizens, it is one that has been shaped by a philosophical commitment to the idea that gender equality is best realized by ensuring that, except at the point of giving birth to and nursing infant children, women are treated in a similar way to men.

Liberal governments have found it relatively straightforward to engage in the development of equal employment opportunity and anti-discrimination policies. However, despite Axworthy's attempts to realize the promises on child care made in the Red Book, the Liberals have proved unable to develop a national child care policy, beyond providing welfare-based subsidies to the provinces, child tax benefits to the working poor, and tax relief for individual parents wishing to purchase child care. More-over, if we compare the Liberals' record on the development of employ-ment equity policies and those concerned with child care, it is clear that although their initiatives in the public sphere are quite extensive, they are reluctant to tackle employment problems that span the public and domes-tic dimensions of women's lives, save for those women on welfare. Indeed, while political theorists have noted that liberals draw "a strict line between the pursuit of equality and the privacy of the family," in fact, the Liberal government's record on child care suggests that the privacy of the family is rather less respected when it is headed by women in receipt of welfare than by adults earning sufficient income to claim tax relief on the pur-chase of child care.[4]

By virtue of being in office for only a small proportion of the time since the 1960s, the Conservatives have had less influence than the Liberals on the development of policies to promote gender equality in the sphere of employment. Nonetheless, as I showed in Chapter 7, the first Mulroney government did attempt to introduce employment equity and child care legislation. However, while the successful implementation of the 1986 EEA came about as a result of Mulroney's commitment to gender equality and Flora MacDonald's ability to drive the legislation through a brokerage-style cabinet, the Act was clearly shaped by the Conservatives' reluctance to regulate the private sector. Similarly, the Conservatives' decision to enter into the field of child care was not motivated by a desire to link child care with policies to promote gender equality in employment but by the competing ideological claims of different groups within the party. These included the pro-family lobby, which sought to reinforce the family as a core institution within Canadian society; the pro-market lobby, which fought to promote commercial as well as state-funded provision of social services; and, finally, the red-Tory camp, which tried to ensure that low-income families could benefit from an enhanced scheme of child tax cred-its. Indeed, the tensions between these three elements within the Con-servative Party made it very difficult for the Mulroney government to maintain its promises to develop a national child care strategy during its second term in office.

It is important to assess the records of Liberal and Conservative gov-ernments against the concerns of feminist theorists that were raised in Chapter 1. In my opinion, they reinforce feminist claims that the social contract that underscores contemporary liberal visions of rights and citi-zenship is, in fact, a highly gendered contract based on a male-defined norm of worker-citizenship. As a result, federal policies to promote gender equality in the paid workplace have failed to take sufficient account of the way that the domestic context of many women's lives impacts on their employment opportunities. Indeed, the only way that Liberal and Conservative governments have acknowledged the problems women can face in juggling paid work and child care is to encourage those women who remain dependent on welfare to participate in the labour force so that the state can take care of their children and ensure that its welfare budget is reduced.

Despite the efforts of feminist theorists to develop concepts of equality that take gender differences into account, federal policies to promote employment equality have repeatedly assumed that, for the most part, men and women should be treated in a similar fashion. As we saw in Chapters 2, 4, and 5, the development of Canadian human rights and equal opportunities legislation sought to ensure that women were treated in a similar way to men. Moreover, although the 1986 and 1995 Employment Equity Acts acknowledged differences among the four target groups at which the legislation was aimed, they both emphasized the need to ensure the equitable treatment of target group members *once they have entered the labour force*. As a result, broader societal questions about the context in which women (and other target groups) assume employment have not been reflected in federal employment equity legislation. Inevitably, therefore, questions of child care provision become disconnected from those of employment equity.

Even though feminist theorists have asserted the need to develop public policies that recognize how questions of care affect citizens' working lives, their concerns have not been fully recognized in the federal government's approach to questions of employment equity and child care. Indeed, when the federal government's relative success at implementing employment equity and anti-discrimination policies is compared with their failure to develop a national child care policy, it is clear that policies to promote gender equality in the workplace in Canada have marginalized considerations of care that worker-citizens face when they assume paid employment. This pattern is alarming not only because it discounts the claims that many women have voiced through a variety of public inquiries but also because it will prove increasingly problematic as workers face the demands of both child care and elder care in a downsized welfare state.[5]

The Impact of Royal Commissions on Debates about Employment Equality and Child Care

Federal governments of both a Liberal and Conservative orientation have either failed or been unable to develop policies that recognize how integral child care is to the promotion of women's employment equality. Nonetheless, as we saw in Chapters 3, 5, and 6, the Liberal governments of Lester

B. Pearson and Pierre Trudeau did establish two important royal commissions that – as it turned out – provided women with major opportunities to articulate the link between the provision of child care and gender equality at work.

At the heart of this book is an analysis of the way that the 1967 Royal Commission on the Status of Women (RCSW) and the 1983 Royal Commission on Equality in Employment (RCEE) enabled women to channel concerns about the gendered nature of their employment opportunities into the federal policy arena. It shows not only how women used these commissions to link together their concerns about employment opportunity and child care but also how the commissioners who conducted these inquiries actively encouraged this process. In each inquiry, women made strong claims that in order to participate in the paid workforce and enjoy the status of worker-citizenship to the same degree as men, assumptions that they were, first and foremost, mother-citizens had to be revised. Moreover, by making clear recommendations that the federal government link the development of employment opportunity policies for women with the provision of a national system of child care, the commissioners heading up the RCSW and the RCEE pushed the federal policy agenda well beyond each commission's terms of reference.

The federal government's inability to respond to the double-edged recommendations of the RCSW and the RCEE does raise serious questions about the capacity of royal commissions to reset the federal policy agenda. Both these commissions were designed to ascertain how governments might develop policies that would not only enhance the status of women as worker-citizens but also improve the country's economic productivity. In each case, the commissioners took the federal government's concern about linking the pursuit of gender equality with the promotion of economic efficiency and argued that in the case of women, neither of these objectives could be achieved unless governments considered how women's responsibilities for child care shaped their employment opportunities. In the process, the commissioners not only radicalized and engendered the federal policy agenda but undermined established assumptions about the best way to include women within the male-defined paradigm of worker-citizenship.

This conclusion reinforces Jenson's observation that royal commissions have often "taken on a life of their own and produced recommendations not at all to the liking – or the expectations – of the government that appointed them."[6] However, it also raises serious problems about the way that federal governments ignore or deflect the more radical recommendations of royal commissions.[7] My own conclusion, drawn from examining the policies that were developed in the wake of the RCSW and the RCEE, is that the federal government kept its policy response narrowly framed within the equity-efficiency paradigm in which each commission's mandate was rooted. While this was a double-edged response of a kind, it did not traverse the boundaries of the public and domestic domains in the way that the commissioners had recommended.

Even though women have not seen the link between employment equality and child care realized in federal public policy, the commissions still served as forums in which women debated and challenged their construction as mother-citizens and put on record their own understanding of the preconditions for enjoying worker-citizenship with men. Although royal commissions do not always lead to the policy outcomes that their commissioners recommend, they, nonetheless, provide textual coherence to policy connections that might otherwise not be articulated. Moreover, while royal commission recommendations can be deflected away from the government's policy agenda, the inquiries themselves can actually encourage citizens' awareness of inequalities and a desire to challenge them. Indeed, I would argue that these connections are often advanced through royal commissions, first, because they are established to examine policy problems that cannot easily be resolved or developed through the normal channels of federal policy making and, second, because they enable citizens to be directly involved in debating policy agendas that affect their daily lives.[8]

While my research provides grounds for optimism about the potential of royal commissions to empower citizens and engender public discourse, it also signals specific ways in which the role of royal commissions needs to be re-evaluated. First, greater attention needs to be paid to the question of whether, by encouraging citizens to provide oral and written testimony, royal commissions have a contradictory impact on Canadian democracy. On the one hand – while their inquiries are in process – royal commissions can act as crucial mechanisms to affirm the relationship between citizens and the state. On the other hand, they may raise citizens' expectations about potential policy developments beyond a level that can be realized either within the ideological framework of the government that receives their reports or within the jurisdictional, fiscal, and institutional parameters of the federal (provincial or territorial) policy system.

Governments need to pay greater attention to the mechanisms through which the recommendations of royal commissions are processed in order to prevent the disjuncture between civic participation in these inquiries and the subsequent development – or nondevelopment – of public policy. Though it may be healthy for any democracy to have periods when the potential policy agenda is first broadened in order to be honed down with the benefit of new insights, greater attention needs to be paid to the most effective and democratic way in which recommendations can be addressed within the policy-making process.

The impact that recommendations of royal commissions can have on the development of public policy is not, however, simply the responsibility of the federal government. Royal commissioners also need to pay close attention to the institutional, fiscal, and jurisdictional ramifications of their recommendations. After all, we need to ask whether the links between women's employment equality and child care, which were made so explicit in the reports of both the RCSW and the RCEE, would have been severed so rapidly if greater attention had been paid to the forces within the federal policy process that drives these issues apart.

Final Reflections

In many respects, the conclusions of this research are depressing. Despite the persistent attempts of female citizens, political activists, and royal commissioners to highlight the importance of developing a contextualized approach to employment equality, federal governments have developed policies that not only maintain a sharp division between the public world of employment and the domestic world of the family but prioritize two forms of public policy to keep these issues apart. First, they have adhered, with greater or lesser degrees of regulation, to promoting employment policies that prioritize the equal, nondiscriminatory treatment of individuals and groups over the recognition of the particular circumstances in which worker-citizens enter the labour market. Second, despite contributing directly to the establishment of an extensive welfare state in the fields of education, income maintenance, and health care, federal governments have failed to do more than subsidize the provision and purchase of child care. Rather than working with the provinces and territories to develop a national system of child care that could fundamentally reshape the lives of many working women, the federal government has focused its energies on developing employment equity and anti-discrimination policies that regulate the working conditions of a very small percentage of the female labour force.

At the same time, my research into royal commissions has provided enormous grounds for optimism. For all their limitations – and these are real and recorded – the royal commissions I have examined suggest that these inquiries have provided women with important public arenas in which to articulate different aspects of their working lives and bring out the multidimensionality of employment inequality. In the process, women have helped to develop frameworks of policy analysis that have fundamentally challenged liberal assumptions that the key goal of an equal employment opportunity policy must be to ensure the similar, nondiscriminatory treatment of all worker-citizens. The fact that governments disregarded the more radical insights of the RCSW and the RCEE because they did not fit with their own political, economic, or ideological perspectives does need to be addressed – particularly as this process negated reflections that citizens had rooted in their own experience. Nonetheless, even though this book has demonstrated the federal government's resistance to linking the public and domestic facets of women's labour, it has also emphasized the capacity of royal commissions to provide civic spaces that bridge this very divide. Their potential, therefore, to continue defining the contours of female citizenship in a way that makes sense to women should not be ignored.

Appendix A
Research Interviews

The author conducted hour-long interviews with key activists and policy makers. Interviews were held in both Canada and the United Kingdom between August 1986 and December 1998. Although interviewees were selected for their expertise in each of the specific areas listed below, their reflections often covered other issues addressed in this book.

The Canadian Women's Movement and the Royal Commission on the Status of Women

Doris Anderson, President, National Action Committee on the Status of Women, 1982-4, and Chair of the Canadian Advisory Council on the Status of Women, 1979-81. Interview, Toronto, December 1988.

Monique Bégin, Executive Secretary, Royal Commission on the Status of Women, 1967-70. Interview, Ottawa, December 1998.

Florence Bird, Chief Commissioner, Royal Commission on the Status of Women, 1967-70. Interview, Ottawa, September 1986.

John English, biographer of Lester B. Pearson and Liberal MP for Kitchener, Ontario, 1993-7. Interview, London, UK, March 1995.

Chaviva Hošek, President, National Action Committee on the Status of Women, 1984-6. Interview, Toronto, September 1986.

Martha Hynna, Coordinator, Status of Women, Privy Council Office, 1973-6. Interview, Hull, QC, September 1986.

Lorna Marsden, Chair, National Action Committee on the Status of Women, 1975-7. Interviews, Toronto, August 1986 and August 1987.

Laura Sabia, Chair, Committee for the Equality of Women in Canada, 1966-71, Chair, National Ad Hoc Action Committee on the Status of Women, 1971-2, and Chair, National Action Committee on the Status of Women, 1972-4. Interview, Toronto, August 1986.

Women and the Labour Movement

Julie Davis, Secretary-Treasurer, Ontario Federation of Labour, 1988-95. Interview, Toronto, November 1988.

Linda Gallant, National Representative, Women's Bureau, Canadian Labour Congress. Interview, Ottawa, December 1988.

Irene Harris, Equal Opportunities Representative, Ontario region, Canadian Union of Public Employees, 1987-94. Interview, Toronto, December 1988.

The Royal Commission on Equality in Employment

Rosalie Silberman Abella, Commissioner, Royal Commission on Equality in Employment, 1983-4. Interviews, Toronto, August 1986 and August 1987.

Lloyd Axworthy, Minister of Employment and Immigration, 1980-3. Interview, Ottawa, September 1986.

Ron Collett, Senior Policy Advisor to Lloyd Axworthy, 1980-3. Interview, Toronto, September 1986.

Patricia Preston, Press Secretary to Lloyd Axworthy, 1980-3. Interview, Ottawa, September 1986.

John Roberts, Minister of Employment and Immigration, 1983-4. Interview, Toronto, April 1997.

Bernadette Sulgit, Executive Coordinator, Royal Commission on Equality in Employment, 1983-4. Interview, Toronto, August 1986.

The 1986 Employment Equity Act

Warren Allmand, former Liberal MP and Chair of the Special Parliamentary Committee/Task Force on Employment Opportunities for the 1980s, 1980-1. Interview, Ottawa, December 1988.

John Bullock, President, Canadian Federation of Independent Businesses, 1971-95. Interview by telephone, December 1988.

Marnie Clarke, Director, Employment Equity Branch, Canadian Employment and Immigration Commission, 1985-94. Interview, Hull, QC, December 1988.

Robert Cooper, Chairman, Northern Ireland Fair Employment Commission, 1990-9. Interview, Belfast, UK, October 1996.

Joanne De Laurentis, Vice-President and Director, Public Affairs, Canadian Bankers Association, 1986-94. Interview, Toronto, December 1988.

David Dodge, Director of the Task Force on Labour Market Development, 1980-1. Interview, Ottawa, December 1988.

Peter S. Doyle, Commissioner for Employers, Canadian Employment and Immigration Commission, 1984-96. Interview, Hull, QC, December 1988.

Katherine Filsinger, Industrial Relations Policy Advisor, Canadian Manufacturers Association. Interview, Toronto, September 1986.

Marsha Gordon, Vice-President, Canadian Chamber of Commerce, 1982-90. Interview, Toronto, December 1988.

Hanne Jensen, Director, Employment and Pay Equity Branch, Canadian Human Rights Commission, 1988-90. Interview, Ottawa, December 1988.

Margueritte Keeley, Director, Pay and Employment Equity Branch, Canadian Human Rights Commission, 1992-6. Interview, Ottawa, September 1995.

Flora MacDonald, Minister of Employment and Immigration, 1984-6. Interview, Leeds, UK, December 1990.

Fazil Mihlar, Policy Analyst, Fraser Institute, Vancouver, 1994-9. Interview, Vancouver, September 1995.

Maureen O'Neil, Secretary General, Canadian Human Rights Commission, 1986-7. Interview, Ottawa, September 1986.

Rhys Phillips, Policy Analyst, Affirmative Action Directorate, Canadian Employment and Immigration Commission, 1978-83. Interview, Hull, QC, September 1986.

Michael Sabia, Senior Policy Advisor to Flora MacDonald, 1984-6. Interview, Ottawa, September 1986.

Michael Walker, Director, Fraser Institute, Vancouver. Interview, Vancouver, September 1995.

The Development of Child Care Policy in the 1980s

Howard Clifford, National Child Care Advisor, Health and Welfare Canada, 1972-94, Human Resources Development Canada, 1994-5. Interview, Ottawa, December 1988.

Susan Colley, Executive Director, Ontario Coalition for Better Child Care, 1985-90. Interview, Toronto, December 1988.

Lyse Corbeil-Vincent, Executive Coordinator, Canadian Day Care Advocacy Association, 1988-90. Interview, Ottawa, December 1988.

Renée Edwards, member of the Katie Cooke Task Force on Child Care, 1984-6, and former

Ontario representative on Executive Board, Canadian Day Care Advocacy Association. Interview, Toronto, December 1988.

Martha Friendly, Coordinator, Childcare Resource and Research Centre, University of Toronto. Interview, Toronto, November 1988.

Debbie Jette, Director of Child Care Programs, Health and Welfare Canada, 1988-91. Interview, Ottawa, December 1988.

Julie Mathien, former member, Executive Board, Canadian Day Care Advocacy Association. Interview, Toronto, November 1988.

Susan Phillips, Professor, School of Public Administration, Carleton University. Interview, Ottawa, June 1998.

The Development of Employment Equity Policy in the 1990s

Elizabeth Bertoldi, Program Officer, Employment Equity Division, Human Resources Branch, Treasury Board of Canada Secretariat. Interview, Ottawa, December 1998.

Wally Boxhill, Senior Program Officer, Employment Equity Division, Human Resources Branch, Treasury Board of Canada Secretariat. Interview, Ottawa, December 1998.

Neil Gavigan, Director, Labour Standards and Workplace Equity, Human Resources Development Canada. Interviews, by telephone, October 1995, and in person, Hull, QC, June and December 1998.

Edna MacKenzie, member of the Task Force on Barriers to Women in the Public Service, 1988-90. Interview, Oxford, UK, March 1993.

Frances MacLellan, Senior Program Officer, Employment Equity Division, Human Resources Branch, Treasury Board of Canada Secretariat, 1990-9. Interview, Ottawa, December 1998.

Michael Paliga, Manager, Workplace Equity Programs, Labour Standards and Workplace Equity, Human Resources Development Canada. Interview, Hull, QC, December 1998.

Rhys Phillips, Chief, Legislation and Program Development, Employment Equity Branch, Canadian Human Rights Commission. Interview, Ottawa, December 1998.

Sheila Regehr, Economic Policy Coordinator, Policy Analysis and Development Directorate, Status of Women Canada. Interview, Ottawa, December 1998.

Kay Stanley, Assistant Secretary, Employment Equity Division, Human Resources Branch, Treasury Board of Canada Secretariat. Interview, December 1998.

Monique Vezina, Minister of Employment and Immigration, 1988-93. Interview, Montreal, October 1995.

The Development of Child Care Policy in the 1990s

Diane Bascombe, Executive Director, Canadian Child Care Federation, 1995-9. Interview, Ottawa, June 1998.

Margaret Biggs, Associate Executive Head of Strategic Policy, Human Resources Development Canada, and Director of the Children's Task Team, Human Resources Development Canada, 1996-8. Interview, Hull, QC, December 1998.

Phyllis Colvin, Director, Health Policy Division, Health Canada. Interview, Ottawa, December 1998.

Martha Friendly, Coordinator, Childcare Resource and Research Unit, University of Toronto. Interview, Toronto, November 1998.

Sandra Harder, Researcher, Political and Social Affairs Division, Research Branch, Library of Parliament. Interview, Ottawa, December 1998.

Marta Juorio, Saskatchewan representative and co-chair, Executive Board, Canadian Child Care Advocacy Association, 1998-2000. Interview, Toronto, November 1998.

Patricia McLaughlin, Policy Analyst, Policy Analysis and Development Directorate, Status of Women Canada. Interview, Ottawa, December 1998.

Alfred MacLeod, Assistant to Chaviva Hošek, Director of the National Liberal Caucus, 1991-3. Interview by telephone, December 1998.

Marti Menard, Policy Analyst, Health Policy Division, Health Canada. Interview, Ottawa, December 1998.

Robert Mundie, Assistant Director Children's Policy, Social Policy Unit, Human Resources Development Canada. Interview, Hull, QC, December 1998.

Jasbir Randhawa, Yukon member, Executive Board, Child Care Advocacy Association of Canada. Interview, Toronto, November 1998.

Laurel Rothman, Director of Social Action, Family Services Association of Toronto. Interview, Toronto, December 1998.

Rebecca Scherer, Alberta representative and co-chair, Executive Board, Child Care Advocacy Association of Canada, 1998-2000. Interview, Toronto, November 1998.

Lynne Westlake, Senior Policy Analyst, Children's Task Team, Social Policy Unit, Human Resources Development Canada. Interview, Hull, QC, December 1998.

Rebecca Will, Policy Analyst, Health Policy Division, Health Canada. Interview, Ottawa, December 1998.

Ron Yzerman, Director of Child Care Programs, Health and Welfare Canada, 1991-4, Human Resources Development Canada, 1994-6. Interview, Ottawa, December 1998.

The Federal Approach to Gender Issues

Hélène Dwyer-Renaud, Director, Women's Bureau, Human Resources Development Canada. Interview, Hull, QC, December 1998.

Scheherzade Rana, Economic Policy Analyst, Policy Analysis and Development Directorate, Status of Women Canada. Interview, Ottawa, December 1998.

Tamra Thomson, former Policy Analyst, Legal Affairs Section, Status of Women Canada. Interview, Ottawa, September 1986.

Appendix B
Turning Points in Canadian Policy Development on Women's Employment Equality and Child Care

Date	Employment Equality	Child Care	Other Events
1942	Federal Department of Labour and National Selective Service begin recruiting women into the war effort.	Dominion-Provincial War-time Agreement on Child Care.	Mackenzie King (Liberal) serving as prime minister.
1943			Subcommittee on Post-War Problems of Women established.
1944			Marsh Report on Social Security published. Report of Subcommittee on Post-War Problems of Women published.
1945	Marriage bar for women re-introduced in federal public service.	Mothers' allowances introduced.	
1946		Dominion-Provincial War-time Agreement on Child Care rescinded.	United Nations Commission on the Status of Women established.
1947			Joint Senate and House of Commons Committee on Human Rights and Fundamental Freedoms established.
1948			Universal Declaration of Human Rights includes "sex" as ground for nondiscrimination.
1951			Louis St. Laurent (Liberal) elected as prime minister. Canada ratifies International Labour Organization's (ILO) Convention 100 on equal pay for work of equal value.

1954	Women's Bureau established within Department of Labour.	
1955	Marriage bar removed for women working in the federal public service.	
1956	Federal Female Employees Equal Pay Act introduced.	
1957		John G. Diefenbaker (Conservative) elected as prime minister.
1958	ILO ratifies Convention 111 on Discrimination (Employment and Occupation).	Canada joins United Nations (UN) Commission on the Status of Women.
1960		Canadian Bill of Rights enacted, outlawing sex discrimination in the federal sphere.
1963		Lester B. Pearson (Liberal) elected as prime minister.
1964		Committee for the Equality of Women in Canada formed.
1966	Canada ratifies ILO Convention 111.	Canada Assistance Plan (CAP) introduced, includes federal provision for welfare-based child care.
1967		Royal Commission on the Status of Women (RCSW) established. UN Declaration on Elimination of Discrimination against Women.

The Trudeau Era

1968		Pierre Trudeau (Liberal) elected as prime minister. International Human Rights Year.
1970	Public Service Employment Act outlaws sex discrimination.	Local Initiatives Project encourages the expansion of community-controlled child care centres. Canadian Labour Congress includes eradication of sex discrimination within its constitution. Report of Royal Commission on the Status of Women published. Interdepartmental Committee on the Status of Women established.

Date	Employment Equality	Child Care	Other Events
1971	Office of Equal Opportunity established within the federal public service.	Child Care Expense Deduction introduced under Income Tax Act. Canadian Council on Social Development (CCSD) organizes first national conference on day care.	Appointment of first minister responsible for Status of Women. National Ad Hoc Committee on the Status of Women formed.
1972	Cabinet Directive 44 encourages ministers to promote more women to middle/upper-echelon posts. Unemployment Insurance Act outlaws discrimination on grounds of sex or marital status.	Canada Assistance Plan regulations changed to permit cost-sharing for the operation of day care. National Day Care Information Centre set up within the Department of Health and Welfare.	National Action Committee on the Status of Women (NAC) established. Office of the Coordinator for Status of Women established within Privy Council Office. Women's Program and Native Women's Program set up within the Office of the Secretary of State. Liberals re-elected to government in October.
1973		Local Initiatives Project funding withdrawn. National Housing Act amended to permit child care centres to be built in federally financed housing units.	Advisory Council on the Status of Women established.
1974			
1975	Equal Opportunities for Women Program established within federal public service. Sylvia Ostry becomes first female deputy minister within the federal government.		Liberal government re-elected in July. International Women's Year. Grace Hartman elected president of the Canadian Union of Public Employees (CUPE), the first woman to head a major Canadian union.
1976			Office of the Coordinator for Status of Women given departmental status. Cabinet directive encourages federal departments to integrate status of women issues in all government activities.

1977			Canadian Human Rights Act passed, prohibiting sex discrimination in federal jurisdiction. Canadian Human Rights Commission (CHRC) established.
1978		Child Tax Credit introduced.	
1979	Canadian Employment and Immigration Commission (CEIC) announces voluntary affirmative action program. Action travail des femmes (ATF) lodges complaint with CHRC about systemic employment discrimination at Canadian National Railway (CNR).	International Year of the Child. CHRC receives complaint of sex discrimination because not all fathers allowed to claim tax relief on child care expenses.	Canadian Advisory Council on the Status of Women publishes *Ten Years Later*, detailing the degree to which RCSW recommendations have been implemented. Federal government publishes *Towards Equality*, detailing its plan of action on the status of women. Joe Clark (Conservative) elected as prime minister in June.
1980	Treasury Board announces pilot affirmative action project in federal public service. Special Parliamentary Committee on Employment Opportunities for the 1980s established. Labour Market Development Task Force established in the CEIC.	CHRC finds it does not have powers to respond to complaint on child care expenses for fathers. Women's Committee of the Ontario Federation of Labour (OFL) mounts major campaign for public day care. Canadian Labour Congress (CLC) endorses public day care.	Pierre Trudeau (Liberal) re-elected as prime minister in February.
1981	Systemic Discrimination Unit established within the CHRC. CHRC establishes tribunal to investigate the complaint brought by ATF against CNR. Report of Task Force on Labour Market Development in the 1980s published. Report of Special Parliamentary Committee on Employment Opportunities in the 1980s published.	NAC's annual meeting endorses CLC/OFL day care campaigns. CUPE establishes a National Day Care Committee. Status of Women Canada publishes report of Interdepartmental Committee on Day Care. Federal government announces that it will establish pilot day care centres in some government buildings.	Ad Hoc Committee on the Constitution formed. Canada ratifies UN Convention opposing all forms of discrimination against women.

Date	Employment Equality	Child Care	Other Events
1982	Federal affirmative action project extended to more departments in federal public service.	CCSD and Department of Health and Welfare organize second national child care conference in Winnipeg. National Steering Committee on Day Care formed at Winnipeg conference. Canadian Day Care Advocacy Association (CDCAA) established.	Charter of Rights and Freedoms entrenched in the Canadian Constitution, including sections 15 and 28.
1983	Royal Commission on Equality in Employment (RCEE) established. Federal government mandatory affirmative action in the federal public service for women, Native people, and disabled persons.	Canadian Child Day Care Federation established. Income Tax Act amended to ensure that men and women are treated equally when applying for Child Care Expense Deduction.	
1984	ATF's complaint of systemic employment discrimination at CNR upheld by CHRC tribunal. CNR required to implement affirmative action program to hire more women in non-traditional jobs.	Status of Women Canada appoints Task Force on Child Care. NAC presents arguments to Royal Commission on Economic Union and Development Prospects for Canada emphasizing link between child care and employment equality.	John Turner (Liberal) replaces Pierre Trudeau as prime minister in June. NAC organizes first ever televised debate on women's issues during an election campaign.

The Mulroney Era

Date	Employment Equality	Child Care	Other Events
1984	Report of the RCEE published.		
1985	Government announces response to RCEE and proposals to develop Employment Equity Act. Affirmative action within the federal public service expanded to include visible minorities. Federal Court of Appeal rules in favour of CNR in its appeal against CHRC's ruling in case of ATF v. CNR.	Special Parliamentary Committee on Child Care established.	Brian Mulroney (Conservative) elected prime minister in September general election. Section 15 of the Charter of Rights and Freedoms comes into force, outlawing sex discrimination and permitting affirmative action to remedy past discrimination.

1986	Employment Equity Act passed. Federal Contractors Program for Employment Equity introduced. Supreme Court rules in favour of ATF in final appeal on case of *ATF v. CNR*.	Report of the Status of Women Task Force on Child Care published.	Shirley Carr elected first female president of the CLC.
1987		Report of the Special Parliamentary Committee on Child Care published. Federal government announces its new National Strategy on Child Care.	
1988	Treasury Board establishes Task Force on Barriers to Women in the Public Service immediately after the November general election.	Child Care Expense Deduction increased. Refundable Child Tax Credit introduced. Child Care Initiatives Fund established. Bill C-144, the proposed Canada Child Care Act, never passed. Mulroney government promises to reintroduce National Strategy on Child Care if re-elected.	NAC and CDCAA both campaign against proposed Free Trade Agreement with the United States. Women's issues debated in second hour of leaders' debate during 1988 general election campaign. Conservative government is re-elected in November.
1989		Government indicates that it cannot proceed with National Strategy on Child Care. UN introduces Convention on the Rights of the Child. House of Commons passes unanimous resolution to eliminate child poverty by the year 2000.	Free Trade Agreement between Canada and the United States introduced.
1990	Report of the Task Force on Barriers to Women in the Public Service published.	Budget caps money cost-shared with Ontario, Alberta, and British Columbia under CAP. Mulroney co-hosts UN World Summit for Children.	

Date	Employment Equality	Child Care	Other Events
1991	Special parliamentary committee established to review the 1986 Employment Equity Act.		
1992	Public Service Reform Act makes employment equity mandatory throughout the federal public service. Report of special committee established to review the 1986 Employment Equity Act published. Earned Income Supplement introduced to offset loss of benefits for low-income workers.	New Child Tax Benefit introduced. New Children's Bureau established. Brighter Futures Program and new child development initiatives introduced. Canadian Day Care Advocacy Association of Canada (CDCAA) becomes Child Care Advocacy Association of Canada (CCAAC). Canadian Child Day Care Federation becomes Canadian Child Care Federation.	
1993	Liberals' "Red Book" promises to strengthen Employment Equity Act if returned to government. Workplace Equity and Labour Standards office set up within new Department of Human Resources Development Canada (HRDC).	Child Care Expense Deduction increased. Liberals' "Red Book" promises an additional $720 million for a new shared-cost child care program, subject to 3 percent annual growth rate and provincial agreement. Children's Task Team set up within HRDC.	NDP government in Ontario introduces employment equity legislation to cover public and private sectors. Kim Campbell, Canada's first female prime minister, replaces Brian Mulroney in June.

The Chrétien Era

Date	Employment Equality	Child Care	Other Events
1993			Jean Chrétien (Liberal) elected as prime minister in October.
1994	New Employment Equity Act tabled in the House of Commons. Treasury Board begins reporting to Parliament on development of employment equity within federal public service.	HRDC organizes meeting, "A Vision for Child Care in the 21st Century," in Montreal. Child care provision addressed as part of HRDC's Social Security Review.	Minister for HRDC announces Social Security Review with public consultation conducted by Standing Committee on Human Resources Development.

1995	New Employment Equity Act passed in December. Federal Contractors Program given legislative mention.	January report of Standing Committee on Human Resources Development acknowledges link between child care and employment equality. Social Security Review closed down prior to budget. February budget introduces Canada Health and Social Transfer (CHST) to replace CAP. Minister for HRDC proposes new federal-provincial shared-cost program on child care in December.	New Conservative government in Ontario passes an act to repeal job quotas and restore merit-based employment practices. Premiers establish Ministerial Council on Social Policy Reform. Quebec referendum in October returns a narrow defeat of the provincial government's proposals for sovereignty.
1996	New Employment Equity Act comes into force. Working Income Supplement replaces Earned Income Supplement, benefit levels increased.	Federal government abandons proposed shared-cost program for child care. Canada Assistance Plan formally abolished. Criteria for claiming Child Care Expense Deduction expanded. Young Child Supplement introduced. First ministers agree to work together to address child poverty.	Federal government announces that it will not create new shared-cost programs in areas of provincial jurisdiction without consent the majority of the provinces.
1997	Working Income Supplement increased.	National Child Benefit announced. National Children's Agenda endorsed by federal, provincial, and territorial governments.	Liberals re-elected to government in June.
1998		National Child Benefit introduced.	
1999		National Children's Agenda announced.	New Social Union framework announced.

Notes

Chapter 1: The Double-Edged Nature of Women's Employment Inequality

1 See Ruth Roach Pierson, *"They're Still Women after All": The Second World War and Canadian Womanhood* (Toronto: McClelland and Stewart, 1986), 1-61, 215; Ruth Abbott and Robert Young, "Cynical and Deliberate Manipulation: Child Care and the Reserve Army of Female Labour in Canada," *Journal of Canadian Studies* 24, 2 (1989): 22-38.

2 See Alison Prentice, Paula Bourne, Gail Cuthbert Brandt, Beth Light, Wendy Mitchinson, and Naomi Black, *Canadian Women: A History*, 2nd ed. (Toronto: Harcourt Brace Canada, 1996), 353-4; Sandra Burt, "The Changing Patterns of Public Policy," in *Changing Patterns: Women in Canada*, 2nd ed., ed. Sandra Burt, Lorraine Code, and Lindsay Dorney (Toronto: McClelland and Stewart, 1993), 220; and Nicole Morgan, *The Equality Game: Women in the Federal Public Service (1908-1987)* (Ottawa: Canadian Advisory Council on the Status of Women, 1988), 9-10.

3 The term "second wave" refers to the renaissance of organized feminism in the early 1960s, and contrasts this era of feminist organizing with the "first wave" of feminism in the late nineteenth and early twentieth centuries. For comparison of these periods, see Sylvia Bashevkin, *Toeing the Lines: Women and Party Politics in English Canada*, 2nd ed. (Toronto: Oxford University Press, 1993), 3-16, 19-31; Sandra Burt, "Variations in an Earlier Theme: The Second Wave of the Canadian Women's Movement," in *Canadian Politics: An Introduction to the Discipline*, ed. Alain-G. Gagnon and James P. Bickerton (Peterborough, ON: Broadview Press, 1990), 542-58; and Prentice et al., *Canadian Women*, 214-42, 414-38, 455-6.

4 Roberta Hamilton, *Gendering the Vertical Mosaic: Feminist Perspectives on Canadian Society* (Toronto: Copp Clark, 1996), 169-70.

5 See, for example, Nancy Adamson, Linda Briskin, and Margaret McPhail, *Feminists Organizing for Change: The Contemporary Women's Movement in Canada* (Toronto: Oxford University Press, 1988), 46-7; Bonnie Fox, ed., *Hidden in the Household: Women's Domestic Labour under Capitalism* (Toronto: Women's Press, 1980); Peggy Morton, "Women's Work Is Never Done ... or the Production, Maintenance and Reproduction of Labour Power," in *Up from the Kitchen, Up from the Bedroom, Up from Under: Women Unite!* ed. Toronto Women's Liberation Movement, Discussion Collective no. 6 (Toronto: Canadian Women's Educational Press, 1970), 46-68; and Meg Luxton, "The Home: A Contested Terrain," in *Still Ain't Satisfied: Canadian Feminism Today*, ed. Maureen Fitzgerald, Connie Guberman, and Margie Wolfe (Toronto: Women's Press, 1982), 112-22.

6 For evidence of women having greater responsibility for child care than men, see Judith L. MacBride-King, *Work and Family: Employment Challenge of the 90s*, Compensation Research Centre, Report 59-90 (Ottawa: Conference Board of Canada, 1990), 10; and Paul Phillips and Erin Phillips, *Women and Work: Inequality in the Labour Market*, rev. ed. (Toronto: James Lorimer, 1993), 42.

7 Pat Schulz, "Minding the Children," in *Still Ain't Satisfied,* ed. Fitzgerald, Guberman, and Wolfe, 124. Schulz was a well-known socialist feminist who lived and worked in Toronto and founded Action Day Care.
8 For evidence of this link in British feminist arguments, see Sheila Rowbotham, *Dreams and Dilemmas* (London: Virago, 1983), 17-20; Vicky Randall, "Feminism and Child Day-care," *Journal of Social Policy* 25, 4 (1996): 485-505; and Sheila Rowbotham, *The Past Is Before Us: Feminism in Action since the 1960s* (London: Pandora Press, 1989), 182.
   For evidence of the link in American feminist arguments, see Eli Zaretsky, "Capitalism, the Family and Personal Life, Part 1," *Socialist Revolution* 3, 1/2 (1973): 69-125; Miriam Schneir, ed., *The Vintage Book of Feminism* (New York: Vintage, 1995), 41-5; Betty Friedan, *The Feminine Mystique,* 20th anniversary ed. (New York: W.W. Norton, 1983), 385, 390, 392; and Shulamith Firestone, *The Dialectic of Sex: The Case for Feminist Revolution* (New York: William Morrow, 1970), 232-7, 269-74.
9 For a discussion of the distinction between American and Canadian women's movements in this regard, see Jill Vickers, Pauline Rankin, and Christine Appelle, *Politics As If Women Mattered: A Political Analysis of the National Action Committee on the Status of Women* (Toronto: University of Toronto Press, 1993), 30-1.
10 On Canadian feminists' engagement with the state, see Sue Findlay, "Feminist Struggles with the Canadian State," *Resources for Feminist Research/Documents sur la recherche féministe* (special issue, *Feminist Perspectives on the Canadian State*) 17, 3 (1988): 5-9; and Christina McCall, "The Unlikely Gladiators: Pearson and Diefenbaker Remembered," in *Pearson: The Unlikely Gladiator,* ed. Norman Hillmer (Montreal and Kingston: McGill-Queen's University Press, 1999), 67.
11 On English Canadian feminists' identification with the federal state, see Vickers et al., *Politics As If Women Mattered,* 16. On the provincial orientation of women's associations in Quebec, see Monique Bégin, "The Royal Commission on the Status of Women in Canada: Twenty Years Later," in *Challenging Times: The Women's Movement in Canada and the United States,* ed. Constance Backhouse and David H. Flaherty (Montreal and Kingston: McGill-Queen's University Press, 1992), 24.
12 See Gail C.A. Cook and Mary Eberts, "Policies Affecting Work," in *Opportunity for Choice: A Goal for Women in Canada,* ed. Gail C.A. Cook (Ottawa: Statistics Canada in association with the C.D. Howe Research Institute, 1976), 162-9, 187-8.
13 See Janine Brodie, *Politics at the Margins: Restructuring and the Canadian Women's Movement* (Halifax: Fernwood Publishing, 1995), 40-4.
14 Royal Commission on the Status of Women in Canada, *Report* (Ottawa: Information Canada, 1970), vii.
15 Paula Bourne, *Women's Paid and Unpaid Work: Historical and Contemporary Perspectives* (Toronto: New Hogtown Press, 1985); Prentice et al., *Canadian Women,* 351-2; Clio Collective, *Quebec Women: A History,* trans. Roger Gannon and Rosalind Gill (Toronto: Women's Press, 1987), 85-93, 170-3, 233-40, 309-12. See also Joan Sangster, "Doing Two Jobs: The Wage Earning Mother, 1945-1970," in *A Diversity of Women: Ontario, 1945-1980,* ed. Joy Parr (Toronto: University of Toronto Press, 1995), 98-132; and Patricia Connelly and Martha MacDonald, "Women's Work: Domestic and Wage Labour in a Nova Scotia Community," in *The Politics of Diversity: Feminism, Marxism and Nationalism,* ed. Roberta Hamilton and Michèle Barrett (London: Verso, 1986), 35-52.
16 Pat Armstrong and Hugh Armstrong, *The Double Ghetto: Canadian Women and Their Segregated Work* (Toronto: McClelland and Stewart, 1978); ibid., rev. ed., 1984; Pat Armstrong and Hugh Armstrong, *A Working Majority: What Women Must Do for Pay* (Ottawa: Canadian Advisory Council on the Status of Women, 1983); Phillips and Phillips, *Women and Work,* 1983 edition; S.J. Wilson, *Women, the Family and the Economy* (Toronto: McGraw-Hill Ryerson, 1982); ibid., 2nd ed., 1986; Pat Armstrong and Hugh Armstrong, "Women, Family and Economy," in *Reconstructing the Canadian Family: Feminist Perspectives,* ed. Nancy Mandell and Ann Duffy (Toronto: Butterworths, 1988), 143-74; and Pat Armstrong and Hugh Armstrong, "The Conflicting Demands of 'Work' and 'Home,'" in *Family Matters: Sociology and Contemporary Canadian Families,* ed. Karen L. Anderson (Scarborough, ON: Nelson Canada, 1988), 113-40.

17 For overviews of the development of equal opportunity and anti-discrimination policies
    in Canada, see Cook and Eberts, "Policies Affecting Work"; Labour Canada, Women's
    Bureau, *Race and Sex Equality in the Workplace: A Challenge and an Opportunity,* ed. Harish
    C. Jain and Dianne Carroll (Ottawa: Supply and Services, 1979); Harish C. Jain, "Race and
    Sex Discrimination in the Workplace: An Analysis of Theory, Research and Public Policy
    in Canada" (paper prepared for the Affirmative Action Directorate, Employment and
    Immigration Canada, March 1981); Morton Weinfield, "The Development of Affirmative
    Action in Canada," *Canadian Ethnic Studies* 13, 2 (1981): 23-39; Carol Agocs, "Affirmative
    Action, Canadian Style: A Reconnaissance," *Canadian Public Policy* 12, 1 (1986): 148-62;
    Stephen G. Petchins, *Women and Work: Discrimination and Response* (Toronto: McClelland
    and Stewart, 1989); and Nan Weiner, *Employment Equity: Making It Work* (Toronto: Butter-
    worths, 1993).
        For comparative perspectives of the development of equal opportunity and anti-
    discrimination policies in Canada, see Ronnie Steinberg Ratner, *Equal Employment Policy
    for Women: Strategies for Implementation in the United States, Canada and Western Europe*
    (Philadelphia, PA: Temple University Press, 1980); and Harish C. Jain and Peter Sloane,
    *Equal Employment Issues: Race and Sex Discrimination in the United States, Canada and
    Britain* (New York: Praeger, 1981).
        For discussions criticizing the development of equal opportunity and anti-discrimination
    policies in Canada, see Rainer Knopff with Thomas Flanagan, *Human Rights and Social
    Technology: The New War on Discrimination* (Ottawa: Carleton University Press, 1989); W.E.
    Block and M.A. Walker, eds., *Discrimination, Affirmative Action and Equal Opportunity:
    An Economic and Social Perspective* (Vancouver: Fraser Institute, 1982); Conrad Winn,
    "Affirmative Action for Women: More than a Case of Simple Justice," *Canadian Public
    Administration* 28, 1 (1985): 24-46; and Martin Loney, *The Pursuit of Division: Race, Gender
    and Preferential Hiring in Canada* (Montreal and Kingston: McGill-Queen's University
    Press, 1998).
        For feminist critiques of equal opportunity and anti-discrimination policies in Canada,
    see Marjorie Cohen, "Employment Equity Is *Not* Affirmative Action," *Canadian Woman
    Studies/Les cahiers de la femme* 6, 4 (1985): 23-5; Lorna R. Marsden, "The Importance of
    Studying Affirmative Action," *Canadian Woman Studies/Les cahiers de la femme* 6, 4 (1985):
    11-15; Sandra Burt, "Voluntary Affirmative Action: Does It Work?" *Rélations indus-
    trielles/Industrial Relations* 41, 3 (1986): 541-50; and Annis May Timpson, "The Politics of
    Employment Inequality in Canada: Gender and the Public Sector," in *Women and Career:
    Themes and Issues in Advanced Industrial Societies,* ed. Julia Evetts (Longman: London,
    1994), 44-58.
18 For historical perspectives on the development of child care, see Patricia Vanderbelt
    Schulz, "Day Care in Canada: 1850-1962," in *Good Day Care: Fighting for It, Getting It,
    Keeping It,* ed. Kathleen Gallagher Ross (Toronto: Women's Press, 1982); Veronica Strong-
    Boag, "Intruders in the Nursery: Childcare Professionals Reshape the Years One to Five,
    1920-1940," in *Childhood and Family History,* ed. Joy Parr (Toronto: McClelland and Stew-
    art, 1982), 160-78; Neil Sutherland, *Children in English-Canadian Society: Framing the Twen-
    tieth Century Consensus* (Toronto: University of Toronto Press, 1976); Susan Prentice,
    "Workers, Mothers, Reds: Toronto's Postwar Daycare Fight," in *Feminism in Action: Studies
    in Political Economy,* ed. M. Patricia Connelly and Pat Armstrong (Toronto: Canadian
    Scholars Press, 1992), 175-200; and Nancy Miller Chenier and Dorothy LaBarge, "Towards
    Universality: An Historical Overview of the Evolution of Education, Health Care, Day
    Care and Maternity Leave," *Background Papers Prepared for the Report of the Task Force on
    Child Care,* Series 2 (Ottawa: Supply and Services, 1985), 1–36.
        For economic analyses of child care options, see Michael Krashinsky, *Day Care and Pub-
    lic Policy in Ontario* (Toronto: Ontario Economic Council, 1977); and Gordon Cleveland
    and Michael Krashinsky, *The Benefits and Costs of Good Child Care: The Economic Rationale
    for Public Investment in Young Children* (Toronto: Childcare Resource and Research Unit,
    1998).
        For different ideological perspectives on the development of child care, see Laura C.
    Johnson and Janice Dineen, *The Kin Trade: The Day Care Crisis in Canada* (Toronto:

McGraw-Hill Ryerson, 1981); Jack Carr, *The Day Care Dilemma: A Critical Analysis of the Options* (Vancouver: Fraser Institute, 1987); Loren Lind and Susan Prentice, *Their Rightful Place: An Essay on Children, Families and Childcare in Canada* (Toronto: Our Schools/Our Selves Education Foundation, 1992); and Marna A. Schecter, *Dealing with the Child Care Challenge,* School of Industrial Relations Research Essay Series no. 32 (Kingston: Industrial Relations Centre, Queen's University, 1990).

For perspectives on organizing for child care, see Sue Colley, "Free Universal Day Care: The OFL Takes a Stand" in *Union Sisters,* ed. Linda Briskin and Lynda Yanz (Toronto: Women's Press, 1983), 307-21; and Ronnie Leah, *Organizing for Daycare* (Kingston, ON: Industrial Relations Centre, Queen's University, 1989).

For overviews of child care policy developments in Canada, see Sandra Harder, *Child Care in Canada,* Current Issue Review 87-11E (Ottawa: Library of Parliament Research Branch, 1995); Martha Friendly, *Child Care Policy in Canada: Putting the Pieces Together* (Don Mills, ON: Addison-Wesley, 1994); Lisa M. Powell, "Toward Child-Care Policy Development in Canada," in *Social Policy in the Global Economy,* ed. Terrance M. Hunsley (Kingston: School of Policy Studies, 1992), 155-81; Maureen Baker, *Canadian Family Policies: Cross-National Comparisons* (Toronto: University of Toronto Press, 1995); and Evelyn Ferguson, "The Child Care Debate: Fading Hopes and Shifting Sands," in *Women's Caring: Feminist Perspectives on Social Welfare,* 2nd ed., ed. Carol T. Baines, Patricia M. Evans, and Sheila M. Neysmith (Toronto: Oxford University Press, 1998), 191-217.

For analyses of the Mulroney government's approach to child care, see Susan D. Phillips, "Rock-a-Bye-Brian: The National Strategy on Child Care," in *How Ottawa Spends 1989-90: The Buck Stops Where?* ed. Katherine A. Graham (Ottawa: Carleton University Press, 1989), 165-208; Derek P.J. Hum, "Compromise and Delay: The Federal Strategy on Child Care," in *Canada: The State of the Federation, 1989,* ed. Ronald L. Watts and Douglas M. Brown (Kingston: Institute of Intergovernmental Relations, Queen's University, 1989), 151-65; Katherine Teghtsoonian, "Institutions and Ideology: Sources of Opposition to Federal Regulation of Child Care Services in Canada and the United States," *Governance* 5, 2 (1992): 197-223; and Katherine Teghtsoonian, "Neo-Conservative Ideology and Opposition to Federal Regulation of Child Care Services in the United States and Canada," *Canadian Journal of Political Science* 16, 1 (1993): 97-122.

For discussions of the Chrétien government's approach to child care, see Sandra Bach and Susan D. Phillips, "Constructing a New Social Union: Child Care beyond Infancy?" in *How Ottawa Spends 1997-98, Seeing Red: A Liberal Report Card,* ed. Gene Swimmer (Ottawa: Carleton University Press, 1997), 235-58; and Martha Friendly and Mab Oloman, "Child Care at the Centre: Child Care on the Social, Economic and Political Agenda in the 1990s," in *Remaking Canadian Social Policy: Social Security in the Late 1990s,* ed. Jane Pulkingham and Gordon Ternowetsky (Halifax: Fernwood, 1996): 273-85.

19 In Canada, see Margrit Eichler, *Families in Canada Today: Recent Changes and Their Policy Consequences* (Toronto: Gage, 1983); Morley Gunderson, *Implications of Daycare Policies on Female Labour Market Behaviour,* Report prepared for the Special Parliamentary Committee on Child Care, 1986; Employment and Immigration Advisory Council, *Workers with Family Responsibilities in a Changing Society: Who Cares?* (Ottawa: Supply and Services, 1987); Maureen Baker, ed., *Canada's Changing Families: Challenges to Public Policy* (Ottawa: Vanier Institute of the Family, 1994); Katherine Teghtsoonian, "Work and/or Motherhood: The Ideological Construction of Women's Options in Canadian Child Care Policy Debates," *Canadian Journal of Women and the Law* 8 (1995): 411-39; and Julia S. O'Connor, "Employment Equality Strategies and Their Representation in the Political Process in Canada, 1970-1994," in *Women and Political Representation in Canada,* ed. Manon Tremblay and Caroline Andrew (Ottawa: University of Ottawa Press, 1998), 85-112.

In the United States, see Louise A. Tilly and Joan W. Scott, *Women, Work and Family* (New York: Holt, Rinehart and Winston, 1978); Irene Diamond, ed., *Families, Politics and Public Policies: A Feminist Dialogue on Women and the State* (New York: Longman, 1983); Carol S. Robb, ed., *Equal Value: An Ethical Approach to Economics and Sex* (Boston: Beacon Press, 1995); and Daphne Spain and Suzanne Bianchi, *Balancing Act: Motherhood, Marriage and Employment among American Women* (New York: Russell Sage Foundation, 1996).

In Australia, see Suzanne Franzway, Diane Court, and R.W. Connell, *Staking a Claim: Feminism, Bureaucracy and the State* (Cambridge: Polity Press, 1989), 59-83, 87-100.

In Europe, see Janet Finch and Dulcie Groves, *A Labour of Love: Women, Work and Caring* (London: Routledge and Kegan Paul, 1983); Gillian Pascall, *Social Policy: A Feminist Analysis* (London: Tavistock, 1986), 34-102; Bronwen Cohen and Karen Clarke, eds., *Childcare and Equal Opportunities: Some Policy Perspectives* (London: Her Majesty's Stationery Office, 1986); Mavis Maclean and Dulcie Groves, eds., *Women's Issues in Social Policy* (London: Routledge, 1991); Jane Lewis, *Women in Britain since 1945: Women, Family, Work and the State in the Post-War Years* (Oxford: Basil Blackwell, 1992); Jane Lewis, "Equality, Difference and State Welfare: Labour Market and Family Policies in Sweden," *Feminist Studies* 18 (1992): 59-87; Arnlang Leira, *Welfare States and Working Mothers: The Scandinavian Experience* (Cambridge: Cambridge University Press, 1992); Kim England, ed., *Who Will Mind the Baby? Geographies of Child Care and Working Mothers* (London: Routledge, 1996); and Eileen Drew, Ruth Emerek, and Ruth Mahon, eds., *Women, Work and Family in Europe* (London: Routledge, 1998).

For comparative work, see Mary Ruggie, *The State and Working Women: A Comparative Study of Britain and Sweden* (Princeton, NJ: Princeton University Press, 1984); Clare Ungerson, ed., *Gender and Caring: Work and Welfare in Britain and Scandinavia* (London: Harvester Wheatsheaf, 1990); Rianne Mahon, "'Both Wage Earner and Mother': Women's Organizing and Child Care Policy in Sweden and Canada," in *Women's Organizing and Public Policy in Canada and Sweden*, ed. Linda Briskin and Mona Eliasson (Montreal and Kingston: McGill-Queen's University Press, 1999), 238-79; and Carol Lee Bacchi, *Women, Policy and Politics: The Construction of Policy Problems* (London: Sage Publications, 1999), 93-111, 130-47.

20 See Isabella Bakker, "Women's Employment in Comparative Perspective," in *Feminization of the Labour Force: Paradoxes and Promises*, ed. Jane Jenson, Elisabeth Hagen, and Cellaigh Reddy (New York: Oxford University Press, 1988), 17-44.

21 Elisabeth Hagen and Jane Jenson, "Paradoxes and Promises: Work and Politics in the Postwar Years," in *Feminization of the Labour Force*, ed. Jenson, Hagen, and Reddy, 8. For a more general discussion of the postwar boom in the service sector, see J.I. Gershuny and I.D. Miles, *The New Service Economy: The Transformation of Employment in Industrial Societies* (New York: Praeger, 1983), 121-30.

22 Helga Maria Hernes, "Women and the Welfare State: The Transition from Private to Public Dependence," in *Women and the State*, ed. Ann Showstack Sassoon (London: Hutchinson, 1987), 78-84; and Annette Borchorst and Birte Siim, "Women and the Advanced Welfare State – A New Kind of Patriarchal Power," in ibid., 134-7.

23 Royal Commission on Equality in Employment, *Report* (Ottawa: Supply and Services, 1984), 62-71.

24 Organization for Economic Co-operation and Development (OECD), *The Integration of Women in the Economy* (Paris: OECD, 1985), 56.

25 See Caroline Andrew, "Women and the Welfare State," *Canadian Journal of Political Science* 17, 4 (1984): 677; Bakker, "Women's Employment in Comparative Perspective," 31; Paul Blyton, "The Changing Canadian Labour Force," *British Journal of Canadian Studies* 5, 2 (1990): 375; OECD, *The Integration of Women*, 17, 55-6; and Hagen and Jenson, "Paradoxes and Promises," 9.

26 Hagen and Jenson, "Paradoxes and Promises," 8.

27 Ibid., 5. See also Labour Canada, *Part-Time Work in Canada: Report of the Commission of Inquiry into Part-Time Work* (Ottawa: Supply and Services, 1983), 73, 77.

28 Morley Gunderson, *Implications of Daycare Policies*, 12-14.

29 Sylvia Ostry, *The Female Worker in Canada* (Ottawa: Dominion Bureau of Statistics, 1968), 19.

30 Phillips and Phillips, *Women and Work*, rev. ed., 35.

31 Sylvia Bashevkin, "The Challenge of Personhood: Women's Citizenship in Contemporary Perspective" (keynote address to the Conference on Women's Equality and Participation in Public Life, Canadian High Commission, London, 21 October 1999).

32 Human Resources Development Canada, *Status of Day Care in Canada 1995 and 1996* (Ottawa: Supply and Services, 1997), 9.

33 Kristin Colwell, "Child Care: A Community Issue," in *Changing Methods: Feminists Transforming Practice,* ed. Sandra Burt and Lorraine Code (Peterborough, ON: Broadview Press, 1995), 169.

34 For a fuller discussion of this tension in Canadian liberalism see Ronald Manzer, *Public Policies and Political Development in Canada* (Toronto: University of Toronto Press, 1985), 17-19.

35 See, for example, Ruth Lister, "Women, Economic Dependency and Citizenship," *Journal of Social Policy* 19, 4 (1990): 445-67; Ruth Lister, "Tracing the Contours of Women's Citizenship," *Policy and Politics* 21, 1 (1993): 3-16; Ruth Lister, "Dilemmas in Engendering Citizenship," *Economy and Society* 24, 1 (1995): 1-40; Ruth Lister, *Citizenship: Feminist Perspectives* (London: Longman, 1997); Anne Phillips, *Engendering Democracy* (Cambridge: Polity Press, 1991); Anne Phillips, "Universal Pretensions in Political Thought," in *Destabilising Theory: Contemporary Feminist Debates,* ed. Anne Phillips and Michèle Barrett (Cambridge: Polity Press, 1992), 10-30; Janine Brodie, "Canadian Women, Changing State Forms, and Public Policy," in *Women and Canadian Public Policy,* ed. Janine Brodie (Toronto: Harcourt Brace, 1996), 1-30; Janine Brodie, "Restructuring and the New Citizenship," in *Rethinking Restructuring: Gender and Change in Canada,* ed. Isabella Bakker (Toronto: University of Toronto Press, 1996), 126-40; Janine Brodie, "Meso-Discourses, State Forms and Gendering of Liberal-Democratic Citizenship," *Citizenship Studies* 1, 2 (1997): 223-42; Helga Maria Hernes, "Scandinavian Citizenship," *Acta Sociologica* 31, 3 (1988): 199-215; Helga Maria Hernes, "The Welfare State Citizenship of Scandinavian Women," in *The Political Interests of Gender: Developing Theory and Research with Feminist Face,* ed. Kathleen B. Jones and Anna G. Jónasdottir (London: Sage, 1988), 187-213; and Hernes, "Women and the Welfare State."

36 Anna Shola Orloff, "Gender and the Social Rights of Citizenship: The Comparative Analysis of Gender Relations and Welfare States," *American Sociological Review* 58, 3 (1993): 308.

37 Elizabeth Meehan and Selma Sevenhuijsen, "Problems in Principles and Policies," in *Equality Politics and Gender,* ed. Meehan and Sevenhuijsen (London: Sage, 1991), 2.

38 See Carole Pateman, "The Patriarchal Welfare State," in *The Disorder of Women: Democracy, Feminism and Political Theory,* ed. Carole Pateman (Cambridge: Polity Press, 1989), 179-204.

39 Joan Tronto, *Moral Boundaries: A Political Argument for an Ethic of Care* (New York: Routledge, 1993), 166.

40 Ibid., 165.

41 Findlay, "Feminist Struggles," 9. See also Jan Barnsley, "Feminist Action, Institutional Reaction," *Resources for Feminist Research/Documents sur la recherche féministe* (special issue, *Feminist Perspectives on the Canadian State*) 17, 3 (1988): 18-21.

42 See Joyce Gelb and Marian Leaf Palley, *Women and Public Policies,* rev. ed. (Princeton, NJ: Princeton University Press, 1987); Sandra Burt, "Women's Issues and the Women's Movement in Canada since 1970," in *The Politics of Gender, Ethnicity and Language in Canada,* vol. 34 of *Research Studies, Royal Commission on the Economic Union and Development Prospects for Canada,* ed. Alan Cairns and Cynthia Williams (Toronto: University of Toronto Press, 1986), 139-56; and Sandra Burt, "Organized Women's Groups and the State," in *Policy Communities and Public Policy in Canada,* ed. William Coleman and Grace Skogstad (Toronto: Copp Clark Pitman, 1990), 204-8.

Chapter 2: Citizenship, Motherhood, and Employment in the Wartime and Welfare States

1 For discussion of the forces that encouraged the development of second-wave feminism in Canada, see Naomi Black, "The Canadian Women's Movement: The Second Wave," in *Changing Patterns: Women in Canada,* 2nd ed., ed. Lorraine Code, Sandra Burt, and Lindsay Dorney (Toronto: McClelland and Stewart, 1993), 151-4; Micheline Dumont, "The Origins of the Women's Movement in Quebec," in *Challenging Times: The Women's Movement in Canada and the United States,* ed. Constance Backhouse and David H. Flaherty (Montreal

and Kingston: McGill-Queen's University Press, 1992), 79-89; Sylvia Bashevkin, *Toeing the Lines: Women and Party Politics in English Canada,* 2nd ed. (Toronto: Oxford University Press, 1993), 16-19; and Jill Vickers, "The Intellectual Origins of the Women's Movement," in *Challenging Times,* ed. Backhouse and Flaherty, 39-60.

2 Bryan D. Palmer, *Working Class Experience: Rethinking the History of Canadian Labour, 1800-1991,* 2nd ed. (Toronto: McClelland and Stewart, 1992), 325.

3 Alison Prentice, Paula Bourne, Gail Cuthbert Brandt, Beth Light, Wendy Mitchinson, and Naomi Black, *Canadian Women: A History,* 2nd ed. (Toronto: Harcourt Brace Canada, 1996), 343-9.

4 Pat Armstrong and Hugh Armstrong, *The Double Ghetto: Canadian Women and Their Segregated Work,* 3rd ed. (Toronto: McClelland and Stewart, 1994), 17.

5 Ruth Roach Pierson, *Canadian Women and the Second World War,* Canadian Historical Association Historical Booklet no. 37 (Ottawa: Canadian Historical Association, 1983), 9.

6 See Ruth Roach Pierson, *"They're Still Women after All": The Second World War and Canadian Womanhood* (Toronto: McClelland and Stewart, 1986), 23-33; Patricia A. Timpson, "My Experiences of Serving in the Royal Canadian Air Force (Women's Division) during World War II" (lecture delivered at the University of Sussex, February 1997).

7 For discussion of the "cult of true womanhood," see Barbara Welter, "The Cult of True Womanhood: 1820-1860," *American Quarterly* 18, 2, part 1 (1966): 152. For discussion of the way that women took on work that had traditionally been carried out by men, see Prentice et al., *Canadian Women,* 345-6.

8 Privy Council Office, P.C. Order in Council 1942-6242, "Order in Council authorizing agreement with Provinces for the care of children whose mothers or foster mothers are employed in war industries in Canada," *Proclamations and Orders in Council Relating to the War* 8 (1942), 79.

9 Although all the provinces were eligible to take part, only Ontario and Quebec took advantage of the agreement. In Ontario, at the end of the war, there were a total of twenty-eight day nurseries for pre-school children and forty-two day care centres for school-age children. See Susan Prentice, "Workers, Mothers, Reds: Toronto's Postwar Daycare Fight," in *Feminism in Action: Studies in Political Economy,* ed. M. Patricia Connelly and Pat Armstrong (Toronto: Canadian Scholars Press, 1992), 176. In Quebec, only six centres were opened. They were all in Montreal and primarily attended by anglophone children. See Martha Friendly, *Child Care Policy in Canada: Putting the Pieces Together* (Don Mills, ON: Addison-Wesley, 1994), 130. Alberta signed the agreement but never acted on it. Other provinces chose not to sign the agreement either, as in the case of Manitoba and British Columbia, because they already had established child care services or, as in the case of Saskatchewan, because women with children were often engaged in farm work. Ironically, this was not considered to be priority work. See Friendly, *Child Care Policy in Canada,* 129.

10 See Pierson, *"They're Still Women,"* 48-61; Prentice et al., *Canadian Women,* 344; and Palmer, *Working Class Experience,* 326.

11 See Carol Lee Bacchi, *Liberation Deferred? The Ideas of the English Canadian Suffragists, 1877-1918* (Toronto: University of Toronto Press, 1983), 142-3; Bashevkin, *Toeing the Lines,* 8-9.

12 Susan Bland, "'Henrietta the Homemaker' and 'Rosie the Riveter': Images of Women in Advertising in *Maclean's* Magazine, 1939-50," *Atlantis* 8, 2 (1983): 82.

13 See Pierson, *Canadian Women and the Second World War,* 12.

14 Ibid., 5, 15. For amusing anecdotes about the way women serving in the Canadian air force rephrased these mottoes to reflect some of the realities of military life, see Patricia A. Timpson, "My Experiences of Serving in the Royal Canadian Air Force."

15 Carole Pateman, "The Patriarchal Welfare State," in *The Disorder of Women: Democracy, Feminism and Political Theory,* ed. Carole Pateman (Cambridge: Polity Press, 1989), 184.

16 Advisory Committee on Reconstruction, *Post-War Problems of Women,* Final Report of the Subcommittee VI (Ottawa: Edmond Cloutier, 1944), 1. On women's efforts to establish the subcommittee, see Pierson, *"They're Still Women,"* 40; and Gail Cuthbert Brandt, "'Pigeon-Holed and Forgotten': The Work of the Subcommittee on the Post-War Problems of Women, 1943," *Histoire sociale/Social History* 15, 29 (1982): 241.

17 Advisory Committee on Reconstruction, *Post-War Problems of Women*, 16, 7.
18 Ibid. 9. For discussion of women's training needs, see p. 17.
19 Ibid., 24.
20 The fact that the postwar dip in women's employment was not larger reflects the way that many older, married women, who had completed their families, decided to keep their foothold in the labour force because they needed the money that wartime employment had brought them and wanted to work for pay. For discussion of these patterns, see Prentice et al., *Canadian Women*, 349-51.
21 Pierson, *Canadian Women and the Second World War*, 22-5; Prentice et al., *Canadian Women*, 350.
22 Prentice et al., *Canadian Women*, 350.
23 Pierson, *Canadian Women and the Second World War*, 23.
24 Prentice et al., *Canadian Women*, 350; Nicole Morgan, *The Equality Game: Women in the Federal Public Service (1908-1987)* (Ottawa: Canadian Advisory Council on the Status of Women, 1988), 9.
25 On the emergence of assumptions about men needing to earn a "family wage," see Elisabeth Hagen and Jane Jenson, "Paradoxes and Promises: Work and Politics in the Postwar Years," in *Feminization of the Labour Force: Paradoxes and Promises,* ed. Jane Jenson, Elisabeth Hagen, and Cellaigh Reddy (New York: Oxford University Press, 1988), 3.
26 Pierson, *"They're Still Women,"* 55-6, 60.
27 For evidence of how links between femininity and domesticity were reasserted in women's magazines, see Susan Bland, "Henrietta the Homemaker," 70; and Pierson, *"They're Still Women,"* 215-18.
28 Leonard Marsh, *Report on Social Security in Canada* (1943; reprint, Toronto: University of Toronto Press, 1975), 196.
29 See Advisory Committee on Reconstruction, *Post-War Problems of Women*, 27-34.
30 Pierson, *Canadian Women and the Second World War*, 20-1.
31 See, for example, Hope Stoddard, "No Women Being Hired," *The Canadian Forum* 26 (June 1946): 58-9; Charlotte Whitton, "The Exploited Sex," *Maclean's* 60 (15 April 1947): 37-8, 40.
32 See, for example, Agnes Macphail, "Men Want to Hog Everything," *Maclean's* 62 (15 September 1949):71-3.
33 T.H. Marshall, "Citizenship and Social Class," in *Citizenship and Social Class and Other Essays* (Cambridge: Cambridge University Press, 1950), 88.
34 Pateman, "The Patriarchal Welfare State," 184.
35 Janine Brodie, "Restructuring and the New Citizenship," in *Rethinking Restructuring: Gender and Change in Canada,* ed. Isabella Bakker (Toronto: University of Toronto Press, 1996), 128-30.
36 David Wolfe, "Mercantilism, Liberalism and Keynesianism," *Canadian Journal of Social and Political Theory* 5, 1-2 (1981): 89.
37 For discussions about the construction of women as recipients of state welfare, see Caroline Andrew, "Women and the Welfare State," *Canadian Journal of Political Science* 17, 4 (1984): 670, 676-7.
38 Catherine Briggs and Sandra Burt, "The Canadian Women's Bureau: Leading the Fight for Justice and Fair Play" (paper prepared for *Canada: Confederation to Present* [Edmonton: Chinook Multimedia, forthcoming]), 33.
39 Linda Geller-Schwartz, "Four Decades of Women in the Workplace" (paper prepared for the Canadian Employment and Immigration Commission, Women's Bureau, 1991), 4.
40 Department of Labour, Economics and Research Branch, *Survey of Married Women Working for Pay in Eight Canadian Cities,* prepared for the Women's Bureau (Ottawa: Queen's Printer, 1958).
41 Briggs and Burt, "The Canadian Women's Bureau," 16.
42 Ibid.
43 Department of Labour, Women's Bureau, "Day Care Services for Children of Working Mothers," *Women's Bureau Bulletin* 11 (January 1964).
44 See Sandra Burt, "Organized Women's Groups and the State," in *Policy Communities and*

Public Policy in Canada, ed. William Coleman and Grace Skogstad (Toronto: Copp Clark Pitman, 1990), 204; and Rianne Mahon, "The Never-Ending Story, Part 1: Feminist Struggle to Reshape Canadian Day Care Policy in the 1970s" (paper presented to the Annual Workshop of the Research Network on Gender, State and Society held in conjunction with the Social Science History Association, Washington, DC, October 1997), 9-13.

45 Burt, "Organized Women's Groups and the State," 201.

46 Mahon, "The Never-Ending Story," 10.

47 Ibid.

48 R. Brian Howe and David Johnson, *Restraining Equality: Human Rights Commissions in Canada* (Toronto: University of Toronto Press, 2000), 6.

49 See House of Commons, *Debates,* 2 April 1946, 513; House of Commons, *Debates,* 16 May 1947, 3149ff; Arthur Lower, "Some Reflections on a Bill of Rights," *Fortnightly Law Journal* 16 (15 February 1947): 216-18 and (1 March 1947): 234-7; John Bracken, *John Bracken Says* (Toronto: Oxford University Press, 1944), all cited in R. Brian Howe, "Human Rights Policy in Ontario: The Tension between Positive and Negative State Values" (PhD diss., University of Toronto, 1988), 50-69.

50 House of Commons, *Debates,* 16 May 1947, 3153.

51 R. Brian Howe, "The Evolution of Human Rights Policy in Ontario," *Canadian Journal of Political Science* 24, 4 (1991): 789.

52 David Lewis and Frank Scott, *Make This Your Canada: A Review of CCF History and Policy* (Toronto: Central Canadian Publishing, 1943), 195; Frank Scott, "Dominion Jurisdiction over Human Rights and Fundamental Freedoms," *Canadian Bar Review* 27, 5 (1949): 513-53; both cited in Howe, "Human Rights Policy," 89, 91, 380.

53 Howe, "Human Rights Policy," 90.

54 Ronald Manzer, *Public Policies and Political Development in Canada* (Toronto: University of Toronto Press, 1985), 145.

55 Howe, "Human Rights Policy," 123.

56 Canadian Labour Congress, "Human Rights and the CLC," *Canadian Labour* 12, 2 (1967): 11, 31. The Canadian Congress of Labour was formed out of the All-Canadian Congress of Labour (ACCL) in 1940. It merged with the Trades and Labour Congress (TLC) in 1956 to form the Canadian Labour Congress (CLC). (Personal communication from Bruce Pearce, Librarian, Newman Industrial Relations Library, University of Toronto, 4 July 2000).

57 Ibid.; Howe, "The Evolution of Human Rights," 787-93.

58 Howe, "Human Rights Policy," 118.

59 Ibid. The increasing participation of ethnic minority groups in the labour force after the war forced the labour movement to address the problem of race discrimination. Nonetheless, there was some criticism of immigrants within the labour movement because of their willingness to work for low wages rather than unionize against them. See Herbert A. Sohn, "Human Rights Legislation in Ontario: A Study of Social Action" (PhD diss., University of Toronto, 1975), 10-11, 102. However, the support of union activists proved crucial in campaigning against discrimination, not least in Ontario, where there was rapid industrialization and unionization during the 1950s. By the end of the decade, 37 percent of the labour force – 550,000 employees – were unionized. See Howe, "Human Rights Policy," 63.

60 On Canada, see Manzer, *Public Policies,* 145. On Australia, see Sophie Watson, ed., *Playing the State: Australian Feminist Interventions* (London: Verso, 1990), 107. On Britain, see Elizabeth M. Meehan, *Women's Rights at Work: Campaigns and Policies in Britain and the United States* (Basingstoke: Macmillan, 1985), 38.

61 Kalmen Kaplansky, "Human Rights and the ILO," *Canadian Labour* 12, 2 (1967): 7, 27. For more general discussion of the impact of international conventions on Canadian human rights law, see David Matas, "Domestic Implementation of Human Rights Agreements," in *Canadian Human Rights Yearbook,* ed. William Pentney and Daniel Proulx (Toronto: Carswell, 1987), 91-118; and Walter S. Tarnopolsky, "The Impact of UN Achievement on Canadian Laws and Practices," in *Human Rights, Federalism and Minorities,* ed. Allan Gotlieb (Toronto: Canadian Institute for International Affairs, 1970).

62 See House of Commons, *Debates*, 23 November 1945, 2455-61; and Canadian Business Association, "A Bill of Rights ... Now," Canadian Business Interviews: John G. Diefenbaker, *Canadian Business* 25 (September 1952): 38-41. Bills of rights were initially developed at the provincial rather than the federal level. In 1947, the government of Saskatchewan created the Saskatchewan Bill of Rights, making it the first government to address discrimination in employment, government services, and housing. See Howe, "Human Rights Policy," 68. However, it took until 1964, when the government of Quebec introduced its Employment Discrimination Act (Bill C-142), for sex discrimination in employment to be prohibited at the provincial level (*Employment Discrimination Act,* Statutes of Quebec, 1964, c. 46, s. 51a).

63 Howe, "Human Rights Policy," 76.

64 *Fair Employment Practices Act,* S.C. 1953, c. 19, s. 4.

65 *Unemployment Insurance Act,* R.S.C. 1970, U-2, s. 21.2(b). See also Joel Silcoff, *Labour Legislation Affecting Women in Canada,* Studies of the Royal Commission on the Status of Women no. 29 (Ottawa: Information Canada, 1970), 145-6.

66 *Federal Female Employees Equal Pay Act,* S.C. 1956, c. 38, s. 4

67 *Bill of Rights,* S.C. 1960, c. 44, s. 1b.

68 *Public Service Employment Act,* S.C. 1967, c. 71, s. 2.

69 Cook and Eberts, "Policies Affecting Work," 178.

70 Black, "The Canadian Women's Movement," 153.

71 Helga Maria Hernes, "Women and the Welfare State: The Transition from Private to Public Dependence," in *Women and the State,* ed. Ann Showstack Sassoon (London: Hutchinson, 1987), 76.

72 Secretary of State, Women's Program, "Pressure for Change: The Role of Canadian Women's Groups," notes prepared for discussion at the United States International Seminar, 1974, 10-11.

73 International Labour Organization, *C-111 Discrimination (Employment and Occupation) Convention,* 1958, Article 2.

74 Mahon, "The Never-Ending Story," 12; Briggs and Burt, "The Canadian Women's Bureau," 6-7.

75 Briggs and Burt, "The Canadian Women's Bureau," 17.

76 Canadian Labour Congress, "CLC Adopts Changes in Structure," *Canadian Labour* 13, 5 (1968): 9; Canadian Labour Congress, "Human Rights," *Canadian Labour* 13, 5 (1968): 37.

77 Meg Luxton and Ester Reiter, "Double, Double, Toil and Trouble ... Women's Experience of Work and Family in Canada, 1980-1995," in *Women and the Canadian Welfare State: Challenges and Change,* ed. Patricia M. Evans and Gerda R. Wekerle (Toronto: University of Toronto Press, 1997), 206-12; and Pat Armstrong and Hugh Armstrong, "Women, Family and Economy," in *Reconstructing the Canadian Family: Feminist Perspectives,* ed. Nancy Mandell and Ann Duffy (Toronto: Butterworths, 1988), 161.

78 Julie White, *Sisters and Solidarity: Women and Unions in Canada* (Toronto: Thompson Educational Publishing, 1993), 45-59, 123-7.

79 Thelma Cartwright, "Twentieth Century Trying Time for Women," *Canadian Labour* 12, 2 (1967): 26.

80 Black, "The Canadian Women's Movement," 153. For a fuller discussion of socialist feminism in Canada, see Nancy Adamson, Linda Briskin, and Margaret McPhail, *Feminists Organizing for Change: The Contemporary Women's Movement in Canada* (Toronto: Oxford University Press, 1988), 97-135.

81 Author's interview with Laura Sabia, Chair of the Committee for the Equality of Women in Canada, 1966-71, Toronto, August 1986.

82 Cerise Morris, "'Determination and Thoroughness': The Movement for a Royal Commission on the Status of Women," *Atlantis* 5, 2 (1980): 11.

Chapter 3: The Royal Commission on the Status of Women

1 For further discussion of this point, see Florence Bird, *Anne Francis: An Autobiography* (Toronto: Clarke Irwin, 1974), 316; Naomi Black, "The Canadian Women's Movement: The Second Wave," in *Changing Patterns: Women in Canada,* 2nd ed., ed. Lorraine Code,

Sandra Burt, and Lindsay Dorney (Toronto: McClelland and Stewart, 1993), 159-60; Annis May Timpson, "Between the Royal Commissions: Women's Employment Equality in Canada, 1966-1986," *London Journal of Canadian Studies* 4 (1987): 68-81; Sandra Burt, "The Changing Patterns of Public Policy," in *Changing Patterns,* ed. Code, Burt, and Dorney (Toronto: McClelland and Stewart, 1993), 222; Lorrenne M.G. Clark, "Reminiscences and Reflections on the Twentieth Anniversary of the Commission's Report," in *Women and the Canadian State/Les femmes et l'État canadien,* ed. Caroline Andrew and Sandra Rodgers (Montreal and Kingston: McGill-Queen's University Press, 1997), 3-4; and Freda L. Paltiel, "State Initiatives: Impetus and Effect," in *Women and the Canadian State,* ed. Andrew and Rodgers, 27.

2 Alison Prentice, Paula Bourne, Gail Cuthbert Brandt, Beth Light, Wendy Mitchinson, and Naomi Black, *Canadian Women: A History* (Toronto: Harcourt Brace Jovanovich, 1988), 352.

3 For a discussion of the RCSW's strategy for collecting evidence in both oral and written testimony, see Cerise Morris, "No More than Simple Justice: The Royal Commission on the Status of Women" (PhD diss., McGill University, 1982), 199-200. The kinds of issues raised at the hearings are also discussed in Christina Newman, "What's So Funny about the Royal Commission on the Status of Women?" *Saturday Night* 84, 1 (1969): 21-4; Bird, *Anne Francis,* 273-86; Barbara M. Freeman, "Framing Feminine/Feminist: English-Language Press Coverage of the Hearings of the Royal Commission on the Status of Women in Canada, 1968," *International Journal of Canadian Studies/Revue internationale d'études canadiennes* 11 (Spring 1995): 11-32; and Florence Bird, "Reminiscences of the Commission Chair," in *Women and the Canadian State,* ed. Andrew and Rodgers, 188-96. However, the written submissions have not yet been subject to the kind of systematic analysis offered here.

4 Both issues are addressed in articles about the RCSW's report. See, for example, Lucia Kowaluk, "The Status of Women in Canada," *Our Generation* 8, 2 (1972): 108-15. They are also addressed in analyses of the federal government's response to the commission's recommendations. See, for example, Lucie Morgado, "Une révolution inachievée: la commission royale d'enquête sur la situation de la femme 20 ans plus tard," *Femmes d'action* 20, 3 (1991): 29-31; Advisory Council on the Status of Women, *What's Been Done? Assessment of the Federal Government's Implementation of the Recommendations of the Royal Commission on the Status of Women* (Ottawa: Advisory Council on the Status of Women, 1974), 2-14, 21-4; and Canadian Advisory Council on the Status of Women, *Ten Years Later: An Assessment of the Federal Government's Implementation of the Recommendations Made by the Royal Commission on the Status of Women* (Ottawa: Canadian Advisory Council on the Status of Women, 1979), 10-31, 48-9. In none of these examples are the two issues linked together.

5 In addition, the commission received a number of confidential briefs. These are stored in the National Archives of Canada (NAC) with the papers of the RCSW, but in deference to their authors' wishes for confidentiality they have not been included in this analysis (NAC, RG 33/89).

6 Bird, "Reminiscences of a Commission Chair," 188-96; Bird, *Anne Francis,* 273-86.

7 For analysis of the media coverage of the RCSW, see Barbara M. Freeman, "The Media and the Royal Commission on the Status of Women in Canada, 1966-1972: Research in Progress," *Resources for Feminist Research/Documents sur la recherche féministe* 23, 3 (1993): 3-9; Morris, "No More Than Simple Justice," 224-6; and Newman, "What's So Funny about the Royal Commission on the Status of Women?" 23.

8 Bird, *Anne Francis,* 269. For a fuller discussion of the ideas of participatory democracy that were taking root at the time, see Carole Pateman, *Participation and Democratic Theory* (Cambridge: Cambridge University Press, 1970). It is interesting that the NDP Provincial Women's Committee of Saskatchewan stated that "the remarks of Mrs. John Bird in Regina, as quoted in the *Leader-Post* of December 7, 1967, were very helpful in showing what we might deal with in the brief" (New Democratic Party Provincial Women's Committee, Saskatchewan Section, Submission to the Royal Commission on the Status of Women, Brief no. 133, 19 March 1968, NAC, RG 33/89, microfilm C-4878).

9 See Annis May Timpson, "Royal Commissions as Sites of Resistance: Women's Challenges

on Child Care in the Royal Commission on the Status of Women," *International Journal of Canadian Studies/Revue international d'études canadiennes* 20 (Fall 1999): 123-48.

10 Ibid.

11 Some attention has been paid to this question by Cerise Morris, "'Determination and Thoroughness': The Movement for a Royal Commission on the Status of Women," *Atlantis* 5, 2 (1980): 11-13. On the politics of the RCSW's creation, see B. Craig, "Women's March May Back Call for Rights Probe," *Globe and Mail,* 5 January 1967, A1; Paltiel, "State Initiatives: Impetus and Effect," 27-51; and Judy LaMarsh, *Memoirs of a Bird in a Gilded Cage* (Toronto: McClelland and Stewart, 1989), 301-2.

12 June Menzies, a member of the CFUW, wrote a letter in the association's March 1966 newsletter, asking what women should do to improve their status in Canada. This letter, and a follow-up communication from Helen Tucker as president of Voice of Women (VOW), led Tucker and Laura Sabia to call the meeting that led to the creation of the CEW. Fifty women from these organizations met, along with members of the press, at the CFUW Club House in Toronto on 3 May 1966 and passed resolutions about ways in which the status of women could be improved in Canada. See Morris, "Determination and Thoroughness," 9-10.

13 Author's emphasis.

14 Morris, "Determination and Thoroughness," 11.

15 The implicit parallels between establishing a commission to review the status of Canada's *two founding nations* and Canada's *two founding sexes* also enabled the activists on the CEW to see their work as promoting national unity among Canadian women. It is interesting to note that through Sabia's own contacts in Montreal, representatives of the Fédération des femmes du Québec (FFQ) were drawn into the lobbying process (author's interview with Laura Sabia, Chair of the CEW, 1966-71, Toronto, August 1986).

16 This decision was confirmed by the CEW on 28 June 1966, just after the July issue of the women's magazine *Chatelaine* published Anderson's editorial calling for a royal commission on the status of women. See Doris Anderson, "Let's Find Out What's Happening to Women," *Chatelaine* 39, 7 (1966): 1. The brief submitted to the federal government was ratified by the CEW on 15 September 1966. An interesting aspect of the work of the CEW, which has not been clarified in the literature to date, is that the Ontario Federation of Women Teachers Associations (which later housed NAC and many other groups at 1260 Bay Street, Toronto) played a very active part in its development. The federation provided free office space in which the CEW headquarters could be based and offered significant financial support to develop the campaign for the RCSW (interview with Laura Sabia, August 1986). Nonetheless, the fact that women in the CEW paid their own travel and accommodation bills to join the Ottawa lobby indicates that this kind of political action was only open to women with adequate financial resources.

17 Morris, "Determination and Thoroughness," 13. The brief was presented to the minister of Justice, Lucien Cardin, by Laura Sabia, Margaret Hyndman, Emile Colas, Julia Schultz, and Margaret MacLellan in the presence of sixty observers, including a delegation from the FFQ (ibid.). The inclusion of the FFQ representatives was not simply to give a show of national unity but to ensure that the CEW delegates had some direct influence on the francophone minister of Justice (interview with Laura Sabia, Toronto, August 1986).

18 The seven areas were: female workers under federal jurisdiction, family law, taxation, education and retraining, immigration, International Labour Organization conventions that had not yet been ratified, and the global status of women in a changing society. See Morris, "Determination and Thoroughness," 13.

19 Indeed, Hyndman argued that the CEW considered a royal commission the only appropriate vehicle to achieve this because it would demand public attention and be made up, primarily, of women. See Morris, "Determination and Thoroughness," 12.

20 Jane Arscott, "Twenty-five Years and Sixty-five Minutes after the Royal Commission on the Status of Women," *International Journal of Canadian Studies/Revue internationale d'études canadiennes* 11 (Spring 1995): 41.

21 See George F. Henderson, *Federal Royal Commissions in Canada, 1867-1966: A Checklist* (Toronto: University of Toronto Press, 1967).

22 For an autobiographical account of Judy LaMarsh's internal cabinet wranglings to get the RCSW established – "one of the hardest things I ever accomplished" – see LaMarsh, *Memoirs*, 301-2. For an account of Laura Sabia's remarks, see Craig, "Women's March." Its significance is reinforced by Bégin's account of the politics surrounding the creation of the commission, in which she argues that the federal government was keen to avoid confrontation. See Monique Bégin, "The Royal Commission on the Status of Women in Canada: Twenty Years Later," in *Challenging Times: The Women's Movement in Canada and the United States*, ed. Constance Backhouse and David H. Flaherty (Montreal and Kingston: McGill-Queen's University Press, 1992), 27.

23 For analyses of the impact of minority government on Pearson, see Morris, "Determination and Thoroughness," 5, 20; and Black, who notes that "in parliament, the New Democratic Party, urged on by their only woman MP, Grace MacInnis, used the issue of a women's commission as yet another handy weapon against a government that lacked an absolute majority" ("The Canadian Women's Movement," 159).

24 Black alludes to the fact that the Royal Commission was an ideal instrument for "appeasing and possibly diffusing any feminist activism" but does not explain why ("The Canadian Women's Movement," 159). John English has suggested that Pearson also believed that the existence of a royal commission would channel second-wave feminist activity (and his daughter's interest) away from the peace movement (author's discussion with John English, MP, Canadian High Commission, London, March 1995). Dumont has argued that by agreeing to a royal commission, the federal government hoped it could contain feminist debate within the sphere of human rights. See Micheline Dumont, *The Women's Movement: Then and Now*, Feminist Perspectives Féministes no. 5b (Ottawa: Canadian Research Institute for the Advancement of Women, 1986), 17.

25 Timpson, "Between the Royal Commissions," 68-81; Black, "The Canadian Women's Movement," 159. It is also important to recognize that this was "the golden age" of royal commissions. See V. Seymour Wilson, "The Role of Royal Commissions and Task Forces," in *The Structures of Policy Making in Canada*, ed. G. Bruce Doern and Peter Aucoin (Toronto: Macmillan, 1971), 115.

26 International Labour Organization, *C-111 Discrimination (Employment and Occupation) Convention*, 1958, Article 2. For discussion of Canada's ratification of ILO Convention 111, see Harish C. Jain and Peter Sloane, *Equal Employment Issues: Race and Sex Discrimination in the United States, Canada and Britain* (New York: Praeger, 1981), 21.

27 In addition to the President's Commission on the Status of Women in the United States (1961-3), similar commissions on the status of women had been established in France (1966), West Germany (1962), Denmark (1965), United Kingdom (1966), Finland (1966), the Netherlands (1966), Austria (1966), Belgium (1966), and Norway (1966) (Royal Commission on the Status of Women in Canada, *Report* [Ottawa: Information Canada, 1970], 1).

28 Anderson, "Let's Find Out," 1.

29 Department of Labour, Address prepared for delivery by Miss Sylva M. Gelber, Director, Women's Bureau, 8 December 1969.

30 Monique Bégin, "The Canadian Government and the Commission's Report," in *Women and the Canadian State*, ed. Andrew and Rodgers, 13.

31 See Royal Commission on Equality in Employment, *Report* (Ottawa: Supply and Services, 1984), 61; and Pat Armstrong and Hugh Armstrong, *The Double Ghetto: Canadian Women and Their Segregated Work*, 3rd ed. (Toronto: McClelland and Stewart, 1994), 23-85.

32 Black, "The Canadian Women's Movement," 159.

33 See Armstrong and Armstrong, *The Double Ghetto*, 3rd ed., 191; Royal Commission on Equality in Employment, *Report*, 59-60.

34 For a fuller discussion of this tension in Canadian liberalism, see Ronald Manzer, *Public Policies and Political Development in Canada* (Toronto: University of Toronto Press, 1985), 9-19.

35 Royal Commission on the Status of Women, *Report*, vii.

36 Ibid.

37 Ibid.

38 Ibid.
39 Ibid., vii-viii.
40 Ibid., viii.
41 See Royal Commission on Equality in Employment, *Report,* 183; Susan A. McDaniel, "The Changing Canadian Family: Women's Roles and the Impact of Feminism," in *Changing Patterns,* ed. Burt, Code, and Dorney, 428.
42 For discussion of femocrats' efforts to address the question of child care for working mothers, see Rianne Mahon, "The Never-Ending Story Part 1: Feminist Struggle to Re-shape Canadian Day Care Policy in the 1970s" (paper presented to the Annual Workshop of the Research Network on Gender, State and Society held in conjunction with the Social Science History Association, Washington, DC, October 1997), 15-16; Burt, "The Changing Patterns of Public Policy," 220.
43 Peter C. Newman, *The Distemper of Our Times: Canadian Politics in Transition, 1963-1968* (Toronto: McClelland and Stewart, 1969), 324.
44 For a fuller discussion of questions about women's roles as worker-citizens and carer-citizens, see Helga Maria Hernes, "Women and the Welfare State: The Transition from Private to Public Dependence," in *Women and the State,* ed. Ann Showstack Sassoon (London: Hutchinson, 1987), 72-92; and Ruth Lister, *Citizenship: Feminist Perspectives* (London: Macmillan, 1997), 177.
45 Author's interview with the Hon. Monique Bégin, Executive Secretary, Royal Commission on the Status of Women, 1967-70, Ottawa, December 1998.
46 A total of 454 nonconfidential briefs can be identified in the records of the commission. Of these, a total of 177 were submitted by individual women, 68 percent (120) of which addressed issues of women's employment and child care. A total of 173 briefs were received from established groups of women, 88 percent (153) of which raised questions about women's employment and child care. The briefs from organizations included twenty-nine from female-dominated professional and trade associations; twenty-eight from women's religious organizations; twenty-one from national, provincial, and community women's organizations; nineteen from women's institutes and home economics associations; seventeen from family service and single-parent associations; sixteen from university women's clubs; ten from business and professional women's clubs; nine from young women's secular associations; eight from women's peace organizations; seven from women's associations within political parties; five from day care organizations; and four from farm women's organizations (Royal Commission on the Status of Women, *Report,* 456-67).
47 Manitoba Volunteer Committee on the Status of Women, Submission to the Royal Commission on the Status of Women, Brief no. 318, 21 March 1968, National Archives of Canada (hereinafter NAC), RG 33/89, microfilm C-4881, 270.
48 Voice of Women, Montreal, Submission to the Royal Commission on the Status of Women, Brief no. 348, May 1968, NAC, RG 33/89, microfilm C-4881, 5. This was the only brief I found with different sections written in French and English. The quotation in English is not a translation from French.
49 Canadian Federation of University Women, New Brunswick Section, Submission to the Royal Commission on the Status of Women, Brief no. 141, March 1968, NAC, RG 33/89, microfilm C-4878, 5.
50 Manitoba Volunteer Committee on the Status of Women, Submission, 2.
51 Canadian Dietetic Association, Submission to the Royal Commission on the Status of Women, Brief no. 239, 19 January 1968, NAC, RG 33/89, microfilm C-4880, 4. At the time of submitting the brief, the Canadian Dietetic Association was an "incorporated association of 1587 Dieticians 3 of whom [were] men" (ibid., 1).
52 Ibid., 11.
53 Anderson, "Let's Find Out," 1.
54 Canadian Federation of University Women, New Brunswick Section, Submission, 4.
55 Canadian Federation of Business and Professional Women's Clubs, Ottawa, Submission to the Royal Commission on the Status of Women, Brief no. 147, 19 March 1968, NAC, RG 33/89, microfilm C-4879, 10.
56 Ibid., 10-11.

57 Women's Group of the London and Middlesex Riding Association of the New Democratic Party, Submission to the Royal Commission on the Status of Women, Brief no. 176, 4 June 1968, NAC, RG 33/89, microfilm C-4879, B.
58 See, for example, Canadian Federation of Business and Professional Women's Clubs, Ottawa, Submission, 10.
59 Canadian Federation of University Women, New Brunswick Section, Submission, 6.
60 Canadian Clubs of Zonta International, Toronto, Submission to the Royal Commission on the Status of Women, Brief no. 97, 15 February 1968, NAC, RG 33/89, microfilm C-4878, 2.
61 Canadian Dietetic Association, Submission, 4.
62 Joan B. Hayes (Halifax), Submission to the Royal Commission on the Status of Women, Brief no. 6, 20 October 1967, NAC, RG 33/89, microfilm C-4878, 2.
63 New Democratic Party Provincial Women's Committee, Saskatchewan Section, Submission, 5.
64 Canadian Dietetic Association, Submission, 3-4.
65 See, for example, New Democratic Party Provincial Women's Committee, Saskatchewan Section, Submission, 16; and Manitoba Volunteer Committee on the Status of Women, Submission, 311. These briefs called on governments both to achieve greater balance between the retraining programs for rural and urban women and to address issues of difference relating to maternity and child care.
66 Anglican Church of Canada, Commission on Women's Work, Submission to the Royal Commission on the Status of Women, Brief no. 52, 1 February 1968, NAC, RG 33/89, microfilm C-4878, 16.
67 Business and Professional Women's Clubs of British Columbia and the Yukon, Submission to the Royal Commission on the Status of Women, Brief no. 261, 17 March 1968, NAC, RG 33/89, microfilm C-4880, 2-3.
68 Canadian Federation of Business and Professional Women Clubs, Ottawa, Submission, 23.
69 Vera G. Alback (Ottawa), Submission to the Royal Commission on the Status of Women, Brief no. 193, 20 March 1968, NAC, RG 33/89, microfilm C-4879, 4.
70 Junior League of Toronto, Submission to the Royal Commission on the Status of Women, Brief no. 98, 7 June 1968, NAC, RG 33/89, microfilm C-4878, 2.
71 Sherrie E. Tutt (Rouleau), Submission to the Royal Commission on the Status of Women, Brief no. 157, March 1968, NAC, RG 33/89, microfilm C-4879, 3.
72 See, for example, Women's Ad Hoc Committee of the Saskatchewan Federation of Labour, Submission to the Royal Commission on the Status of Women, Brief no. 296, 20 March 1968, NAC, RG 33/89, microfilm C-4880, 4.
73 Betty Cooper (Calgary), Submission to the Royal Commission on the Status of Women, Brief no. 399, 1968, NAC, RG 33/89, microfilm C-4882, 3.
74 Zenny Burton (Regina), Submission to the Royal Commission on the Status of Women, Brief no. 211, 22 March 1968, NAC, RG 33/89, microfilm C-4880, 10.
75 The translation reads: "by also creating work for other mothers in the area, who either have the appropriate training or are capable of looking after children." Suzel T. Perron (Westmount), Submission to the Royal Commission on the Status of Women, Brief no. 336, 9 March 1968, NAC, RG 33/89, microfilm C-4881, 4.
76 Bonita Bridge (Winnipeg), Submission to the Royal Commission on the Status of Women, Brief no. 279, March 1968, NAC, RG 33/89, microfilm C-4880, 3.
77 Bégin, "The Canadian Government and the Commission's Report," 13.
78 Interestingly, this perspective gained legitimacy in the late twentieth century. As Lister notes, "the 1995 UN Platform for Action agreed at Beijing for women's unpaid caring work to be treated as part of the gross national product" (*Citizenship: Feminist Perspectives* [London: Macmillan, 1997], 235).
79 Soroptomist Club of Halifax, Submission to the Royal Commission on the Status of Women, Brief no. 86, 27 February 1968, NAC, RG 33/89, microfilm C-4878, 5.
80 Bonita Bridge, Submission, 3.
81 Victoria Day Care Services, Toronto, Submission to the Royal Commission on the Status of Women, Brief no. 168, 19 March 1968, NAC, RG 33/89, microfilm C-4879, 2.

82 Eleanor S. Dunn (Ottawa), Submission to the Royal Commission on the Status of Women, Brief no. 55, February 1968, NAC, RG 33/89, microfilm C-4878, 3.
83 Young Women's Christian Association of Canada, Toronto, Submission to the Royal Commission on the Status of Women, Brief no. 160, 20 March 1968, NAC, RG 33/89, microfilm C-4879, 3.
84 University of British Columbia, Committee of Mature Women Students, Submission to the Royal Commission on the Status of Women, Brief no. 217, March 1968, NAC, RG 33/89, microfilm C-4880, 1.
85 The report of the Royal Commission on Taxation was tabled in the House of Commons on 24 February 1967 by Mitchell Sharp as Minister of Finance (House of Commons, *Debates,* 24 February 1967, 13479). For reactions to this commission's recommendations, see Pioneer Women's Organization of Canada, Submission to the Royal Commission on the Status of Women, Brief no. 65, 11 March 1968, NAC, RG 33/89, microfilm C-4878, 4; and Business and Professional Women's Clubs of British Columbia and the Yukon, Submission, 23. See also Alan Edmonds, "This is Anne Francis, Chairman of the Royal Commission on the Status of Women. She's never been exploited, discriminated against, patronized or bored. She's trying to find out why most women are," *Maclean's* 81, 1 (1968): 11.
86 Royal Commission on Taxation, *Report* (Ottawa: Queen's Printer, 1966), 3: 290.
87 Pioneer Women's Organization of Canada, Submission, 4.
88 Dawson Creek Business and Professional Women's Club, Submission to the Royal Commission on the Status of Women, Brief no. 219, March 1968, NAC, RG 33/89, microfilm C-4880, 4.
89 Alice James (Vancouver), Submission to the Royal Commission on the Status of Women, Brief no. 92, 25 February 1968, NAC, RG 33/89, microfilm C-4878, 10.
90 Ibid.
91 University of British Columbia, Committee of Mature Women Students, Submission, 2.
92 Junior League of Toronto, Submission, 4.
93 Mrs. W.D. Hall (Weston), Submission to the Royal Commission on the Status of Women, Brief no. 345, 28 March 1968, NAC, RG 33/89, microfilm C-4881, 5. See also Alberta Association of Registered Nurses, Submission to the Royal Commission on the Status of Women, Brief no. 26, January 1968, NAC RG 33/89, microfilm C-4878, 5; Canadian Federation of University Women, Sudbury, Ontario, Submission to the Royal Commission on the Status of Women, Brief no. 192, 3 October 1968, NAC, RG 33/89, microfilm C-4879, 13.
94 Dawson Creek Business and Professional Women's Club, Submission, 4.
95 United Nations Association, Women's Section, Toronto, Submission to the Royal Commission on the Status of Women, Brief no. 58, 5 June 1968, NAC, RG 33/89, microfilm C-4878, 3.
96 Lorraine Code, "Feminist Theory," in *Changing Patterns,* ed. Burt, Code, and Dorney, 37.
97 See, for example, Parents Without Partners, Ottawa Chapter, Submission to the Royal Commission on the Status of Women, Brief no. 319, 30 April 1968, NAC, RG 33/89, microfilm C-4881, 2; Alberta Association of Registered Nurses, Submission, 6; United Nations Association, Submission, 1.
98 See, for example Sherrill Jackson's call for free nursery and after-school care (Submission to the Royal Commission on the Status of Women, Brief no. 28, 12 June 1968, NAC, RG 33/89, microfilm C-4878, 2); and Alice James's call for pre-school and after-school care (Submission, 3).
99 The translation reads: while "the budget of a married woman who must work rarely allows her to hire competent household help ... in fact there is a shortage of such people because their role in society is undervalued." L'association féminine d'éducation et d'action sociale, Submission to the Royal Commission on the Status of Women, Brief no. 303, March 1968, NAC, RG 33/89, microfilm C-4880, 3.
100 See, for example, University of British Columbia, Committee of Mature Women Students, Submission, 9; Young Men's and Young Women's Hebrew Association and Neighbourhood House Services, Submission to the Royal Commission on the Status of Women, Brief no. 314, 21 March 1968, NAC, RG 33/89, microfilm, C-4881, 12; and Thelma Cartwright (Ottawa), Submission to the Royal Commission on the Status of Women, Brief no. 407, 1968, NAC, RG 33/89, microfilm C-4882, 1.

101 See, for example, Fédération des services sociaux à la famille du Québec, Submission to the Royal Commission on the Status of Women, Brief no. 256, 20 March 1968, NAC, RG 33/89, microfilm C-4880, 6.

102 For discussion of Canadian campaigns for free universal child care, see Martha Friendly, *Child Care Policy in Canada: Putting the Pieces Together* (Don Mills, ON: Addison-Wesley, 1994), 142-9.

103 Voice of Women, Edmonton, Submission to the Royal Commission on the Status of Women, Brief no. 159, 25 April 1968, NAC, RG 33/89, microfilm C-4879, 4 .

104 Briefs calling for subsidized child care places included Marianne Lafon (Montreal), Submission to the Royal Commission on the Status of Women, Brief no. 40, 29 January 1968, NAC, RG 33/89, microfilm C-4878, 4; Margaret Smith (Whitehorse), Submission to the Royal Commission on the Status of Women, Brief no. 414, 1968, NAC, RG 33/89, microfilm C-4882, 2. For a good example of a brief calling for subsidized child care spaces and tax relief, see Sherrie E. Tutt, Submission, 4.

105 Junior League of Toronto, Submission, 1.

106 The translation reads: "Each municipality must ensure that it has a sufficient number of day nurseries [to meet] the needs of the poor." Louyse Ouelet-Savoie (Montreal), Submission to the Royal Commission on the Status of Women, Brief no. 144, 10 March 1968, NAC, RG 33/89, microfilm C-4878, 8.

107 Dunn, Submission, 3.

108 The translation reads: Suzanne Pelletier looked forward to the day when "day nurseries [would] be integrated into the services already provided by the ministry of Family and Health," and envisaged that, like health insurance, "these services would be paid for by parents, the government, and the employer." Suzanne Pelletier (Quebec), Submission to the Royal Commission on the Status of Women, Brief no. 210, 21 March 1968, NAC, RG 33/89, microfilm C-4880, 5.

109 Committee of the Day Care Section of the Citizens' Committee on Children, Submission to the Royal Commission on the Status of Women, Brief no. 324, 29 April 1968, NAC, RG 33/89, microfilm C-4881, 1.

110 Ibid.

111 Ibid., 7. For a broader discussion of the way in which jurisdictional divisions affect the development of issues that concern Canadian women, see Audrey Doerr, "Overlapping Jurisdictions and Women's Issues," in *Women and the Constitution in Canada,* ed. Audrey Doerr and Micheline Carrier (Ottawa: Canadian Advisory Council on the Status of Women, 1981), 123-48.

112 Committee of the Day Care Section of the Citizens' Committee on Children, Submission, 1.

113 Victoria Day Care Services, Submission, 2.

114 Ibid.

115 Ibid.

116 St. Andrew's United Church, Group of Women, Beloeil, Submission to the Royal Commission on the Status of Women, Brief no. 166, 17 March 1968, NAC, RG 33/89, microfilm C-4879, 1.

117 Ibid., 2.

118 Ibid.

119 Ontario Jaycettes, Chatham, Submission to the Royal Commission on the Status of Women, Brief no. 89, 5 June 1968, NAC, RG 33/89, microfilm C-4878, 2.

120 The translation reads: "In the list of items suggested by the Commission, there is a strong emphasis on the acquisition of rights for married or single women who work. It is just and reasonable that certain measures that would help resolve the problems faced by women who work outside the home. In our opinion, it is necessary to attach the greatest importance to the role of married women, who run the home and uphold family values ... In the course of the inquiries being undertaken it will be desirable to address the fact that women who stay home are undervalued in comparison to those who return to the labour market." L'Ordre des Dames Hélène-de-Champlain Inc., Ste. Agathe-des-Monts, Submission to the Royal Commission on the Status of Women, Brief no. 129, 28 February 1968, NAC, RG 33/89, microfilm C-4878, 2.

121 See, for example, Joan C. Tronto, *Moral Boundaries: A Political Argument for an Ethic of Care* (New York: Routledge, 1993); Peta Bowden, *Caring: Gender-Sensitive Ethics* (London and New York: Routledge, 1997); Ruth Lister, *Citizenship: Feminist Perspectives* (London: Macmillan, 1997), 168-94; Selma Sevenhuijsen, *Citizenship and the Ethics of Care: Feminist Considerations on Justice, Morality and Politics*, trans. from Dutch by Liz Savage (London and New York: Routledge, 1998).

122 Imperial Order Daughters of the Empire, Toronto, Submission to the Royal Commission on the Status of Women, Brief no. 311, March 1968, NAC, RG 33/89, microfilm C-4881, 23.

123 National Council of Women of Canada, Ottawa, Submission to the Royal Commission on the Status of Women, Brief no. 131, March 1968, NAC, RG 33/89, microfilm C-4878, 6.

124 Alberta Association of Registered Nurses, Submission, 19.

125 L'Ordre des Dames Hélène, Submission, 15.

126 Montreal Council of Women, Submission to the Royal Commission on the Status of Women, Brief no. 183, February 1968, NAC, RG 33/89, microfilm C-4879, 9.

127 Ibid.

128 Salvation Army of Canada, Women's Organization, Toronto, Submission to the Royal Commission on the Status of Women, Brief no. 110, February 1968, NAC, RG 33/89, microfilm C-4878, 1.

129 Margaret M. Gaudreau (Ste. Thérèse), Submission to the Royal Commission on the Status of Women, Brief no. 337, April 1968, NAC, RG 33/89, microfilm C-4881, 2.

130 For a fuller discussion of anti-maternalism in early second-wave feminism, see Anna Snitow, "A Gender Diary," in *Conflicts in Feminism,* ed. Marianne Hirsch and Evelyn Fox Keller (New York: Routledge, 1990), 31.

131 Royal Commission on the Status of Women, *Report,* xi. The commissioners' concern to frame their report in terms of concepts of citizenship was apparent in their assertion that "there should be equality of opportunity to share the responsibilities of society as well as its privileges and prerogatives" (ibid).

132 Ibid. With the exception of John Humphrey, who wrote a minority report, all the commissioners agreed on these principles. See Bird, *Anne Francis,* 287.

133 Royal Commission on the Status of Women, *Report,* 90-8, 105-21.

134 Ibid., 90-1.

135 Ibid., 92.

136 Ibid., 93.

137 Ibid., 20.

138 Ibid., 105.

139 Ibid., 403.

140 Ibid., 400.

141 Ibid., 37.

142 Ibid., 400.

143 Ibid., 91.

144 Ibid., xii. For further discussion of the extent to which the commissioners were prepared to address the concerns of women who were ambivalent about mothers of young children working outside the home, see Patricia Marchak, "A Critical Review of the Status of Women *Report,*" *Canadian Review of Sociology and Anthropology* 9, 1 (1972): 74-5.

145 Royal Commission on the Status of Women, *Report,* xii.

146 Although Jacques Henripin was not averse to the federal government providing parents with tax relief for child care, he was opposed to national child care legislation on various grounds. In a separate statement, he asserted that "it would be rash to assume that the majority of Canadian taxpayers would be willing to subsidize families sending children under four or five years of age to a day-care centre rather than caring for them themselves" (Jacques Henripin, "Separate Statement," in Royal Commission on the Status of Women, *Report,* 424). He also believed that a new shared-cost program would not only "further accentuate the social and economic disparities between provinces" but might also be interpreted as an encroachment on areas of provincial jurisdiction, which, he believed, "may not be a wise approach ... in the present political climate" (ibid., 425). In addition, Henripin opposed national child care legislation on fiscal grounds, arguing that

"any subsidy to day-care centres beyond what is necessary to take care of the requirements of needy families [would divert too much money] from other social objectives which may be in greater need of government assistance" (ibid.).

John Humphrey's opposition to national child care legislation was evident in his minority report. While Humphrey argued that without day care centres "there can be no question of mothers of young children having equality of opportunity in the labour market," he stressed that "the provision and operation of day-care centres obviously comes under provincial jurisdiction and that is where I think it should remain" (John Humphrey, "Minority Report," in Royal Commission on the Status of Women, *Report,* 444). Indeed, concern about the emergence of a new sovereigntist movement in Quebec undoubtedly triggered his comment that any attempt to "force [the] hands" of the provinces "in a matter falling within provincial jurisdiction ... is dangerous advice at a time when in some provinces, political parties are challenging the very basis of Confederation" (ibid., 446).

147 Royal Commission on the Status of Women, *Report,* 263.
148 Ibid., 230, xii.
149 Ibid., 104.
150 Ibid., 303. This recommendation was opposed by Humphrey on the grounds that it would absorb money that could be spent on old age pensions, encourage large families, increase the burden on taxpayers, and detract from the creation of a more comprehensive approach to a guaranteed annual income (Humphrey, "Minority Report," 443).
151 Royal Commission on the Status of Women, *Report,* 302.
152 Ibid., 270.
153 Ibid., 271. Both Henripin and Humphrey opposed this recommendation (Henripin, "Separate Statement," 424-5; Humphrey, "Minority Report," 446).
154 Royal Commission on the Status of Women, *Report,* 271.
155 Interview with Monique Bégin, Ottawa, December 1998. This bias was also evident in the research that Bégin commissioned as executive director of the RCSW. See, for example, Françoise D. Lacasse, *Women at Home: The Cost to the Canadian Economy of the Withdrawal from the Labour Force of a Major Proportion of the Female Population,* Studies of the Royal Commission on the Status of Women no. 2 (Ottawa: Information Canada, 1970); and Alice Parizeau, *Day-Care Services and Pre-School Education in Selected Countries,* Studies of the Royal Commission on the Status of Women no. 31 (Ottawa: Information Canada, 1970).
156 Royal Commission on the Status of Women, *Report,* xii.

Chapter 4: A Just Society?

1 Speech to the Young Liberals, Ottawa, 5 April 1968, cited in *Dictionary of Canadian Quotations and Phrases,* ed. Robert M. Hamilton and Dorothy Shields (Toronto: McClelland and Stewart, 1979), 706. See also "Trudeau's Era Was Full of Surprises," *Globe and Mail,* 1 March 1984, T5.
2 Royal Commission on the Status of Women in Canada, *Report* (Ottawa: Information Canada, 1970), 388.
3 Freda Paltiel, "Quest for Equality," in *Our Own Agendas: Autobiographical Essays by Women Associated with McGill University,* ed. Margaret Gillet and Ann Beer (Montreal and Kingston: McGill-Queen's University Press, 1995), 117.
4 From *Trailblazers,* by Judith Finlayson, p. 14. Copyright 1999 Judith Finlayson. Published by Doubleday Canada, a division of Random House of Canada Limited. Reprinted with the permission of the publisher.
5 Interdepartmental Committee on the Status of Women, Minutes of the Meetings of Working Party I: Economic Participation of Women, 1970. National Archives of Canada, RG 106, vol. 1; Interdepartmental Committee on the Status of Women, Minutes of the Meetings of Working Party IV: Family and Community Service, 1970; National Archives of Canada, RG 106, vol. 4.
6 Interdepartmental Committee, Minutes of Working Party I and IV.
7 See Kenneth Kernaghan, "Representative Bureaucracy: The Canadian Perspective," *Canadian Public Administration* 21, 4 (1978): 489-512; and V. Seymour Wilson and Willard A.

Mullins, "Representative Bureaucracy: Linguistic/Ethnic Aspects in Canadian Public Policy," *Canadian Public Administration* 21, 4 (1978): 512-38.

8 Roger Gibbins, *Conflict and Unity: An Introduction to Canadian Political Life*, 3rd ed. (Scarborough, ON: Nelson Canada, 1994), 69. For an interesting discussion of "making Ottawa bilingual," see Kenneth McRoberts, *Misconceiving Canada: The Struggle for National Unity* (Toronto: Oxford University Press, 1997), 79-84.

9 Raymond Breton, "Multiculturalism and Canadian Nation Building," in *The Politics of Gender, Ethnicity and Language in Canada*, vol. 34 of *Research Studies, Royal Commission on the Economic Union and Development Prospects for Canada*, ed. Alan Cairns and Cynthia Williams (Toronto: University of Toronto Press, 1986), 29.

10 On the links between the promotion of bilingualism and equal opportunities for women in the FPS, see O.P. Dwivedi and James Iain Gow, *From Bureaucracy to Public Management: The Administrative Culture of the Government of Canada* (Toronto: Institute of Public Administration of Canada; Peterborough, ON: Broadview Press, 1999), 109.

11 The francophone initiative also actively encouraged the creation of a federal public service that reflected the proportion of francophones in the population. This target was reached by 1977, when francophones accounted for 27 percent of the total public service staff. They also accounted for 21 percent of those employed in the senior executive category. See Kernaghan, "Representative Bureaucracy," 500.

12 Public Service Commission of Canada, *Annual Report 1971* (Ottawa: Public Service Commission of Canada, 1972), 14.

13 Nicole Morgan, *The Equality Game: Women in the Federal Public Service (1908-1987)* (Ottawa: Canadian Advisory Council on the Status of Women, 1988), 24.

14 Ibid.

15 Treasury Board of Canada, Personnel Policy Branch, *Equal Opportunities for Women in the Public Service of Canada* (Ottawa: Personnel Policy Branch, Treasury Board of Canada, 1979), 1, 39.

16 Ibid., 39.

17 Canadian Advisory Council on the Status of Women, *Women in the Public Service: Overlooked and Undervalued* (Ottawa: Canadian Advisory Council on the Status of Women, 1980), 30.

18 Royal Commission on the Status of Women, *Report*, 50, 395.

19 Treasury Board of Canada, Personnel Policy Branch, *Equal Opportunities for Women*, 1.

20 On Trudeau's rational style of governing, see Peter Aucoin, "Organizational Change in the Machinery of Canadian Government: From Rational Management to Brokerage Politics," *Canadian Journal of Political Science* 19, 1 (1986): 17.

21 Treasury Board of Canada, Personnel Policy Branch, *Equal Opportunities for Women*, 1.

22 Ibid., 4.

23 Canadian Advisory Council on the Status of Women, *Women in the Public Service*, 1.

24 Ibid.

25 Employment and Immigration Canada, *Annual Report for the Fiscal Year 1977-1978* (Ottawa: Supply and Services, 1978), 8.

26 Patricia Dale, *Women and Jobs: The Impact of Federal Government Employment Strategies on Women* (Ottawa: Canadian Advisory Council on the Status of Women, 1980), 42.

27 Under this legislation, "the federal government undertook to cover the full cost of occupational training for adult members of the labour force, leaving the provinces the responsibility for education and training for the non-adult members of the population" (Barbara Cameron, "From Equal Opportunity to Symbolic Equity: Three Decades of Federal Training Policy for Women," in *Rethinking Restructuring: Gender and Change in Canada*, ed. Isabella Bakker [Toronto: University of Toronto Press, 1996], 57).

28 Employment and Immigration Canada, *Labour Market Development in the 1980s* (Ottawa: Supply and Services, 1981), 91.

29 Dale, *Women and Jobs*, 48; Employment and Immigration Canada, *Labour Market Development in the 1980s*, 91.

30 The exception was enrolment in the student and youth employment scheme. See Dale, *Women and Jobs*, 43, Table III.

31 The discrepancy on the apprenticeship scheme was particularly noticeable given that 32 percent of all new trainees admitted to job creation programs in 1978 were placed in the apprenticeship scheme (ibid., 52, and Appendix II, 19, Table 12).

32 Ibid., 53.

33 Ibid., 15.

34 Ibid., 55.

35 Status of Women Canada, *Towards Equality for Women* (Ottawa: Supply and Services, 1979), 17.

36 Dale, *Women and Jobs,* 56.

37 Ibid., 5, Appendix 1.

38 Ibid., 71.

39 Martha Friendly, *Child Care Policy in Canada: Putting the Pieces Together* (Don Mills, ON: Addison-Wesley, 1994), 137.

40 Ibid., 146.

41 Dale, *Women and Jobs,* 29.

42 Royal Commission on the Status of Women, *Report,* 105.

43 Ibid., 98.

44 The 1970 Public Service Employment Act stipulated that "the Public Service Commission in prescribing selection standards for public servants shall not discriminate against any person by reasons of sex, race, national origin, colour, or religion" (*Public Service Employment Act,* R.S.C. 1970, P-32, s. 12.2). The 1972 Unemployment Insurance Act required the minister of Manpower to ensure that "in referring a worker seeking employment there is no discrimination because of race, national origin, colour, religion, sex, marital status, age or political affiliation" on the part of the national employment services (*Unemployment Insurance Act,* S.C. 1972, c. 48, s. 140.2b).

45 Royal Commission on the Status of Women, *Report,* 389.

46 For the RCSW's discussion of this point, see Royal Commission on the Status of Women, *Report,* 388-9. For a fuller discussion of the development of human rights policies in Canada, see Ronald Manzer, *Public Policies and Political Development in Canada* (Toronto: University of Toronto Press, 1985), 145-75; and R. Brian Howe and David Johnson, *Restraining Equality: Human Rights Commissions in Canada* (Toronto: University of Toronto Press, 2000), 3-36.

47 *Canadian Human Rights Act,* S.C. 1977, c. 33, s. 28.4.

48 Ibid., s. 1.13.

49 Ibid., s. 11.1.

50 For the CHRC's powers to demand "special programs to prevent future disadvantage," see *Canadian Human Rights Act,* S.C. 1977, c. 33. s. 15; for its powers to demand contract compliance, see *Canadian Human Rights Act,* S.C. 1977, c. 33, s. 19.

51 Morgan, *The Equality Game,* 45.

52 For further discussion of the resistance of male managers to the idea of women achieving equal employment opportunities with men, see ibid., 23-48.

53 On the more general failure of Canadian training programs to assess the nature of employment demand, see Thomas R. Klassen, *Precarious Values: Organizations, Politics and Labour Market Policy in Ontario* (Montreal and Kingston: McGill-Queen's University Press, 2000), 16-24.

54 Royal Commission on the Status of Women, *Report,* vii.

55 Ibid., 270-1.

56 Ibid., 303.

57 *Canada Assistance Plan,* S.C. 1966-7, c. 45, s. 2. For a further discussion of CAP, see Allan Moscovitch, "The Canada Assistance Plan: A Twenty Year Assessment, 1966-1986," in *How Ottawa Spends 1988-89: The Conservatives Heading into the Stretch,* ed. Katherine A. Graham (Ottawa: Carleton University Press, 1998), 269-307.

58 Ibid.

59 Rodney S. Haddow, *Poverty Reform in Canada, 1958-1978: State and Class Influences on Policy Making* (Montreal and Kingston: McGill-Queen's University Press, 1993), 89. Bégin's influence on the report is interesting, particularly given that later in her career (as minister

of National Health and Welfare) she managed to secure the Child Tax Credit as "the only concrete by-product" of the 1978 Social Security Review (ibid., 152).

60 Ibid., 151.

61 Ibid., 152.

62 Friendly, *Child Care Policy in Canada*, 76. These amounts were increased to $2,000 in 1983; $4,000 in 1987; and $5,000 per child in 1993 (ibid., 197).

63 Canadian Advisory Council on the Status of Women, *Ten Years Later: An Assessment of the Federal Government's Implementation of the Recommendations Made by the Royal Commission on the Status of Women* (Ottawa: Canadian Advisory Council on the Status of Women, 1979), 22.

64 House of Commons, *Debates*, 12 October 1976, 3. A sliding scale of fees related to income had been recommendation 115 of the RCSW. See Royal Commission on the Status of Women, *Report*, 411.

65 Author's interview with Martha Hynna, Coordinator, Status of Women, Privy Council Office, 1973-6, Hull, QC, December 1988.

66 Interestingly, this point had also been made by Jacques Henripin in the separate statement that he attached to the report of the RCSW, where he noted that "the Commission did not make a survey of public opinion regarding these matters. In my view, it would be rash to assume that the majority of Canadian taxpayers would be willing to subsidize families sending children under four or five years of age to a day-care centre rather than caring for them themselves" (Royal Commission on the Status of Women, *Report*, 424).

67 Labour Canada, Women's Bureau, *Canadian Attitudes towards Women: Thirty Years of Change* (Ottawa: Supply and Services, 1984), 46-7.

68 Helen Tucker, "Federal Council on the Status of Women," *Status of Women News* 1, 1 (1973): 2. Similar proposals were made by the Fédération des femmes du Québec, when delegates at its sixth annual congress in May 1973 emphasized "la necessité de garderies publiques" – the need for public daycare (Caroline Pesiteau "Quebec: 6e Congrès de la Fédération des femmes du Québec," *Status of Women News* 1, 1 [1973]: 5). They were also made by delegates at the Saskatchewan Status of Women Conference, in June 1973, where delegates called for "free, universal 24-hour child care facilities" in the province ("Saskatchewan Status of Women Conference," *Status of Women News* 1, 1 [1973]: 6).

69 Royal Commission on the Status of Women, *Report*, 411.

70 National Ad Hoc Action Committee on the Status of Women in Canada, Submission to the Government of Canada, February 1972, National Action Committee on the Status of Women Files, Toronto, 6.

71 Ibid.

72 Ibid., 4.

73 Ibid.

74 Nancy Adamson, Linda Briskin, and Margaret McPhail, *Feminists Organizing for Change: The Contemporary Women's Movement in Canada* (Toronto: Oxford University Press, 1988), 47.

Chapter 5: Redefining the Issues

1 See, for example, Pat Armstrong and Hugh Armstrong, *The Double Ghetto: Canadian Women and Their Segregated Work*, rev. ed. (Toronto: McClelland and Stewart, 1984), 25-41; Paul Phillips and Erin Phillips, *Women and Work: Inequality in the Labour Market* (Toronto: James Lorimer, 1983), 47-51; and S.J. Wilson, *Women, the Family and the Economy* (Toronto: McGraw-Hill Ryerson Limited, 1982), 101-4.

2 Canadian Advisory Council on the Status of Women, *Women in the Public Service: Overlooked and Undervalued* (Ottawa: Canadian Advisory Council on the Status of Women, 1980).

3 Employment and Immigration Canada, *Labour Market Development in the 1980s* (Ottawa: Supply and Services, 1981), 91. From Human Resources Development Canada, reproduced with the permission of the Minister of Public Works and Government Services Canada, 2000.

4 Ibid., 91-2. From Human Resources Development Canada, reproduced with the permission of the Minister of Public Works and Government Services Canada, 2000.

5 For a fuller discussion of the American affirmative action programs, see Carol Lee Bacchi, *Same Difference: Feminism and Sexual Difference* (St. Leonards, NSW: Allen and Unwin, 1990), 156-64; and Carol Lee Bacchi, *The Politics of Affirmative Action: "Women," Equality and Category Politics* (London: Sage Publications, 1996), 31-56. For a discussion of the application of American models to Canada, see Walter S. Tarnopolsky, "Discrimination and Affirmative Action – Definitions: American Experience and Application in Canada," in Labour Canada, Women's Bureau, *Race and Sex Equality in the Workplace: A Challenge and an Opportunity*, ed. Harish C. Jain and Dianne Carroll (Ottawa: Supply and Services, 1980), 72-98.

6 The variation of opinions became particularly evident in the briefs submitted to the Royal Commission on Equality in Employment. Evidence of feminist support for the mandatory affirmative action programs developed in the United States was explicit in the submission made by the National Action Committee on the Status of Women – even though, as I demonstrate in Chapter 6, its brief advocated the adoption of goals and timetables (rather than specifying quotas) in the development of a Canadian model. This declared "our conviction that the American model is one which Canada would do well to emulate in that it provides for two mechanisms. To wit: mandatory affirmative action programs in the U.S. can be the result of a complaint involving systemic discrimination *or* they can be established within the framework of contract compliance. It is our position that *both* mechanisms are necessary and can be implemented by the federal government in Canada without major legislative changes" (National Action Committee on the Status of Women, "The Implementation of Mandatory Affirmative Action: A Blueprint for Federal Government Policy," 31 January 1984, Submission to the Royal Commission on Equality in Employment, National Archives of Canada, RG 33/133, box no. 1, 2). Evidence of business opposition to the idea of mandatory affirmative action can be found, for example, in the brief submitted by Westinghouse Canada, which stated, "We are strongly opposed to mandatory affirmative action. We believe that a voluntary program results in less tokenism, backlash, and resentment from other employees in the organization. We believe that a voluntary program better allows our organization to develop a program that addresses its own unique nature" (Westinghouse Canada, Submission to the Royal Commission on Equality in Employment, National Archives of Canada, 13 December 1983, RG 33/133, box no. 2, 8-9). Business opposition to affirmative action was also evident in "Hiring Quotas May Creep North," *Business Week* 2744 (21 June 1982): 137.

7 For studies documenting the persistence of gender discrimination in the public sphere see, for example, Patricia Connelly, *Last Hired, First Fired: Women and the Canadian Work Force* (Toronto: Women's Press, 1978); Canadian Advisory Council on the Status of Women, *Ten Years Later: An Assessment of the Federal Government's Implementation of the Recommendations Made by the Royal Commission on the Status of Women* (Ottawa: Canadian Advisory Council on the Status of Women, 1979). On women's concern to see strong anti-discrimination measures entrenched in the Charter, see Chaviva Hošek, "Women and the Constitutional Process," in *And No One Cheered: Federalism, Democracy and the Constitution Act*, ed. Keith Banting and Richard Simeon (Toronto: Methuen, 1983), 280-300; and Alexandra Dobrowolsky, *The Politics of Pragmatism: Women, Representation, and Constitutionalism in Canada* (Toronto: Oxford University Press, 2000), 39-74.

8 Lise Gotell, *Feminism, Equality Rights and the Charter of Rights and Freedoms*, Feminist Perspectives Féministes no. 16 (Ottawa: Canadian Research Institute for the Advancement of Women, 1990), 4.

9 Sandra Burt, "The Changing Patterns of Public Policy," in *Changing Patterns: Women in Canada*, 2nd ed., ed. Sandra Burt, Lorraine Code, and Lindsay Dorney (Toronto: McClelland and Stewart, 1993), 221.

10 Gotell, *Feminism, Equality Rights and the Charter*, 9.

11 *Canada (Attorney General)* v. *Lavell et al.*, [1974] S.C.R. 1349. For a fuller discussion of the case, see Peter Kulchyski, ed., *Unjust Relations: Aboriginal Rights in Canadian Courts* (Toronto: Oxford University Press, 1994), 127-50.

12 *Bliss* v. *Canada (Attorney General)*, [1979] 1 S.C.R. 183.

13 See Penney Kome, *The Taking of Twenty-Eight: Women Challenge the Constitution* (Toronto: Women's Press, 1983), 39-42; and Doris Anderson, *Rebel Daughter: An Autobiography* (Toronto: Key Porter Books, 1996), 239-40.

14 For further discussion of this débâcle, see Dobrowolsky, *Politics of Pragmatism,* 50-8.

15 Gotell, *Feminism, Equality Rights and the Charter,* 48.

16 Ibid.

17 Alison Prentice, Paula Bourne, Gail Cuthbert Brandt, Beth Light, Wendy Mitchinson, and Naomi Black, *Canadian Women: A History,* 2nd ed. (Toronto: Harcourt Brace Canada, 1996), 447.

18 Penney Kome, *The Taking of Twenty-Eight,* 43-95.

19 Catherine Mackinnon, Presentation to the Ontario Select Committee on Constitutional Reform, 1998, excerpt reprinted in Ad Hoc Committee on Women and the Constitution, Toronto, "We Can Afford a Better Accord: The Meech Lake Accord," *Resources for Feminist Research/Documents sur la recherche féministe* 17, 3 (1988): 144.

20 *Constitution Act,* S.C. 1982. [en. by the *Canada Act* 1982 (U.K.), c. 11, s. 1], pt 1 (Canadian Charter of Rights and Freedoms), p. iii, s. 15.1.

21 Ibid., s. 15.2.

22 Quotations from House of Commons, *Debates,* 14 April 1980, 4-7.

23 Christina McCall and Stephen Clarkson, *The Heroic Delusion,* vol. 2 of *Trudeau and Our Times* (Toronto: McClelland and Stewart, 1994), 137-61.

24 See Ronald Manzer, *Public Policies and Political Development in Canada* (Toronto: University of Toronto Press, 1985), 13-19.

25 For fuller discussion of American and Canadian women's efforts to entrench gender equality clauses in their countries' constitutions, see Melissa H. Haussman, "The Personal Is Constitutional: Feminist Struggles for Equality Rights in the United States and Canada," in *Women Transforming Politics: Worldwide Strategies for Empowerment,* ed. Jill Bystydzienski (Bloomington and Indianapolis: Indiana University Press, 1992), 108-23.

26 Canadian Human Rights Commission, *Annual Report 1980* (Ottawa: Supply and Services, 1981), 92.

27 Author interview with Hanne Jensen, Director, Pay and Employment Equity Branch, Canadian Human Rights Commission, 1988-90, Ottawa, December 1988.

28 Ibid. Interestingly, in a vein that would prove similar to the subsequent recommendations of the Royal Commission on Equality in Employment, the CHRC argued that "it would be important, if such a step were taken, also to ensure the development of labour force availability data, by sex and minority status. This data would be valuable for employers under both federal and provincial jurisdiction" (Canadian Human Rights Commission, *Annual Report 1980,* 92).

29 Canadian Human Rights Commission, *Annual Report 1981* (Ottawa: Supply and Services, 1982), 18. Reproduced with the permission of the Minister of Public Works and Government Services Canada, 2000.

30 Canadian Human Rights Commission, *Annual Report 1978* (Ottawa: Supply and Services, 1979), 21.

31 Canadian Human Rights Commission, *Annual Report 1981,* 17. Reproduced with the permission of the Minister of Public Works and Government Services Canada, 2000.

32 Patricia McDermott, "Pay and Employment Equity: Why Separate Policies?" in *Women and Canadian Public Policy,* ed. Janine Brodie (Toronto: Harcourt Brace, 1996), 95.

33 *Action travail des femmes* v. *Canadian National Railway Co. et al.,* [1987], 40 D.L.R. (4th), 195.

34 Canadian Human Rights Commission, *Annual Report 1981,* 36, 41.

35 Section 10 of the 1977 Canadian Human Rights Act reads, "It is a discriminatory practice for an employer or an employee organization (a) to establish or pursue a policy or practice, or (b) to enter into an agreement affecting recruitment, referral, hiring, promotion, training, apprenticeship, transfer or any other matter relating to employment or prospective employment, that deprives or tends to deprive an individual or class of individuals of any employment opportunities on a prohibited ground of discrimination" (*Canadian Human Rights Act,* S.C. 1977, c. 33. s. 10).

36 *Griggs* v. *Duke Power Company,* 401 U.S. 424 (1971).
37 For US Supreme Court rulings that have weakened the precedents set by the *Griggs* case, see *Personnel Administrator of Massachusetts* v. *Feeney,* 442 U.S. 256 (1979), which sustained a state employment preference for veterans, most of whom were men. In this case, the court held that despite the disparate effect of the employment preference, the purpose was not to discriminate against women but to reward veterans, male and female, over civilians. See also *Wards Cove Packing Co.* v. *Antonio,* 490 U.S. 642 (1989), in which a conservative group of judges held that when a racially disparate outcome of a test is shown, the defending company must produce evidence that the test is related to business requirements, but the burden of proving discriminatory intent remains with the plaintiff (personal communication from Professor M.L. Benedict, Ohio State University, 30 June 2000).
38 McDermott, "Pay and Employment Equity," 95.
39 *Action travail des femmes* v. *Canadian National Railway Co. et al.,* [1987] 40 D.L.R. (4th), 200.
40 Ibid., 201.
41 Ibid., 200-1.
42 On the reactions of the feminist community to the development and results of this appeal, see Carole Wallace, "Action travail des femmes vs. CN Rail," *Status of Women News* 10 (December 1984): 26-7. Doris Anderson, "How a Tiny Women's Group Defeated a Corporate Giant," *Toronto Star,* 18 July 1988, K1.
43 With regard to this argument it is particularly interesting to note that, just two years earlier, the Supreme Court ruled against the CHRC's decision obliging CNR to accommodate religious difference, on a continuous rather than a temporary basis, by allowing their Sikh employee, Karnaial S. Bhinder, to wear a turban rather than a hard hat in the company's work yards. See Canadian Human Rights Commission, *Annual Report 1983* (Ottawa: Supply and Services, 1984), 30; Canadian Human Rights Commission, *Annual Report 1984* (Ottawa: Supply and Services, 1985), 1; and *Re Bhinder et al.* and *Canadian National Railway Co.,* [1985] 23 D.L.R. (4th) 481. For a more extensive discussion on Supreme Court decisions on the duty to accommodate difference, see Katherine Swinton, "Accommodating Equality in a Unionized Workplace," *Osgoode Hall Law Journal* 33, 4 (1995): 713-22.
44 Canadian Human Rights Commission, *Annual Report 1980,* 92.
45 Canadian Human Rights Commission, *Annual Report 1978,* 9.
46 Canadian Human Rights Commission, *Annual Report 1979,* 7. In fact, an amendment outlawing these dimensions of sex discrimination was subsequently inserted at s. 3(2) of the Canadian Human Rights Act (*Canadian Human Rights Act,* S.C. 1976-77, c. 33; 1980-81-82-83, c. 143, s. 2).
47 Canadian Human Rights Commission, *Annual Report 1979,* 7. The concern was reiterated in Canadian Human Rights Commission, *Annual Report 1980,* 8.
48 Canadian Human Rights Commission, *Annual Report 1983,* 9.
49 Canadian Human Rights Commission, *Annual Report 1978,* 8.
50 Canadian Human Rights Commission, *Annual Report 1980,* 34.
51 Canadian Human Rights Commission, *Annual Report 1979,* 58. Reproduced with the permission of the Minister of Public Works and Government Services Canada, 2000.
52 Canadian Human Rights Commission, *Annual Report 1983,* 15.
53 Harish C. Jain, "Race and Sex Discrimination in the Workplace: An Analysis of Theory, Research and Public Policy in Canada" (paper prepared for the Affirmative Action Directorate, Canadian Employment and Immigration Commission, March 1981), 13.
54 The total number of immigrants admitted annually to Canada fell from 218,000 in 1974 to 86,313 in 1978, rising again to 142,634 by 1980. See Employment and Immigration Canada, *Labour Market Development in the 1980s,* 180.
55 Sue Findlay, "Representation and Regulation: The Role of the State Bureaucracy in Limiting Equal Employment Opportunities for Women," *Canadian Woman Studies/Les cahiers de la femme* 6, 4 (1985): 32.
56 Carol Agocs, "Affirmative Action, Canadian Style: A Reconnaissance," *Canadian Public Policy* 12, 1 (1986): 154.

57 Employment and Immigration Canada, *Annual Report 1979* (Ottawa: Supply and Services, 1980), 2.

58 D. Rhys Phillips, *Affirmative Action As an Effective Labour Market Planning Tool of the 1980s,* Technical Study no. 29, prepared for the Task Force on Labour Market Development, July 1981, 52.

59 Lise Hendlisz, Brenda Lazare, Mario Lebrun, Alix Parlour, and Jackie Tatebe, *Affirmative Action for Women in Canada* (Montreal: Montreal Association for Women and the Law, 1982), 63.

60 Mona Kornberg, "Employment Equity: The Quiet Revolution?" *Canadian Woman Studies/Les cahiers de la femme* 6, 4 (1985): 17.

61 Northwest Territories, Justice and Public Services, Submission to Judge R. Abella, Commission of Inquiry on Equality in Employment, 18 October 1983, National Archives of Canada, RG 33/133, box no. 1, 3.

62 Kornberg, "Employment Equity," 17.

63 Author's interview with Rhys Phillips, Policy Analyst, Affirmative Action Directorate, CEIC, 1978-83, Hull, QC, September 1986.

64 Public Service Commission of Canada, *Annual Report 1981* (Ottawa: Public Service Commission of Canada, 1982), 19.

65 Public Service Commission of Canada, *Annual Report 1982* (Ottawa: Public Service Commission of Canada, 1983), 19.

66 Public Service Commission of Canada, *Annual Report 1983* (Ottawa: Public Service Commission of Canada, 1984), 19.

67 Nicole Morgan, *The Equality Game: Women in the Federal Public Service (1908-1987)* (Ottawa: Canadian Advisory Council on the Status of Women, 1988), 49.

68 Public Service Commission of Canada, *Annual Report 1983,* 16.

69 Treasury Board of Canada, *Annual Report 1980* (Ottawa: Supply and Services, 1981), 2.

70 House of Commons, *Minutes of Proceedings and Evidence of the Special Committee on Employment Opportunities for the '80s* (Ottawa: Queen's Printer, 1980), 3.

71 House of Commons, *Work for Tomorrow: Employment Opportunities for the '80s,* Report of the Task Force on Employment Opportunities for the '80s (Ottawa: Supply and Services, 1981), 4.

72 Ibid., recommendation 105, 19.

73 Employment and Immigration Canada, *Labour Market Development in the 1980s,* 1.

74 Ibid., 91.

75 Ibid., 16.

76 Ibid., 60. However, as Dodge went on to argue, "Such bottlenecks and wage pressures and the associated costs to the economy in terms of higher inflation and foregone production, can be reduced to the extent that public policy can facilitate the introduction of women into a more diverse set of occupations and industries before imbalances occur" (ibid., 62).

77 Ibid., 92.

78 Ibid.

79 Ibid., 102.

80 Interestingly, Sue Findlay argues that "the recommendations on affirmative action that had emerged from the analysis of groups with special employment needs by the Task Force on Labour Market Development were carefully edited by the analysts from the central agencies to emphasize the development of progressive practices and disavow the need for quotas or timetables" (Findlay, "Representation and Regulation," 33). For details of the assessment of women's employment needs prepared for the task force, see Carole Swan, *Women in the Canadian Labour Market,* Technical Study no. 36, prepared for the Task Force on Labour Market Development, July 1981.

81 Employment and Immigration Canada, *Labour Market Development in the 1980s,* 92.

82 Ibid., 95.

83 Ibid., 95. From Human Resources Development Canada, reproduced with the permission of the Minister of Public Works and Government Services Canada, 2000.

84 Author's interview with the Hon. Lloyd Axworthy, Minister of Employment and Immigration, 1980-3, Ottawa, September 1986.

85 "The decision to carry out the review was taken after the Commission had received a number of complaints of discrimination in the areas of job referrals, training programs and labour market programs" (Canadian Human Rights Commission, *Annual Report 1980*, 48). The review was implemented on 14 May 1980, following an agreement signed by Gordon Fairweather (Chairman of the CHRC) and J.D. Lowe (Chairman of the CEIC).

86 Author's interview with Ron Collett, Senior Policy Advisor to Lloyd Axworthy, 1980-3, Toronto, September 1986.

87 The first conference had been held a decade earlier. See Canadian Council on Social Development, *Proceedings/Canadian Conference on Day Care* (Ottawa: Canadian Council on Social Development, 1972).

88 Author's interview with Martha Friendly, Coordinator, Childcare Resource and Research Unit, University of Toronto, November 1988.

89 Martha Friendly, *Child Care Policy in Canada: Putting the Pieces Together* (Don Mills, ON: Addison-Wesley, 1994), 148.

90 Quoted in Barbara Huck, "Day-Care Conference Seeks Answers to Many Concerns: 700 Delegates Gather for Three Days of Workshops," *Winnipeg Free Press*, 24 September 1982, 2.

91 Author's interview with Laurel Rothman, member of Action Day Care and Director of Social Action, Family Services Association of Toronto, Toronto, December 1998.

92 Ibid.

93 Delegates from Quebec were concerned that child care should remain under provincial jurisdiction. As their minority report noted, "given that the procedure used for the approval of resolutions did not permit nuances [or the opportunity to clarify] the meaning of the vote through the absence of the right to amendment and to a justified and registered abstention, we propose that the different levels of government involved (federal and provincial) receive the resolutions, keeping in mind the spirit underlying them, which is the improvement of the quality of day care, and not invalidate them on the basis that they can be interpreted as forms of interference with the responsibilities already defined by the conference" (Canadian Council on Social Development, *The Second Canadian Conference on Day Care: Proceedings and Reflections* [Ottawa: Canadian Council on Social Development, 1983], 159). Indeed, as an editorial in the *Winnipeg Free Press* noted, "education is unmistakably a provincial power and, even if other provinces accepted a federal move into the early childhood education field, no Quebec government would consider tolerating it" ("Who Can Run Day Care?" *Winnipeg Free Press*, 28 September 1982, 6). Although delegates from Alberta were not completely opposed to federal legislation, they wanted to ensure that the financing of such a system would allow child care in Alberta to stay "firmly hinged on private day-care" (Huck, "Day-Care Conference," 2). As the minority report from its delegates noted, "any funding or cost sharing from the provincial or federal government should be made available to all day cares regardless of delivery models" (Canadian Council on Social Development, *Second Canadian Conference on Day Care,* 157). For further discussion of the dynamics of the Winnipeg conference, see Jane Stinson, "The Day Care Fight Goes On: Report on the Second National Conference on Day Care," *The Facts* 4, 10 (1982-3): 16-18.

94 Canadian Council on Social Development, *Second Canadian Conference on Day Care*, 7.

95 Ibid., 8. This resolution was also carried by 75 percent of the delegates voting in its favour.

96 Ibid., 6. Once again, 75 percent of the delegates voted in favour of this resolution.

97 Ibid., 7.

98 In October 1992, the CDCAA was renamed the Child Care Advocacy Association of Canada (CCAAC) (Canadian Day Care Advocacy Association, *Bulletin* [Winter 1992]: 8).

99 "Day Care Advocacy Assn. to Co-ordinate Campaigns for Greater Govt. Funding," *The Facts* 5, 5 (1983): 12.

100 Two examples of the way that child care advocates have linked their demands for a universal child care service to questions of women's employment can be found in Canadian Day Care Advocacy Association, "Beginning to Solve Canada's Daycare Crisis: Short-Term

and Long-Term Proposals," Submission to the Commission of Inquiry on Equality in Employment, November 1983. National Archives of Canada, RG 33/133, box no. 1; and Gillian Doherty, Martha Friendly, and Mab Oloman, *Women's Support, Women's Work: Child Care in an Era of Deficit Reduction, Devolution, Downsizing and Deregulation* (Ottawa: Status of Women Canada, 1998), 1-3.

101 Author's interview with Sue Colley, Executive Director of Ontario Coalition for Better Child Care, 1985-90, Toronto, December 1988.

102 See "Common Day Care Strategy Needed," *Public Employee* 3 (Spring 1981): 7.

103 "Free Universal Child Care Curbed by Spending Restraint," *Labour Scene* 3 (April 1981): 6.

104 Interestingly, this reflects the process of agenda displacement that first-wave feminists went through in Canada, when they sought to build support for suffrage by taking their campaign into more broadly based temperance organizations. For further discussion of this dynamic, see Carol Lee Bacchi, *Liberation Deferred? The Ideas of the English Canadian Suffragists, 1877-1918* (Toronto: University of Toronto Press, 1983), 29-30.

105 Ontario Federation of Labour, "Statement on Day Care," presented at the 24th annual OFL convention, 24-7 November 1980, 1.

106 Nancy Adamson, Linda Briskin, and Margaret McPhail, *Feminists Organizing for Change: The Contemporary Women's Movement in Canada* (Toronto: Oxford University Press, 1988), 47.

107 In a letter to Prime Minister Trudeau, Doris Anderson, then president of the National Action Committee on the Status of Women, stated that "we also view quality child care as a right of all children" (letter written as president of NAC to Prime Minister Pierre Trudeau, 2 June 1982, National Action Committee on the Status of Women Files, Toronto).

108 Letter from Donald S. Macdonald, Chairman of the Royal Commission on the Economic Union and Development Prospects for Canada, to Doris Anderson, President, National Action Committee on the Status of Women, 14 March 1984, attaching TV Ontario's transcript of NAC's intervention before the commission, National Action Committee on the Status of Women Files, p. 12898. Emphasis added.

109 Ibid., 12898-9.

110 Ibid., 12897.

111 Status of Women Canada, *Report of the Task Force on Child Care* (Ottawa: Supply and Services, 1986), 68.

112 Pierre Trudeau, letter written as prime minister to Doris Anderson, President, National Action Committee on the Status of Women, 29 June 1982, National Action Committee on the Status of Women Files, Toronto.

113 Royal Commission on Equality in Employment, *Report* (Ottawa: Supply and Services, 1984), ii. The eleven crown corporations were "Petro-Canada, Air Canada, Canadian National Railway, Canada Mortgage and Housing Corporation, Canada Post Corporation, Canadian Broadcasting Corporation, Atomic Energy of Canada Limited, Export Development Corporation, Teleglobe Canada, the de Havilland Aircraft of Canada Ltd., and the Federal Business Development Bank" (ibid.).

114 Ibid.

115 Status of Women Canada, *Report of the Task Force on Child Care*, xxiii. John Turner replaced Pierre Trudeau as prime minister on 30 June 1984, having been elected leader of the Liberal Party on 16 June 1984.

116 Ibid., xxiii.

117 Author's interview with Judge Rosalie Silberman Abella, Commissioner, Royal Commission on Equality in Employment, 1983-4, Toronto, August 1986.

Chapter 6: The Royal Commission on Equality in Employment

1 Royal Commission on Equality in Employment, *Report* (Ottawa: Supply and Services, 1984), ii.

2 Ibid., 1.

3 Ibid.

4 Ibid., iii. Although the RCEE had been established to ascertain the most efficient, effective, and equitable method of "assisting all individuals to compete for employment opportunities on an equal basis," Abella was instructed to pay particular attention to "the views of associations representing women, native people, disabled persons and visible minorities" (ibid.).

5 See Carole Ann Reed, "Contradictions and Assumptions: A Report on Employment Equity in Canada," *Resources for Feminist Research/Documentation sur la recherche féministe* 24, 3 and 4 (1995-6): 46.

6 Lorna R. Marsden, "The Importance of Studying Affirmative Action," *Canadian Woman Studies/Les cahiers de la femme* 6, 4 (1985): 12.

7 Royal Commission on Equality in Employment, *Report,* ii.

8 Ibid.

9 Royal Commission on Financial Management and Accountability, *Final Report* (Ottawa: Supply and Services, 1979), 328-9, cited in Royal Commission on Equality in Employment, *Report,* 101. For further discussion of the reasons why politicians choose crown corporations as policy instruments in particular settings, see J. Robert S. Prichard and Michael J. Trebilcock, "Crown Corporations in Canada: The Choice of Policy Instrument," in *The Politics of Canadian Public Policy,* ed. Michael M. Atkinson and Marsha A. Chandler, (Toronto: University of Toronto Press, 1983), 199-222.

10 Author's interview with the Hon. Lloyd Axworthy, Minister of Employment and Immigration 1980-3, Ottawa, September 1986.

11 Ibid.

12 See, for example, Employment and Immigration Canada, *Labour Market Development in the 1980s* (Ottawa: Supply and Services, 1981), 108; House of Commons, *Obstacles,* Report of the Special Committee on the Disabled and the Handicapped (Ottawa: Supply and Services, 1981), 31-2, 35-6, 51; and House of Commons, *Work for Tomorrow: Employment Opportunities for the '80s,* Report of the Task Force on Employment Opportunities for the '80s (Ottawa: Supply and Services, 1981), 98-9.

13 Interview with Lloyd Axworthy, September 1986.

14 For an interesting discussion of a provincial government's proactive approach to reviewing provincial statutes after the entrenchment of the Charter, see the discussion of the procedures adopted by the government of Saskatchewan in Hon. Justice J.C. Macpherson, "The Impact of the Canadian Charter of Rights and Freedoms on Executive and Judicial Behaviour," in *Rights and Democracy: Essays in UK-Canadian Constitutionalism,* ed. G.W. Anderson (London: Blackstone Press, 1999), 125-38.

15 On the government side, lobbyists included Judy Erola and Monique Bégin in the House of Commons, and Lorna Marsden in the Senate. Opposition lobbyists included Flora MacDonald (Progressive Conservative), Margaret Mitchell (NDP), and Pauline Jewett (NDP) (interview with Lloyd Axworthy, September 1986).

16 Royal Commission on Equality in Employment, *Report,* 197.

17 Author's interview with Ron Collett, Senior Policy Advisor to Lloyd Axworthy, 1980-3, Toronto, September 1986.

18 See Christina McCall and Stephen Clarkson, *The Heroic Delusion,* vol. 2 of *Trudeau and Our Times* (Toronto: McClelland and Stewart, 1994), 255-61.

19 Interview with Lloyd Axworthy, September 1986.

20 Interview with Ron Collett, September 1986.

21 Interview with Lloyd Axworthy, September 1986.

22 Ibid.

23 Ibid.

24 Author's interviews with Patricia Preston, Press Secretary to Lloyd Axworthy, 1980-3, Ottawa, September 1986; and Ron Collett, September 1986. According to Collett the logistics of Abella securing a leave from the Ontario Provincial Court (Family Division) and the question of whether federal funds could be paid to the province of Ontario in order to cover her salary during this period were complicated. Abella's position on the Ontario Bench required her to be given total independence from the CEIC. Indeed, it was for this reason that a royal commission, rather than a parliamentary task force or departmental

study, became the preferred form of inquiry (author's interview with Judge Rosalie Silberman Abella, Commissioner, Royal Commission on Equality in Employment, 1983-4, Toronto, August 1986). For further evidence of the complexities involved in establishing the RCEE, see Lorna Marsden, "The Importance of Studying Affirmative Action," 12.

25 Interview with Lloyd Axworthy, September 1986.

26 Interviews with Patricia Preston and Ron Collett, September 1986.

27 See Rosalie S. Abella, *Access to Legal Services by the Disabled: The Report of a Study Submitted to the Attorney General of Ontario* (Toronto: Queen's Printer of Ontario, 1983).

28 Interview with Ron Collett, September 1986.

29 For an "exuberant" account of her own history, first delivered on 13 May 1992 when Abella was sworn into the Ontario Court of Appeal as Canada's hundredth woman judge, see Rosalie Silberman Abella, "An Exuberant Rebuke to History," in *Our Own Agendas: Autobiographical Essays by Women Associated with McGill University,* ed. Margaret Gillett and Ann Beer (Montreal and Kingston: McGill-Queen's University Press, 1995), 72-5.

30 Royal Commission on Equality in Employment, *Report,* v.

31 Ibid., 271.

32 Ibid.

33 Ibid., 275.

34 Ibid., 271.

35 Ibid., 274.

36 Ibid.

37 Ibid.

38 This perspective was also evident in some of the background research papers that Abella commissioned for the RCEE. See Kathleen Mahoney, "Daycare and Equality in Canada," in *Research Studies of the Commission on Equality in Employment,* ed. Judge Rosalie Silberman Abella, Commissioner (Ottawa: Supply and Services, 1985), 159-81; and Margrit Eichler, "The Connection between Paid and Unpaid Labour and Its Implications for Creating Equality for Women in Employment," ibid., 539-46.

39 Royal Commission on Equality in Employment, *Report,* 278-81.

40 Interview with Rosalie Abella, Toronto, August 1986.

41 From the Privy Council Office, Royal Commission on Equality in Employment, *Report,* 20, reproduced with the permission of the Minister of Public Works and Government Services Canada, 2000. She also noted that "native people pointed to a range of studies released but ignored in the past decade; disabled persons pointed to the slow progress of the implementation of some of the key recommendations of *Obstacles,* a report of the Special Committee on the Disabled and the Handicapped; and visible minorities pointed to an emphasis in funding for multiculturalism rather than for racial discrimination issues" (ibid.).

42 Royal Commission on Equality in Employment, *Report,* 19.

43 Canadian Psychological Association, Submission to the Commission of Inquiry on Equality in Employment, 8 November 1983, National Archives of Canada (NAC), RG 33/133, box no. 1, 2. Submissions to the RCEE are listed in the front section of the Bibliography.

44 Congress of Canadian Women, Submission to the Commission of Inquiry on Equality in Employment, 15 October 1983, NAC, RG 33/133, box no. 1, 3.

45 Ibid.

46 Ottawa Valley Chapter of Women in Science and Engineering, Submission to the Royal Commission on Equality in Employment, 19 December 1983, NAC, RG 33/133, box no. 1, 1.

47 National Action Committee on the Status of Women, "The Implementation of Mandatory Affirmative Action: A Blueprint for Federal Government Policy," Submission to the Royal Commission on Equality in Employment, 31 January 1984, NAC, RG 33/133, box no. 1, 6.

48 Canadian Congress for Learning Opportunities for Women, Submission to the Commission of Inquiry on Equality in Employment, 13 October 1983, NAC, RG 33/133, box no. 1, 9.

49 Ottawa Women's Lobby, Submission to the Commission of Enquiry on Equality in Employment, 20 October 1983, NAC, RG 33/133, box no. 1, 2.

50 Federal Progressive Conservative Women's Caucus of Peel-Halton, Submission to the Royal Commission on Equality in Employment, 17 October 1983, NAC, RG 33/133, box no. 1, 6-7.
51 Federal Progressive Conservative Women's Caucus of Calgary, Submission to the Commission of Inquiry on Equality in Employment, 27 September 1983, NAC, RG 33/133, box no. 1, 5.
52 Ontario Native Women's Association, "Factors that Affect Native People's Participation in the Labour Force," Submission to the Royal Commission on Equality in Employment, 25 November 1983, NAC, RG 33/133, box no. 1, 3.
53 Federated Women's Institutes of Canada, Submission to the Commission of Inquiry on Equality in Employment, November 1983, NAC, RG 33/133, box no. 1, 3.
54 Ottawa Women's Lobby, Submission, 4-5.
55 Ottawa Valley Chapter of Women in Science and Engineering, Submission, 1.
56 Battlefords Interval House Society, Submission to the Royal Commission on Equality in Employment, 29 September 1983, NAC, RG 33/133, box no. 1; BC Native Women's Society, "Barriers to Women Entering the Labour Market," Submission to the Royal Commission on Equality in Employment, NAC, RG 33/133, box no. 1.
57 Ottawa Women's Lobby, Submission, 5.
58 Business and Professional Women's Clubs of BC and the Yukon, Submission to the Royal Commission on Equality in Employment, 26 September 1983, NAC, RG 33/133, box no. 1, 4.
59 University Women's Club of Ottawa, Standing Committees for the Status of Women and Legislation, Submission to the Royal Commission on Equality in Employment, 10 November 1983, NAC, RG 33/133, box no. 1, 1.
60 Federation of Women Teachers' Associations of Ontario, Submission to the Royal Commission on Equality in Employment, 1983, NAC, RG 33/133, box no. 1, 4.
61 BC Native Women's Society, Submission, 2.
62 Nova Scotia Advisory Council on the Status of Women, Brief presented to the Royal Commission on Equality in Employment, 26 September 1983, NAC, RG 33/133, box no. 1, 2.
63 Ibid.
64 Federation of Junior Leagues of Canada, Submission to the Royal Commission on Equality in Employment, 24 September 1983, NAC, RG 33/133, box no. 1, 3.
65 Federation of Women Teachers' Associations of Ontario, Submission, 4.
66 Battlefords Interval House Society, Submission, 3.
67 Ottawa Valley Chapter of Women in Science and Engineering, Submission, 2.
68 Federal Progressive Conservative Women's Caucus of Calgary, Submission, 15.
69 See, for example, Business and Professional Women's Clubs of BC and the Yukon, Submission, 3; Federated Women's Institutes of Canada, Submission, 3.
70 Infant Formula Action Coalition, "Infact Submission," Submission to the Royal Commission on Equality in Employment, 13 January 1983, NAC, RG 33/133, box no. 1, 1-3, 5.
71 Ontario Native Women's Association, "Factors that Affect Native People's Participation," Submission, 1.
72 Battlefords Interval House Society, Submission, 4.
73 See, for example, Congress of Canadian Women, Submission, 3; and Vancouver Women in Trades Association, Brief submitted to Commission of Inquiry on Equality in Employment, 26 October 1983, NAC, RG 33/133, box no. 1, 6.
74 See, for example, Federal Progressive Conservative Women's Caucus of Ottawa, Submission to the Commission of Inquiry on Equality in Employment, 25 November 1983, NAC, RG 33/133, box no. 1, 4; and University Women's Club of Ottawa, Submission, 3.
75 Quesnel Tillicum Society, Submission to the Royal Commission on Equality in Employment, 19 October 1983, NAC, RG 33/133, box no. 1, 4; Native Women's Association of the Northwest Territories. Submission to the Royal Commission on Equality in Employment, 19 October 1983, NAC, RG 33/133, box no. 1, 11.
76 Canadian Day Care Advocacy Association, "Beginning to Solve Canada's Daycare Crisis: Short-Term and Long-Term Proposals," Submission to the Commission of Inquiry on Equality in Employment, November 1983, NAC, RG 33/133, box no. 1, 1.

77 Ibid., 2.

78 Ibid., 6.

79 Ibid., 9.

80 Royal Commission on Equality in Employment, *Report,* 177.

81 National Action Committee on the Status of Women, "The Implementation of Manda-tory Affirmative Action"; Canadian Day Care Advocacy Association, "Beginning to Solve Canada's Daycare Crisis: Short-Term and Long-Term Proposals," 1.

82 See covering letter accompanying NAC's submission to the RCEE from Doris Anderson, president of NAC, to Judge Rosalie S. Abella, Commissioner, Commission of Inquiry on Equality in Employment, 31 January 1984, attached to National Action Committee on the Status of Women, "The Implementation of Mandatory Affirmative Action." The let-ter indicates that Carole Wallace of the NAC Employment Committee had prepared the brief.

83 See covering letter accompanying CDCAA's submission to the RCEE from Judith Martin, chair of the CDCAA, to Judge Rosalie S. Abella, Commissioner, Commission of Inquiry on Equality in Employment, 2 December 1983, attached to Canadian Day Care Advocacy Association, "Beginning to Solve Canada's Day Care Crisis."

84 Royal Commission on Equality in Employment, *Report,* 102.

85 Ibid., 103.

86 Ibid., 104.

87 Ibid., 116.

88 Ibid., 107.

89 Ibid., 116.

90 Ibid., 125.

91 Ibid.

92 Ibid., 123.

93 Ibid., 126.

94 Ibid., 124.

95 Ibid., 122.

96 Ibid.

97 Ibid., 125. For evidence of Canada Mortgage and Housing Corporation's success in encour-aging the participation and promotion of women, see ibid., 107-21.

98 Ibid., 123.

99 Ibid., 124.

100 Ibid., 123-4.

101 Ibid., 125.

102 Ibid., 126.

103 Ibid., 125.

104 Ibid., 3.

105 Carole Geller, "A Critique of the Abella Report," *Canadian Woman Studies/Les cahiers de la femme* 6, 4 (1985): 20-2.

106 Royal Commission on Equality in Employment, *Report,* 3.

107 Ibid., 13.

108 Her decision to hold the RCEE's hearings *in camera* was unusual in the context of a royal commission. It was made in an attempt to "get away from the confrontational tactics of the courtroom" and increase Abella's ability to get to the root of demands and concerns articulated by representatives of the business, labour, and target groups with whom she met. Indeed Abella believed that in getting the different interest groups to be "frank, very frank" in these closed sessions, she increased her potential to produce recommendations that reflected a consensus among the divergent organizations with whom she consulted (interview with Rosalie Abella, August 1986).

109 Royal Commission on Equality in Employment, *Report,* 23.

110 Ibid., 6.

111 Ibid., 4. The heterosexual assumptions underscoring this argument should be noted.

112 Ibid.

113 Ibid., 17.

114   Ibid., 13.
115   Ibid., 18.
116   Ibid., 4. Indeed, later in the report, Abella noted that "equal pay is an integral element in the implementation of employment equity. It must be included in any undertaking by employers to make the practices in the workplace more equitable" (ibid., 232). For an analysis of federal and provincial governments' failure to maintain the link between these two issues, see Patricia McDermott, "Pay and Employment Equity: Why Separate Policies?" in *Women and Canadian Public Policy,* ed. Janine Brodie (Toronto: Harcourt Brace, 1996), 89-104.
117   Royal Commission on Equality in Employment, *Report,* 212-13. Interestingly, the fact that Abella's recommendations and the subsequent employment equity legislation did not develop quota-based employment equity led to British government interest in the Canadian model. In the mid-1980s, when the British government was forced by American investors in Northern Ireland to address the systemic employment discrimination against Catholics in the province, the Canadian model was considered closely in the development of Northern Ireland's fair employment legislation (author's interview with Sir Robert Cooper, Chairman, Northern Ireland Fair Employment Commission, 1990-9, Belfast, October 1995).

 For a fuller discussion of the politics behind the development of fair employment legislation in Northern Ireland, see Richard Jay and Rick Wilford, "The Politics of the Fair Employment Act in Northern Ireland: Internal and External Dimensions" (paper presented at the 40th Annual Conference of the Political Studies Association, University of Durham, April 1990).

 For a comparison of the development of employment equity legislation in Canada and fair employment legislation in Northern Ireland, see Robert Cormack and Robert Osborne, "Employment Equity in Canada and Fair Employment in Northern Ireland," *British Journal of Canadian Studies* 4, 2 (1989): 219-32.
118   Rosalie Abella, "Equality in Employment: A Royal Commission Report," *Canadian Woman Studies/Les cahiers de la femme* 6, 4 (1985): 6. For further discussion of Abella's rationale for avoiding the term "affirmative action," see Paul Scott, "Equality in Employment: A Royal Commission Report," *Currents* 4, 2 (1984-5): 3-11.
119   Royal Commission on Equality in Employment, *Report,* 7.
120   *An Act to Repeal Job Quotas and Restore Merit-Based Employment Practices in Ontario [Job Quotas Repeal Act],* Statutes of Ontario 1995, c. 4.
121   Royal Commission on Equality in Employment, *Report,* 203.
122   Ibid., 205.
123   Ibid., 203.
124   Ibid., 213.
125   Ibid., 212.
126   Ibid.
127   Ibid., 214.
128   Ibid., 205.
129   Ibid., 195.
130   Ibid.
131   Ibid., 197.
132   Ibid., 202.
133   Ibid., 226-7.
134   Ibid., 229, 227.
135   Ibid., 229.
136   Ibid., 231.
137   Ibid., 228.
138   Ibid., 214-15.
139   Ibid., 215-19.
140   Ibid., 215.
141   Ibid., 257.
142   Ibid., 177.

143 Ibid., 28.
144 Ibid.
145 Ibid., 178.
146 Ibid., 182.
147 Ibid., 180.
148 Ibid., 192.
149 Ibid., 180. On the relationship between parents and the state in the provision of education, Abella argued that "education is seen as part of the care of children and no one thinks women – or for that matter either parent – should stay home so their children will not have to go to school. The parents are still primary, the state indispensable auxiliary" (ibid.).
150 Ibid., 189.
151 Ibid., 179. Recommendations are listed at ibid., 267-8.
152 Ibid., 182.
153 Rosalie Abella, "Equality in Employment: A Royal Commission Report," 7. See also Royal Commission on Equality in Employment, *Report*, 179.
154 Royal Commission on Equality in Employment, *Report*, 267.
155 Ibid., 191-2.
156 Ibid.
157 Interview with Rosalie Abella, August 1986.
158 Ibid.
159 Privy Council Office, P.C. Order in Council, 1983-4048, 22 December 1983. In *Orders in Council* 4, 46 (31 December 1983), 4.
160 Privy Council Office, P.C. Order in Council, 1984-1390, 18 April 1984. In *Orders in Council* 5, 14 (20 April 1984), 2. A further P.C. Order in Council was issued on 23 August 1984 to extend the period for producing the report of the Royal Commission on Equality in Employment (Privy Council Office, P.C. Order in Council, 1984-2882, 23 August 1984, *Orders in Council* 5, 30 [24 August 1984], 12).
161 John Roberts, Letter to Judge Rosalie Abella, Commissioner to Commission of Enquiry on Equality in Employment from the Minister of Employment and Immigration, 21 March 1984, NAC, RG 33/133, box 20, file 14.
162 Ibid.
163 Jackie Smith, "Where These Men Stand on Women's Issues," *Toronto Star*, 12 May 1984, F1, F3.
164 The Conservatives won the largest number of seats ever attained by a single party, with a majority of seats in every province. See Howard Penniman, ed., *Canada at the Polls, 1984: A Study of the Federal General Election* (Durham: Duke University Press, 1988); and Frank Feigert, "National Results: Individual Elections," in *Party Politics in Canada*, 7th ed., ed. Hugh G. Thorburn (Scarborough, ON: Prentice-Hall Canada, 1996), 546-7.

Chapter 7: Breaking the Links
1 Brian Mulroney made this infamous statement in his first major public speech as prime minister, delivered to the Economic Club in New York, when he confirmed the demise of the Foreign Investment Review Agency, its replacement with Investment Canada, and his government's intention to rescind the National Energy Program. See Stephen Clarkson, *Canada and the Reagan Challenge: Crisis and Adjustment 1981-1985* (Toronto: James Lorimer, 1985), 358. For an analysis of "The Mulroney Outlook" that addresses the range of his concerns on taking office, see Sylvia Bashevkin, "Losing Common Ground: Feminists, Conservatives and Public Policy in Canada during the Mulroney Years," *Canadian Journal of Political Science* 29, 2 (1996): 216-19.
2 Author's interview with Michael Sabia, Senior Policy Advisor to Flora MacDonald, Minister of Employment and Immigration, 1984-6, Ottawa, September 1986. For discussions of the pro-family lobby in Canada and its operation both inside and outside the federal Parliament, see Katherine Teghtsoonian, "Neo-Conservative Ideology and Opposition to Federal Regulation of Child Care Services in the United States and Canada," *Canadian Journal of Political Science* 16, 1 (1993): 118-20; Lorna Erwin, "What Feminists Should

Know about the Pro-Family Movement in Canada: A Report on a Recent Survey of Rank-and-File Members," in *Feminist Research: Prospect and Retrospect*, ed. Peta Tancred-Sherriff (Montreal and Kingston: McGill-Queen's University Press, 1988), 266-78; and Margrit Eichler, *The Pro-Family Movement: Are They for or against Families?* Feminist Perspectives Féministes no. 4a (Ottawa: Canadian Research Institute for the Advancement of Women, 1985).

3 For details of the proposed Canada Child Care Act, see House of Commons, *Bill C-144: Canada Child Care Act*, 33rd Parliament, 2nd Session, 1988. See also House of Commons, *Debates*, 26 September 1988, 19649. For details of its failure to proceed through the senate, see Senate of Canada, *Proceedings of the Standing Committee on Social Affairs, Science and Technology*, Issue no. 15, 1 October 1988.

4 For a discussion of the Mulroney brand of neo-conservatism, see Andrew B. Gollner and Daniel Salée, "A Turn to the Right? Canada in the Post-Trudeau Era," in *Canada under Mulroney: An End of Term Report*, ed. Andrew B. Gollner and Daniel Salée (Montreal: Véhicule Press, 1988), 14-17; and Teghtsoonian, "Neo-Conservative Ideology." For a discussion of the concept of red-Toryism, see William Christian and Colin Campbell, *Parties, Leaders and Ideologies in Canada* (Toronto: McGraw-Hill Ryerson, 1996), 9-10.

5 Author's interview with the Hon. Flora MacDonald, Minister of Employment and Immigration, 1984-6, Leeds, England, December 1990.

6 This three-hour debate, held on 15 August 1984, demonstrated the influence that the organized women's movement had in Canadian politics in the early 1980s. (In 1988, their time slot was reduced to one hour in the three-hour leaders' debate.) For a fuller discussion of the debate, see Penney Kome, *Women of Influence: Canadian Women and Politics* (Toronto: Doubleday Canada, 1985), 142-6; and Bashevkin, "Losing Common Ground," 219. For analysis of the equality issues discussed during the debate, see C. Lynch, "Women's Issues Debate Brings Campaign Full Circle," *Montreal Gazette*, 16 August 1984, B1.

7 An Ottawa (CP) press wire for 21 November 1984, reporting the release of the RCEE, noted how in March 1984 Mulroney had promised that a Conservative government would "ensure that companies seeking to provide service to the federal government hire increasing numbers of women to perform those services" (Employment and Immigration Canada, Public Affairs, "AM-Parl-Abella, Night Lead," by Nicole Baer, press clippings, 22 November 1988). See also Charlotte Montgomery, "Tories Consider Buying Policy As Lever for Job Equality Laws," *Globe and Mail*, 22 November 1988, A5.

8 For a fuller discussion of Mulroney's clear commitment to improving the political position of women in both his government and party, see Sydney Sharpe, *The Gilded Ghetto: Women and Political Power in Canada* (Toronto: HarperCollins, 1994), 111-27.

9 For a comparison of broader policy developments affecting women during the Mulroney, Reagan, and Thatcher years, see Sylvia Bashevkin, *Women on the Defensive: Living through Conservative Times* (Toronto: University of Toronto Press, 1998), 47-129.

10 Interview with Michael Sabia, September 1986.

11 Ibid.

12 Donald J. Savoie, *Thatcher, Reagan, Mulroney: In Search of a New Bureaucracy* (Pittsburgh, PA: University of Pittsburgh Press, 1994), 268.

13 Peter Aucoin, "Organizational Change in the Machinery of Canadian Government: From Rational Management to Brokerage Politics," *Canadian Journal of Political Science* 19, 1 (1986): 17.

14 Robert Fulford, "Surrendering Canada," *Saturday Night* 102, 8 (1987): 5.

15 Interview with Flora MacDonald, December 1990.

16 Ibid. The 1984 general election saw a larger number of women elected to Parliament than ever before. Even though women accounted for just 10 percent of the total membership of the House of Commons, the number of female MPs increased from sixteen (in 1980) to twenty-eight (in 1984). The election of more female Conservative MPs was particularly marked. While only two Conservative women candidates had been elected in 1980, a total of nineteen were returned to the House in 1984. See Lisa Young, "Fulfilling the Mandate of Difference: Women in the Canadian House of Commons," in *In the Presence*

of Women: Representations in Canadian Governments, ed. Jane Arscott and Linda Trimble (Toronto: Harcourt Brace, 1997), 84.

17 Interview with Flora MacDonald, December 1990.

18 Canada, Statement to the House of Commons by the Hon. Flora MacDonald, Minister of Employment and Immigration, on the federal government's response to the Royal Commission Report on Equality in Employment, 8 March 1985, 5, 10. See also House of Commons, *Debates,* 8 March 1985, 2820-1.

19 Canada, *Employment Equity and Economic Growth,* Background paper, 8 March 1985, 1.

20 Treasury Board of Canada, President of the Treasury Board, Notes for a statement by the Hon. Robert R. De Cotret, President of the Treasury Board, announcing measures on employment equity, 8 March 1985, 3.

21 Ibid.

22 Ibid.

23 Canada, Notes for a statement by the Hon. Walter F. McLean, Secretary of State of Canada, Minister Responsible for the Status of Women and Minister Responsible for the Status of Disabled Persons, on the federal government's response to the Royal Commission Report on Equality in Employment, Ottawa, 8 March 1985 (GC 194 7540-21-886-3757), 2.

24 Kome, *Women of Influence,* 187.

25 Interview with Flora MacDonald, December 1990.

26 Canada, Notes for a statement by the Hon. Walter McLean, 2. Emphasis added.

27 The four alternative models, all itemized in recommendation 25 of the RCEE were (i) to expand jurisdiction of CHRC and make it responsible for employment equity; (ii) to set up a new independent agency with responsibility for monitoring and enforcement of employment equity and jurisdiction over contract compliance; (iii) to follow model (i) above but ensure that the Canadian Labour Market and Productivity Centre assist the CHRC with the development of employment equity guidelines and encourage input from the designated groups, business and labour; (iv) to give the CHRC jurisdiction over employment equity and contract compliance but require labour inspectors to supplement investigations by the CHRC and refer possible violations back to the CHRC for enforcement (Royal Commission on Equality in Employment, *Report* [Ottawa: Supply and Services, 1984], 258-60).

28 Analyses of the implementation of the EEA at a micro-organizational level can be found in Joanne D. Leck and David Saunders, "Hiring Women: The Effects of Canada's Employment Equity Act," *Canadian Public Policy* 18, 2 (1992): 203-20; and Janet M. Lum, "The Federal Employment Equity Act: Goals vs. Implementation," *Canadian Public Administration* 38, 1 (1995): 45-76.

29 Author's interviews with Hanne Jensen, Director, Pay and Equity Branch, Canadian Human Rights Commission, 1988-90, Ottawa, December 1988, and Peter S. Doyle, Commissioner for Employers, 1984-6, Canadian Employment and Immigration Commission, Hull, QC, December, 1988.

30 *Employment Equity Act,* S.C. 1986, c. 31, s. 5.

31 Employment and Immigration Canada, "Employment Equity Legislation Introduced," press release, 85-28 (E&I 2014E [5-85]), 8 March 1985.

32 Interview with Michael Sabia, September 1986.

33 Royal Commission on Equality in Employment, *Report,* 257-8, recommendations 15-21.

34 Ibid., recommendations 18-21.

35 Ibid.

36 For Abella's recommendations on pay equity, see recommendations 32 and 33 of Royal Commission on Equality in Employment, *Report,* 261.

37 For Abella's recommendations about the protection of part-time and domestic workers, see recommendations 103 and 10 of the report of the RCEE (ibid., 268); for her suggestions about the recognition of home work and volunteer work, see recommendation 105 (ibid.). Recommendation 107 of the report of the RCEE calls for the development of processes to deal with sexual harassment in the workplace (ibid., 268). Recommendation 83 addresses the need to improve training programs for women re-entering the labour

market (ibid., 266). It is interesting to note that Abella's recommendations on recognizing home work and volunteer work as legitimate employment experience were also recommendations in the report of the RCSW (Royal Commission on the Status of Women
in Canada, *Report* [Ottawa: Information Canada, 1970], 49).

38 *Employment Equity Act,* S.C. 1986, c. 31, s. 13.

39 Employment and Immigration Canada, Federal Contractors Program, Employment
Equity Branch, "Federal Contractors Program: Criteria for Implementation," Internal
document, 1986, 2.

40 Employment and Immigration Canada, Office of the Minister, press release, 27 June
1986, (86-20).

41 Mona Kornberg, "Employment Equity: The Quiet Revolution?" *Canadian Woman Studies/
Les cahiers de la femme* 6, 4 (1985): 17.

42 Employment and Immigration Canada, Office of the Minister, Notes for an address by
the Hon. Flora MacDonald, P.C., M.P., Minister of Employment and Immigration, to the
Institute for Research on Public Policy, Montreal, 4 March 1986, 9-10.

43 Bashevkin, "Losing Common Ground," 227.

44 For feminist criticisms of the EEA see Kornberg, "Employment Equity," 17; Patricia
McDermott, "Pay and Employment Equity: Why Separate Policies?" in *Women and Cana-
dian Public Policy,* ed. Janine Brodie (Toronto: Harcourt Brace, 1996), 96; Marjorie Cohen,
"Employment Equity Is *Not* Affirmative Action," *Canadian Woman Studies/Les cahiers de la
femme* 6, 4 (1985): 23-5; and Lorna R. Marsden, "The Importance of Studying Affirmative
Action," *Canadian Woman Studies/Les cahiers de la femme* 6, 4 (1985): 14.

45 Interview with Flora MacDonald, December 1990.

46 House of Commons, *Sharing the Responsibility,* Report of the Special Committee on Child
Care (Ottawa: Queen's Printer for Canada, 1987), 1.

47 Ibid.

48 Derek P.J. Hum, "Compromise and Delay: The Federal Strategy on Child Care," in *Canada:
The State of the Federation 1989,* ed. Ronald L. Watts and Douglas M. Brown (Kingston:
Institute of Intergovernmental Relations, Queen's University, 1989), 153.

49 For discussions on the discrepancy between the reports of the Cooke Task Force and the
Special Committee on Child Care, see Martha Friendly, Julie Mathien, and Tricia Willis,
*Childcare: What the Public Said, An Analysis of the Transcripts of the Public Hearings Held
across Canada by the Parliamentary Special Committee on Child Care* (Ottawa: Canadian
Day Care Advocacy Association, 1987), 2-5; Susan D. Phillips, "Rock-a-Bye, Brian: The
National Strategy on Child Care," in *How Ottawa Spends 1989-90: The Buck Stops Where?,*
ed. Katherine A. Graham (Ottawa: Carleton University Press, 1989), 165-208; Hum,
"Compromise and Delay," 153-8; and Martha Friendly, *Child Care Policy in Canada:
Putting the Pieces Together* (Don Mills, ON: Addison-Wesley, 1994), 152-9.

50 It is important to note that the Liberal (Lucie Pépin) and New Democratic Party (Margaret
Mitchell) members of the SPCCC did not wish the committee to shift the policy agenda
away from the recommendations in the report of the Cooke Task Force. Their differences
with the Conservative members of the committee are recorded in New Democratic Party,
Caring for Canada's Children: A Special Report on the Crisis in Child Care, Minority Report of
the Special Parliamentary Committee on Child Care, prepared by Margaret Mitchell
(Ottawa: New Democratic Party, 1987); and Liberal Party of Canada, *Choices for Childcare:
Now and the Future,* Minority Report of the Special Parliamentary Committee on Child
Care, prepared by Lucie Pépin (Ottawa: Liberal Party of Canada, 1987). For a comparison
of the positions taken by the Conservative, Liberal, and New Democrat members of the
committee in their respective reports, see Canadian Day Care Advocacy Association,
"Child Care: Three Federal Reports at a Glance," 30 March 1997.

51 Recommendation 92 of the RCEE stated that "the ideal childcare system should be publicly funded, of acceptable quality, and universally accessible, though not compulsory"
(Royal Commission on Equality in Employment, *Report,* 267). Recommendation 1 of the
Cooke Report suggested that "the federal, provincial and territorial governments jointly
develop complementary systems of child care and parental leave that are as comprehensive, accessible and competent as our systems of health care and education" (Status of

Women Canada, *Report of the Task Force on Child Care* [Ottawa: Supply and Services, 1986], 373).

52 Recommendation 93 of the RCEE argued that "the Canada Assistance Plan is an inappropriate funding mechanism for childcare as it perpetuates the suggestion that childcare is part of the welfare system" (Royal Commission on Equality in Employment, *Report*, 267). Similarly, recommendation 16 in the Cooke Report argued that "the Canada Assistance Plan provisions applying to child care should be subsumed under legislation that governs the new cost-shared financing" (Status of Women Canada, *Report of the Task Force on Child Care*, 374-5).

53 Recommendation 10 of the SPCCC report suggested that "the federal government introduce a Family and Child Care Act, complementing the Canada Assistance Plan, to provide federal funds for licensed child care centres" (House of Commons, *Sharing the Responsibility*, 87). Recommendation 9 suggested that "Health and Welfare Canada encourage the provinces and territories to use existing matching funds available under the Canada Assistance Plan for high-quality, developmental head-start programs for disadvantaged children" (ibid., 86). Recommendation 8 suggested that "Health and Welfare Canada discuss with the provinces and territories ways and means of publicizing the income levels that currently determine eligibility for day care subsidies under the Canada Assistance Plan" (ibid.).

54 Royal Commission on Equality in Employment, *Report*, 267-8.

55 Status of Women Canada, *Report of the Task Force on Child Care*, 373.

56 For a detailed comparison, see Annis May Timpson, "Driven Apart: The Construction of Women as Worker-Citizens and Mother-Citizens in Canadian Employment and Child Care Policies 1940-1988" (PhD diss., University of Toronto, 1997), 374-5.

57 Ibid.

58 Royal Commission on Equality in Employment, *Report*, 192.

59 Status of Women Canada, *Report of the Task Force on Child Care*, 375.

60 House of Commons, *Sharing the Responsibility*, 3 (recommendation 2).

61 Ibid., 85 (recommendation 3).

62 Ibid.

63 Recommendation 20 of the Cooke Report suggested that "all capital costs of child care facilities incurred either by employers on behalf of employees, or by owners of revenue producing property shall form a new and separate class of depreciable property under the Income Tax Act, with a capital cost allowance rate of 100 per cent" (Status of Women Canada, *Report of the Task Force on Child Care*, 375). Recommendation 21 of the Cooke Report suggested that "the provision by an employer of a child care benefit to employees (whether in the form of cash payments, facilities or services) should *not* be considered a taxable benefit so long as (i) the services are provided in a licensed program; and (ii) the benefit is available to all employees, of whatever rank, within the employer's organization, whether or not all such employees avail themselves of the benefit" (ibid.). Recommendation 25 of the SPCCC report suggested that "amendments be introduced to the *Income Tax Act* to authorize for a period of three years from the date to be specified by the Minister of Health and Welfare, a 100% Capital Cost Allowance for expenditures to provide new child care spaces by employers for their employees in the year in which such costs are incurred, with the provision that should these spaces not remain available for their intended purpose for a period of five years, this Capital Cost Allowance may be revoked in full" (House of Commons, *Sharing the Responsibility*, 90).

64 Recommendations 22 and 23 of the Cooke Report called upon the federal government "to provide an example to other Canadian employers by announcing a policy of establishing child care centres in federal government buildings wherever numbers warrant" (recommendation 22) and ensure that "new resources be provided to departments to fully equip these new centres" (recommendation 23) (Status of Women Canada, *Report of the Task Force on Child Care*, 375). Recommendation 24 of the Cooke Report called on the minister of National Defence to "establish licensed child care programs on each Canadian armed forces base in Canada and abroad, and to provide at least the same level of financing to these programs as is provided for other government employees" (ibid.).

Recommendation 25 of the Cooke Report suggested that "when a member of the armed forces, who is also a single parent, is serving in a capacity that requires him or her to be separated from his or her children, the Department of National Defence underwrite the *full* cost of care for that member's children during the period of duty" (ibid., 376). Recommendation 27 of the SPCCC report suggested that the Treasury Board "encourage establishing and equipping child care centres in federal buildings where feasible and where there are sufficient numbers of employees who will need and use the service" (House of Commons, *Sharing the Responsibility*, 90). Recommendation 22 of the SPCCC report proposed that "the Department of National Defence promote, where needs warrant, the establishment of family resource programs on armed forces bases" (ibid., 89).

65 House of Commons, *Sharing the Responsibility*, 9.
66 Ibid., 23-4.
67 Ibid., 10-11, 24, 43.
68 Health and Welfare Canada, *National Strategy on Child Care* (Ottawa: Health and Welfare Canada, 1987), 6.
69 Ibid.
70 Ibid.
71 Ibid., 2.
72 Ibid., 3.
73 Ibid. This increase was to be phased in at $100 per year in 1988 and 1989.
74 Ibid., 2.
75 Ibid., 4.
76 Ibid., 5.
77 Ibid. An additional $940 million was added to this budget in July 1988.
78 Ibid.
79 Ibid.
80 Ibid.
81 Ibid., 1.
82 Ibid.
83 Employment and Immigration Canada, Office of the Minister, Statement by the Hon. Benoît Bouchard, Minister of Employment and Immigration, 3 December 1987, 2.
84 Status of Women Canada, Office of the Minister, Statement by the Hon. Barbara McDougall, Minister Responsible for the Status of Women, 3 December 1987, 2.
85 Ibid.
86 Health and Welfare Canada, Office of the Minister, Statement by the Hon. Jake Epp, Minister of Health and Welfare, 1987, 3.
87 As he noted, the National Strategy was designed to ensure that "working parents have no greater claim to consideration than parents in general, including those who choose to stay at home with their children, or those who employ informal day care and do not have receipts." The strategy also allowed the federal government to "remain agnostic on ... whether the child-care strategy is to address the needs of the working parent or the custodial requirements of the child. By accommodating all parents without distinction, the strategy is conveniently left standing as a matter of parental choice whether one chooses to work or not, and whether one chooses formal child care or not" (Hum, "Compromise and Delay," 161).
88 Ibid., 160; and Phillips, "Rock-a-Bye, Brian," 174-80.
89 Phillips, "Rock-a-Bye Brian," 167.
90 Ibid., 199.
91 House of Commons, *Bill C-144: Canada Child Care Act*, 1988, 1.
92 Ibid., s. 5. In the case of very poor provinces or territories, the federal government was, for a temporary period, prepared to provide up to 90 percent of the capital costs to help create new nonprofit spaces (Phillips, "Rock-a-Bye, Brian," 183).
93 Phillips, "Rock-a-Bye, Brian," 183.
94 House of Commons, *Bill C-144: Canada Child Care Act*, 1988, s. 5.
95 House of Commons, *Debates*, 11 August 1988, 18184.

96 Ibid., 18187.
97 Ibid.
98 Phillips, "Rock-a-Bye, Brian," 173.
99 House of Commons, *Debates,* 11 August 1988, 18187.
100 On the resistance of provincial ministers, see ibid., 18186. In view of this, it is interesting that no provincial ministers openly criticized the National Strategy or Bill C-144, although, as Phillips notes, Connie Osterman, the minister of Social Services in the government of Alberta, did express some concern about federal infringement on provincial jurisdiction when the Bill was introduced into Parliament (Phillips, "Rock-a-Bye, Brian," 199).
101 Author's interviews with Sue Colley, Executive Director of the Ontario Coalition for Better Child Care, 1985-90, Toronto, December 1988; and Martha Friendly, Coordinator, Childcare Research and Resource Unit, University of Toronto, November 1988.
102 National Action Committee on the Status of Women, Brief to the Special Committee on Child Care, prepared by Martha Friendly, presented by Louise Dulude, President of NAC, and Debbie Hughes-Geoffrion, Past Chair of NAC Social Services Committee, 12 June 1986, NAC files, Toronto.
103 National Action Committee on the Status of Women, Brief to the House of Commons Legislative Committee on Bill C-144, prepared and presented by Tricia Willis and Lynn Kaye, 8 September 1988, NAC files, Toronto.
104 Interview with Sue Colley, December 1988.
105 On the broader debate about social programs during the 1988 election, see Hum, "Compromise and Delay," 152.
106 National Action Committee on the Status of Women, Brief to the House of Commons Legislative Committee on Bill C-144, 1.
107 Canadian Day Care Advocacy Association, "Bill C-144: A Critique of the Proposed Canada Child Care Act," 1988, Childcare Resource and Research Unit files, Toronto, 1.
108 National Action Committee on the Status of Women, Brief to the House of Commons Legislative Committee on Bill C-144, 6-7; Canadian Day Care Advocacy Association, "A Real Canadian Child Care Act: A Reality or Still an Illusive Dream," Brief to the House of Commons Legislative Committee on Bill C-144, September 1988, 2, 4.
109 National Action Committee on the Status of Women, Brief to the House of Commons Legislative Committee on Bill C-144, 5-6; and Martha Friendly, *Child Care Policy in Canada,* 175.
110 See, for example, Martha Friendly, "Free Trade Forum: The Threat to Non-Profit Child Care in Canada," *Toronto Star,* 21 April 1988, A23; Leonard Shifrin, "Social Policy: Free Trade Threatens Our Social Programs," *Toronto Star,* 31 October 1988, A19; and Sylvia Bashevkin, "Free Trade and Canadian Feminism: The Case of the National Action Committee on the Status of Women," *Canadian Public Policy* 15, 4 (1989): 363-75.

Chapter 8: Tiny Timid Steps
1 For evidence of the backlash against employment equity, see Conrad Winn, "Affirmative Action for Women: More than a Case of Simple Justice," *Canadian Public Administration* 28, 1 (1985): 24-46; and Walter Block and Michael A. Walker, *On Employment Equity: A Critique of the Abella Royal Commission Report,* Focus no. 17 (Vancouver: Fraser Institute, 1985). For more recent criticism of the federal government's employment equity policies, see Martin Loney, *The Pursuit of Division: Race, Gender, and Preferential Hiring in Canada* (Montreal and Kingston: McGill-Queen's University Press, 1998), 160-211.
2 House of Commons, *A Matter of Fairness,* Report of the Special Committee on the Review of the Employment Equity Act (Ottawa: Queen's Printer, 1992), xviii.
3 For a more general discussion of this very significant "valley" in Canadian feminism, see Sylvia Bashevkin, *Women on the Defensive: Living through Conservative Times* (Toronto: University of Toronto Press, 1998), 3.
4 Only one submission was received from an individual woman. This addressed the exclusion of age discrimination from employment equity legislation. See Kathleen Sullivan, "Include the Reporting of Age (40 and Over) in Employment Equity Reports," Submission

268 Notes to pages 157-8

to the Special Committee on the Review of the Employment Equity Act, 14 January 1992, Archives of the Committees and Parliamentary Associations Directorate (ACPAD), House of Commons, 5700-343-E2, Wallet 16. A list of all the submissions cited in this chapter can be found at the front of the Bibliography.

5 See Canadian Advisory Council on the Status of Women, "Re-Evaluating Employment Equity," Submission to the Special Committee on the Review of the Employment Equity Act, 18 March 1992, ACPAD, House of Commons, 5700-343-E2, Wallet 7, 5-13; Congress of Black Women of Canada, Submission to the Special Committee to Review the Employment Equity Act (Bill C-62), January 1992, ACPAD, House of Commons, 5700-343-E2, Wallet 11, 3-4; and Native Women's Association of Canada, "NWAC Comments and Recommendations on the Special Review of the Employment Equity Act," Submission to the Special Committee to Review the Employment Equity Act Bill (Bill C-62), 4 February 1992, ACPAD, House of Commons, 5700-343-E2, Wallet 15, 3-4.

6 National Action Committee on the Status of Women, "Not Another Hundred Years," Submission to the Special Committee to Review the Employment Equity Act (Bill C-62), prepared by Judy Rebick, January 1992, ACPAD, House of Commons, 5700-343-E2, Wallet 14, 2-5.

7 See, for example, Canadian Congress for Learning Opportunities for Women, "More than Numbers: A Review of the Employment Equity Act," Submission to the Special Committee on the Review of the Employment Equity Act, 20 January 1992, ACPAD, House of Commons, 5700-343-E2, Wallet 7, 6; National Action Committee on the Status of Women, "Not Another Hundred Years," 7; and Congress of Black Women of Canada, Submission, 3. For discussions of the growing awareness of diversity issues in the Canadian women's movement, see Amy Gottleib, ed., "What about Us? Organizing Inclusively in the National Action Committee on the Status of Women," in *And Still We Rise: Feminist Political Mobilizing in Contemporary Canada,* ed. Linda Carty (Toronto: Women's Press, 1993), 371-85; and Vijay Agnew, *Resisting Discrimination: Women from Asia, Africa, and the Caribbean and the Women's Movement in Canada* (Toronto: University of Toronto Press, 1996), 52-65. See also Judy Rebick and Kiké Roach, *Politically Speaking* (Vancouver: Douglas and McIntyre, 1996), 72-87, 105-22.

8 Canadian Advisory Council on the Status of Women, "Re-Evaluating Employment Equity," 21.

9 National Action Committee on the Status of Women, "Not Another Hundred Years," 2-5.

10 Native Women's Association of Canada, "NWAC Comments and Recommendations," 3.

11 National Organization of Immigrant and Visible Minority Women of Canada, Brief to the Special Committee on the Review of the Employment Equity Act, 24 January 1992, ACPAD, House of Commons, 5700-343-E2, Wallet 15, 2; Congress of Black Women of Canada, Submission, 3.

12 Canadian Advisory Council on the Status of Women, "Re-Evaluating Employment Equity," 20; Native Women's Association of Canada, "NWAC Comments and Recommendations," 4.

13 Congress of Black Women of Canada, Submission, 6.

14 See Canadian Congress for Learning Opportunities for Women, "More than Numbers," 3; Canadian Federation of Business and Professional Women's Clubs, Brief to the Special Committee on the Review of the Employment Equity Act, January 1992, ACPAD, House of Commons, 5700-343-E2, Wallet 7, 8; National Action Committee on the Status of Women, "Not Another Hundred Years," 14; National Association of Women and the Law, "A Brief on Employment Equity," Submission to the Special Committee on the Review of the Employment Equity Act, June 1991, ACPAD, House of Commons, 5700-343-E2, Wallet 14, 2; Native Women's Association of Canada, "NWAC Comments and Recommendations," 7; Toronto Women in Film and Television, Submission to the Special Committee on the Review of the Employment Equity Act, 16 January 1992, ACPAD, House of Commons, 5700-343-E2, Wallet 16, 21.

15 Canadian Federation of Business and Professional Women's Clubs, Brief to the Special Committee, 11.

16 National Association of Women and the Law, "A Brief on Employment Equity," 1.

17 National Action Committee on the Status of Women, "Not Another Hundred Years," 14.
18 See Canadian Advisory Council on the Status of Women, "Re-Evaluating Employment Equity," 8; National Action Committee on the Status of Women, "Not Another Hundred Years," 12.
19 See Canadian Congress for Learning Opportunities for Women, "More than Numbers," 4; Canadian Federation of Business and Professional Women's Clubs, Brief to the Special Committee, 8-9; Congress of Black Women of Canada, Submission, 7.
20 National Action Committee on the Status of Women, "Not Another Hundred Years," 14.
21 Toronto Women in Film and Television, Submission, 11.
22 See Canadian Congress for Learning Opportunities for Women, "More than Numbers," 7; National Association of Women and the Law, "A Brief on Employment Equity," 4; Congress of Black Women of Canada, Submission, 8; and Young Women's Christian Association of Canada, Brief to the Parliamentary Committee Reviewing [Bill] C-62 an Act Respecting Employment Equity, January 1992, ACPAD, House of Commons, 5700-343-E2, Wallet 16, 11.
23 See, for example, National Action Committee on the Status of Women, "Not Another Hundred Years," 12; and Canadian Advisory Council on the Status of Women, "Re-Evaluating Employment Equity," 27-8.
24 National Association of Women and the Law, "A Brief on Employment Equity," 6.
25 See Canadian Advisory Council on the Status of Women, "Re-Evaluating Employment Equity," 28; National Action Committee on the Status of Women, "Not Another Hundred Years," 12; Canadian Congress for Learning Opportunities for Women, "More Than Numbers," 16.
26 Quotation from National Action Committee on the Status of Women, "Not Another Hundred Years," 12. See also Congress of Black Women of Canada, Submission, 10-11; National Association of Women and the Law, "A Brief on Employment Equity," 6; and the Young Women's Christian Association of Canada, Brief to the Parliamentary Committee, 10.
27 See Canadian Advisory Council on the Status of Women, "Re-Evaluating Employment Equity," 22-4; Canadian Congress for Learning Opportunities for Women, "More than Numbers," 2-3; Canadian Federation of Business and Professional Women's Clubs, Brief to the Special Committee, 4-6; National Action Committee on the Status of Women, "Not Another Hundred Years," 6-7; National Association of Women and the Law, "A Brief on Employment Equity," 5; Native Women's Association of Canada, "NWAC Comments and Recommendations," 5; and Toronto Women in Film and Television, Submission, 10.
28 Quotation from Canadian Congress for Learning Opportunities for Women, "More than Numbers," 1, 5. See also National Action Committee on the Status of Women, "Not Another Hundred Years," 10.
29 See National Association of Women and the Law, "A Brief on Employment Equity," 4; Association of Lesbians and Gays of Ottawa, "Equality and Equity: Lesbians, Gays and the Employment Equity Act," Submission to the Special Committee on the Review of the Employment Equity Act, 15 January 1992, ACPAD, House of Commons, 5700-343-E2, Wallet 6, 7-9; Canadian Congress of Learning Opportunities for Women, "More than Numbers," 2; Coalition for Lesbian and Gay Rights in Ontario, "We Count: Lesbians, Gay Men and Employment Equity," Submission to the Special Committee on the Review of the Employment Equity Act (Brief originally written for the Ontario Legislature), October 1991, ACPAD, House of Commons, 5700-343-E2, Wallet 10, 1; and Congress of Black Women of Canada, Submission, 3; and Toronto Women in Film and Television, Submission, 20.
30 National Action Committee on the Status of Women, "Not Another Hundred Years," 10.
31 Canadian Advisory Council on the Status of Women, "Re-Evaluating Employment Equity," 30.
32 See Canadian Congress for Learning Opportunities for Women, "More Than Numbers," 8; Congress of Black Women of Canada, Submission, 5; Native Women's Association of Canada, "NWAC Comments and Recommendations," 7; and Toronto Women in Film and Television, Submission, 15.
33 National Action Committee on the Status of Women, "Not Another Hundred Years," 10.

34 See House of Commons, "Not Fair Enough: Liberal Minority Report on the Review of the Employment Equity Act," in *A Matter of Fairness,* Report of the Special Committee on the Review of the Employment Equity Act (Ottawa: Queen's Printer, 1992), Appendix C, 61-8; and House of Commons, "Five Year Review of the Employment Equity Act: Minority Report of the Employment Equity Act," in *A Matter of Fairness,* Appendix D, 69-75.
35 House of Commons, *A Matter of Fairness,* recommendation 1.1, 39.
36 Ibid., recommendation 1.10, 40.
37 Ibid., p. 24 and recommendation 3.5, 42.
38 Ibid., recommendation 1.3, 39.
39 Ibid., recommendations 1.2 and 1.8, 39-40.
40 Ibid., p. 3.
41 Ibid., recommendations 2.1 and 2.2, 40.
42 Ibid., recommendations 4.1, 4.2, 4.3, 4.4, 42.
43 Ibid., recommendation 5.4, 44.
44 Ibid., recommendation 5.1, 43.
45 Ibid., recommendation 1.9, 40.
46 Ibid., recommendation 3.1, 41.
47 Ibid., recommendation 3.5, 42.
48 House of Commons, "Not Fair Enough," 63.
49 Task Force on Barriers to Women in the Public Service, *Beneath the Veneer: The Report of the Task Force on Barriers to Women in the Public Service,* vol. 1 (Ottawa: Supply and Services, 1990), Foreword.
50 Author's interview with Kay Stanley, Assistant Secretary, Employment Equity Division, Human Resources Branch, Treasury Board of Canada Secretariat, Ottawa, December 1990.
51 Task Force on Barriers to Women in the Public Service, *Beneath the Veneer,* vol. 1, Preface.
52 Ibid.
53 Ibid.
54 Ibid., 5.
55 Ibid., 37-8.
56 Task Force on Barriers to Women in the Public Service, *Beneath the Veneer,* vol. 2, 70.
57 Ibid., 73.
58 Ibid., 85.
59 Task Force on Barriers to Women in the Public Service, *Beneath the Veneer,* vol. 1, 80.
60 Ibid., 80.
61 Ibid., 82.
62 Ibid., 83.
63 Ibid., 80.
64 Ibid., 124.
65 Ibid.
66 Ibid.
67 Ibid.
68 Treasury Board of Canada, Secretariat, "More Than the Numbers: Case Studies on Best Practices in the Employment of Women," A Report by the Consultation Group on Employment Equity for Women, Study no. 1, 1993, 20.
69 Treasury Board of Canada, Secretariat, "Exploding the Myths: Employment Equity in the Public Service of Canada," Internal document, 1995, 4; Treasury Board of Canada, *Employment Equity in the Public Service: Annual Report 1992-93* (Ottawa: Communications and Coordination Directorate, Treasury Board of Canada, 1994).
70 This contradicted Mulroney's promise that "the Government of Canada shall, even in difficult circumstances, find the resources necessary to do our share in making a child care program a national reality" (House of Commons, *Debates,* 9 March 1987, 3770).
71 Author's interview with Martha Friendly, Coordinator, Childcare Resource and Research Unit, University of Toronto, November 1998.
72 Sandra Bach and Susan Phillips, "Constructing a New Social Union: Child Care beyond Infancy?" in *How Ottawa Spends 1997-98, Seeing Red: A Liberal Report Card,* ed. Gene Swimmer (Ottawa: Carleton University Press, 1997), 238.

73 Author's interview with Ron Yzerman, Director of Child Care Programs, 1991-4 (Health and Welfare Canada), 1994-6 (Human Resources Development Canada), Ottawa, December 1998.
74 Gillian Doherty, Martha Friendly, and Mab Oloman, *Women's Support, Women's Work: Child Care in an Era of Deficit Reduction, Devolution, Downsizing and Deregulation* (Ottawa: Status of Women Canada, 1998), 47.
75 Author's interview with Laurel Rothman, Director of Social Action, Family Services Association, Toronto, December 1998.
76 Interviewee requested anonymity.
77 For details of the 1990 World Summit for Children, see Canadian Child Care Federation, "National Child Care Policy in Canada 1966-1995: An Overview" (background paper by Anne Maxwell and Catherine Ryerse, May 1995), 7. Quotation from interview with Laurel Rothman, December 1998.
78 United Nations, *Convention on the Rights of the Child* (New York: United Nations, 1991), 24, Article 18.3.
79 Health Canada, *Community Action Program for Children* (Ottawa: Health Canada, 1992), 1.
80 Canadian Child Care Federation, "National Child Care Policy," 15.
81 Ibid., 16.
82 Interviewee requested anonymity.
83 Ken Battle, "The Politics of Stealth: Child Benefits under the Tories," in *How Ottawa Spends: A More Democratic Canada ...?* ed. Susan D. Phillips (Ottawa: Carleton University Press, 1993), 417-48.
84 For further discussion of the politics behind the creation of HRDC, see Herman Bakvis, "Shrinking the House of HRIF: Program Review and the Department of Human Resources and Development," in *How Ottawa Spends, 1996-97: Life under the Knife,* ed. Gene Swimmer (Ottawa: Carleton University Press, 1996), 138.
85 For a more general discussion of the potential of HRDC to link policy issues, see Donald J. Savoie, *Governing from the Centre: The Concentration of Power in Canadian Politics* (Toronto: University of Toronto Press, 1999), 181.
86 On Campbell's 1993 election campaign, see David McLaughlin, *Poisoned Chalice: The Last Campaign of the Progressive Conservative Party* (Toronto: Dundurn Press, 1994), 175-276; on the decimation of the Progressive Conservative Party in the 1993 election, see Annis May Timpson, "Canada's Electoral Earthquake," *World Today* 50, 1 (1994): 6-7.

Chapter 9: Creating Opportunity?
1 Liberal Party of Canada, *Creating Opportunity: The Liberal Plan for Canada* (Ottawa: Liberal Party of Canada, 1993), 86-7.
2 Ibid., 39.
3 Ibid., 39, 111.
4 Ibid., 38-40.
5 Ibid., 35.
6 Ibid., 40.
7 Royal Commission on Equality in Employment, *Report* (Ottawa: Supply and Services, 1984), 178.
8 Interviewee requested anonymity.
9 House of Commons, "Not Fair Enough: Liberal Minority Report on the Review of the Employment Equity Act," in *A Matter of Fairness,* Report of the Special Committee on the Review of the Employment Equity Act, Appendix C (Ottawa: Queen's Printer, 1992), 61-8.
10 Ibid., 64-5.
11 Author's interview with Neil Gavigan, Director of Labour Standards and Workplace Equity, Human Resources Development Canada, Hull, QC, June 1998.
12 Author's interview with Kay Stanley, Assistant Secretary, Employment Equity Division, Human Resources Branch, Treasury Board of Canada Secretariat, Ottawa, December 1998.
13 Interview with Neil Gavigan, December 1998.
14 Ibid.
15 Interview with Neil Gavigan, June 1998.

16 Author's interview with Rhys Phillips, Chief of Legislation and Program Development, Employment Equity Branch, Canadian Human Rights Commission, Ottawa, December 1998.
17 Ibid.
18 Ibid.
19 Interview with Neil Gavigan, December 1998.
20 Ibid.
21 Interview with Neil Gavigan, June 1998. The contact between HRDC and CHRC was also noted in author's interview with Michael Paliga, Manager, Workplace Equity Programs, Labour Standards and Workplace Equity, Human Resources Development Canada, Hull, QC, December 1998.
22 Author's interview with Elizabeth Bertoldi, Program Officer, Employment Equity Division, Human Resources Branch, Treasury Board of Canada Secretariat, Ottawa, December 1998.
23 Author's interview with Wally Boxhill, Senior Program Officer, Employment Equity Division, Human Resources Branch, Treasury Board of Canada Secretariat, December 1998.
24 Interview with Michael Paliga, December 1998.
25 Ibid.
26 Ibid.
27 Ibid.
28 House of Commons, *Debates,* 5 October 1995, 15297.
29 *Employment Equity Act,* S.C. 1986, c. 31, s. 2; *Employment Equity Act,* S.C. 1995, c. 44, s. 2.
30 Ibid.
31 It is worth noting that the four target groups did not change as they might have done, for example, to include gay and lesbian worker-citizens. For more recent discussion of this issue, see David Rayside, "Advances Understated," *University of Toronto Bulletin,* 21 July 1997, 4; and David Rayside, *On the Fringe: Gays and Lesbians in Politics* (Ithaca, NY: Cornell University Press, 1998), 109.
32 Human Resources Development Canada, *Employment Equity Act: Annual Report 1997* (Ottawa: Supply and Services, 1997); Human Resources Development Canada, *Employment Equity Act: Annual Report 1998* (Ottawa: Supply and Services, 1998); and Human Resources Development Canada, *Employment Equity Act: Annual Report 1999* (Ottawa: Supply and Services, 1999), 7-11.
33 House of Commons, *Debates,* 5 October 1995, 15297.
34 Author's interview with Martha Friendly, Coordinator, Childcare Resource and Research Unit, University of Toronto, November 1998.
35 Liberal Party of Canada, *Creating Opportunity,* 5.
36 Ibid.
37 Interviewee requested anonymity.
38 Interviewee requested anonymity.
39 Interviewee requested anonymity.
40 Author's interview with Sandra Harder, Researcher, Political and Social Affairs Division, Library of Parliament, Ottawa, December 1998.
41 Author's interview with Ron Yzerman, Director of Child Care Programs, Health and Welfare Canada (1991-4), Human Resources Development Canada (1994-6), Ottawa, December 1998.
42 Ibid.
43 Interview with Martha Friendly, November 1998.
44 See Sylvia Bashevkin, "Rethinking Retrenchment: North American Social Policy during the Early Clinton and Chrétien Years," *Canadian Journal of Political Science* 33, 1 (March 2000): 26-33.
45 Interview with Ron Yzerman, December 1998.
46 Ibid.
47 Ibid.
48 Human Resources Development Canada, *A Vision for Child Care into the 21st Century,* Report of the National Child Care Workshop, Montreal, 2-3 February 1994 (Ottawa: Supply and Services, 1994), 3.

49 Interview with Ron Yzerman, December 1998.
50 Human Resources Development Canada, *A Vision for Child Care*, 27-33.
51 Ibid., 5.
52 Ibid., 19.
53 Ibid., 11.
54 Ibid., 12.
55 House of Commons, *Debates*, 31 January 1994, 609.
56 House of Commons, *Security, Opportunities and Fairness: Canadians Renewing Their Social Programs*, Report of the Standing Committee on Human Resources Development (Ottawa: Queen's Printer, 1995), 1.
57 Ibid.
58 Interview with Martha Friendly, November 1998.
59 Interview with Sandra Harder, December 1998.
60 Human Resources Development Canada, *Agenda: Jobs and Growth, Improving Social Security in Canada,* discussion paper (Ottawa: Supply and Services, 1994), 8. From Human Resources Development Canada, reproduced with the permission of the Minister of Public Works and Government Services Canada, 2000.
61 Ibid., 5.
62 Ibid., 25.
63 Ibid.
64 Ibid., 53.
65 Ibid.
66 Ibid.
67 Ibid., 54.
68 Human Resources Development Canada, *Improving Social Security in Canada: Child Care and Development*, supplementary paper (Ottawa: Supply and Services, 1994).
69 Ibid., 1.
70 Ibid.
71 Ibid.
72 Ibid., 3.
73 Ibid.
74 Interviewee requested anonymity.
75 House of Commons, *Security, Opportunities and Fairness*, 1.
76 Ibid.
77 Michelle Turiano, "Analysis of Testimony Presented to the 1994 Social Security Review," Childcare Research and Resource Unit files, University of Toronto, 1995.
78 Ibid.
79 National Action Committee on the Status of Women, Presentation to the Standing Committee on Social Security Reform, November 1994, Archives of the Committees and Parliamentary Associations Directorate (ACPAD), House of Commons, 5900-351-R1, Wallet 48, 11. All references to submissions made to the Standing Committee on Human Resources Development are listed in the front section of the Bibliography.
80 Child Care Advocacy Association of Canada, "Taking the First Steps – Child Care: An Investment in Canada's Future," Submission to the Standing Committee on Human Resources Development, 13 December 1994, ACPAD, House of Commons, 5900-351-R1, Wallet 30, 4, 5-6.
81 National Women's Consultation on Social Security Review, "Final Report of Recommendations," Ottawa, 3-5 December 1994, ACPAD, House of Commons, 5900-351-R1, Wallet 48, 1.
82 National Action Committee on the Status of Women, Presentation to the Standing Committee, 3.
83 Child Care Advocacy Association of Canada, "Taking First Steps," 5-6; Canadian Child Care Federation, Brief to the Standing Committee on Human Resources Development, 1994, ACPAD, House of Commons, 5900-351-R1, Wallet 26, 4-5.
84 Gillian Doherty, Martha Friendly, and Mab Oloman, *Women's Support, Women's Work: Child Care in an Era of Deficit Reduction, Devolution, Downsizing and Deregulation* (Ottawa: Status of Women Canada, 1998), 39.

85　House of Commons, *Security, Opportunities and Fairness*, 99-100.
86　Ibid., 100.
87　Ibid., 101.
88　Ibid., 92-3.
89　Ibid., 73.
90　Ibid.
91　Ibid.
92　Ibid., 25.
93　Ibid., 28-9.
94　Ibid., 29-30.
95　Ibid., 27.
96　Interview with Martha Friendly, November 1998.
97　House of Commons, *Security, Opportunities and Fairness*, 51, 27.
98　Ibid., 74.
99　See Edward Greenspon and Anthony Wilson-Smith, *Double Vision: The Inside Story of the Liberals in Power* (Toronto: Doubleday, 1996), 245-50.
100　Interviewee requested anonymity.
101　Interviewee requested anonymity.
102　Interview with Martha Friendly, November 1998.
103　Interviewee requested anonymity.
104　Doherty, Friendly, and Oloman, *Women's Support, Women's Work*, 79.
105　The CHST combined the existing federal block grant for health and postsecondary education (Established Program Financing) with the shared-cost grant for welfare programs (the Canada Assistance Plan) into a new, super block grant. Sandra Bach and Susan D. Phillips, "Constructing a New Social Union: Child Care beyond Infancy?" in *How Ottawa Spends 1997-98, Seeing Red: A Liberal Report Card*, ed. Gene Swimmer (Ottawa: Carleton University Press, 1997), 239-40. For further discussion of the CHST, see Allan M. Maslowe, "The Canada Health and Social Transfer: Forcing Issues," in *How Ottawa Spends 1996-97: Life under the Knife*, ed. Gene Swimmer (Ottawa: Carleton University Press, 1996), 283-302.
106　Ibid., 247. Cash transfers to the provinces declined by 33 percent, from $18.6 billion (1995-6) to $12.5 billion in 1997-8 (ibid., 241).
107　Ibid.
108　Interview with Martha Friendly, November 1998.
109　Human Resources Development Canada, Transcript of the press conference held by the Hon. Lloyd Axworthy, Room 130-S, Centre Block, House of Commons, Ottawa, 13 December 1995, 2.
110　Ibid., 2-3.
111　Human Resources Development Canada, Minister of Human Resources Development, Letter from Lloyd Axworthy to provincial and territorial ministers of social services, 13 December 1995, Childcare Resources and Research Unit files, Toronto.
112　Interview with Ron Yzerman, December 1998.
113　Human Resources Development Canada, Minister of Human Resources Development, Letter from Lloyd Axworthy.
114　Interview with Ron Yzerman, December 1998.
115　Ibid.
116　On the impact of the 1995 Quebec referendum, see Annis May Timpson, "Lessons from a House Divided," *The World Today* 51, 12 (1995): 234-6; and Kenneth McRoberts, *Misconceiving Canada: The Struggle for National Unity* (Toronto: Oxford University Press, 1997), 222-4.
117　See Annis May Timpson, "Western Canadian Perspectives on the Quebec Referendum" (paper presented to the Annual Conference of the Centre for Canadian Studies, Queens University Belfast, 28 October 1995), 8. For a more general discussion of the political relationship between Quebec and Western Canada, see Roger Gibbins and Sonia Arrison, *Western Visions: Perspectives on the West in Canada* (Peterborough, ON: Broadview, 1995), 137-40; and Bashevkin, "Rethinking Retrenchment," 27-30.

118 Intergovernmental Conference Secretariat, Conference Communiqué, 35th Annual Premiers Conference, Toronto, 1 September 1994, 830-054/016.
119 Intergovernmental Conference Secretariat, Final Communiqué, 36th Annual Premiers Conference, St. John's, NF, 25 August 1995, 850-057/008.
120 Human Resources Development Canada, Minister of Human Resources Development, Letter from Lloyd Axworthy, 2.
121 Interview with Ron Yzerman, December 1998.
122 Ministerial Council on Social Policy Reform and Renewal, *Report to Premiers* (St. John's, NF: The Council, 1995), 2.
123 Ibid.
124 "Federal child-care plan reported doomed," *Globe and Mail,* 16 February 1995, A3.
125 Interview with Ron Yzerman, December 1998.
126 Human Resources Development Canada, Minister of Human Resources Development, Statement by the Hon. Douglas Young Concerning Child Care, 21 February 1996, 1.
127 Ibid.
128 House of Commons, *Debates,* 27 February 1996, 4.
129 Human Resources Development Canada, *The National Child Benefit: Building a Better Future for Canadian Children,* SC 126-04-98, Catalogue no. MP43-472/1998, September 1997, 4-6.
130 Ibid., 1.
131 Douglas Durst, "Phoenix or Fizzle? Background to Canada's New National Child Benefit," in *Canada's National Child Benefit: Phoenix or Fizzle?* ed. Douglas Durst (Halifax: Fernwood Publishing, 1999), 13.
132 Martha Friendly, "Child Care and Canadian Federalism in the 1990s: Canary in a Coal Mine" (paper presented at a special conference on Good Child Care in Canada in the 21st Century: Preparing the Policy Map, University of Toronto, May 1999), 15.
133 See, for example, "Manitoba Grits Run on Anti-Poverty Program," *Globe and Mail,* 1 September 1999, A5.
134 Martha Friendly, "Child Care and Canadian Federalism in the 1990s," 15.
135 Interview with Ron Yzerman, December 1998.
136 G. Boismenu and Jane Jenson, "A Social Union or a Federal State? Competing Visions of Intergovernmental Relations in the New Liberal Era," in *How Ottawa Spends 1998-99: Balancing Act – The Post-Deficit Mandate,* ed. Leslie A. Pal (Don Mills, ON: Oxford University Press, 1998), 63.
137 Bach and Phillips, "Constructing a New Social Union," 249.
138 Ibid., 249. The scheme was initially introduced in 1992 by the Conservatives as the Earned Income Supplement to offset the costs of working for low-income workers. The Working Income Supplement was increased from $500 per family in 1996 to $750 per family in 1997 and $1,000 per family in 1998.
139 Ibid.
140 House of Commons, *Debates,* 23 September 1997, 8.
141 Quoted in Child Care Advocacy Association of Canada, "Early Childhood Care and Education and the National Children's Agenda: A Policy Discussion Paper" (prepared by Jane Beach, August 1998), Childcare Resource and Research Unit files, Toronto, 2.
142 Federal-Provincial-Territorial Council of Ministers on Social Policy Renewal, *A National Children's Agenda: Measuring Child Well Being and Monitoring Progress,* Supplementary Discussion Paper, May 1999, 3.
143 Ibid., 10.
144 Ibid.

Chapter 10: Linked Together, Yet Driven Apart
1 Author's interview with Neil Gavigan, Director, Labour Standards and Workplace Equity, Human Resources Development Canada, Hull, QC, December 1998. As Arthur Kroeger notes, "as a result of the 1994-95 program review exercise, HRDC's staff was cut to 20,000 from 25,000. In 1996, a further 2,000 employees were transferred to the provinces. Thus,

in the span of three years, the department lost 7,000 experienced employees, more than a quarter of its strength" ("Everyone Loses," *Globe and Mail,* 23 March 2000, A15).

2 Gordon Cleveland and Michael Krashinsky, *The Benefits and Costs of Good Child Care: The Economic Rationale for Public Investment in Young Children* (Toronto: Childcare Resource and Research Unit, 1998), 10-11.

3 Quotation by Julie Mathien, cited in author's interview with Martha Friendly, Coordinator, Childcare Resource and Research Unit, University of Toronto, November 1998.

4 Elizabeth Meehan and Selma Sevenhuijsen, "Problems in Principles and Policies," in *Equality Politics and Gender,* ed. Elizabeth Meehan and Selma Sevenhuijsen (London: Sage, 1991), 12.

5 See Irene Hoskins, ed., *Combining Work and Elder Care: A Challenge for Now and the Future* (Geneva: International Labour Office, 1996); Dorothy Lipovenko, "Care of an Aging Relative Beginning at Home," *Globe and Mail,* 29 July 1994, A1, A5; and Alvi Shahid, *Eldercare and the Workplace,* Report 150-95 (Ottawa: Conference Board of Canada, 1995).

6 Jane Jenson, "Commissioning Ideas: Representations and Royal Commissions," in *How Ottawa Spends 1994-95: Making Change,* ed. Susan D. Phillips (Ottawa: Carleton University Press, 1994), 54.

7 For further discussion of this point, see Peter Aucoin, "Contributions of Commissions of Inquiry to Policy Analysis: An Evaluation," in *Commissions of Inquiry,* ed. A. Paul Pross, Innis Christie, and John A. Yogis (Toronto: Carswell, 1990), 198.

8 For discussion of the way in which royal commissions examine policy problems that cannot easily be resolved through other channels, see Neil Bradford, *Commissioning Ideas: Canadian National Policy Innovation in Comparative Perspective* (Toronto: Oxford University, 1998), 158-60; and Neil Bradford, "Innovation by Commission: Policy Paradigms and the Canadian Political System," in *Canadian Politics,* 3rd ed., ed. James Bickerton and Alain-G. Gagnon (Peterborough, ON: Broadview Press), 541-64.

Bibliography

Documents in Federal Government Archives

Submissions to the 1967 Royal Commission on the Status of Women in Canada
Alback, Vera G. (Ottawa). Submission to the Royal Commission on the Status of Women. Brief no. 193, 20 March 1968. National Archives of Canada (NAC), RG 33/89, microfilm C-4879.

Alberta Association of Registered Nurses. Submission to the Royal Commission on the Status of Women. Brief no. 26, January 1968. NAC, RG 33/89, microfilm C-4878.

Anglican Church of Canada, Commission on Women's Work. Submission to the Royal Commission on the Status of Women. Brief no. 52, 1 February 1968. NAC, RG 33/89, microfilm C-4878.

L'association féminine d'éducation et d'action sociale. Submission to the Royal Commission on the Status of Women. Brief no. 303, March 1968. NAC, RG 33/89, microfilm C-4880.

Bridge, Bonita (Winnipeg). Submission to the Royal Commission on the Status of Women. Brief no. 279, March 1968. NAC, RG 33/89, microfilm C-4880.

Burton, Zenny (Regina). Submission to the Royal Commission on the Status of Women. Brief no. 211, 22 March 1968. NAC, RG 33/89, microfilm C-4880.

Business and Professional Women's Clubs of British Columbia and the Yukon. Submission to the Royal Commission on the Status of Women. Brief no. 261, 17 March 1968. NAC, RG 33/89, microfilm C-4880.

Canadian Clubs of Zonta International, Toronto. Submission to the Royal Commission on the Status of Women. Brief no. 97, 15 February 1968. NAC, RG 33/89, microfilm C-4878.

Canadian Dietetic Association. Submission to the Royal Commission on the Status of Women. Brief no. 239, 19 January 1968. NAC, RG 33/89, microfilm C-4880.

Canadian Federation of Business and Professional Women's Clubs, Ottawa. Submission to the Royal Commission on the Status of Women. Brief no. 147, 19 March 1968. NAC, RG 33/89, microfilm C-4879.

Canadian Federation of University Women, New Brunswick Section. Submission to the Royal Commission on the Status of Women. Brief no. 141, March 1968. NAC, RG 33/89, microfilm C-4878.

Canadian Federation of University Women, Sudbury, Ontario. Submission to the Royal Commission on the Status of Women. Brief no. 192, 3 October 1968. NAC, RG 33/89, microfilm C-4879.

Cartwright, Thelma (Ottawa). Submission to the Royal Commission on the Status of Women. Brief no. 407, 1968. NAC, RG 33/89, microfilm C-4882.

Committee of the Day Care Section of the Citizens' Committee on Children. Submission to the Royal Commission on the Status of Women. Brief no. 324, 29 April 1968. NAC, RG 33/89, microfilm C-4881.

Cooper, Betty (Calgary). Submission to the Royal Commission on the Status of Women. Brief no. 399, 1968. NAC, RG 33/89, microfilm C-4882.

Dawson Creek Business and Professional Women's Club. Submission to the Royal Commission on the Status of Women. Brief no. 219, March 1968. NAC, RG 33/89, microfilm C-4880.

Dunn, Eleanor S. (Ottawa). Submission to the Royal Commission on the Status of Women. Brief no. 55, February 1968. NAC, RG 33/89, microfilm C-4878.

Fédération des services sociaux à la famille du Québec. Submission to the Royal Commission on the Status of Women. Brief no. 256, 20 March 1968. NAC, RG 33/89, microfilm C-4880.

Gaudreau, Margaret M. (Ste. Thérèse). Submission to the Royal Commission on the Status of Women. Brief no. 337, April 1968. NAC, RG 33/89, microfilm C-4881.

Hall, Mrs. W.D. (Weston). Submission to the Royal Commission on the Status of Women. Brief no. 345, 28 March 1968. NAC, RG 33/89, microfilm C-4881.

Hayes, Joan B. (Halifax). Submission to the Royal Commission on the Status of Women. Brief no. 6, 20 October 1967. NAC, RG 33/89, microfilm C-4878.

Imperial Order Daughters of the Empire, Toronto. Submission to the Royal Commission on the Status of Women. Brief no. 311, March 1968. NAC, RG 33/89, microfilm C-4881.

Jackson, Sherrill (Montreal). Submission to the Royal Commission on the Status of Women. Brief no. 28, 12 June 1968. NAC, RG 33/89, microfilm C-4878.

James, Alice (Vancouver). Submission to the Royal Commission on the Status of Women. Brief no. 92, 25 February 1968. NAC, RG 33/89, microfilm C-4878.

Junior League of Toronto. Submission to the Royal Commission on the Status of Women. Brief no. 98, 7 June 1968. NAC, RG 33/89, microfilm C-4878.

Lafon, Marianne (Montreal). Submission to the Royal Commission on the Status of Women. Brief no. 40, 29 January 1968. NAC, RG 33/89, microfilm C-4878.

Manitoba Volunteer Committee on the Status of Women. Submission to the Royal Commission on the Status of Women. Brief no. 318, 21 March 1968. NAC, RG 33/89, microfilm C-4881.

Montreal Council of Women. Submission to the Royal Commission on the Status of Women. Brief no. 183, February 1968. NAC, RG 33/89, microfilm C-4879.

National Council of Women of Canada, Ottawa. Submission to the Royal Commission on the Status of Women. Brief no. 131, March 1968. NAC, RG 33/89, microfilm C-4878.

New Democratic Party Provincial Women's Committee, Saskatchewan Section. Submission to the Royal Commission on the Status of Women. Brief no. 133, 19 March 1968. NAC, RG 33/89, microfilm C-4878.

Ontario Jaycettes, Chatham. Submission to the Royal Commission on the Status of Women. Brief no. 89, 5 June 1968. NAC, RG 33/89, microfilm C-4878.

L'Ordre des Dames Hélène-de-Champlain Inc., Ste. Agathe-des-Monts. Submission to the Royal Commission on the Status of Women. Brief no. 129, 28 February 1968. NAC, RG 33/89, microfilm C-4878.

Ouelet-Savoie, Louyse (Montreal). Submission to the Royal Commission on the Status of Women. Brief no. 144, 10 March 1968. NAC, RG 33/89, microfilm C-4878.

Parents Without Partners, Ottawa Chapter. Submission to the Royal Commission on the Status of Women. Brief no. 319, 30 April 1968. NAC, RG 33/89, microfilm C-4881.

Pelletier, Suzanne (Quebec). Submission to the Royal Commission on the Status of Women. Brief no. 210, 21 March 1968. NAC, RG 33/89, microfilm C-4880.

Perron, Suzel T. (Westmount). Submission to the Royal Commission on the Status of Women. Brief no. 336, 9 March 1968. NAC, RG 33/89, microfilm C-4881.

Pioneer Women's Organization of Canada. Submission to the Royal Commission on the Status of Women. Brief no. 65, 11 March 1968. NAC, RG 33/89, microfilm C-4878.

St. Andrew's United Church, A Group of Women, Beloeil. Submission to the Royal Commission on the Status of Women. Brief no. 166, 17 March 1968. NAC, RG 33/89, microfilm C-4879.

Salvation Army of Canada, Women's Organization, Toronto. Submission to the Royal

Commission on the Status of Women. Brief no. 110, February 1968. NAC, RG 33/89, microfilm C-4878.

Smith, Margaret (Whitehorse). Submission to the Royal Commission on the Status of Women. Brief no. 414, 1968. NAC, RG 33/89, microfilm C-4882.

Soroptomist Club of Halifax. Submission to the Royal Commission on the Status of Women. Brief no. 86, 27 February 1968. NAC, RG 33/89, microfilm C-4878.

Tutt, Sherrie E. (Rouleau). Submission to the Royal Commission on the Status of Women. Brief no. 157, March 1968. NAC, RG 33/89, microfilm C-4879.

United Nations Association, Women's Section, Toronto. Submission to the Royal Commission on the Status of Women. Brief no. 58, 5 June 1968. NAC, RG 33/89, microfilm C-4878.

University of British Columbia, Committee of Mature Women Students. Submission to the Royal Commission on the Status of Women. Brief no. 217, March 1968. NAC, RG 33/89, microfilm C-4880.

Victoria Day Care Services, Toronto. Submission to the Royal Commission on the Status of Women. Brief no. 168, 19 March 1968. NAC, RG 33/89, microfilm C-4879.

Voice of Women, Edmonton. Submission to the Royal Commission on the Status of Women. Brief no. 159, 25 April 1968. NAC, RG 33/89, microfilm C-4879.

Voice of Women, Montreal. Submission to the Royal Commission on the Status of Women. Brief no. 348, May 1968. NAC, RG 33/89, microfilm C-4881.

Women's Ad Hoc Committee of the Saskatchewan Federation of Labour. Submission to the Royal Commission on the Status of Women. Brief no. 296, 20 March 1968. NAC, RG 33/89, microfilm C-4880.

Women's Group of the London and Middlesex Riding Association of the New Democratic Party. Submission to the Royal Commission on the Status of Women. Brief no. 176, 4 June 1968. NAC, RG 33/89, microfilm C-4879.

Young Men's and Young Women's Hebrew Association and Neighbourhood House Services. Submission to the Royal Commission on the Status of Women. Brief no. 314, 21 March 1968. NAC, RG 33/89, microfilm C-4881.

Young Women's Christian Association of Canada, Toronto. Submission to the Royal Commission on the Status of Women. Brief no. 160, 20 March 1968. NAC, RG 33/89, microfilm C-4879.

Submissions to the 1983 Royal Commission on Equality in Employment

Battlefords Interval House Society. Submission to the Royal Commission on Equality in Employment, 29 September 1983. NAC, RG 33/133, box no. 1.

BC Native Women's Society. "Barriers to Women Entering the Labour Market." Submission to the Royal Commission on Equality in Employment. NAC, RG 33/133, box no. 1.

Business and Professional Women's Clubs of BC and the Yukon. Submission to the Royal Commission on Equality in Employment, 26 September 1983. NAC, RG 33/133, box no. 1.

Canadian Congress for Learning Opportunities for Women. Submission to the Commission of Inquiry on Equality in Employment, 13 October 1983. NAC, RG 33/133, box no. 1.

Canadian Day Care Advocacy Association. "Beginning to Solve Canada's Daycare Crisis: Short-Term and Long-Term Proposals." Submission to the Commission of Inquiry on Equality in Employment, November 1983. NAC, RG 33/133, box no. 1.

Canadian Psychological Association. Submission to the Commission of Inquiry on Equality in Employment, 8 November 1983. NAC, RG 33/133, box no. 1.

Congress of Canadian Women. Submission to the Commission of Inquiry on Equality in Employment, 15 October 1983. NAC, RG 33/133, box no. 1.

Federal Progressive Conservative Women's Caucus of Calgary. Submission to the Commission of Inquiry on Equality in Employment, 27 September 1983. NAC, RG 33/133, box no. 1.

Federal Progressive Conservative Women's Caucus of Ottawa. Submission to the Commission of Inquiry on Equality in Employment, 25 November 1983. NAC, RG 33/133, box no. 1.

Federal Progressive Conservative Women's Caucus of Peel-Halton. Submission to the Royal Commission on Equality in Employment, 17 October 1983. NAC, RG 33/133, box no. 1.

Federated Women's Institutes of Canada. Submission to the Commission of Inquiry on Equality in Employment, November 1983. NAC, RG 33/133, box no. 1.

Federation of Junior Leagues of Canada. Submission to the Royal Commission on Equality in Employment, 24 September 1983. NAC, RG 33/133, box no. 1.

Federation of Women Teachers' Associations of Ontario. Submission to the Royal Commission on Equality in Employment, 1983. NAC, RG 33/133, box no. 1.

Infant Formula Action Coalition. "Infact Submission." Submission to the Royal Commission on Equality in Employment, 13 January 1983. NAC, RG 33/133, box no. 1.

National Action Committee on the Status of Women. "The Implementation of Mandatory Affirmative Action: A Blueprint for Federal Government Policy." Submission to the Royal Commission on Equality in Employment, 31 January 1984. NAC, RG 33/133, box no. 1.

Native Women's Association of the Northwest Territories. Submission to the Royal Commission on Equality in Employment, 19 October 1983. NAC, RG 33/133, box no. 1.

Northwest Territories, Justice and Public Services. Submission to Judge R. Abella, Commission of Inquiry on Equality in Employment, 18 October 1983. NAC, RG 33/133, box no. 1.

Nova Scotia Advisory Council on the Status of Women. Brief presented to the Royal Commission on Equality in Employment, 26 September 1983. NAC, RG 33/133, box no. 1.

Ontario Native Women's Association. "Factors that Affect Native People's Participation in the Labour Force." Submission to the Royal Commission on Equality in Employment, 25 November 1983. NAC, RG 33/133, box no. 1.

Ottawa Valley Chapter of Women in Science and Engineering. Submission to the Royal Commission on Equality in Employment, 19 December 1983. NAC, RG 33/133, box no. 1.

Ottawa Women's Lobby. Submission to the Commission of Enquiry on Equality in Employment, 20 October 1983. NAC, RG 33/133, box no. 1.

Quesnel Tillicum Society. Submission to the Royal Commission on Equality in Employment, 19 October 1983. NAC, RG 33/133, box no. 1.

University Women's Club, Standing Committees for the Status of Women and Legislation, Ottawa. Submission to the Royal Commission on Equality in Employment, 10 November 1983. NAC, RG 33/133, box no. 1.

Vancouver Women in Trades Association. Brief submitted to Commission of Inquiry on Equality in Employment, 26 October 1983. NAC, RG 33/133, box no. 1.

Westinghouse Canada, Submission to the Royal Commission on Equality in Employment, 13 December 1983. NAC, RG 33/133, box no. 2.

Submissions to the 1991 House of Commons Special Committee on the Review of the Employment Equity Act

Association of Lesbians and Gays of Ottawa. "Equality and Equity: Lesbians, Gays and the Employment Equity Act." Submission to the Special Committee on the Review of the Employment Equity Act, 15 January 1992. Archives of the Committees and Parliamentary Associations Directorate (ACPAD), House of Commons, 5700-343-E2, Wallet 6.

Canadian Advisory Council on the Status of Women. "Re-Evaluating Employment Equity." Submission to the Special Committee on the Review of the Employment Equity Act, 18 March 1992. ACPAD, House of Commons, 5700-343-E2, Wallet 7.

Canadian Congress for Learning Opportunities for Women. "More than Numbers: A Review of the Employment Equity Act." Submission to the Special Committee on the Review of the Employment Equity Act, 20 January 1992. ACPAD, House of Commons, 5700-343-E2, Wallet 7.

Canadian Federation of Business and Professional Women's Clubs. Brief to the Special Committee on the Review of the Employment Equity Act, January 1992. ACPAD, House of Commons, 5700-343-E2, Wallet 8.

Coalition for Lesbian and Gay Rights in Ontario. "We Count: Lesbians, Gay Men and Employment Equity." Submission to the Special Committee on the Review of the Employment Equity Act. (Brief originally written for the Ontario Legislature), October 1991. ACPAD, House of Commons, 5700-343-E2, Wallet 10.

Congress of Black Women of Canada. Submission to the Special Committee to Review the Employment Equity Act (Bill C-62). January 1992. ACPAD, House of Commons, 5700-343-E2, Wallet 11.

National Action Committee on the Status of Women. "Not Another Hundred Years." Submission to the Special Committee to Review the Employment Equity Act (Bill C-62). Prepared by Judy Rebick, January 1992. ACPAD, House of Commons, 5700-343-E2, Wallet 14.

National Association of Women and the Law. "A Brief on Employment Equity." Submission to the Special Committee on the Review of the Employment Equity Act, June 1991. ACPAD, House of Commons, 5700-343-E2, Wallet 14.

National Organization of Immigrant and Visible Minority Women of Canada. Brief to the Special Committee on the Review of the Employment Equity Act, 24 January 1992. ACPAD, House of Commons, 5700-343-E2, Wallet 15.

Native Women's Association of Canada. "NWAC Comments and Recommendations on the Special Review of the Employment Equity Act." Submission to the Special Committee on the Review of the Employment Equity Act, 4 February 1992. ACPAD, House of Commons, 5700-343-E2, Wallet 15.

Sullivan, Kathleen. "Include the Reporting of Age (40 and Over) in Employment Equity Reports." Submission to the Special Committee on the Review of the Employment Equity Act, 14 January 1992. ACPAD, House of Commons, 5700-343-E2, Wallet 16.

Toronto Women in Film and Television. Submission to the Special Committee on the Review of the Employment Equity Act, 16 January 1992. ACPAD, House of Commons, 5700-343-E2, Wallet 16.

Young Women's Christian Association of Canada. Brief to the Parliamentary Committee Reviewing C-62 an Act Respecting Employment Equity, January 1992. ACPAD, House of Commons, 5700-343-E2, Wallet 16.

Submissions to the 1994 House of Commons Standing Committee on Human Resource Development (Social Security Review)

Canadian Child Care Federation. Brief to the Standing Committee on Human Resources Development, 1994, ACPAD, House of Commons, 5900-351-R1, Wallet 26.

Child Care Advocacy Association of Canada. "Taking the First Steps – Child Care: An Investment in Canada's Future." Submission to the Standing Committee on Human Resources Development, 13 December 1994, ACPAD, House of Commons, 5900-351-R1, Wallet 30.

National Action Committee on the Status of Women. Presentation to the Standing Committee on Social Security Reform, November 1994, ACPAD, House of Commons, 5900-351-R1, Wallet 48.

National Women's Consultation on Social Security Review, "Final Report of Recommendations," Ottawa, 3-5 December 1994, ACPAD, House of Commons, 5900-351-R1, Wallet 48.

Parliamentary Debates, Statutes, and Cases

Parliamentary Debates

House of Commons. *Debates*. 23 November 1945.

–. 2 April 1946.

–. 16 May 1947.

–. 24 February 1967.

–. 12 October 1976.
–. 14 April 1980.
–. 8 March 1985.
–. 3 October 1985.
–. 9 March 1987.
–. 25 July 1988.
–. 11 August 1988.
–. 26 September 1988.
–. 31 January 1994.
–. 5 October 1995.
–. 27 February 1996.
–. 23 September 1997.

Federal Statutes
Bill of Rights, S.C. 1960, c. 44.
Canada Assistance Plan, S.C. 1966-67, c. 45.
Canadian Human Rights Act, S.C. 1977, c. 33; 1980-81-82-83, c. 143.
Constitution Act, S.C. 1982. [en. by the *Canada Act* 1982 (U.K.), c. 11, s. 1], pt 1 (Canadian Charter of Rights and Freedoms).
Employment Equity Act, S.C. 1986, c. 31.
Employment Equity Act, S.C. 1995, c. 44.
Fair Employment Practices Act, S.C. 1953, c. 19.
Federal Female Employees Equal Pay Act, S.C. 1956, c. 38.
Public Service Employment Act, S.C. 1967, c. 71.
Public Service Employment Act, R.S.C. 1970, c. P-32.
Public Service Reform Act, S.C. 1992, c. 54.
Unemployment Insurance Act, R.S.C. 1970, c. U-2.
Unemployment Insurance Act, S.C. 1972, c. 48.

Provincial Statutes
Employment Discrimination Act, Statutes of Quebec 1964, c. 46.
An Act to Repeal Job Quotas and Restore Merit-Based Employment Practices in Ontario [Job Quotas Repeal Act], Statutes of Ontario 1995, c. 4.

Canadian Cases
Action travail des femmes v. *Canadian National Railway Co. et al.,* [1987] 40 D.L.R. (4th) 193-216.
Re Bhinder et al. and *Canadian National Railway Co.,* [1985] 23 D.L.R. (4th) 481.
Bliss v. *Canada (Attorney General),* [1979] 1 S.C.R. 183.
Canada (Attorney General) v. *Lavell et al.,* [1974] S.C.R. 1349.

U.S. Cases
Griggs v. *Duke Power Company,* 401 U.S. 424 (1971).
Personnel Administrator of Massachusetts v. *Feeney,* 442 U.S. 256 (1979).
Wards Cove Packing Co. v. *Antonio,* 490 U.S. 642 (1989).

Other Material
Abbott, Ruth, and Robert Young. "Cynical and Deliberate Manipulation: Child Care and the Reserve Army of Female Labour in Canada." *Journal of Canadian Studies* 24, 2 (1989): 22-38.
Abella, Rosalie S. *Access to Legal Services by the Disabled: The Report of a Study Submitted to the Attorney General of Ontario.* Toronto: Queen's Printer of Ontario, 1983.
–. *Employment Equity: Implications for Industrial Relations.* Kingston: Industrial Relations Centre, Queen's University, 1987.
–. "Equality in Employment: A Royal Commission Report." *Canadian Woman Studies/Les cahiers de la femme* 6, 4 (1985): 5-7.

–. "An Exuberant Rebuke to History." In *Our Own Agendas: Autobiographical Essays by Women Associated with McGill University,* ed. Margaret Gillett and Ann Beer, 72-5. Montreal and Kingston: McGill-Queen's University Press, 1995.

Adamson, Nancy, Linda Briskin, and Margaret McPhail. *Feminists Organizing for Change: The Contemporary Women's Movement in Canada.* Toronto: Oxford University Press, 1988.

Advisory Committee on Reconstruction. *Post-War Problems of Women.* Final Report of the Subcommittee VI. Ottawa: Edmond Cloutier, 1944.

Advisory Council on the Status of Women. *What's Been Done? Assessment of the Federal Government's Implementation of the Recommendations of the Royal Commission on the Status of Women.* Ottawa: Advisory Council on the Status of Women, 1974.

Agnew, Vijay. *Resisting Discrimination: Women from Asia, Africa, and the Caribbean and the Women's Movement in Canada.* Toronto: University of Toronto Press, 1996.

Agocs, Carol. "Affirmative Action, Canadian Style: A Reconnaissance." *Canadian Public Policy* 12, 1 (1986): 148-62.

Andersen, Margaret, ed. *Mother Was Not a Person.* Montreal: Content Publishing and Black Rose Books, 1972.

Anderson, Doris. "How a Tiny Women's Group Defeated a Corporate Giant." *Toronto Star,* 18 July 1988, K1.

–. "Let's Find Out What's Happening to Women." *Chatelaine* 39, 7 (1966): 1.

–. "Yes, Dear Governments, We *Can* Afford Day Care." *Chatelaine* 44, 3 (1971): 1.

–. Letter written as president of the National Action Committee on the Status of Women to Prime Minister Pierre Trudeau, 2 June 1982. National Action Committee on the Status of Women Files, Toronto.

–. *Rebel Daughter: An Autobiography.* Toronto: Key Porter Books, 1996.

Andrew, Caroline. "Women and the Welfare State." *Canadian Journal of Political Science* 17, 4 (1984): 667-83.

Archibald, Kathleen. *Sex and the Public Service.* Ottawa: Queen's Printer, 1970.

Armstrong, Pat, and Hugh Armstrong. "The Conflicting Demands of 'Work' and 'Home.'" In *Family Matters: Sociology and Contemporary Canadian Families,* ed. Karen L. Anderson, 113-40. Scarborough, ON: Nelson Canada, 1988.

–. *The Double Ghetto: Canadian Women and Their Segregated Work.* Toronto: McClelland and Stewart, 1978.

–. *The Double Ghetto: Canadian Women and Their Segregated Work,* Rev. ed. Toronto: McClelland and Stewart, 1984.

–. *The Double Ghetto: Canadian Women and Their Segregated Work,* 3rd ed. Toronto: McClelland and Stewart, 1994.

–. *A Working Majority: What Women Must Do for Pay.* Ottawa: Canadian Advisory Council on the Status of Women, 1983.

–. "Women, Family and Economy." In *Reconstructing the Canadian Family: Feminist Perspectives,* ed. Nancy Mandell and Ann Duffy, 143-74. Toronto: Butterworths, 1988.

Arscott, Jane. "Twenty-Five Years and Sixty-Five Minutes after the Royal Commission on the Status of Women." *International Journal of Canadian Studies/Revue internationale d'études canadiennes* 11 (Spring 1995): 33-58.

Aucoin, Peter. "Contributions of Commissions of Inquiry to Policy Analysis: An Evaluation." In *Commissions of Inquiry,* ed. A. Paul Pross, Innis Christie, and John A. Yogis, 197-207. Toronto: Carswell, 1990.

–. "Organizational Change in the Machinery of Canadian Government: From Rational Management to Brokerage Politics," *Canadian Journal of Political Science* 19, 1 (1986): 3-27.

Bach, Sandra, and Susan D. Phillips. "Constructing a New Social Union: Child Care beyond Infancy?" In *How Ottawa Spends 1997-98, Seeing Red: A Liberal Report Card,* ed. Gene Swimmer, 235-58. Ottawa: Carleton University Press, 1997.

Bacchi, Carol Lee. *Liberation Deferred? The Ideas of the English Canadian Suffragists, 1877-1918.* Toronto: University of Toronto Press, 1983.

–. *The Politics of Affirmative Action: "Women," Equality and Category Politics.* London: Sage Publications, 1996.

–. *Same Difference: Feminism and Sexual Difference*. St. Leonards, NSW: Allen and Unwin, 1990.

–. *Women, Policy and Politics: The Construction of Policy Problems*. London: Sage Publications, 1999.

Baines, Beverley. "Women, Human Rights and the Constitution." In *Women and the Constitution in Canada*, ed. Audrey Doerr and Micheline Carrier, 31-63. Ottawa: Canadian Advisory Council on the Status of Women, 1981.

Baker, Maureen. *Canadian Family Policies: Cross-National Comparisons*. Toronto: University of Toronto Press, 1995.

–. *Part-Time Work*. Current Issue Review 85-7E. Ottawa: Library of Parliament Research Branch, 1987.

–, ed. *Canada's Changing Families: Challenges to Public Policy*. Ottawa: Vanier Institute of the Family, 1994.

Baker, Maureen, and Sandra Harder. *Child Care in Canada*. Current Issue Review 87-11E. Ottawa: Library of Parliament Research Branch, 1990.

Bakker, Isabella. "Women's Employment in Comparative Perspective." In *Feminization of the Labour Force: Paradoxes and Promises*, ed. Jane Jenson, Elisabeth Hagen, and Cellaigh Reddy, 17-44. New York: Oxford University Press, 1988.

Bakvis, Herman. "Shrinking the House of HRIF: Program Review and the Department of Human Resources and Development." In *How Ottawa Spends 1996-97: Life under the Knife*, ed. Gene Swimmer, 133-70. Ottawa: Carleton University Press, 1996.

Banting, Keith G. *The Welfare State and Canadian Federalism*, 2nd ed. Montreal and Kingston: McGill-Queen's University Press, 1987.

Barnsley, Jan. "Feminist Action, Institutional Reaction." *Resources for Feminist Research/ Documents sur la recherche féministe*. Special issue, *Feminist Perspectives on the Canadian State* 17, 3 (1988): 18-21.

Bashevkin, Sylvia. "The Challenge of Personhood: Women's Citizenship in Contemporary Perspective." Keynote address to the Conference on Women's Equality and Participation in Public Life, Canadian High Commission, London, 21 October 1999.

–. "Confronting Neo-Conservatism: Anglo-American Women's Movements under Thatcher, Reagan and Mulroney." *International Political Science Review* 15, 3 (1994): 275-96.

–. "Free Trade and Canadian Feminism: The Case of the National Action Committee on the Status of Women." *Canadian Public Policy* 15, 4 (1989): 363-75.

–. "Losing Common Ground: Feminists, Conservatives and Public Policy in Canada during the Mulroney Years." *Canadian Journal of Political Science* 29, 2 (1996): 211-42.

–. "Rethinking Retrenchment: North American Social Policy during the Early Clinton and Chrétien Years." *Canadian Journal of Political Science* 33, 1 (2000): 7-36.

–. *Toeing the Lines: Women and Party Politics in English Canada*, 2nd ed. Toronto: Oxford University Press, 1993.

–. *Women on the Defensive: Living through Conservative Times*. Toronto: University of Toronto Press, 1998.

Battle, Ken. "The Politics of Stealth: Child Benefits under the Tories." In *How Ottawa Spends: A More Democratic Canada ...? 1993-94*, ed. Susan D. Phillips, 417-48. Ottawa: Carleton University Press, 1993.

Beatty, David M. "The Canadian Concept of Equality." *University of Toronto Law Journal*, 46 (1996): 349-74.

Bégin, Monique. "The Canadian Government and the Commission's Report." In *Women and the Canadian State/Les femmes et l'État canadien*, ed. Caroline Andrew and Sandra Rodgers, 12-26. Montreal and Kingston: McGill-Queen's University Press, 1997.

–. "The Royal Commission on the Status of Women in Canada: Twenty Years Later." In *Challenging Times: The Women's Movement in Canada and the United States*, ed. Constance Backhouse and David H. Flaherty, 21-38. Montreal and Kingston: McGill-Queen's University Press, 1992.

Bird, Florence. *Anne Francis: An Autobiography*. Toronto: Clarke Irwin, 1974.

–. "Reminiscences of the Commission Chair." In *Women and the Canadian State/Les femmes et l'État canadien,* ed. Caroline Andrew and Sandra Rodgers, 185-96. Montreal and Kingston: McGill-Queen's University Press, 1997.

Black, Naomi. "The Canadian Women's Movement: The Second Wave." In *Changing Patterns: Women in Canada,* 2nd ed., ed. Lorraine Code, Sandra Burt, and Lindsay Dorney, 151-77. Toronto: McClelland and Stewart, 1993.

Black, William. "From Intent to Effect: New Standards in Human Rights." *Canadian Human Rights Reporter,* 1 February 1980, c/2.

Bland, Susan. "'Henrietta the Homemaker' and 'Rosie the Riveter': Images of Women in Advertising in *Maclean's* Magazine, 1939-50." *Atlantis* 8, 2 (1983): 61-86.

Block, W.E., and M.A. Walker, eds. *Discrimination, Affirmative Action and Equal Opportunity: An Economic and Social Perspective.* Vancouver: The Fraser Institute, 1982.

Block, Walter, and Michael A. Walker. *On Employment Equity: A Critique of the Abella Royal Commission Report.* Focus no. 17. Vancouver: The Fraser Institute, 1985.

Blyton, Paul. "The Changing Canadian Labour Force." *British Journal of Canadian Studies* 5, 2 (1990): 368-77.

Bock, Gisela, and Susan James, ed. *Beyond Equality and Difference: Citizenship, Feminist Politics and Female Subjectivity.* London: Routledge, 1992.

Boismenu, G., and Jane Jenson. "A Social Union or a Federal State? Competing Visions of Intergovernmental Relations in the New Liberal Era." In *How Ottawa Spends 1998-99: Balancing Act – The Post-Deficit Mandate,* ed. Leslie A. Pal, 56-79. Don Mills, ON: Oxford University Press, 1998.

Borchorst, Annette, and Birte Siim. "Women and the Advanced Welfare State – a New Kind of Patriarchal Power." In *Women and the State,* ed. Anne Showstack Sassoon, 128-57. London: Hutchinson, 1987.

Boulet, Jac-André, and Laval Lavallée. *The Changing Economic Status of Women.* Ottawa: Supply and Services, 1984.

Bourne, Paula. *Women's Paid and Unpaid Work: Historical and Contemporary Perspectives.* Toronto: New Hogtown Press, 1985.

Bowden, Peta. *Caring: Gender-Sensitive Ethics.* London and New York: Routledge, 1997.

Boyd, Monica. "Changing Canadian Family Forms: Issues for Women." In *Reconstructing the Canadian Family: Feminist Perspectives,* ed. Nancy Mandell and Ann Duffy, 85-110. Toronto: Butterworths, 1988.

Boyd, Susan B., ed. *Challenging the Public/Private Divide: Feminism, Law and Public Policy.* Toronto: University of Toronto Press, 1997.

Bracken, John. *John Bracken Says.* Toronto: Oxford University Press, 1944.

Bradford, Neil. *Commissioning Ideas: Canadian National Policy Innovation in Comparative Perspective.* Toronto: Oxford University Press, 1998.

–. "Innovation by Commission: Policy Paradigms and the Canadian Political System." In *Canadian Politics,* 3rd ed., ed. James Bickerton and Alain-G. Gagnon, 541-64. Peterborough, ON: Broadview Press, 1999.

Brandt, Gail Cuthbert. "'Pigeon-Holed and Forgotten': The Work of the Subcommittee on the Post-War Problems of Women, 1943." *Histoire sociale/Social History* 15, 29 (1982): 239-59.

Breton, Albert. *Marriage, Population, and the Labour Force Participation of Women.* An essay prepared for the Economic Council of Canada. Ottawa: Supply and Services, 1984.

Breton, Raymond. "Multiculturalism and Canadian Nation Building." In *The Politics of Gender, Ethnicity and Language in Canada.* Vol. 34 of *Research Studies, Royal Commission, on the Economic Union and Development Prospects for Canada,* ed. Alan Cairns and Cynthia Williams. Toronto: University of Toronto Press, 1986.

Briggs, Catherine, and Sandra Burt. "The Canadian Women's Bureau: Leading the Fight for Justice and Fair Play." Paper prepared for *Canada, Confederation to Present.* Edmonton: Chinook Multimedia, forthcoming.

Brodie, Janine. "Canadian Women, Changing State Forms, and Public Policy." In *Women and Canadian Public Policy,* ed. Janine Brodie, 1-30. Toronto: Harcourt Brace, 1996.

–. "Meso-Discourses, State Forms and the Gendering of Liberal-Democratic Citizenship." *Citizenship Studies* 1, 2 (1997): 223-42.

–. *Politics at the Margins: Restructuring and the Canadian Women's Movement.* Halifax: Fernwood, 1995.

–. "Restructuring and the New Citizenship." In *Rethinking Restructuring: Gender and Change in Canada,* ed. Isabella Bakker, 126-40. Toronto: University of Toronto Press, 1996.

–. "Shifting the Boundaries: Gender and the Politics of Restructuring." In *The Strategic Silence: Gender and Economic Policy,* ed. Isabella Bakker, 46-60. London: Zed Books, 1994.

Brodsky, Gwen, and Shelagh Day. *Canadian Charter Equality Rights for Women: One Step Forward or Two Steps Back?* Ottawa: Canadian Advisory Council on the Status of Women, 1989.

Burt, Sandra. "Canadian Women's Groups in the 1980s: Organizational Development and Policy Influence." *Canadian Public Policy* 16, 1 (1990): 17-28.

–. "The Changing Patterns of Public Policy." In *Changing Patterns: Women in Canada,* 2nd ed., ed. Sandra Burt, Lorraine Code, and Lindsay Dorney, 212-42. Toronto: McClelland and Stewart, 1993.

–. "Organized Women's Groups and the State." In *Policy Communities and Public Policy in Canada: A Structural Approach,* ed. William Coleman and Grace Skogstad, 191-211. Toronto: Copp Clark Pitman, 1990.

–. "The Status of Women: Learning to Live without the State." In *Canadian Public Policy,* ed. Andrew F. Johnson and Andrew Stritcheds, 251-74. Toronto: Copp Clark, 1997.

–. "Variations in an Earlier Theme: The Second Wave of the Canadian Women's Movement." In *Canadian Politics: An Introduction to the Discipline,* ed. Alain-G. Gagnon and James P. Bickerton, 542-58. Peterborough, ON: Broadview Press, 1990.

–. "Voluntary Affirmative Action: Does It Work?" *Rélations industrielles/Industrial Relations* 41, 3 (1986): 541-50.

–. "Women's Issues and the Women's Movement in Canada since 1970." In *The Politics of Gender, Ethnicity and Language in Canada.* Vol. 34 of *Research Studies, Royal Commission on the Economic Union and Development Prospects for Canada,* ed. Alan Cairns and Cynthia Williams, 111-69. Toronto: University of Toronto Press, 1986.

Cameron, Barbara. "From Equal Opportunity to Symbolic Equity: Three Decades of Federal Training Policy for Women." In *Rethinking Restructuring: Gender and Change in Canada,* ed. Isabella Bakker, 55-81. Toronto: University of Toronto Press, 1996.

Campbell, Claire. "Le rapport de la Commission royale d'enquête sur le statut de la femme au Canada," *Rélations* 29 (March 1970): 86.

Campbell, Claire. "Une clé ... pour la compréhension du Rapport," *Rélations* 31 (March 1971): 85.

Canada. *Employment Equity and Economic Growth,* Background paper, 8 March 1985.

–. *Employment Equity: A Response to the Abella Commission of Enquiry on Equality in Employment,* pamphlet, 1985.

–. *Employment Equity ... Discussion Paper: Information and Proposed Contents of Regulations for Reports.* Cat. no. MP43-178/1985. Ottawa: Supply and Services, 1985.

–. Notes for a statement by the Hon. Walter F. McLean, Secretary of State of Canada, Minister Responsible for the Status of Women and Minister Responsible for the Status of Disabled Persons, on the federal government's response to the Royal Commission Report on Equality in Employment, Ottawa, 8 March 1985 (GC 194 7540-21-886-3757).

–. Statement to the House of Commons by the Hon. Flora MacDonald, Minister of Employment and Immigration, on the federal government's response to the Royal Commission Report on Equality in Employment, 8 March 1985.

Canadian Advisory Council on the Status of Women. Brief to the House of Commons Legislative Committee on Bill C-144. 6 September 1988. Ottawa: Canadian Advisory Council on the Status of Women, 1988.

–. "Caring for Our Children." Brief to the Special Committee on Child Care. Ottawa: Canadian Advisory Council on the Status of Women, 1986.

–. "On Employment Equity." Brief by the Canadian Advisory Council on the Status of Women to the Legislative Committee on Employment Equity (Bill C-62). December 1985.

–. *Summary of Recommendations of the Canadian Advisory Council on the Status of Women.* Ottawa: Canadian Advisory Council on the Status of Women, 1982.

–. *Ten Years Later: An Assessment of the Federal Government's Implementation of the Recommendations Made by the Royal Commission on the Status of Women.* Ottawa: Canadian Advisory Council on the Status of Women, 1979.

–. *Women in the Public Service: Overlooked and Undervalued.* Ottawa: Canadian Advisory Council on the Status of Women, 1980.

Canadian Association of Adult Education. *What's in It?* Toronto: Canadian Association of Adult Education, 1970.

Canadian Business Association. "A Bill of Rights ... Now." Canadian Business Interviews: John G. Diefenbaker, *Canadian Business* 25 (September 1952): 38-41.

Canadian Child Care Federation. "National Child Care Policy in Canada, 1966-1995: An Overview." Background paper by Anne Maxwell and Catherine Ryerse, May 1995.

Canadian Council on Social Development. *Proceedings/Canadian Conference on Day Care.* Ottawa: Canadian Council on Social Development, 1972.

–. *The Second Canadian Conference on Day Care: Proceedings and Reflections.* Ottawa: Canadian Council on Social Development, 1983.

Canadian Day Care Advocacy Association. "Bill C-144: A Critique of the Proposed Canada Child Care Act," 1988. Childcare Resource and Research Unit files, Toronto.

–. *Bulletin* (Winter 1992): 8.

–. "Child Care: Three Federal Reports at a Glance," 30 March 1997. Childcare Resource and Research Unit files, Toronto.

–. "A Real Canadian Child Care Act: A Reality or Still an Illusive Dream." Brief to the House of Commons Legislative Committee on Bill C-144, September 1988. Childcare Resource and Research Unit files, Toronto.

Canadian Human Rights Commission. *Annual Report 1978.* Ottawa: Supply and Services, 1979.

–. *Annual Report 1979.* Ottawa: Supply and Services, 1980.

–. *Annual Report 1980.* Ottawa: Supply and Services, 1981.

–. *Annual Report 1981.* Ottawa: Supply and Services, 1982.

–. *Annual Report 1982.* Ottawa: Supply and Services, 1983.

–. *Annual Report 1983.* Ottawa: Supply and Services, 1984.

–. *Annual Report 1984.* Ottawa: Supply and Services, 1985.

Canadian Labour Congress. "CLC Adopts Changes in Structure." *Canadian Labour* 13, 5 (1968): 9.

–. "Human Rights." *Canadian Labour* 13, 5 (1968): 37.

–. "Human Rights and the CLC." *Canadian Labour* 12, 2 (1967): 11, 31.

–. "No Working Women on Royal Commission." *Canadian Labour* 12, 3 (1967): 26.

–. "Women Suffer Job Discrimination." *Canadian Labour* 13, 10 (1968): 7, 40.

Carr, Jack. *The Day Care Dilemma: A Critical Analysis of the Options.* Vancouver: Fraser Institute, 1987.

Cartwright, Thelma. "Twentieth Century Trying Time for Women." *Canadian Labour* 12, 2 (1967): 26.

Chenier, Nancy Miller, and Dorothy LaBarge. "Towards Universality: An Historical Overview of the Evolution of Education, Health Care, Day Care and Maternity Leave." *Background Papers Prepared for the Report of the Task Force on Child Care.* Series 2, 1-36. Ottawa: Supply and Services, 1985.

Child Care Advocacy Association of Canada. "Early Childhood Care and Education and the National Children's Agenda: A Policy Discussion Paper." Prepared by Jane Beach, August 1998. Childcare Resource and Research Unit files, Toronto.

–. "Federal Government Flip-Flops on Child Care," 1995. Childcare Resource and Research Unit files, Toronto.

Childcare Resource and Research Unit. *Child Care in Canada: Provinces and Territories.* Toronto: Childcare Resource and Research Unit, 1993.

–. "Childcare in Canada: A Key Federal Policy Issue." November Fact Sheet, 1988.

–. <www.childcarecanada.org>. September 1999.

Christian, William, and Colin Campbell. *Parties, Leaders and Ideologies in Canada.* Toronto: McGraw-Hill Ryerson, 1996.

Clark, Lorrenne M.G. "Reminiscences and Reflections on the Twentieth Anniversary of the Commission's Report." In *Women and the Canadian State/Les femmes et l'État canadien,* ed. Caroline Andrew and Sandra Rodgers, 3-11. Montreal and Kingston: McGill-Queen's University Press, 1997.

Clarkson, Stephen. *Canada and the Reagan Challenge: Crisis and Adjustment 1981-1985.* Toronto: James Lorimer, 1985.

Clarkson, Stephen, and Christina McCall. *The Heroic Delusion.* Vol. 2 of *Trudeau and Our Times.* Toronto: McClelland and Stewart, 1994.

–. *The Magnificent Obsession.* Vol. 1 of *Trudeau and Our Times.* Toronto: McClelland and Stewart, 1990.

Cleveland, Gordon, and Michael Krashinsky. *The Benefits and Costs of Good Child Care: The Economic Rationale for Public Investment in Young Children.* Toronto: Childcare Resource and Research Unit, 1998.

Clio Collective. *Quebec Women: A History,* trans. Roger Gannon and Rosalind Gill. Toronto: Women's Press, 1987.

Coates, Mary Lou. *Employment Equity: Issues, Approaches and Public Policy Framework.* Kingston: Industrial Relations Centre, Queen's University, 1986.

–. *Part-Time Employment: Labour Market Flexibility and Equity Issues.* Kingston: Industrial Relations Centre, 1988.

–. *Pay and Employment Equity.* Kingston: Industrial Relations Centre, 1989.

Code, Lorraine. "Feminist Theory." In *Changing Patterns: Women in Canada,* 2nd ed., ed. Lorraine Code, Sandra Burt, and Lindsay Dorney, 19-59. Toronto: McClelland and Stewart, 1993.

Cohen, Bronwen, and Karen Clarke, eds. *Childcare and Equal Opportunities: Some Policy Perspectives.* London: Her Majesty's Stationery Office, 1986.

Cohen, Leah. "Mandatory Affirmative Action: A Discussion Paper." Prepared for Federation of Women Teachers' Associations of Ontario, July 1983.

Cohen, Marjorie. "Employment Equity Is *Not* Affirmative Action." *Canadian Woman Studies/Les cahiers de la femme* 6, 4 (1985): 23-5.

Colley, Susan. "Free Universal Day Care: The OFL Takes a Stand." In *Union Sisters: Women in the Labour Movement,* ed. Linda Briskin and Lynda Yanz, 307-21. Toronto: Women's Press, 1983.

Colwell, Kristin. "Child Care: A Community Issue." In *Changing Methods: Feminists Transforming Practice,* ed. Sandra Burt and Lorraine Code, 163-94. Peterborough, ON: Broadview, 1995.

"Common Day Care Strategy Needed." *Public Employee* 3 (Spring 1981): 7.

Connelly, Patricia. *Last Hired, First Fired: Women and the Canadian Work Force.* Toronto: Women's Press, 1978.

Connelly, Patricia, and Martha MacDonald. "Women's Work: Domestic and Wage Labour in a Nova Scotia Community." In *The Politics of Diversity: Feminism, Marxism and Nationalism,* ed. Roberta Hamilton and Michèle Barrett, 35-52. London: Verso, 1986.

Cook, Gail C.A., and Mary Eberts. "Policies Affecting Work." In *Opportunity for Choice: A Goal for Women in Canada,* ed. Gail C.A. Cook, 145-202. Ottawa: Statistics Canada in association with the C.D. Howe Research Institute, 1976.

Cormack, Robert, and Robert Osborne. "Employment Equity in Canada and Fair Employment in Northern Ireland." *British Journal of Canadian Studies* 4, 2 (1989): 219-32.

Courtney, John. "In Defence of Royal Commissions." *Canadian Public Administration* 12, 2 (1969): 198-212.

Craig, B. "Women's March May Back Call for Rights Probe." *Globe and Mail,* 5 January 1967, A1.

Dale, Patricia. *Women and Jobs: The Impact of Federal Government Employment Strategies on Women.* Ottawa: Canadian Advisory Council on the Status of Women, 1980.

"Day Care Advocacy Assn. to Co-ordinate Campaigns for Greater Govt. Funding." *The Facts* 5, 5 (1983): 12.

Diamond, Irene, ed. *Families, Politics and Public Policies: A Feminist Dialogue on Women and the State.* New York: Longman, 1983.

Dobrowolsky, Alexandra. *The Politics of Pragmatism: Women, Representation, and Constitutionalism in Canada.* Toronto: Oxford University Press, 2000.

Doerr, Audrey. "Overlapping Jurisdictions and Women's Issues." In *Women and the Constitution in Canada,* ed. Audrey Doerr and Micheline Carrier, 123-48. Ottawa: Canadian Advisory Council on the Status of Women, 1981.

Doherty, Gillian. *Child Care Policy in Canada: An Annotated Bibliography.* Toronto: Childcare Resource and Research Unit, 1994.

Doherty, Gillian, Martha Friendly, and Mab Oloman. *Women's Support, Women's Work: Child Care in an Era of Deficit Reduction, Devolution, Downsizing and Deregulation.* Ottawa: Status of Women Canada, 1998.

Dominelli, Lena. *Women across Continents: Feminist Comparative Social Policy.* London: Harvester Wheatsheaf, 1991.

Drew, Eileen, Ruth Emerek, and Ruth Mahon, eds. *Women, Work and Family in Europe.* London: Routledge, 1998.

Dulude, Louise. *Seniority and Employment Equity for Women.* Kingston: IRC Press, 1995.

Dumont, Micheline. "The Origins of the Women's Movement in Quebec." In *Challenging Times: The Women's Movement in Canada and the United States,* ed. Constance Backhouse and David H. Flaherty, 72-93. Montreal and Kingston: McGill-Queen's University Press, 1992.

–. *The Women's Movement: Then and Now.* Feminist Perspectives Féministes no. 5b. Ottawa: Canadian Research Institute for the Advancement of Women, 1986.

Durst, Douglas. "Phoenix or Fizzle? Background to Canada's New National Child Benefit." In *Canada's National Child Benefit: Phoenix or Fizzle?* ed. Douglas Durst. Halifax: Fernwood Publishing, 1999.

Dwivedi, O.P., and James Iain Gow. *From Bureaucracy to Public Management: The Administrative Culture of the Government of Canada.* Toronto: Institute of Public Administration of Canada; Peterborough, ON: Broadview Press, 1999.

Eberts, Mary. "Women and Constitutional Renewal." In *Women and the Constitution in Canada,* ed. Audrey Doerr and Micheline Carrier, 3-28. Ottawa: Canadian Advisory Council on the Status of Women, 1985.

Economic Council of Canada. *Towards Equity.* Ottawa: Supply and Services, 1985.

Edmonds, Alan. "This is Anne Francis, Chairman of the Royal Commission on the Status of Women. She's never been exploited, discriminated against, patronized or bored. She's trying to find out why most women are." *Maclean's* 81, 1 (1968): 10-11, 52, 56.

Eichler, Margrit. "The Connection between Paid and Unpaid Labour and Its Implication for Creating Equality for Women in Employment." In *Research Studies of the Commission on Equality in Employment,* ed. Judge Rosalie Silberman Abella, Commissioner, 539-546. Ottawa: Supply and Services, 1985.

–. *Families in Canada Today: Recent Changes and Their Policy Consequences.* Toronto: Gage, 1983.

–. *The Pro-Family Movement: Are They for or against Families?* Feminist Perspectives Féministes no. 4a. Ottawa: Canadian Research Institute for the Advancement of Women, 1985.

–. "Social Policy Concerning Women." In *Canadian Social Policy,* ed. Yelaja Shankar, 139-56. Waterloo: Wilfrid Laurier University Press, 1987.

Employment and Immigration Advisory Council. *Workers with Family Responsibilities in a Changing Society: Who Cares?* Ottawa: Supply and Services, 1987.

Employment and Immigration Canada. "Affirmative Action in Canada." Speech delivered by Hon. Lloyd Axworthy, Minister of Employment and Immigration, Public Affairs International Conference, Toronto, 22 April 1980.

–. *Annual Report for the Fiscal Year 1977-1978.* Ottawa: Supply and Services, 1978.

–. *Annual Report 1979.* Ottawa: Supply and Services, 1980.

–. *Consultations in Preparation for the Review of the Employment Equity Act.* Ottawa: Employment and Immigration Canada, 1991.

–. *Employment Equity: A Working Paper.* Ottawa: Employment and Immigration Canada, June 1985.

–. *Employment Equity Act and Reporting Requirements*. Ottawa: Employment and Immigration Canada, 1986.

–. *Labour Market Development in the 1980s*. Ottawa: Supply and Services, 1981.

–. *Where to Find Employers' Reports*. Ottawa: Supply and Services, 1989.

Employment and Immigration Canada, Federal Contractors Program, Employment Equity Branch. *Employment Equity: Federal Contractors Program, Questions and Answers*. Ottawa: Supply and Services, 1987.

–. "Federal Contractors Program: Criteria for Implementation." Internal document,1986.

–. "Federal Contractors Program for Employment Equity." Internal document, 1986.

Employment and Immigration Canada, Minister of Employment and Immigration. "Employment Equity Legislation Introduced." Press release 85-28 (E&I 2014E [5-85]), 8 March 1985.

–. Press release. 27 June 1986 (86-20).

Employment and Immigration Canada, Office of the Minister. Notes for an address by the Hon. Flora MacDonald, P.C., M.P., Minister of Employment and Immigration, to the Institute for Research on Public Policy, Montreal, 4 March 1986.

–. Statement by the Hon. Benoît Bouchard, Minister of Employment and Immigration, 3 December 1987.

Employment and Immigration Canada, Public Affairs. "AM-Parl-Abella, Night Lead," by Nicole Baer. Press clippings, 22 November 1988.

England, Kim, ed. *Who Will Mind the Baby? Geographies of Child Care and Working Mothers*. London: Routledge, 1996.

Erwin, Lorna. "What Feminists Should Know about the Pro-Family Movement in Canada: A Report on a Recent Survey of Rank-and-File Members." In *Feminist Research: Prospect and Retrospect,* ed. Peta Tancred-Sherriff, 266-78. Montreal and Kingston: McGill-Queen's University Press, 1988.

Fairweather, R.G.L. "Affirmative Action – The Time Is Now." Notes for an address by R.G.L. Fairweather, Chief Commissioner, Canadian Human Rights Commission, to the 55th Annual Meeting of the Canadian Chamber of Commerce, Royal York Hotel, Toronto, 25 September 1984.

"Federal Child-Care Plan Reported Doomed." *Globe and Mail*, 16 February 1995, A1, A3.

Federal-Provincial-Territorial Council of Ministers on Social Policy Renewal. *A National Children's Agenda: Developing a Shared Vision*, May 1999.

–. *A National Children's Agenda: Measuring Child Well Being and Monitoring Progress*. Supplementary Discussion Paper, May 1999.

Fédération des femmes du Québec. *Guide de discussion et resumé du rapport de la Commission royale d'enqûete sur la situation de la femme au Canada*. Montreal: Fédération des femmes du Québec, 1971.

Feigert, Frank. "National Results: Individual Elections." In *Party Politics in Canada*, 7th ed., ed. Hugh G. Thorburn, 537-48. Scarborough, ON: Prentice-Hall Canada, 1996.

Ferguson, Evelyn. "The Child-Care Debate: Fading Hopes and Shifting Sands." In *Women's Caring: Feminist Perspectives on Social Welfare*, 2nd ed., ed. Carol T. Baines, Patricia M. Evans, and Sheila M. Neysmith, 191-217. Toronto: Oxford University Press, 1998.

Fillion, Kate. "The Daycare Decision." *Saturday Night* 104, 1 (1989): 23-30.

Finch, Janet, and Dulcie Groves. *A Labour of Love: Women, Work and Caring*. London: Routledge and Kegan Paul, 1983.

Findlay, Sue. "Representation and Regulation: The Role of the State Bureaucracy in Limiting Equal Employment Opportunities for Women." *Canadian Woman Studies/Les cahiers de la femme* 6, 4 (1985): 30-3.

–. "Feminist Struggles with the Canadian State." *Resources for Feminist Research/Documents sur la recherche féministe*. Special issue, *Feminist Perspectives on the Canadian State* 17, 3 (1988): 5-9.

Finlayson, Judith. "Freda Paltiel, Social Worker and First Coordinator, Status of Women." In *Trailblazers: Women Talk about Changing Canada*, 13-20. Toronto: Doubleday Canada, 1999.

Firestone, Shulamith. *The Dialectic of Sex: The Case for Feminist Revolution*. New York: William Morrow, 1970.

Forbes, Ian. "Equal Opportunity: Radical, Liberal and Conservative Critiques." In *Equality Politics and Gender,* ed. Elizabeth Meehan and Selma Sevenhuijsen, 17-35. London: Sage, 1991.

Fox, Bonnie, ed. *Hidden in the Household: Women's Domestic Labour under Capitalism.* Toronto: Women's Press, 1980.

Franzway, Suzanne, Diane Court, and R.W. Connell. *Staking a Claim: Feminism, Bureaucracy and the State.* Cambridge: Polity Press, 1989.

Fréchette, Jean-Denis. "Federal-Provincial Fiscal Arrangements." Current Issue Review 86-23E. Ottawa: Library of Parliament, 1992.

"Free Universal Child Care Curbed by Spending Restraint." *Labour Scene* 3 (April 1981): 5-6.

Freeman, Barbara M. "Framing Feminine/Feminist: English-Language Press Coverage of the Hearings of the Royal Commission on the Status of Women in Canada, 1968." *International Journal of Canadian Studies/Revue internationale d'études canadiennes* 11 (Spring 1995): 11-32.

–. "The Media and the Royal Commission on the Status of Women in Canada, 1966-1972: Research in Progress." *Resources for Feminist Research/Documents sur la recherche féministe* 23, 3 (1993): 3-9.

Friedan, Betty. *The Feminine Mystique,* 20th anniversary ed. New York: W.W. Norton, 1983.

Friendly, Martha. "Child Care and Canadian Federalism in the 1990s: Canary in a Coal Mine." Paper presented at a special conference on Good Child Care in Canada in the 21st Century: Preparing the Policy Map, University of Toronto, May 1999.

–. *Child Care Policy in Canada, 1990: Selected Topics, An Annotated Bibliography.* Toronto: Childcare Resource and Research Unit, 1990.

–. *Child Care Policy in Canada: Putting the Pieces Together.* Don Mills, ON: Addison-Wesley, 1994.

–. "Free Trade Forum: The Threat to Non-Profit Child Care in Canada." *Toronto Star,* 21 April 1988, A23.

Friendly, Martha, Julie Mathien, and Tricia Willis. *Childcare: What the Public Said, An Analysis of the Transcripts of the Public Hearings Held across Canada by the Parliamentary Special Committee on Child Care.* Ottawa: Canadian Day Care Advocacy Association, February 1987.

Friendly, Martha, and Mab Oloman. "Child Care at the Centre: Child Care on the Social, Economic and Political Agenda in the 1990s." In *Remaking Canadian Social Policy: Social Security in the Late 1990s,* ed. Jane Pulkingham and Gordon Ternowetsky, 273-85. Halifax: Fernwood, 1996.

Fulford, Robert. "Surrendering Canada." *Saturday Night* 102, 8 (1987): 5-7.

Gelb, Joyce, and Marian Lief Palley. *Women and Public Policies.* Rev. ed. Princeton, NJ: Princeton University Press, 1987.

Geller, Carole. "A Critique of the Abella Report." *Canadian Woman Studies/Les cahiers de la femme* 6, 4 (1985): 20-2.

–. "Equality in Employment for Women: The Role of Affirmative Action." *Canadian Journal of Women and the Law* 4, 2 (1987): 373-406.

Geller-Schwartz, Linda. "Four Decades of Women in the Workplace." Paper prepared for Canadian Employment and Immigration Commission, Women's Bureau, 1991.

Gershuny, J.I., and I.D. Miles. *The New Service Economy: The Transformation of Employment in Industrial Societies.* New York: Praeger, 1983.

Gibbins, Roger. *Conflict and Unity: An Introduction to Canadian Political Life,* 3rd ed. Scarborough, ON: Nelson Canada, 1994.

Gibbins, Roger, and Sonia Arrison. *Western Visions: Perspectives on the West in Canada.* Peterborough, ON: Broadview, 1995.

Gollner, Andrew B., and Daniel Salée. "A Turn to the Right? Canada in the Post-Trudeau Era." In *Canada under Mulroney: An End of Term Report,* ed. Andrew B. Gollner and Daniel Salée, 14-17. Montreal: Véhicule Press, 1988.

Gotell, Lise. "The Canadian Women's Movement, Equality Rights and the Charter of

Rights in Canada, 1980-1992: 'The Radical Future of Liberal Feminism?'" PhD diss., York University, 1993.

–. *Feminism, Equality Rights and the Charter of Rights and Freedoms.* Feminist Perspectives Féministes no. 16. Ottawa: Canadian Research Institute for the Advancement of Women, 1990.

Gottleib, Amy, ed. "What about Us? Organizing Inclusively in the National Action Committee on the Status of Women." In *And Still We Rise: Feminist Political Mobilizing in Contemporary Canada,* ed. Linda Carty, 371-85. Toronto: Women's Press, 1993.

Greenspon, Edward, and Anthony Wilson-Smith. *Double Vision: The Inside Story of the Liberals in Power.* Toronto: Doubleday, 1996.

Greschner, Donna. "Affirmative Action and the Charter of Rights and Freedoms." *Canadian Woman Studies/Les cahiers de la femme* 6, 4 (1985): 34-6.

Guest, Dennis. "World War II and the Welfare State in Canada." In *The "Benevolent" State: The Growth of Welfare in Canada,* ed. Allan Moscovitch and Jim Albert, 205-21. Toronto: Garamond Press, 1987.

Gunderson, Morley. "Discrimination, Equal Pay and Equal Opportunities in the Labour Market." In Work *and Pay: The Canadian Labour Market.* Vol. 17 of *Research Studies, Royal Commission on the Economic Union and Development Prospects for Canada,* ed. W. Craig Riddell, 219-66. Toronto: University of Toronto Press, 1985.

–. *Implications of Daycare Policies on Female Labour Market Behaviour.* Report prepared for the Special Parliamentary Committee on Child Care, 1986.

Gunderson, Morley, Leon Muszynski with Jennifer Keck. *Women and Labour Market Poverty.* Ottawa: Canadian Advisory Council on the Status of Women, 1990.

Haddow, Rodney S. *Poverty Reform in Canada, 1958-1978: State and Class Influences on Policy Making.* Montreal and Kingston: McGill-Queen's University Press, 1993.

Hagen, Elisabeth, and Jane Jenson. "Paradoxes and Promises: Work and Politics in the Postwar Years." In *Feminization of the Labour Force: Paradoxes and Promises,* ed. Jane Jenson, Elisabeth Hagen, and Cellaigh Reddy, 3-16. New York: Oxford University Press, 1988.

Hamilton, Roberta. *Gendering the Vertical Mosaic: Feminist Perspectives on Canadian Society.* Toronto: Copp Clark, 1996.

Hamilton, Robert M., and Dorothy Shields, ed. *Dictionary of Canadian Quotations and Phrases.* Toronto: McClelland and Stewart, 1979.

Harder, Sandra. *Child Care in Canada.* Current Issue Review 87-11E. Ottawa: Library of Parliament Research Branch, 1995.

Haussman, Melissa H. "The Personal Is Constitutional: Feminist Struggles for Equality Rights in the United States and Canada." In *Women Transforming Politics: Worldwide Strategies for Empowerment,* ed. Jill Bystydzienski, 108-23. Bloomington and Indianapolis: Indiana University Press, 1992.

Health and Welfare Canada. *National Strategy on Child Care.* Ottawa: Health and Welfare Canada, 1987.

–. *Status of Day Care in Canada, 1984.* Ottawa: Supply and Services, 1985.

–. *Status of Day Care in Canada, 1990.* Ottawa: Supply and Services, 1991.

Health and Welfare Canada, Office of the Minister. Statement by the Hon. Jake Epp, Minister of National Health and Welfare, 3 December 1987.

Health Canada. *Community Action Program for Children.* Ottawa: Health Canada, 1992.

Henderson, George F. *Federal Royal Commissions in Canada, 1867-1966: A Checklist.* Toronto: University of Toronto Press, 1967.

Hendlisz, Lise, Brenda Lazare, Mario Lebrun, Alix Parlour, and Jackie Tatebe. *Affirmative Action for Women in Canada.* Montreal: Montreal Association for Women and the Law, 1982.

Henripin, Jacques. Separate statement. In Royal Commission on the Status of Women in Canada, *Report,* 421-428. Ottawa: Information Canada, 1970.

Hepworth, H. Philip. *Day Care Services for Children.* Ottawa: Canadian Council on Social Development, 1975.

Hernes, Helga Maria. "Scandinavian Citizenship." *Acta Sociologica* 31, 3 (1988): 199-215.

–. "Women and the Welfare State: The Transition from Private to Public Dependence." In *Women and the State,* ed. Ann Showstack Sassoon, 72-92. London: Hutchinson, 1987.

–. "The Welfare State Citizenship of Scandinavian Women." In *The Political Interests of Gender: Developing Theory and Research with a Feminist Face,* ed. Kathleen B. Jones and Anna G. Jónasdottir, 187-213. London: Sage, 1988.

"Hiring Quotas May Creep North." *Business Week* 2744 (21 June 1982): 137.

Hošek, Chaviva. "Women and the Constitutional Process." In *And No One Cheered: Federalism, Democracy and the Constitution Act,* ed. Keith Banting and Richard Simeon, 280-300. Toronto: Methuen, 1983.

Hoskins, Irene, ed. *Combining Work and Elder Care: A Challenge for Now and the Future.* Geneva: International Labour Office, 1996.

House of Commons. *Bill C-144: Canada Child Care Act.* 33rd Parliament, 2nd Session, 1988.

–. "Five Year Review of the Employment Equity Act: Minority Report of the Employment Equity Act." In *A Matter of Fairness.* Report of the Special Committee on the Review of the Employment Equity Act, 69-75 (Appendix D). Ottawa: Queen's Printer, 1992.

–. *A Matter of Fairness.* Report of the Special Committee on the Review of the Employment Equity Act. Ottawa: Queen's Printer, 1992.

–. *Minutes of Proceedings and Evidence of the Special Committee on Employment Opportunities for the '80s.* Ottawa: Queen's Printer for Canada, 1980.

–. *Minutes of Proceedings and Evidence of the Special Committee on the Review of the Employment Equity Act.* Ottawa: Queen's Printer for Canada, 1991.

–. "Not Fair Enough: Liberal Minority Report on the Review of the Employment Equity Act." In *A Matter of Fairness.* Report of the Special Committee on the Review of the Employment Equity Act, 61-8 (Appendix C). Ottawa: Queen's Printer, 1992.

–. *Obstacles.* Report of the Special Committee on the Disabled and Handicapped. Ottawa: Supply and Services, 1981.

–. *Security, Opportunities and Fairness: Canadians Renewing Their Social Programs.* Report of the Standing Committee on Human Resources Development. Ottawa: Queen's Printer, 1995.

–. *Sharing the Responsibility.* Report of the Special Committee on Child Care. Ottawa: Queen's Printer for Canada, 1987.

–. *Work for Tomorrow: Employment Opportunities for the '80s.* Report of the Task Force on Employment Opportunities for the '80s. Ottawa: Supply and Services, 1981.

Howe, R. Brian. "The Evolution of Human Rights Policy in Ontario." *Canadian Journal of Political Science* 24, 4 (1991): 783-802.

–. "Human Rights Policy in Ontario: The Tension between Positive and Negative State Values." PhD diss., University of Toronto, 1988.

Howe, R. Brian, and David Johnson. *Restraining Equality: Human Rights Commissions in Canada.* Toronto: University of Toronto Press, 2000.

Huck, Barbara. "Day-Care Conference Seeks Answers to Many Concerns: 700 Delegates Gather for Three Days of Workshops." *Winnipeg Free Press,* 24 September 1982, 2.

Hum, Derek P.J. "Compromise and Delay: The Federal Strategy on Child Care." In *Canada: The State of the Federation 1989,* ed. Ronald L. Watts and Douglas M. Brown, 151-65. Kingston: Institute of Intergovernmental Relations, Queen's University, 1989.

Human Resources Development Canada. *Agenda: Jobs and Growth, Improving Social Security in Canada.* Discussion paper. Ottawa: Supply and Services, 1994.

–. *Employment Equity Act: Annual Report.* Ottawa: Supply and Services, 1997.

–. *Employment Equity Act: Annual Report.* Ottawa: Supply and Services, 1998.

–. *Employment Equity Act: Annual Report.* Ottawa: Supply and Services, 1999.

–. *Improving Social Security in Canada: Child Care and Development.* Supplementary paper. Ottawa: Supply and Services, 1994.

–. *The National Child Benefit: Building a Better Future for Canadian Children,* SC 126-04-98, Catalogue no. MP43-472/1998, September 1997.

–. *Status of Day Care in Canada 1995 and 1996.* Ottawa: Supply and Services, 1997.

–. Transcript of the press conference held by the Hon. Lloyd Axworthy, Room 130-S, Centre Block, House of Commons, Ottawa, 13 December 1995.

–. *A Vision for Child Care into the 21st Century.* Report of the National Child Care Workshop, Montreal, 2-3 February 1994. Ottawa: Supply and Services, 1994.

Human Resources Development Canada, Minister of Human Resources Development. Letter from Lloyd Axworthy to provincial and territorial ministers of social services, 13 December 1995. Childcare Resources and Research Unit files, Toronto.

–. Statement by the Hon. Douglas Young concerning child care, 2 February 1996. Childcare Resources and Research Unit files, Toronto.

Humphrey, John. "Minority Report." In Royal Commission on the Status of Women in Canada, *Report,* 433-51. Ottawa: Information Canada, 1970.

Hunt, Audrey, ed. *Women and Paid Work: Issues of Equality.* Basingstoke: Macmillan, 1988.

Interdepartmental Committee on the Status of Women. Minutes of the Meetings of Working Party I: Economic Participation of Women, 1970. National Archives of Canada, RG 106, vol. 1.

–. Minutes of the Meetings of Working Party IV: Family and Community Service, 1970. National Archives of Canada, RG 106, vol. 4.

Intergovernmental Conference Secretariat. Conference Communiqué, 35th Annual Premiers Conference, Toronto. 1 September 1994. 830-054/016.

–. Final Communiqué, 36th Annual Premiers Conference. St. John's, NF, 25 August 1995. 850-057/008.

International Labour Conference. *The Employment of Women with Family Responsibilities.* Report V(1) and V(2). Geneva: International Labour Office, 1965.

International Labour Organization. *C-111 Discrimination (Employment and Occupation) Convention,* 1958.

Irving, Allan. "Federal-Provincial Issues in Social Policy." In *Canadian Social Policy,* ed. Shankar Yelaja, 326-49. Waterloo: Wilfrid Laurier University Press, 1987.

Jacobs, Lesley A. "Equality and Opportunity." In *Gender Politics in Contemporary Canada,* ed. François-Pierre Gingras, 106-20. Toronto: Oxford University Press, 1995.

Jain, Harish C. "Race and Sex Discrimination in the Workplace: An Analysis of Theory, Research and Public Policy in Canada." Paper prepared for the Affirmative Action Directorate, Employment and Immigration Canada, March 1981.

Jain, Harish C., and Rick D. Hackett. "A Comparison of Employment Equity and Non-Employment Equity Organizations on Desired Group Representation and Views towards Staffing." *Canadian Public Administration* 35, 1 (1992): 103-9.

–. "Measuring Effectiveness of Employment Equity Programs in Canada: Public Policy and a Survey." *Canadian Public Policy* 15, 2 (1989): 189-204.

Jain, Harish C., and Peter Sloane. *Equal Employment Issues: Race and Sex Discrimination in the United States, Canada and Britain.* New York: Praeger, 1981.

Jay, Richard, and Rick Wilford. "The Politics of the Fair Employment Act in Northern Ireland: Internal and External Dimensions." Paper presented at the 40th Annual Conference of the Political Studies Association, University of Durham, April 1990.

Jenson, Jane. "Commissioning Ideas: Representations and Royal Commissions." In *How Ottawa Spends 1994-95: Making Change,* ed. Susan D. Phillips, 39-69. Ottawa: Carleton University Press, 1994.

Johnson, Andrew F. "Canadian Social Services beyond 1984: A Neo-Liberal Agenda." In *Canada under Mulroney: An End of Term Report,* ed. Andrew B. Gollner and Daniel Salée, 265-83. Montreal: Véhicule Press, 1988.

Johnson, Laura C., and Janice Dineen. *The Kin Trade: The Day Care Crisis in Canada.* Toronto: McGraw Hill Ryerson, 1981.

Johnston, Larry. "Breaking the Impasse: Moving Child Care Up the Agenda." Paper presented to the Canadian Political Science Association, Université d'Ottawa, 31 May 1988.

Judek, Stanislaw. *Women in the Public Service.* Ottawa: Queen's Printer, 1968.

Kaplansky, Kalmen. "Human Rights and the ILO." *Canadian Labour* 12, 2 (1967): 7, 27.

Kernaghan, Kenneth. "Representative Bureaucracy: The Canadian Perspective." *Canadian Public Administration* 21, 4 (1978): 489-512.

Killean, Emer, ed. *Equality in the Economy: A Synthesis of the Proceedings of a Workshop.* Montreal: Institute for Research on Public Policy, 1987.

Klassen, Thomas R. *Precarious Values: Organizations, Politics and Labour Market Policy in Ontario*. Montreal and Kingston: McGill-Queen's University Press, 2000.

Knopff, Rainer with Thomas Flanagan. *Human Rights and Social Technology: The New War on Discrimination*. Ottawa: Carleton University Press, 1989.

Kome, Penney. *The Taking of Twenty-Eight: Women Challenge the Constitution*. Toronto: Women's Press, 1983.

–. *Women of Influence: Canadian Women and Politics*. Toronto: Doubleday Canada, 1985.

Kornberg, Mona. "Employment Equity: The Quiet Revolution?" *Canadian Woman Studies/Les cahiers de la femme* 6, 4 (1985): 17-19.

Kowaluk, Lucia. "The Status of Women in Canada." *Our Generation* 8, 2 (1972): 108-15.

Krashinsky, Michael. *Day Care and Public Policy in Ontario*. Toronto: Ontario Economic Council, 1977.

Kroeger, Arthur. "Everyone Loses." *Globe and Mail*, 23 March 2000, A15.

Kulchyski, Peter, ed. *Unjust Relations: Aboriginal Rights in Canadian Courts*. Toronto: Oxford University Press, 1994.

Kyle, Irene, and Martha Friendly, eds. *Proceedings from the Child Care Policy and Research Symposium 1991, Kingston, Ontario*. Toronto: Childcare Resource and Research Unit and the Centre for Urban and Community Studies.

Labour Canada. *Part-Time Work in Canada: Report of the Commission of Inquiry into Part-Time Work*. Ottawa: Supply and Services, 1983.

–. *Sex Discrimination in the Canadian Labour Market: Theories, Data and Evidence*. Equality in the Workplace discussion paper no. 3. Prepared for the Women's Bureau, Labour Canada, by Morley Gunderson and Frank Reid, Labour Canada, 1983.

–. *Women in the Labour Force: 1990-91 Edition*. Ottawa: Supply and Services, 1990.

Labour Canada, Women's Bureau. *Canadian Attitudes towards Women: Thirty Years of Change*. Ottawa: Supply and Services, 1984.

–. *Race and Sex Equality in the Workplace: A Challenge and an Opportunity*, ed. Harish C. Jain and Dianne Carroll. Ottawa: Supply and Services, 1980.

–. *Working Mothers and their Child-Care Arrangements*. Ottawa: Queen's Printer, 1970.

Labour, Department of, Economics and Research Branch. *Survey of Married Women Working for Pay in Eight Canadian Cities*. Prepared for the Women's Bureau. Ottawa: Queen's Printer, 1958.

Labour, Department of, Women's Bureau. Address prepared for delivery by Miss Sylva M. Gelber, Director, Women's Bureau, 8 December 1969.

–. *Changing Patterns in Women's Employment*. Report of a Consultation held on 18 March 1966. Ottawa: Department of Labour, 1966.

–. "Day Care Services for Children of Working Mothers," *Women's Bureau Bulletin* 11, January 1964.

Lacasse, Françoise D. *Women at Home: The Cost to the Canadian Economy of the Withdrawal from the Labour Force of a Major Proportion of the Female Population*. Studies of the Royal Commission on the Status of Women no. 2. Ottawa: Information Canada, 1970.

LaMarsh, Judy. *Memoirs of a Bird in a Gilded Cage*. Toronto: McClelland and Stewart, 1989.

Larkin, Jackie. "The Status of Women Report: Fundamental Questions Remain Unanswered." *Canadian Dimension* 7 (January/February 1970): 6-8.

"Le statut de la femme." *La Presse*, 12 June 1968, 58-9.

Leah, Ronnie. *Organizing for Daycare*. Kingston: Industrial Relations Centre, Queen's University, 1989.

Leck, Joanne D., and David Saunders. "Hiring Women: The Effects of Canada's Employment Equity Act." *Canadian Public Policy* 18, 2 (1992): 203-20.

Lee, Ian, and Clem Hobbs. "Pink Slips and Running Shoes: The Liberal Government's Downsizing of the Public Service." In *How Ottawa Spends 1996-97: Life under the Knife*, ed. Gene Swimmer, 337-78. Ottawa: Carleton University Press, 1996.

Leira, Arnlang, *Welfare States and Working Mothers: The Scandinavian Experience*. Cambridge: Cambridge University Press, 1992.

Lewis, David, and Frank Scott. *Make This Your Canada: A Review of CCF History and Policy*. Toronto: Central Canadian Publishing, 1943.

Lewis, Jane. "Equality, Difference and State Welfare: Labour Market and Family Policies in Sweden." *Feminist Studies* 18 (1992): 59-87.

–. *Women in Britain since 1945: Women, Family, Work and the State in the Post-War Years.* Oxford: Basil Blackwell, 1992.

–, ed. *Women and Social Policies in Europe: Work, Family and the State.* Aldershot: Edward Elgar, 1993.

Liberal Party of Canada. *Choices for Childcare: Now and the Future.* Minority Report of the Special Parliamentary Committee on Child Care. Prepared by Lucie Pépin. Ottawa: Liberal Party of Canada, 1987.

–. *Creating Opportunity: The Liberal Plan for Canada.* Ottawa: Liberal Party of Canada, 1993.

–. *A Record of Achievement: A Report on the Liberal Government's 36 Months in Office.* Ottawa: Liberal Party of Canada, 1996.

Lightman, Ernie, and Allan Irving. "Restructuring Canada's Welfare State." *Journal of Social Policy* 20, 1 (1991): 65-156.

Lind, Loren, and Susan Prentice. *Their Rightful Place: An Essay on Children, Families and Childcare in Canada.* Toronto: Our Schools/Our Selves Education Foundation, 1992.

Lipovenko, Dorothy. "Care of an Aging Relative Beginning at Home." *Globe and Mail,* 29 July 1994, A1, A5.

Lister, Ruth. *Citizenship: Feminist Perspectives.* London: Macmillan, 1997.

–. "Dilemmas in Engendering Citizenship." *Economy and Society* 24, 1 (1995): 1-40.

–. "Tracing the Contours of Women's Citizenship." *Policy and Politics* 21, 1 (1993): 3-16.

–. "Women, Economic Dependency and Citizenship." *Journal of Social Policy* 19, 4 (1990): 445-67.

Loney, Martin. *The Pursuit of Division: Race, Gender and Preferential Hiring in Canada.* Montreal and Kingston: McGill-Queen's University Press, 1998.

Lower, Arthur. "Some Reflections on a Bill of Rights." *Fortnightly Law Journal* 16 (15 February 1947): 216-18 and (1 March 1947): 234-7.

Lum, Janet M. "The Federal Employment Equity Act: Goals vs. Implementation." *Canadian Public Administration* 38, 1 (1995): 45-76.

Luxton, Meg. "The Home: A Contested Terrain." In *Still Ain't Satisfied: Canadian Feminism Today,* ed. Maureen Fitzgerald, Connie Guberman, and Margie Wolfe, 112-22. Toronto: Women's Press, 1982.

Luxton, Meg, and Ester Reiter. "Double, Double, Toil and Trouble ... Women's Experience of Work and Family in Canada 1980-1995." In *Women and the Canadian Welfare State: Challenges and Change,* ed. Patricia M. Evans and Gerda R. Wekerle, 197-221. Toronto: University of Toronto Press, 1997.

Lynch, C. "Women's Issues Debate Brings Campaign Full Circle." *Montreal Gazette,* 16 August 1984, B1.

MacBride-King, Judith L. *Work and Family: Employment Challenge of the '90s.* Compensation Research Centre, Report 59-90. Ottawa: Conference Board of Canada, 1990.

McCall, Christina. "The Unlikely Gladiators: Pearson and Diefenbaker Remembered." In *Pearson: The Unlikely Gladiator,* ed. Norman Hillmer, 58-67. Montreal and Kingston: McGill-Queen's University Press, 1999.

McCormack, Thelma. *Politics and the Hidden Injuries of Gender: Feminism and the Making of the Welfare State.* The CRIAW Papers/Les Documents de l'ICREF, no. 28. Ottawa: Canadian Research Institute for the Advancement of Women, 1991.

McDaniel, Susan A. "The Changing Canadian Family: Women's Roles and the Impact of Feminism." In *Changing Patterns: Women in Canada,* 2nd ed., ed. Sandra Burt, Lorraine Code, and Lindsay Dorney, 422-51. Toronto: McClelland and Stewart, 1993.

–. *Towards Family Policies with Women in Mind.* Feminist Perspectives Féministes no. 17. Ottawa: Canadian Research Institute for the Advancement of Women, 1989.

McDermott, Patricia. "Employment Equity." *Canadian Woman Studies/Les cahiers de la femme* 12, 3 (1992): 24-7.

–. "Pay and Employment Equity: Why Separate Policies?" In *Women and Canadian Public Policy,* ed. Janine Brodie, 89-103. Toronto: Harcourt Brace, 1996.

Macdonald, Donald S., Chairman of the Royal Commission on the Economic Union and

Development Prospects for Canada. Letter to Doris Anderson, President, National Action Committee on the Status of Women, 14 March 1984, attaching TV Ontario's transcript of NAC's intervention before the Commission, National Action Committee on the Status of Women Files, Toronto.

MacIvor, Heather. *Women and Politics in Canada.* Peterborough, ON: Broadview Press, 1996.

Mackinnon, Catherine. Excerpt from presentation to the Ontario Select Committee on Constitutional Reform, 1988, reprinted in the Ad Hoc Committee on Women and the Constitution, Toronto, "We Can Afford a Better Accord: The Meech Lake Accord," *Resources for Feminist Research/Documents sur la recherche féministe* 17, 3 (1988): 144.

McLaughlin, David. *Poisoned Chalice: The Last Campaign of the Progressive Conservative Party.* Toronto: Dundurn Press, 1994.

Maclean, Mavis, and Dulcie Groves, ed. *Women's Issues in Social Policy.* London: Routledge, 1991.

Macphail, Agnes. "Men Want to Hog Everything." *Maclean's* 62 (15 September 1949): 71-3.

Macpherson, Hon. Justice J.C. "The Impact of the Canadian Charter of Rights and Freedoms on Executive and Judicial Behaviour." In *Rights and Democracy: Essays in UK-Canadian Constitutionalism,* ed. G.W. Anderson, 125-38. London: Blackstone Press, 1999.

McRoberts, Kenneth. "Federal Structures and the Policy Process." In *Governing Canada: Institutions and Public Policy,* ed. Michael M. Atkinson, 149-77. Toronto: Harcourt Brace, 1993.

–. *Misconceiving Canada: The Struggle for National Unity.* Toronto: Oxford University Press, 1997.

Mahon, Rianne. "'Both Wage-Earner and Mother': Women Organizing and Child Care Policy in Sweden and Canada." In *Women's Organizing and Public Policy in Canada and Sweden,* ed. Linda Briskin and Mona Eliasson, 238-79. Montreal and Kingston: McGill-Queen's University Press, 1999.

–. "The Never-Ending Story Part 1: Feminist Struggles to Reshape Canadian Day Care Policy in the 1970s." Paper presented to the Annual Workshop of the Research Network on Gender, State and Society held in conjunction with the Social Science History Association, Washington, DC, October 1997.

Mahoney, Kathleen. "Daycare and Equality in Canada." In *Research Studies of the Commission on Equality in Employment,* ed. Judge Rosalie Silberman Abella, Commissioner, 159-81. Ottawa: Supply and Services, 1985.

"Manitoba Grits Run on Antipoverty Program." *Globe and Mail,* 1 September 1999, A5.

Manzer, Ronald. *Public Policies and Political Development in Canada.* Toronto: University of Toronto Press, 1985.

Marchak, Patricia. "A Critical Review of the Status of Women *Report.*" *Canadian Review of Sociology and Anthropology* 9, 1 (1972): 73-85.

Marcotte, Marcel. "Être femme aujourd'hui." *Rélations* 31 (February 1971): 47-50.

Maroney, Heather Jon, and Meg Luxton. *Feminism and Political Economy: Women's Work, Women's Struggles.* Toronto: Methuen, 1987.

Marsden, Lorna R. "The Importance of Studying Affirmative Action." *Canadian Woman Studies/Les cahiers de la femme* 6, 4 (1985): 11-15.

Marsh, Leonard. *Report on Social Security in Canada.* 1943. Reprint, Toronto: University of Toronto Press, 1975.

Marshall, T.H. "Citizenship and Social Class." In *Citizenship and Social Class and Other Essays.* Cambridge: Cambridge University Press, 1950.

Maslowe, Allan M. "The Canada Health and Social Transfer: Forcing Issues." In *How Ottawa Spends 1996-97: Life under the Knife,* ed. Gene Swimmer, 283-302. Ottawa: Carleton University Press, 1996.

Matas, David. "Domestic Implementation of Human Rights Agreements." In *Canadian Human Rights Yearbook,* ed. William Pentney and Daniel Proulx, 91-118. Toronto: Carswell, 1987.

Meehan, Elizabeth M. *Women's Rights at Work: Campaigns and Policies in Britain and the United States.* Basingstoke: Macmillan, 1985.

Meehan, Elizabeth, and Selma Sevenhuijsen. "Problems in Principles and Policies." In *Equality Politics and Gender,* ed. Elizabeth Meehan and Selma Sevenhuijsen, 1-16. London: Sage, 1991.

Ministerial Council on Social Policy Reform and Renewal. *Report to Premiers.* St. John's, NF: The Council, 1995.

Montgomery, Charlotte. "Tories Consider Buying Policy As Lever for Job Equality Laws." *Globe and Mail,* 22 November 1988, A5.

Morgado, Lucie. "Une révolution inachevée: la commission royale d'enquête sur la situation de la femme 20 ans plus tard." *Femmes d'action* 20, 3 (1991): 29-31.

Morgan, Nicole. *The Equality Game: Women in the Federal Public Service (1908-1987).* Ottawa: Canadian Advisory Council on the Status of Women, 1988.

–. *Implosion: An Analysis of the Growth of the Federal Public Service in Canada (1945-1985).* Ottawa: Institute for Research on Public Policy, 1986.

Morris, Cerise. "'Determination and Thoroughness': The Movement for a Royal Commission on the Status of Women." *Atlantis* 5, 2 (1980): 1-21.

–. "No More than Simple Justice: The Royal Commission on the Status of Women." PhD diss., McGill University, 1982.

–. "Pressuring the Canadian State for Women's Rights: The Role of the National Action Committee on the Status of Women." *Alternate Routes* 6 (1983): 87-108.

Morton, Elizabeth Homer. "Raising the Status of Canadian Women." *Queen's Quarterly* 78 (1971): 304-7.

Morton, Peggy. "Women's Work Is Never Done ... or the Production, Maintenance and Reproduction of Labour Power." In *Up from the Kitchen, Up from the Bedroom, Up from Under: Women Unite!* ed. Toronto Women's Liberation Movement, Discussion Collective no. 6, 46-68. Toronto: Canadian Women's Educational Press, 1970.

Moscovitch, Allan. "The Canada Assistance Plan: A Twenty Year Assessment, 1966-1986." In *How Ottawa Spends 1988-89: The Conservatives Heading into the Stretch,* ed. Katherine A. Graham, 269-307. Ottawa: Carleton University Press, 1988.

–. "Citizenship, Social Rights and Canadian Social Welfare." *Canadian Review of Social Policy* 28 (Winter 1991): 28-44.

Moscovitch, Allan, and Jim Albert, ed. *The "Benevolent" State: The Growth of Welfare in Canada.* Toronto: Garamond Press, 1987.

Nakamura, Alice, and Masao Nakamura. "A Survey on the Work Behaviour of Canadian Women." In *Work and Pay: The Canadian Labour Market.* Vol. 17 of *Research Studies, Royal Commission on the Economic Union and Development Prospects for Canada,* ed. W. Craig Riddell, 171-218. Toronto: University of Toronto Press, 1985.

Nanton, Philip. "Extending the Boundaries: Equal Opportunities as Social Regulation." *Policy and Politics* 23, 3 (1995): 203-12.

National Action Committee on the Status of Women. Brief to the Legislative Committee on Bill C-62. Prepared by Lynn Kaye, 1985. National Action Committee on the Status of Women (NAC) files, Toronto.

–. Brief to the House of Commons Legislative Committee on Bill C-144: The Canada Child Care Act. Prepared and presented by Tricia Willis and Lynn Kaye, 8 September 1988. NAC files, Toronto.

–. Brief to the Royal Commission on Economic Union and Development Prospects for Canada on the Status of Women, 1984. NAC files, Toronto.

–. Brief to the Special Committee on Child Care. Prepared by Martha Friendly. Presented by Louise Dulude, President of NAC, and Debbie Hughes-Geoffrion, Past Chair of NAC Social Services Committee, 12 June 1986. NAC files, Toronto.

–. "Child Care Act Moves Canada Three Steps to the Rear!" Press Release, 25 July 1988. NAC files, Toronto.

National Ad Hoc Action Committee on the Status of Women in Canada, Submission to the Government of Canada, February 1972, NAC files, Toronto.

National Council of Welfare. *Child Care: A Better Alternative.* Ottawa: National Council of Welfare, 1988.

New Democratic Party. *Caring for Canada's Children: A Special Report on the Crisis in Child*

Care. Minority Report of the Special Parliamentary Committee on Child Care. Prepared by Margaret Mitchell. Ottawa: New Democratic Party, 1987.

Newman, Christina. "The Body Politic: Some Awkward Truths about Women That the Royal Commission Missed." *Chatelaine*, 44, 3 (1971): 14.

–. "What's So Funny about the Royal Commission on the Status of Women?" *Saturday Night* 84, 1 (1969): 21-4.

Newman, Peter. C. *The Distemper of Our Times: Canadian Politics in Transition, 1963-1968.* Toronto: McClelland and Stewart, 1969.

Nicholson, Linda J. "Feminist Theory: The Private and the Public." In *Defining Women: Social Institutions and Gender Divisions,* ed. Linda McDowell and Rosemary Pringle, 36-44. Cambridge: Polity Press, 1992.

O'Connor, Julia S. "Employment Equality Strategies and Their Representation in the Political Process in Canada, 1970-1994." In *Women and Political Representation in Canada,* ed. Manon Tremblay and Caroline Andrew, 85-112. Ottawa: University of Ottawa Press, 1998.

"OFL Forums Show Broad Support for Free Childcare." *Solidarity* (April 1981): 4.

Okin, Susan Moller. *Justice, Gender and the Family.* New York: Basic Books, 1989.

O'Neil, Maureen, and Sharon Sutherland. "The Machinery of Women's Policy: Implementing the RCSW." In *Women and the Canadian State/Les femmes et l'État canadien,* ed. Caroline Andrew and Sandra Rodgers, 197-219. Montreal and Kingston: McGill-Queen's University Press, 1997.

Ontario Federation of Labour. "Statement on Day Care." Presented at the 24th annual Ontario Federation of Labour convention, 24-7 November 1980.

–. "Working Women: Feds to Make Daycare a Major Issue." *Ontario Labour* (November/December 1980): 12.

"Oppose Profit Day Care." *The Public Employee* (Autumn 1981): 6.

Organization for Economic Co-operation and Development (OECD). *Equal Opportunities for Women.* Paris: OECD, 1979.

–. *The Integration of Women in the Economy.* Paris: OECD, 1985.

–. *Women and Employment: Policies for Equal Opportunities.* Paris: OECD, 1980.

Orloff, Anna Shola. "Gender and the Social Rights of Citizenship: The Comparative Analysis of Gender Relations and Welfare States." In *American Sociological Review* 58, 3 (1993): 303-28.

Ostry, Sylvia. *The Female Worker in Canada.* Ottawa: Dominion Bureau of Statistics, 1968.

Palmer, Bryan D. *Working Class Experience: Rethinking the History of Canadian Labour, 1800-1991,* 2nd ed. Toronto: McClelland and Stewart, 1992.

Paltiel, Freda. "Quest for Equality." In *Our Own Agendas: Autobiographical Essays by Women Associated with McGill University,* ed. Margaret Gillet and Ann Beer, 111-20. Montreal and Kingston: McGill-Queen's University Press, 1995.

–. "State Initiatives: Impetus and Effect." In *Women and the Canadian State/Les femmes et l'État canadien,* ed. Caroline Andrew and Sandra Rodgers, 27-51. Montreal and Kingston: McGill-Queen's University Press, 1997.

Paltiel, R. "'Stop Harping about a Royal Commission': Judy LaMarsh Warns Women's Groups." *Globe and Mail,* 9 January 1967, 13.

Parizeau, Alice. *Day-Care Services and Pre-School Education in Selected Countries.* Studies of the Royal Commission on the Status of Women no. 31. Ottawa: Information Canada, 1970.

Parr, Elizabeth. "Who Cares for the Children?" *Chatelaine* 55, 3 (1982): 51, 72-8.

Pascall, Gillian. *Social Policy: A Feminist Analysis.* London: Tavistock, 1986.

Pateman, Carole. *Participation and Democratic Theory.* Cambridge: Cambridge University Press, 1970.

–. "The Patriarchal Welfare State." In *The Disorder of Women: Democracy, Feminism and Political Theory,* ed. Carole Pateman, 179-204. Cambridge: Polity Press, 1989.

–. *The Sexual Contract.* Cambridge: Polity Press, 1988.

Patmore, G.A. *An Inquiry into the Norm of Non-Discrimination in Canada.* Research and Current Issues Series no. 63. Kingston: Industrial Relations Centre, Queen's University, 1990.

Penniman, Howard, ed. *Canada at the Polls, 1984: A Study of the Federal General Election.* Durham: Duke University Press, 1988.

Pesiteau, Caroline. "Quebec: 6e Congrès de la Fédération des femmes du Québec." *Status of Women News* 1, 1 (1973): 5.

Petchins, Stephen G. *Women at Work: Discrimination and Response.* Toronto: McClelland and Stewart, 1989.

Phillips, Anne. *Democracy and Difference.* Cambridge: Polity Press, 1993.

–. "Democracy and Difference: Some Problems for Feminist Theory." *The Political Quarterly* 63, 1 (1992): 77-90.

–. *Engendering Democracy.* Cambridge: Polity Press, 1991.

–. "Universal Pretensions in Political Thought." In *Destabilising Theory: Contemporary Feminist Debates,* ed. Anne Phillips and Michèle Barrett, 10-30. Cambridge: Polity Press, 1992.

Phillips, D. Rhys. *Affirmative Action As an Effective Labour Market Planning Tool of the 1980s.* Technical Study 29 prepared for the Task Force on Labour Market Development, June 1981.

–. "Equality in the Labour Market: The Potential of Affirmative Action." In *Research Studies of the Commission on Equality in Employment,* ed. Judge Rosalie Silberman Abella, Commissioner, 49-111. Ottawa: Supply and Services, 1985.

Phillips, Paul, and Erin Phillips. *Women and Work: Inequality in the Labour Market.* Toronto: James Lorimer, 1983.

–. *Women and Work: Inequality in the Labour Market.* Rev. ed. Toronto: James Lorimer, 1993.

Phillips, Susan D. "Discourse, Identity, and Voice: Feminist Contributions to Policy Studies." In *Policy Studies in Canada: The State of the Art,* ed. Laurent Dobuzinskis, Michael Howlett, and David Laycock, 242-65. Toronto: University of Toronto Press, 1996.

–. "Meaning and Structure in Social Movements: Mapping the Network of National Canadian Women's Organizations." *Canadian Journal of Political Science* 24, 4 (1991): 755-82.

–. "Rock-a-Bye, Brian: The National Strategy on Child Care." In *How Ottawa Spends 1989-90: The Buck Stops Where?* ed. Katherine A. Graham, 165-208. Ottawa: Carleton University Press, 1989.

Pierson, Ruth. "Women's Emancipation and the Recruitment of Women into the Canadian Labour Force in World War II." In *The Neglected Majority: Essays in Canadian Women's History,* Volume 1, ed. Alison Prentice and Susan Mann Trofimenkoff, 125-91. Toronto: McClelland and Stewart, 1977.

Pierson, Ruth Roach. *Canadian Women and the Second World War.* Canadian Historical Association Historical Booklet no. 37. Ottawa: Canadian Historical Association, 1983.

–. *"They're Still Women after All": The Second World War and Canadian Womanhood.* Toronto: McClelland and Stewart, 1986.

Pierson, Ruth Roach, and Marjorie Griffin Cohen. *Canadian Women's Issues Volume II : Bold Visions.* Toronto: James Lorimer and Company, 1995.

Pierson, Ruth Roach, Marjorie Griffin Cohen, Paula Bourne, and Philinda Masters. *Canadian Women's Issues Volume I: Strong Voices – Twenty Five Years of Women's Activism in Canada.* Toronto: James Lorimer and Company, 1993.

Piven, Frances Fox. "Women and the State: Ideology, Power and the Welfare State." *Socialist Review* 14, 2 (1984): 11-19.

Poole, Phebe. "Canada's Federal Employment Equity Legislation: An Evaluation and Proposals for Change." PhD diss., University of Toronto, 1993.

Powell, Lisa M. "Toward Child-Care Policy Development in Canada." In *Social Policy in the Global Economy,* ed. Terrance M. Hunsley, 155-81. Kingston: School of Policy Studies, 1992.

Prentice, Alison, Paula Bourne, Gail Cuthbert Brandt, Beth Light, Wendy Mitchinson, and Naomi Black. *Canadian Women: A History.* Toronto: Harcourt Brace Jovanovich, 1988.

–. *Canadian Women: A History.* 2nd ed. Toronto: Harcourt Brace Canada, 1996.

Prentice, Susan. "Militant Mothers in Domestic Times: Toronto's Postwar Childcare Struggle." PhD diss., York University, 1993.

–. "Workers, Mothers, Reds: Toronto's Postwar Daycare Fight." In *Feminism in Action: Studies in Political Economy*, ed. M. Patricia Connelly and Pat Armstrong, 175-200. Toronto: Canadian Scholars Press, 1992.

Prichard, J. Robert S., and Michael J. Trebilcock. "Crown Corporations in Canada: The Choice of an Instrument." In *The Politics of Canadian Public Policy*, ed. Michael M. Atkinson and Marsha A. Chandler, 199-222. Toronto: University of Toronto Press, 1983.

Prince, Michael J. "The Mulroney Agenda: A Right Turn for Ottawa?" In *How Ottawa Spends 1986-87: Tracking the Tories*, ed. Michael J. Prince, 1-64. Toronto: Methuen, 1986.

Privy Council Office. P.C. Order in Council 1942-6242, 20 July 1942. In *Proclamations and Orders in Council Relating to the War* 8 (1942), 79.

–. P.C. Order in Council 1983-1924, 24 June 1983. In *Orders in Council* 4, 24 (2 July 1983), 2.

–. P.C. Order in Council 1983-4048, 22 December 1983. In *Orders in Council* 4, 46 (31 December 1983), 4.

–. P.C. Order in Council 1984-1390, 18 April 1984. In *Orders in Council* 5, 14 (20 April 1984), 2.

–. P.C. Order in Council 1984-2882, 23 August 1984. In *Orders in Council* 5, 30 (24 August 1984), 12.

Public Service Commission of Canada. *Annual Report 1971*. Ottawa: Public Service Commission of Canada, 1972.

–. *Annual Report 1981*. Ottawa: Public Service Commission of Canada, 1982.

–. *Annual Report 1982*. Ottawa: Public Service Commission of Canada, 1983.

–. *Annual Report 1983*. Ottawa: Public Service Commission of Canada, 1984.

Pulkingham, Jane. "Social Policy in the Late 1990s and Beyond: What Is to Be Done?" *Canadian Review of Social Policy* 37 (Spring 1996): 51-3.

Pulkingham, Jane, and Gordon Ternowetsky, ed. *Remaking Canadian Social Policy: Social Security in the Late 1990s*. Halifax: Fernwood, 1996.

Randall, Melanie. "Feminism and the State: Questions for Theory and Practice." *Resources for Feminist Research/Documents sur la recherche féministe* 17, 3 (1988): 10-17.

Randall, Vicky. "Feminism and Child Daycare." *Journal of Social Policy* 25, 4 (1996): 485-505.

–. "The Irresponsible State? The Politics of Child Daycare Provision in Britain." *British Journal of Political Science* 25 (1995): 327-48.

Ratner, Ronnie Steinberg. *Equal Employment Policy for Women: Strategies for Implementation in the United States, Canada and Western Europe*. Philadelphia, PA: Temple University Press, 1980.

Rayside, David. "Advances Understated." *University of Toronto Bulletin*, 21 July 1997, 4.

–. *On the Fringe: Gays and Lesbians in Politics*. Ithaca, NY: Cornell University Press, 1998.

Razack, Sherene. *Canadian Feminism and the Law: The Women's Legal Education and Action Fund and the Pursuit of Equality*. Toronto: Second Story Press, 1991.

Rebick, Judy, and Kiké Roach. *Politically Speaking*. Vancouver: Douglas and McIntyre, 1996.

Reed, Carole Ann. "Contradictions and Assumptions: A Report on Employment Equity in Canada." *Resources for Feminist Research/Documentation sur la recherche féministe* 24, 3 and 4 (1995-6): 46-8.

Rice, James J., and Michael J. Prince. "Lowering the Safety Net and Weakening the Bonds of Nationhood: Social Policy in the Mulroney Years." In *How Ottawa Spends: A More Democratic Canada ...?* ed. Susan D. Phillips, 381-416. Ottawa: Carleton University Press, 1993.

Robb, Carol S., ed. *Equal Value: An Ethical Approach to Economics and Sex*. Boston: Beacon Press, 1995.

Roberts, John. Letter to Judge Rosalie Abella, Commissioner, Commission of Enquiry on Equality in Employment from the Minister for Employment and Immigration, 21 March 1984. National Archives of Canada, RG 33/133, box no. 20, file 14.

Robertson, Peter C. "Affirmative Action: What's It All About?" Transcript of Audio-Visual prepared for the Affirmative Action Division, Employment and Immigration Canada, March 1980.

–. "Some Thoughts about Affirmative Action in Canada in the 1980s." Paper prepared for the Affirmative Action Division, Employment and Immigration Canada, March 1980.

Rocher, François, and Miriam Smith, ed. *New Trends in Canadian Federalism.* Peterborough, ON: Broadview Press, 1995.

Ronalds, Chris. "Government Action against Employment Discrimination." In *Playing the State: Australian Feminist Interventions,* ed. Sophie Watson. London: Verso, 1990.

Rosenthal, Joyce. "Unionist Call for Day Care Campaign." *Union Woman* 4 (November 1980): 1-2.

Ross, Kathleen Gallagher. *Good Day Care: Fighting for It, Getting It, Keeping It.* Toronto: Women's Press, 1978.

Rowbotham, Sheila. *Dreams and Dilemmas.* London: Virago, 1983.

–. *The Past Is before Us: Feminism in Action since the 1960s.* London: Pandora Press, 1989.

–. *Woman's Consciousness, Man's World.* Harmondsworth: Penguin, 1973.

Royal Commission on Equality in Employment. *Report.* Ottawa: Supply and Services, 1984.

Royal Commission on Financial Management and Accountability. *Final Report.* Ottawa: Supply and Services, 1979.

Royal Commission on the Status of Women in Canada. *Report.* Ottawa: Information Canada, 1970.

Royal Commission on Taxation. *Report.* Ottawa: Queen's Printer, 1966.

Ruggie, Mary. *The State and Working Women: A Comparative Study of Britain and Sweden.* Princeton: Princeton University Press, 1984.

Russell, Peter H. *Constitutional Odyssey: Can Canadians Become a Sovereign People?* 2nd ed. Toronto: University of Toronto Press, 1993.

Sandwell, B.K. *The State and Human Rights.* Toronto: Canadian Association of Adult Learning, 1947.

–. *You Take Out What You Put In.* Toronto: Canadian Association for Adult Education, 1947.

Sangster, Joan. "Doing Two Jobs: The Wage Earning Mother, 1945-1970." In *A Diversity of Women: Ontario, 1945-1980,* ed. Joy Parr, 98-132. Toronto: University of Toronto Press, 1995.

"Saskatchewan Status of Women Conference." *Status of Women News* 1, 1 (1973): 6.

Sassoon, Anne Showstack. "Women's New Social Role: Contradictions of the Welfare State." In *Women and the State,* ed. Anne Showstack Sassoon, 158-90. London: Hutchinson, 1987.

Sauvé, Jeanne. "Commentaires sur la Commission Royale sur la situation de la femme au Canada." *The Canadian Banker* 78, 1 (1971): 30-3.

Savoie, Donald J. *Governing from the Centre: The Concentration of Power in Canadian Politics.* Toronto: University of Toronto Press, 1999.

–. *Thatcher, Reagan, Mulroney: In Search of a New Bureaucracy.* Pittsburgh, PA: University of Pittsburgh Press, 1994.

Schecter, Marna A. *Dealing with the Child Care Challenge.* School of Industrial Relations Research Essay Series no. 32. Kingston: Industrial Relations Centre, Queen's University, 1990.

Schneir, Miriam, ed. *The Vintage Book of Feminism.* New York: Vintage, 1995.

Schulz, Pat. "Minding the Children." In *Still Ain't Satisfied: Canadian Feminism Today,* ed. Maureen Fitzgerald, Connie Guberman, and Margie Wolfe, 122-31. Toronto: Women's Press, 1982.

Schulz, Patricia Vanderbelt. "Day Care in Canada: 1850-1962." In *Good Day Care: Fighting for It, Getting It, Keeping It,* ed. Kathleen Gallagher Ross, 137-58. Toronto: Women's Press, 1978.

Scott, Frank. "Dominion Jurisdiction over Human Rights and Fundamental Freedoms." *Canadian Bar Review* 27, 5 (1949): 497-651.

Scott, Joan W. "Deconstructing Equality-Versus-Difference: Or, the Uses of Poststructuralist Theory for Feminism." *Feminist Studies* 14, 1 (1988): 33-50.

Scott, Paul. "Equality in Employment: A Royal Commission Report." *Currents* 4, 2 (1984/85): 3-11.

Secretary of State, Women's Program. "Pressure for Change: The Role of Canadian Women's Groups." Notes prepared for discussion at the United States International Seminar, 1974.

Senate of Canada. *Proceedings of the Standing Committee on Social Affairs, Science and Technology,* Issue no. 15, 1 October 1988. Ottawa: Senate of Canada, 1988.

Sevenhuijsen, Selma. *Citizenship and the Ethics of Care: Feminist Considerations on Justice, Morality and Politics.* Translated from Dutch by Liz Savage. London and New York: Routledge, 1998.

Shahid, Alvi. *Eldercare and the Workplace,* Report 150-95. Ottawa: Conference Board of Canada, 1995.

Sharpe, Sydney. *The Gilded Ghetto: Women and Political Power in Canada.* Toronto: HarperCollins, 1994.

Sheppard, Colleen. "Affirmative Action in Times of Recession: The Dilemma of Seniority-Based Layoffs." Paper presented to the National Association of Women and the Law, Victoria, BC, February 1982.

Shifrin, Leonard. "Social Policy: Free Trade Threatens Our Social Programs." *Toronto Star,* 31 October 1988, A19.

Shillington, Richard. Facsimile to Martha Friendly, Coordinator, Childcare Resource and Research Unit, University of Toronto, detailing Statistics Canada data on mothers in the labour force, 13 October 1999. Childcare Resource and Research Unit files, Toronto.

Siim, Birte. "Welfare State, Gender Politics and Equality Policies: Women's Citizenship in the Scandinavian Welfare States." In *Equality Politics and Gender,* ed. Elizabeth Meehan and Selma Sevenhuijsen, 175-92. London: Sage, 1991.

Silcoff, Joel. *Labour Legislation Affecting Women in Canada.* Studies of the Royal Commission on the Status of Women no. 29. Ottawa: Information Canada, 1970.

Simard, Carolle. *L'administration contre les femmes: la reproduction des différences sexuelles dans la fonction publique canadienne.* Montreal: Boréal Express, 1983.

Smith, Arthur. "Affirmative Action Job Placement." Paper prepared for the Affirmative Action Division, Employment and Immigration Canada, March 1980.

Smith, Jackie. "Where These Men Stand on Women's Issues." *Toronto Star,* 12 May 1984, F1, F3.

Snitow, Anna. "A Gender Diary." In *Conflicts in Feminism,* ed. Marianne Hirsch and Evelyn Fox Keller, 9-43. New York: Routledge, 1990.

Sohn, Herbert A. "Human Rights Legislation in Ontario: A Study of Social Action." PhD diss., University of Toronto, 1975.

Spain, Daphne, and Suzanne Bianchi. *Balancing Act: Motherhood, Marriage and Employment among American Women.* New York: Russell Sage Foundation, 1996.

Speirs, Rosemary. "Will This Woman Change Your Life?" *Maclean's* 42, 7 (1969): 32, 52-3.

Statistics Canada. *Canadian National Child Care Study: Where Are the Children? An Overview of Child Care Arrangements.* Ottawa: Statistics Canada, 1992.

–. *Women in the Labour Force, 1994 Edition.* Catalogue no. 75-507E. Ottawa: Statistics Canada, 1994.

Status of Women Canada. *Background Papers to the Report of the Task Force on Child Care.* Series 1-6. Ottawa: Supply and Services, 1985.

–. *Report of the Task Force on Child Care.* Ottawa: Supply and Services, 1986.

–. *Towards Equality for Women.* Ottawa: Supply and Services, 1979.

Status of Women Canada, Office of the Minister. Statement by the Hon. Barbara McDougall, Minister Responsible for the Status of Women, 3 December 1987.

–. Statement by the Hon. Walter McLean, Minister Responsible for the Status of Women, 8 March 1985.

Status of Women Council. *Status Anyone?* Vancouver: City Wide Print, 1972.

Stilborn, Jack. *Federal-Provincial Relations.* Current Issue Review 86-2E. Ottawa: Library of Parliament Research Branch, 1993.

Stinson, Jane. "The Day Care Fight Goes On: Report on the Second National Conference on Day Care." *The Facts* 4, 10 (1982-3): 16-18.

Stoddard, Hope. "No Women Being Hired." *The Canadian Forum* 26 (June 1946): 58-9.

Strong-Boag, Veronica. "Intruders in the Nursery: Childcare Professionals Reshape the Years One to Five, 1920-1940." In *Childhood and Family in Canadian History,* ed. Joy Parr, 160-78. Toronto: McClelland and Stewart, 1982.

Sutherland, Neil. *Children in English-Canadian Society: Framing the Twentieth Century Consensus.* Toronto: University of Toronto Press, 1976.

Swan, Carole. *Women in the Canadian Labour Market,* Technical Study 36 prepared for the Task Force on Labour Market Development, July 1981.

Swinton, Katherine. "Accommodating Equality in a Unionized Workplace." *Osgoode Hall Law Journal* 33, 4 (1995): 703-47.

Tarnopolsky, Walter S. "Discrimination and Affirmative Action – Definitions: American Experience and Application in Canada." In *Race and Sex Equality in the Workplace: A Challenge and an Opportunity,* ed. Harish C. Jain and Dianne Carroll, 72-98. Ottawa: Supply and Services, 1980.

–. "The Impact of UN Achievement on Canadian Laws and Practices." In *Human Rights, Federalism and Minorities,* ed. Allan Gotlieb. Toronto: Canadian Institute for International Affairs, 1970.

Task Force on Barriers to Women in the Public Service. *Beneath the Veneer: The Report of the Task Force on Barriers to Women in the Public Service.* Vols. 1-4. Ottawa: Supply and Services, 1990.

Teghtsoonian, Katherine. "Institutions and Ideology: Sources of Opposition to Federal Regulation of Child Care Services in Canada and the United States." *Governance* 5, 2 (1992): 197-223.

–. "Neo-Conservative Ideology and Opposition to Federal Regulation of Child Care Services in the United States and Canada." *Canadian Journal of Political Science* 16, 1 (1993): 97-122.

–. "Work and/or Motherhood: The Ideological Construction of Women's Options in Canadian Child Care Policy Debates." *Canadian Journal of Women and the Law* 8 (1995): 411-39.

Tilly, Louise A., and Joan W. Scott. *Women, Work and Family.* New York: Holt, Rinehart and Winston, 1978.

Timpson, Annis May. "Between the Royal Commissions: Women's Employment Equality in Canada, 1966-1986." *London Journal of Canadian Studies* 4 (1987): 68-81.

–. "Canada's Electoral Earthquake." *The World Today* 50, 1 (1994): 6-7.

–. "Driven Apart: The Construction of Women as Worker-Citizens and Mother-Citizens in Canadian Employment and Child Care Policies, 1940-1988." PhD diss., University of Toronto, 1997.

–. "Florence Bird: A Way for Canadian Women." *Guardian,* 5 August 1998, 12.

–. "Lessons from a House Divided." *World Today* 51, 12 (1995): 234-36.

–. "The Politics of Employment Inequality in Canada: Gender and the Public Sector." In *Women and Career: Themes and Issues in Advanced Industrial Societies,* ed. Julia Evetts, 44-58. Longman: London, 1994.

–. "Royal Commissions as Sites of Resistance: Women's Challenges on Child Care in the Royal Commission on the Status of Women." *International Journal of Canadian Studies/ Revue internationale d'études canadiennes* 20 (Fall 1999): 123-48.

–. "Western Canadian Perspectives on the Quebec Referendum." Paper presented to the Annual Conference of the Centre for Canadian Studies, Queens University, Belfast, 28 October 1995.

Timpson, Patricia A. "My Experiences of Serving in the Royal Canadian Air Force (Women's Division) during World War II." Lecture delivered at the University of Sussex, February 1997.

Townson, Monica. "The Management of Affirmative Action in Hard Times: The Implications of the Current Recession for Affirmative Action Programs." Paper prepared for the Affirmative Action Directorate, Employment and Immigration Canada, May 1983.

Treasury Board of Canada. *Annual Report 1980.* Ottawa: Supply and Services, 1981.

–. *Employment Equity in the Public Service: Annual Report 1992-93.* Ottawa: Communications and Coordination Directorate, Treasury Board of Canada, 1994.

Treasury Board of Canada, Human Resources Division, Personnel Policy Branch. *Employment Equity for Crown Corporations: Policy and Reference Guide.* Ottawa: Communications Division, Treasury Board of Canada, 1986.

Treasury Board of Canada, Personnel Policy Branch. *Equal Opportunities for Women in the Public Service of Canada.* Ottawa: Personnel Policy Branch, Treasury Board of Canada, 1979.

–. *On Target: Progress in Employment Equity in the Federal Public Service.* Ottawa: Communications Division, Treasury Board of Canada, 1988.

Treasury Board of Canada, President of the Treasury Board. Notes for a statement by the Hon. Robert R. De Cotret, President of the Treasury Board, announcing measures on employment equity. 8 March 1985.

Treasury Board of Canada, Secretariat. "Exploding the Myths: Employment Equity in the Public Service of Canada." Internal document, 1995.

–. "More Than the Numbers: Case Studies on Best Practices in the Employment of Women." A Report by the Consultation Group on Employment Equity for Women, Study no. 1, 1993.

–. "Work-Life Balance in the Public Sector." Internal document, 1988.

–. Consultation Group on Employment Equity for Women. *Looking to the Future: Challenging the Cultural and Attitudinal Barriers to Women in the Public Service.* Ottawa: Planning and Communications Directorate, Treasury Board of Canada, 1995.

Tronto, Joan C. *Moral Boundaries: A Political Argument for an Ethic of Care.* New York: Routledge, 1993.

Trudeau, Pierre. Letter written as prime minister to Doris Anderson, President, National Action Committee on the Status of Women. 29 June, 1982. National Action Committee on the Status of Women Files, Toronto.

"Trudeau's Era Was Full of Surprises." *Globe and Mail,* 1 March 1984, T5.

Tucker, Helen. "Federal Council on the Status of Women." *Status of Women News* 1, 1 (1973): 1-2.

Tuohy, Carolyn. "Social Policy: Two Worlds." In *Governing Canada: Institutions and Public Policy,* ed. Michael M. Atkinson, 275-305. Toronto: Harcourt Brace, 1993.

Turiano, Michelle. "Analysis of Testimony Presented to the 1994 Social Security Review." Childcare Research and Resource Unit files, University of Toronto, 1995.

Tyskš, Vappu K. "The Women's Movement and the Welfare State: Child Care Policy in Canada and Finland, 1960-1990." PhD diss., University of Toronto, 1993.

Ungerson, Clare, ed. *Gender and Caring: Work and Welfare in Britain and Scandinavia.* London: Harvester Wheatsheaf, 1990.

United Nations. *Convention on the Elimination of All Forms of Discrimination against Women.* New York: United Nations, 1979.

–. *Convention on the Rights of the Child.* New York: United Nations, 1991.

Vickers, Jill. "The Intellectual Origins of the Women's Movement." In *Challenging Times: The Women's Movement in Canada and the United States,* ed. Constance Backhouse and David H. Flaherty, 39-60. Montreal and Kingston: McGill-Queen's University Press, 1992.

–. "Major Equality Issues of the Eighties." In *Canadian Human Rights Yearbook,* ed. Jean-Denis Archambault and R. Paul Nadin-Davis, 47-72. Toronto: Carswell, 1983.

–. "Why *Should* Women Care about Federalism?" In *Canada: The State of the Federation 1994,* ed. Douglas M. Brown and Janet Hiebert, 135-52. Kingston: Institute of Intergovernmental Relations, Queen's University, 1994.

Vickers, Jill, Pauline Rankin, and Christine Appelle. *Politics As If Women Mattered: A Political Analysis of the National Action Committee on the Status of Women.* Toronto: University of Toronto Press, 1993.

Wadell, Eric. "State, Language and Society: The Vicissitudes of French in Quebec and Canada." In *The Politics of Gender, Ethnicity and Language in Canada.* Vol. 34 of *Research Studies, Royal Commission on the Economic Union and Development Prospects for Canada,* ed. Alan Cairns and Cynthia Williams, 67-110. Toronto: University of Toronto Press, 1996.

Wallace, Carole. "Action travail des femmes vs. CN Rail." *Status of Women News* 10 (December 1984): 26-7.

Watson, Sophie, ed. *Playing the State: Australian Feminist Interventions.* London: Verso, 1990.

Weiner, Nan. *Employment Equity: Making It Work.* Toronto: Butterworths, 1993.

Weinfeld, Morton. "The Development of Affirmative Action in Canada." *Canadian Ethnic Studies* 13, 2 (1981): 23-39.

Welter, Barbara. "The Cult of True Womanhood: 1820-1860." *American Quarterly* 18, 2, Part 1 (1966): 151-74.

White, Julie. *Sisters and Solidarity: Women and Unions in Canada.* Toronto: Thompson Educational Publishing, 1993.

–. *Women and Part-Time Work.* Ottawa: Canadian Advisory Council on the Status of Women, 1983.

–. *Women and Unions.* Ottawa: Canadian Advisory Council on the Status of Women, 1980.

Whitton, Charlotte. "The Exploited Sex." *Maclean's* 60 (15 April 1947): 37-8, 40.

"Who Can Run Day Care?" *Winnipeg Free Press,* 28 September 1982: 6.

Williams, Fiona. "Somewhere over the Rainbow: Universality and Diversity in Social Policy." In *Social Policy Review 1991-2,* ed. Nick Manning and Robert Page, 1-19. Canterbury: Social Policy Association, 1992.

Williams, Toni. "Re-forming 'Women's' Truth: A Critique of the Report of the Royal Commission on the Status of Women in Canada." *Ottawa Law Review* 22, 3 (1990): 725-59.

Wilson, Elizabeth. *Women and the Welfare State.* London: Tavistock Publications, 1977.

Wilson, S.J. *Women, Families and Work,* 3rd ed. Toronto: McGraw-Hill Ryerson, 1991.

–. *Women, Families and Work,* 4th ed. Toronto: McGraw-Hill Ryerson, 1996.

–. *Women, the Family and the Economy.* Toronto: McGraw-Hill Ryerson, 1982.

–. *Women, the Family and the Economy,* 2nd ed. Toronto: McGraw-Hill Ryerson, 1986.

Wilson, V. Seymour. "The Role of Royal Commissions and Task Forces." In *The Structures of Policy Making in Canada,* ed. G. Bruce Doern and Peter Aucoin, 113-29. Toronto: Macmillan, 1971.

Wilson, V. Seymour, and Willard A. Mullins. "Representative Bureaucracy: Linguistic/Ethnic Aspects in Canadian Public Policy." *Canadian Public Administration* 21, 4 (1978): 512-38.

Winn, Conrad. "Affirmative Action for Women: More than a Case of Simple Justice." *Canadian Public Administration* 28, 1 (1985): 24-46.

Woodsworth, J.S. *My Neighbour: A Study of City Conditions: A Plea for Social Service.* Toronto: Toronto Missionary Society of the Methodist Church, 1911.

Wolfe, David. "Mercantilism, Liberalism and Keynesianism." *Canadian Journal of Social and Political Theory* 5, 1/2 (1981): 69-96.

Young, Claire F.L. "Child Care and the Charter: Privileging the Privileged." *Review of Constitutional Studies* 2, 1 (1994): 20-38.

Young, Lisa. "Fulfilling the Mandate of Difference: Women in the Canadian House of Commons." In *In the Presence of Women: Representations in Canadian Governments,* ed. Jane Arscott and Linda Trimble, 82-103. Harcourt Brace, 1997.

Young, Margaret. *Affirmative Action/Employment Equity.* Current Issue Review 84-31E. Ottawa: Library of Parliament, Research Branch, 1989.

Young Women's Christian Association. *Women and Employment: A Canadian Perspective.* Toronto: YWCA of Metropolitan Toronto, 1987.

Zaretsky, Eli. "Capitalism, the Family and Personal Life, Part 1." *Socialist Revolution* 3, 1/2 (1973): 69-125.

Index

Mulroney, Brian. *See* Mulroney government (1984-8); Mulroney government (1988-93)
Mulroney government (1984-8): anti-regulation bias, 127, 129, 131, 133, 155, 210; Bill C-144 (Canada Child Care Act), 126, 149, 151-4; Child Care Expense Deduction (1988), 151; Child Care Initiatives Fund (1988), 126, 149, 151; Child Care Tax Credit (1988), 151; difficulty in getting employment equity legislation approved, 127-9; employment equity and child care separated, 126-7, 130-1, 140, 141, 150-1, 154-5, 206-7; *Employment Equity and Economic Growth* (1985), 130; employment equity and economic growth linked, 129-31; Federal Contractors Program (1986), 137-8, 139(t); Mulroney as brokerage politician, 128-9, 210; National Strategy on Child Care, 126, 148-51; neo-conservative ideology, 126-7, 155, 210; pro-family lobby, 127, 128, 129, 155, 210; public response to government actions, 138, 140; red-Tory elements, 125, 210; *Sharing the Responsibility* (1987), 148; SPCCC (1985), 141, 142(t)-145(t), 146-8; turning points in employment equity and child care policy, 224(t)-225(t); women appointed to senior positions, 127
Mulroney government (1988-93): Brighter Futures Program (1992), 170, 172; Child Development Initiative (1992), 170; child poverty new focus (1989), 168-71; Child Tax Benefit (1993), 170-1; Children's Bureau (1992), 170; Community Action Program for Children (CAP-C) (1992), 170, 172; EEA review (*see* Employment Equity Act [1986], Redway Committee 1991 review); Task Force on Barriers to Women in the Public Service (1988), 165-8; turning points in employment equity and child care policy, 225(t)-226(t); World Summit for Children (UN, 1990), 170

National Action Committee on the Status of Women (NAC): brief to 1991 Redway Committee, 157, 158, 159, 160; brief to RCEE, 107, 113; established 1972, 41, 67; links between women's employment equality and child care, 92-3, 113, 193, 208-9; relationship with child care movement, 92, 153, 208-9;

response to Bill C-144, 153-4; stance on national child care legislation (1970s), 67-8; testimony to Social Security Review (1994), 193
National Ad Hoc Action Committee on the Status of Women in Canada (NAHAC), 67
National Association of Women and the Law, 158
National Child Benefit (1998), 201-2, 205
National Child Care Program proposed (1995): components of proposal, 197-8; provinces and federal transfers, 199; provinces' reaction, 198-9; and report of Ministerial Council for Social Policy Reform, 199-200; shared-cost program, 198; withdrawal of proposal, 200
National Children's Agenda (NCA), 201, 202-3
National Council of Women of Canada, 47
National Organization of Immigrant and Visible Minority Women, 158
National Strategy on Child Care (1987): Bill C-144 (Canada Child Care Act), 126, 149, 151-4; cancelled in 1992, 168, 169; centrality of family emphasized, 150-1; Child Care Expense Deduction, 151; Child Care Initiatives Fund, 149, 151; Child Care Tax Credit, 151; child care's link with women's employment, 150, 151; and "economic equality" of women, 150; partial implementation by Mulroney government, 126, 168; proposal re national system, 148-50; tax policies proposed, 148-9
National Women's Consultation on the Social Security Review, 193
Native Women's Association of Canada, 158
Native Women's Program, 222
New Democratic Party: London and Middlesex Riding Association, Women's Group, 35; Saskatchewan Provincial Women's Committee, 36
Nova Scotia Advisory Council on the Status of Women, 110
Nunziata, John, 174

Office of Equal Opportunity (1971), 57
Official Languages Act (1969), and employment opportunities for women, 56
Ogston, Don, 187-8
Ontario Federation of Labour: institutional support for child care campaigns, 91; Statement on Day Care (1980), 91-2